DATE DUE

i1: 1390 6 867			
12-2-05			
DEC 0 8 2005			
GAYLORD			PRINTED IN U S A

RILEY   NICHOLSON
        ADE   TARKINGTON

A HISTORY OF

INDIANA LITERATURE

*A special printing of three thousand copies by the Indiana
Historical Society for distribution to its
membership in 1962*

Issued also as

Indiana Historical Collections

Volume XLII

A HISTORY OF
INDIANA LITERATURE

With Emphasis on the Authors of Imaginative Works
Who Commenced Writing Prior to World War II

by

ARTHUR W. SHUMAKER

INDIANA HISTORICAL SOCIETY

1962

This Book Is Dedicated
to
My Understanding and Helpful Wife and Daughter
Who
During My Years of Labor
Were Continually Sacrificed
on the Altar
of
Indiana Literature

CONTENTS

ACKNOWLEDGMENTS

ANY BOOK as detailed as this must certainly represent debts which should be acknowledged, though they can hardly be paid.

First, I wish to declare my indebtedness especially to the works of four writers, in ascending order of importance: Orah Cole Briscoe, "The Hoosier School of Fiction. Part I: Indiana Fiction before 1870" (unpublished M.A. thesis, Indiana University, 1934); Thomas J. Barry, "A Biographical and Bibliographical Dictionary of Indiana Authors" (unpublished M.A. thesis, University of Notre Dame, 1943); James Woodress, *Booth Tarkington. Gentleman from Indiana* (Philadelphia, 1954); and Richard E. Banta, *Indiana Authors and Their Books, 1816-1916* (Wabash College, 1949). This last volume has been of great use to me, for the author did much of the spade work prerequisite to a book such as my own, supplying quantities of biographical and bibliographical information which would have required much time for me to ferret out. Mr. Banta also offered helpful suggestions when I first began my research.

To many other persons heartfelt thanks are due: to Dr. Ward S. Miller, professor of English at the University of Redlands, who first suggested that I write a literary history of my home state; to my brother, Dr. Wayne Shumaker, professor of English at the University of California at

Berkeley, who offered advice about the organization of the project; to Dr. Raymond W. Pence, former head of the English Department of DePauw University and to Professor Oliver W. Robinson of the English staff, both of whom read portions of the manuscript and gave valuable suggestions; to Lorena Lovett, of Indianapolis, who supplied information about Indianapolis authors and who aided me in many ways; to Caroline Dunn, librarian of the William Henry Smith Memorial Library of the Indiana Historical Society, and to the entire staff of the Indiana State Library, who were always helpful. I wish to acknowledge especially the constant, cheerful assistance given by Mrs. Hazel Hopper, head of the Indiana Division of the State Library, and her staff—Mrs. Leona Alig, Mrs. Ferne Roseman, Lila Brady, Martha Wright, Carol Deschler, and Louise Wood. My gratitude can not be sufficiently expressed to the women of the Indiana Division for their constant, cheerful assistance to this writer, who occupied a place at a certain table during so many years that the good ladies finally threatened to erect there a commemorative bronze plaque!

Mr. Hubert H. Hawkins, head of the Indiana Historical Bureau, and secretary of the Indiana Historical Society, has been more than helpful in many ways; I have much for which to be grateful to him. Mr. D. Laurence Chambers, former president and chairman of the board of directors of The Bobbs-Merrill Company, read most of the manuscript and gave it very searching, detailed criticism, from which I profited much. Dorothy Riker, editor of the Historical Bureau, and Gayle Thornbrough, editor of the Indiana Historical Society, are to be thanked for their patience, their many suggestions, and assistance in numerous ways. In addition, many friends have provided intangible aid in the form of interest in the project and encouragement.

Finally, in spite of the strenuous objections of my wife (in fact, practically over her dead body), I wish to record my indebtedness to her of many sorts: for typing the manuscript, for aiding with the research necessary to the last two chapters, for accepting from me only my best in thought, arrangement of materials, and phraseology, and particularly for her tolerance of her absentee husband.

ARTHUR W. SHUMAKER

DEPAUW UNIVERSITY
GREENCASTLE, INDIANA
September 4, 1961

Introduction

INTRODUCTION

INDIANA'S HIGH LITERARY PRODUCTION

THE FAMOUS INDIANA HUMORIST, George Ade, tells the story of how once an eastern writer, lecturing to an Indiana audience on a literary subject, began his address by saying that he was well aware of the literary reputation of the inhabitants of the state of Indiana and that he would like, therefore, to invite any authors present in the audience to come forward and sit on the platform during his lecture—whereupon great confusion broke out in the hall as the entire audience arose from their seats and attempted to move toward the platform. According to another version of the incident everyone in the audience started in the direction of the platform except one old man, who remained stolidly in his seat. The lecturer, appalled at the result of his invitation, finally recovered himself enough to remark that he observed that there was at least one person in the audience who did not consider himself an author. Whereupon, someone replied, "Oh, he writes too. He's just deaf and didn't hear what you said."

Of course, the number of writers in the state of Indiana is absurdly exaggerated in such jokes; nevertheless, they contain a modicum of truth. For the production of Indiana writers is one of the more significant contributions to American literature made by any state or region. It is the purpose of this literary history to substantiate the above statement.

Thus, we shall see that Indiana authors have made
signal contributions in poetry and the novel, with lesser
offerings in the fields of the drama, the short story, the
essay, humor, and even in travel and confession writings.
We shall observe that in the annals of Hoosier literature
appear such well-known names, of varying literary merit,
as Alice Cary, Lew Wallace, George Cary Eggleston,
Maurice Thompson, James Whitcomb Riley, Charles
Major, George Ade, George Barr McCutcheon, Meredith
Nicholson, Kin Hubbard, and Gene Stratton Porter—to
say nothing of Edward Eggleston, Booth Tarkington, and
William Vaughn Moody. In short, the literary output of
the state has been vast in quantity and high in quality.
The people of Indiana from the very first, as an early
writer said in 1827, have been "a scribbling and a forth-
putting people."

William T. Coggeshall, publishing in 1860 an anthology
of Western (what today would be called Midwestern)
poetry, listed 152 writers, 23 of whom were from Indiana.
Of the 23 Indiana poets, 13 were natives of the state.[1]
Only one state, Ohio, had a larger number of poets—60;
other states represented in the anthology included Kentucky, Illinois, Michigan, Wisconsin, Missouri, Iowa,
Minnesota, and Kansas with one to fourteen poets each.

Then, in 1934 Edward Weeks, in behalf of the Columbia University Institute of Arts and Sciences, compiled a list of American books which have had the largest
sales since 1875. Five of the twenty titles listed were from
the pens of Indiana writers, three of the five being novels
of Gene Stratton Porter.[2] Indeed, Indiana authors have
long made the lists of the "best sellers" with such titles as

[1] William T. Coggeshall, *The Poets and Poetry of the West: With
Biographical and Critical Notices* (Columbus, Ohio, 1860), v.

[2] Editorial, "Indiana Authors," in Indianapolis *News,* April 11, 1934,
pt. 1, p. 6.

Edward Eggleston's *The Hoosier School-Master*, in 1871; Lew Wallace's *Ben-Hur*, in 1880; Riley's *"The Old Swimmin'-Hole,"* in 1883; Charles Major's *When Knighthood Was in Flower*, in 1899; George Barr McCutcheon's *Graustark*, in 1901; Gene Stratton Porter's *Freckles*, in 1904; *A Girl of the Limberlost*, in 1909; *The Harvester*, in 1911; *Laddie*, in 1913; and *Michael O'Halloran*, in 1915; Booth Tarkington's *Penrod*, in 1914; Ernie Pyle's *Here Is Your War*, in 1943; *Brave Men*, in 1944; and *Last Chapter*, in 1946; Ross F. Lockridge, Jr.'s *Raintree County*, in 1948; and Elmer Davis' *But We were Born Free*, in 1954. In fact, the new *Encyclopedia of American History* lists approximately 136 books which were the most widely read in the ninety-year period, 1861 to 1951; and 19 of them, or about 15 per cent, were by Hoosier authors.[3] The popularity of Indiana authors is also evident in the large number of their novels and stories that have been converted into the form of motion pictures.

The prevalence of writing in Indiana, thus, scarcely can be overstated. People of all walks of life have continually turned aside to compose literature of varying quality. Poetry, especially, has been the favored form of expression, particularly since the acclaim of Riley.

The successes of several Indiana authors were a great stimulus to literary ambition in Indiana; and the literary clubs were an additional encouragement. Poetry seems to the amateur much more easily achieved than prose, and poets rose in every quarter of the State following the general recognition of James Whitcomb Riley and Maurice Thompson. There was a time in Indiana when it was difficult to forecast who would next turn poet, suggesting the Tractarian period in England, of which Birrell writes that so prolific were the pamphleteers

[3] *Encyclopedia of American History*, edited by Richard B. Morris (New York, 1953), 571-72; Corbin Patrick, "Hoosier Past Fine, How About Literary Future?" in Indianapolis *Star*, April 26, 1953, Sec. 2, p. 10.

at the high tide of the movement that a tract might at any time be served upon one suddenly, like a sheriff's process. At Indianapolis the end seemed to have been reached when a retired banker, who had never been suspected, began to inveigle friends into his office on the pretense of business but really to read them his own verses. Charles Dennis, a local journalist, declared that there had appeared in the community a peculiar crooking of the right elbow and a furtive sliding of the hand into the left inside pocket, which was an unfailing preliminary to the reading of a poem.[4]

Literary interest and activity in the state is indicated by the poetry pages in newspapers, books of verse, poetry anthologies, poetry clubs, poetry days, and poetry prizes, collections of short stories, of essays, and of plays, books of many sorts of humor, and novels by the hundreds. Authors' nights were held and railroad excursions were run to see plays.

The sales of such popular writers as George Barr Mc-Cutcheon and Gene Stratton Porter reached into the millions of copies. Many Hoosier writers, like Riley and Tarkington, made a fortune from their pens, some from one book alone, such as Wallace from *Ben-Hur,* Thompson from *Alice of Old Vincennes,* and Ade from *Fables in Slang.*

Perhaps the best of all analyses of the production of Hoosier "best sellers" was made in 1947 by a fresh arrival in the state, John H. Moriarty, the new librarian of Purdue University, who wondered if the reputation of Hoosier letters was at all deserved. After a study of the data in Alice Payne Hackett's *Fifty Years of Best Sellers* he reported that in the preceding fifty years books of Indiana authors sold better than the works of the writers of any other state save New York—and the Hoosier record nearly equaled that of the Empire State.

[4] Meredith Nicholson, *The Hoosiers* (New York, 1900), 27-28.

Mr. Moriarty writes:

We took the period from the turn of the century to the beginning of World War II, and assigned the score of ten for each top best seller during those years. The second novel on the list was scored as nine, the third as eight and so on. The birthplace of each author was then ascertained (foreign-born authors were ignored as not of interest for this study and co-authors were divided equally if two states were involved). The various states were then credited with the total score of the authors born in them. And Indiana, during the forty years checked, was second state in the Union, and a fighting second at that. The top ten were:

1. New York, with a score of 218
2. Indiana, with a score of 213
3. Pennsylvania, with a score of 125
4. Virginia, with a score of 102
5. Kentucky, with a score of 94
6. Missouri, with a score of 80
7. Ohio, with a score of 73
8. Michigan, with a score of 70
9. Minnesota, with a score of 67
10. California, with a score of 64

—rather an amazing result in view of the fact that New York's population—and therefore the potential authors of best sellers—averaged almost four times that of Indiana during the forty-year period analyzed.[5]

Hoosier soil, therefore, has been fertile not only for the development of agriculture and politics but also for the production of writers. Yet, why has this interesting phenomenon occurred? What has there been about Indiana which causes writers to spring forth in each generation as the milkweed or the golden rod, so familiar to the Hoosier landscape, is reborn each season?

[5] *Indiana Quarterly for Bookmen* (Bloomington), January, 1947. I have used R. E. Banta's reprinting of a portion of the report in *Indiana Authors and Their Books, 1816-1916* (Crawfordsville, Ind., 1949), xi, since this includes Moriarty's revision.

The answer is not readily found. As a matter of fact, a completely satisfactory answer can hardly be given at all. For the problem is closely interwoven with the difficult question of why does anyone write, or why has anyone ever written.

Now people write, evidently, because they have something to say—or at least, think they have—and because for some reason they are inspired to attempt to say it. This much of the writing process is universal and timeless in aspect. Our question, then, is why did this desire for communication move so many Indiana people.

Probably the best single reason is so elementary as not to appear worth while even to mention—that somehow Indiana has been blessed with a large number of imaginative people who have wished to express themselves in written form. Why this is more true of Indiana than of most other states it is almost impossible to say. Another good reason is that after the pioneer period in the history of the state a literary climate developed which inspired new writers, who, in turn, inspired still others, so that a resulting cross-fertilization kept up a lively interest in reading and writing. Yet, this inspiration served simply to encourage people to write, not necessarily to form particular schools of writing or organizations of writers.

Nevertheless, there are more concrete reasons which can be cited. One of these is that the Hoosiers developed into a very articulate people, a people who wished to communicate with others and to be understood. They had no use for any cult of obscurity, and they developed nothing in the way of synthetic intellectual centers such as Greenwich Village.[6]

[6] The genesis of some of the following ideas was Howard H. Peckham's "What Made Hoosiers Write?" in *American Heritage,* Autumn, 1950, pp. 25-27, 59-60.

The reason for this articulateness is seen as a result of the mingling of the various strains making up the state's population. Indiana became the home of many Southerners—indeed, more than any other state north of the Ohio —and these were joined, somewhat later, by the immigrants from Ohio, Pennsylvania, New Jersey, and New York, with a trickle from New England and Europe. It was the melting pot of the nation. Practically no islands of nationality developed, and assimilation was rapid. The result was that to live in the state meant being in constant contact with people of different backgrounds, cultures, ideas, and religious faiths. Indiana was large enough and rich enough to make possible a good living for all the immigrants coming into it, regardless of their geographical or national origin, culture, and religion. Competition for security was eliminated; yet everyone felt called upon to state and defend his position. He had, to some extent, to be vocal.

In addition, there were many other conditions which had a signal effect upon the rise of literature. One of these centered in the situation in education. On the one hand, we have the establishment of several denominational colleges, which not only turned out authors but also created an atmosphere in which it was very respectable to be a writer. On the other hand, elementary and secondary education did not fare so well. The provision of the Constitution of 1816 for a general system of education could not be realized because of the resistance to taxation for local schools. In 1840 Indiana stood sixteenth among the twenty-six states in adult literacy, surpassed by three southern states and all other northern states, and in 1850 ranked twenty-fifth among the thirty-one states.

Naturally, there were many far-reaching results of this lack of education. In the first place, folklore, brought in mostly by Southerners, not only was preserved but was greatly encouraged; and today Indiana boasts a body of folklore larger than that of any other Midwestern state, except, perhaps, Illinois. In addition, Indiana became known for the "tall story," the product of the "liar's bench," which was a social institution in many towns, where the best tales excited much admiration on the part of the hearers. Today this imaginative institution has declined, but not entirely disappeared. The second result may be seen in the language; for archaisms, colloquialisms, peculiar pronunciations, and bad grammar developed, or, at least, were not impeded by the leveling effect of good schools. The language thereby became enriched, although it did not attain the status of a real dialect. The close relationship between a rich language and a good literature is evident, as in the case of Elizabethan England.

Then, a third result of the lack of education was the attempt of early residents to satisfy their desire for knowledge through libraries and literary clubs. For example, Vevay, founded in 1814 by a group of Swiss in an attempt to develop vineyards, boasted three years later some 84 dwellings, eight stores, 34 shops, three taverns, a courthouse, a church, a school, a jail, a library of some three hundred volumes, and also a literary society. And Vevay is only one example; there are many others. In addition to literary clubs, lyceums with lecture courses were in vogue. Also libraries, both public and private, flourished.[7] Thus, perhaps, lack of schools did hold some advantages.

[7] In 1852 the Indiana General Assembly established township school libraries, the books of which were purchased by revenue from a state tax. Over two thirds of the state's townships secured these libraries, and even though they declined later, a good beginning had been made, and the circulation was very high. See Richard G. Boone, *A History of Education in Indiana* (New York, 1892, reprinted by offset process by the Indiana Historical Bureau, 1941), 339-45.

A Hoosier character was developing by the beginning of the Civil War, if not before, with traits emanating from influences of population and geography. Because he lived close to the soil, the Hoosier was a rustic, but without social crudeness; because of the southern influence, the rural isolation, and the bountiful aspects of nature, he was friendly and hospitable; because he believed in equality and co-operation, he was neighborly. As early as 1839 a pioneer poet, Joseph S. Welsh, referred to these characteristics in his "Indiana Georgics," published in his small volume entitled *Harp of the West*.[8]

And added to these characteristics was the Hoosier's pride in his state, his independence of thought, and a tolerance which at times permitted him to hold himself up to ridicule, as in the case of the veteran of the Civil War home guard in Salem who was proud of his own service but who, in telling of his part in resisting Confederate General Morgan's raid into Indiana, said that with the first appearance of Morgan's men "I run like hell, jes' like ever'body else did."[9]

The Indianan was also gregarious, a confirmed joiner —of political parties, clubs, and lodges, in all of which conversation was the common medium of expression and entertainment. So the Hoosier was complex, yet a type. George Ade called him "a puzzling combination of shy provincial, unfettered democrat and Fourth of July orator. He is a student by choice, a poet by sneaking inclination, and a story-teller by reason of his nativity."[10]

But granted that early Indiana people did write, what opportunities did they have for publication of the fruit

[8] See pages 78-79.

[9] Peckham, *op. cit.*, 59.

[10] *George Ade 1866-1944 (The Magazine of Sigma Chi*, Memorial Issue, October-November, 1944), 68.

of their minds? Happily, there were several magazines available which welcomed the contributions of Hoosier authors, whether or not any remuneration was forthcoming. For example, in Cincinnati, the literary center of the West for many years, the *Western Monthly Magazine* was published from 1833 to 1837, the *Western Messenger* from 1835 to 1841, and the famous *Ladies' Repository* for thirty-five years, beginning in 1841. In addition, there were anthologies in which writers could be recognized. William D. Gallagher of Cincinnati issued in 1841 the first anthology of poetry of the West, entitled *Selections from the Poetical Literature of the West,* in which three of the thirty-eight writers represented were from Indiana; and as before noted, when William T. Coggeshall issued his *Poets and Poetry of the West* in 1860 at Columbus, Ohio, he included 152 writers, of whom 23 were Indiana residents.

The printing presses of local newspapers offered still another opportunity for publication. Although often unpaid for their contributions, writers found the columns of these papers hospitable to their efforts. Newspapers developed early and have maintained up till the present an influential, and usually moral, voice in affairs, civic, political, religious—and literary. Newspaper publishers also used their printing presses to issue separate literary works. The first of these was an anonymous *Life of Bonaparte,* published at Salem in 1818 by Patrick and Booth, printers of *The Tocsin,* and the next was a popular edition of Joel Barlow's *Vision of Columbus,* printed in Centerville in 1824 by John Scott of the *Western Emporium.* After this, other Indiana printers began to risk ventures on local authors.

Another strong influence in the development of literature was oratory. In the days of few books and newspapers, oratory supplied the need for news and discussion or debate of problems of a national, local, political, or religious nature and rose rapidly to the level of fine art. Hoosier political leaders were orators possessing distinctive styles. Men like Vice-president Hendricks, Governor Morton, Vice-president Colfax, Daniel Voorhees (known as "the Tall Sycamore of the Wabash"), and President Benjamin Harrison, to say nothing of later figures like Albert J. Beveridge, were famous for their successful appearances. The texts of many of their orations come close to the status of literature.

Moreover, as Indiana became less isolated from the East, "the flowering of New England" undoubtedly had some effect in the West, exciting both appreciation and envy. But when it became apparent to the Midwest that the East failed to understand it sufficiently to appreciate its literature and that the eastern writers did not portray the frontier accurately, Hoosier writers felt impelled to provide evidence for themselves (and for the East) that they and their country could not be ignored or misrepresented.

Altogether, then, many subsidiary factors influenced the rise of a state literature: the melting pot of population; the development of articulateness; the lack of elementary education with its resulting impetus toward folklore, toward richness of language, and toward a hunger for knowledge as seen in the rise of libraries and literary societies; also, the emergence of a Hoosier character; the opportunities for publication; the popularity of eloquent oratory; the example of the East and a desire to express and defend their own individuality. Once the literary movement was well under way, it quickly achieved momentum.

This sudden urge to write demanded more than the

usual literary outlets, and they were not slow in appearing. A fresh crop of literary societies for both men and women arose. The Indianapolis Literary Club, for men, was established in 1877 and still meets regularly; the Terre Haute Literary Club, also a men's group, began in 1881; and the Ouiatenon Club, in Crawfordsville, was founded in 1883. Thirty-seven literary clubs for women that were established before 1890 were still flourishing in 1950. In addition, The Western Association of Writers was organized in 1886 at Indianapolis and was monopolized by Hoosiers, who honored such fellow members as Riley, Lew Wallace, Charles Major, Mary H. Catherwood, Maurice Thompson, Meredith Nicholson, and Booth Tarkington. The Association met yearly in the summer at Eagle (now Winona) Lake in the northern part of the state for a week-long literary festival, when the members read their best works to one another and conversed in an atmosphere of enthusiasm and mutual stimulation. The twenty-year history of this group is intimately connected with the spirit which produced the Golden Age of Indiana literature.

Along with a growing sense of the importance of its literature, Indiana began to develop a sense of being typical. The statistical center of population of the United States was found in 1890 to be in eastern Indiana, and because of its slow progress across the state it moved into Illinois only in 1950. The state thus was located in the center of things, at the "crossroads of America." In national elections Indiana voted with the majority of the nation, and she began to be known as a reliable political barometer. State pride thus rose in the feeling that Hoosiers were the real, typical Americans; and this pride boosted interest in local self-expression.

By no means the least of the factors in the rise of Indi-

ana literature was the establishment in Indianapolis, in
1883, of the publishing house of Merrill, Meigs and Company, which became in 1885 the Bowen-Merrill Company
and in 1903 the Bobbs-Merrill Company. Their first
publication was the second printing of Riley's *"The Old
Swimmin'-Hole."* The appearance of a house that could
publish local materials and market them nationally was a
great stimulus to writers. The company did publish the
works of many Indiana authors; Riley, Nicholson, Porter,
and many others reached their wide audiences at least
partly through the efforts of Bobbs-Merrill.

THE APPROACH USED IN THIS STUDY

Up until the present time nearly all criticism of Indiana literature has concerned itself with the individual
writers rather than with the entire field and, of course,
largely with the figures of greatest importance, such as Edward Eggleston and William Vaughn Moody. There have
been three previous investigations of portions of the history of Indiana literature. Two are unpublished Master
of Arts theses: one by Orah Cole Briscoe, "The Hoosier
School of Fiction. Part I: Indiana Fiction before 1870"
(Indiana University, 1934); and the other by Thomas J.
Barry, "A Biographical and Bibliographical Dictionary of
Indiana Authors" (University of Notre Dame, 1943). The
third, edited by Richard E. Banta, is entitled *Indiana
Authors and Their Books, 1816-1916* (Wabash College,
1949). It represents an alphabetical listing of the authors
who wrote in the first century of Indiana statehood and
who were considered by Mr. Banta and his committee to
be the most significant.[11] This book gives for each writer

[11] The other members of this committee seem to have occupied mostly
an honorary position; evidently Mr. Banta, with the aid of two or three
researchers, did the actual work represented by the book.

a biography—usually brief but sometimes more in detail—
and a list of his works in order of publication. The Briscoe
thesis is brief and in some respects rather sketchy. The
Barry thesis is lengthy and follows the general plan of
the Banta book.[12] The last has been the most helpful and
authoritative study in the field,[13] but Banta has not en-
deavored to give a literary history of the state. Rather,
except for his biographical summaries, there is provided
only a listing of source materials, and practically no attempt to offer analysis or criticism or to indicate the development of Indiana literature. Of course, authors who
began publishing after 1916 are not included.

A literary history as here conceived is an analysis and
criticism of the production, together with pertinent biographical facts, of each Indiana author of creative literature who had begun writing by 1939, who, according to
the considered judgment of this writer, deserves to be
included in a literary history of Indiana. Also, it is an
arrangement of these authors in such a way as to present
the development of Indiana literature by chronology and
by type. It is hoped that by writing the literary history of
a state (and that of a state which has been significant in
American literature) some contribution will be made to
the criticism of American literature.

The first problem that presents itself is that of defining an Indiana author. This is one of the thorniest of
all problems, not only in this present study but also in
any regional literary history. Various scholars have tried
to solve it in various ways. Here are some of the ques-

[12] It goes without saying, of course, that the criteria for inclusion in
the Barry thesis are much more liberal than those which the author of
the present volume has used.

[13] Perhaps one should also list here the early study in the field, Nicholson's *The Hoosiers* (1900), although only a portion of the book deals with
literature.

tions pertinent to the present work. Is an Indiana writer one who was merely born in the state, regardless of where he spent the rest of his life? Or, is he a Hoosier if he moved here in childhood—or, if he spent only a few years here—or, if he wrote about the state, regardless of residence?

The Indiana State Library and Indiana libraries in general are obliged by the needs of their patrons to regard as a Hoosier almost anyone who has had any remote connection with the state. For example, there is seldom any differentiation in the cataloguing or shelving of materials by Indiana writers and materials about Indiana; and these libraries usually include as Hoosiers such people as Joaquin Miller, who was born about 1840 near Liberty, Indiana, and left the state in 1852. Similarly are included Edgar Watson Howe, who left the state at about age fourteen or fifteen, and who became associated mostly thereafter with Kansas, and Jessamyn West, who departed at about the age of six.

From the point of view of the present author, however, all the definitions, stated or implied, used by various people and groups have merit for their own projects; but they all are sufficiently broad to admit as Hoosiers many people who have had little connection with the state. Sometime after beginning work on the present volume, the author decided that if this literary history was to be of a size that could be easily used and if it was to represent primarily people who have had a strong connection with Indiana and, therefore, should be properly identified with it, the following definition of an Indiana author should be followed:

1. A person born in Indiana who spent all or most of his life in the state.

2. A person not born in Indiana who spent all or most of his life in the state.

3. A writer not born in Indiana who spent a few years here which were very productive in his literary career.

4. A person whose Indiana background influenced strongly his later writing.

The following have been excluded:

1. An author who was born in Indiana but who moved elsewhere before producing any significant writing.

2. A person who spent only a few years in the state and whose literary work seems not to have been particularly affected by residence here.

3. A writer who may have fulfilled our definition but did not publish at least one book.

In short, my definition of an Indiana author is a person who shows evidence in his life or in his works of the influence of an Indiana environment—that is, one whose residence here has really affected him.

According to this definition, authors of recognized Indiana residence and influence, like Sarah T. Bolton, Lew Wallace, and Gene Stratton Porter, are included; but there are many borderline cases. People like William Vaughn Moody, the dramatist, who had a long Indiana residence before he began writing, are in, as are Alice and Phoebe Cary, who lived long enough in Indiana to be influenced by the environment. But people like Edgar Watson Howe and Jessamyn West did not spend enough time here to merit inclusion; and George Jean Nathan, for example, does not show any Hoosier influence in his works and is therefore out. Very reluctantly David Graham Phillips and Theodore Dreiser have been excluded because of insufficient residence and Indiana influence in their works.

So much for the problem of definition. The second

problem has also been a big one—that of compiling a list
of authors who might fit this definition. A bibliography
on the subject of Indiana literature in general was built
up; then an author file was started. Names for the latter
were obtained from lists of Indiana writers supplied by
the Indiana State Library and the Indianapolis Public
Library, from Banta's book, and the theses of Barry and
Briscoe. The *Hoosier Caravan, A Treasury of Indiana
Life and Lore,* an anthology of Indiana literature published by Banta in 1951, was also read. By this time several hundred names had been amassed.

The next step was to consult the various collections of
Indiana and Middle Western poetry and prose, including
William D. Gallagher's *Selections from the Poetical Lit-
erature of the West* (1841); William T. Coggeshall's
Poets and Poetry of the West (1860); Parker and Heiney's
Poets and Poetry of Indiana (1900); and Eletha M.
Taylor's *Indiana Poetry* (1925). These collections yielded
still more names. So also did the few critical works touching on Indiana materials, such as William H. Venable's
Beginnings of Literary Culture in the Ohio Valley (1891)
and Meredith Nicholson's *The Hoosiers* (1900). The card
catalogue in the State Library was checked, newspaper
clippings by the hundred in the same library were examined, and the file of authors that the bibliographical
committee of the Indiana Historical Society once assembled was searched for additional names. The result of all
this seaching was a list of 1,563 names of possible Hoosier
creative writers, a rather staggering number.

This led to the third main problem, that of cutting the
list down to a workable size. By establishing the closing
date as 1939, the beginning of World War II, at which
time people became interested in writing about the war,
some were eliminated. Then the question of including

juveniles arose. It was surprising to learn that for many years Indiana has had so strong a representation in this field as to approach, according to some critics, a monopoly. One hundred and twenty-four writers of this type were listed. Are juveniles literature in the sense being considered? Certainly they are important and interesting; yet they are tangential to this study and have been excluded.

To reduce the list still further it was decided to exclude writers on the following specific grounds: (1) an insufficient quantity of works published to justify inclusion; (2) inferior quality of works published; (3) insufficient residence in Indiana; (4) insufficient quantity of works obtainable; (5) insufficient quantity of works of the type included in this study; and (6) no creative works published during the period included in this study.

This method of elimination necessitated working with biography and bibliography, and when the quality of an author's work was in question, enough of his books were read to justify making a decision. In poetry, writers of doggerel were eliminated as well as those whose verse was so feeble from the point of view of expression or thought as to be unworthy of consideration. Prose of obviously careless mechanics, construction, or thought was likewise eliminated. The general criterion that has been used in this process of evaluation is how the particular piece of literature under examination compares with English and particularly American literature which is considered, by consensus of literary historians, to be worthwhile. Of course, to justify inclusion a poet does not have to be a Wordsworth, a dramatist a Shakespeare, or a novelist a Dickens; still, he should have *some* of the qualities of the best writers. By the above process of exclusion 1,421 names were weeded out, leaving 142 to be included in this study. If there have been errors, the author is alone responsible.

The fourth problem was a mechanical one, that of actually laying hands on all the items published by an author. Even though the Indiana State Library has the best collection of Indiana materials, still it does not contain everything, and I have had to utilize the facilities of other libraries for a few authors and sources.

As the work proceeded, it became evident that Indiana literature falls naturally and logically into three different periods. The first comprises the early material, beginning at the dawn of Hoosier writing, about 1821, and extending through the Civil War until 1870. This first grouping includes particularly the early poets and novelists, with some additions, such as travel and confession literature. Then, with the publication of Edward Eggleston's *Hoosier School-Master* in 1871 Indiana literature, heretofore not much noticed and not too significant, attracted widespread attention. From Eggleston on through several decades this literature swelled into a flood tide, bearing such names as George Cary Eggleston, Mary H. Catherwood, Lew Wallace, Maurice Thompson, James Whitcomb Riley, Meredith Nicholson, George Ade, Evaleen Stein, Charles Major, Booth Tarkington, Caroline V. Krout, William Vaughn Moody, George Barr McCutcheon, Gene Stratton Porter, and Kin Hubbard. Of course, some of these writers, like Tarkington, continued publishing past the limit of the period; but we shall end the Golden Age of Hoosier letters in 1921, with the publication of his *Alice Adams*. For after the appearance of this Pulitzer prize novel Tarkington could never again reach that level, and the heyday of Indiana literature was past. It was a glorious period, the fifty years from 1871 to 1921, peopled with the greatest names in the out-

put of Hoosier pens. The period from 1922 to 1939 represents an afterglow, but it must be noticed that a few
names of more or less significant writers still are to be
counted, such as Marguerite Young. The works of each
author are treated as a unit, even though in certain cases
his or her list of publications transcends the period.

A SUMMARY AND EVALUATION OF INDIANA LITERATURE

Let us approach the field of Indiana literature by
types, briefly analyzing and evaluating each; then perhaps
we can draw a few conclusions.

The confession literature, which was confined to six
writers who wrote mostly during the period of early literature, was hardly literary, yet often smacks of Daniel Defoe. It is significant almost entirely because of the early
dates of publication; indeed, Indiana literature began
with one such book.   Confession literature is the most
bizarre type of writing to be encountered.

The travel materials, both the emigrants' guides and
the Hoosier travel narratives, often provide fascinating
reading and afford much valuable historical information;
but they make no pretense of being literature and, again,
are significant mostly because of their early appearance.
These documents evidence a very romantic spirit, and in
spite of—partly, perhaps, because of—their simplicity and
artlessness, are near the status of literature.

Poetry was the dominant literary genre in the period of
early literature; the strongest voices before 1871 are those
of poets, the outstanding writers, many heretofore neglected in literary history, being Dr. Joseph S. Welsh,
George W. Cutter, John S. Reid, Alice Cary, Phoebe Cary,
Mary Louisa Chitwood, Sandford C. Cox, Sarah T. Bolton,
and Forceythe Willson. The best poets of all were the

Cary sisters and Mrs. Bolton. In this body of verse one sees the strong mark of the frontier, the literary influence of Edgar Allan Poe, and a cultural lag in the retention here and there of the heroic couplet. Temperance, abolition, and the Civil War form the favorite subjects of the verse; and there is much reflection of sorrow, part of which, perhaps, may be in the nature of a pose.

Though the Golden Age was overshadowed by the novel, it produced much significant verse, the best poets being James Whitcomb Riley, Evaleen Stein, Max Ehrmann, and William Vaughn Moody. Miss Stein and Maurice Thompson were Indiana's main nature poets. William Vaughn Moody is by far the best poet, with the sentimental Riley as the very popular runner-up. If one can stomach sentimentalism, Riley must be accorded first place in his type of verse; but if one cannot agree to its use in good literature, then much of Riley must be counted sub-literary. The verse of this period represents in many ways a refinement upon the verse before 1871: the subjects are more diverse; the verse forms are more varied.

The poetry following the Golden Age continued the tradition of that era. Although there was no one of the stature of Moody or of the popularity of Riley, still there were idealists with a sensitive imagination and an awareness of beauty and of life and its hidden meanings. The verse form that marks this period by its excellent use is the sonnet; and the best poets are Marguerite Young, Margaret Bruner, and E. Merrill Root. The verse of this late period is at least as good as the novel.

The greatest Indiana poet of all three periods is Moody; and no one before or since his time can compare with him. However, for nearly everyone Riley is the popular poet and, in a sense, *is* Indiana *literature*.

Before 1871 production of the novel was insignificant; most of the few volumes published were weighted heavily with propaganda, such as preachments in behalf of temperance, or contained much sentiment and thin romance. The majority of these novels appeared in the 1850's. The most interesting of them were records of personal dissatisfaction with Indiana—*The New Purchase* (1843), by Baynard Rush Hall, and *From Dawn to Daylight* (1859), by Mrs. Henry Ward Beecher—and yet these two novels were the most famous—and infamous—books published in Indiana before 1871.

The Golden Age marked the flowering of the novel, which dominated all other forms of literature, even the effusions of Riley. The novel was predominantly romantic; and the typical novel was a wholesome, innocuous story written primarily for entertainment — very few Hoosier novels were burdened with message. The genre divides itself into certain recognizable types, with some overlapping. As a favorite comes the historical novel, the greatest period of its production being 1900-1910 with most of these books being highly romantic, such as *The Circuit Rider* (1874), by Edward Eggleston, Wallace's *Ben-Hur* (1880), Major's *When Knighthood Was in Flower* (1898), and Tarkington's *Monsieur Beaucaire* (1900). Edward Eggleston's *The Hoosier School-Master* (1871) is, of course, more realistic than romantic; and it began the Golden Age. These novels were the best of the historical.

The romantic novel of the Golden Age was slight and entertaining and carried little permanent value. It was concentrated from about 1900 to 1910 or 1915, and the best are George Barr McCutcheon's *Graustark* (1901) and Nicholson's *The House of a Thousand Candles* (1905).

The only thoroughgoing realist was Edward Eggleston, sharing the honors of the highest level of attainment with Tarkington, who dominates the realistic novel. The dates of concentration of this type are from about 1908 to 1921; and the best realistic novels are *The Hoosier School-Master* (1871), Tarkington's *The Gentleman from Indiana* (1899), George Eggleston's *Blind Alleys* (1906), George Barr McCutcheon's *Mary Midthorne* (1911), Tarkington's *Penrod* (1914), *Penrod and Sam* (1916), *Seventeen* (1916), *The Magnificent Ambersons* (1918), *Alice Adams* (1921), and *The Midlanders* (1924).

Satire in the Golden Age was negligible and is embodied in only a few novels: Tarkington's *Cherry* (1903), George W. Louttit's *The Gentleman from Jay* (1903), and John T. McCutcheon's *Congressman Pumphrey* (1907).

In contrast to the Golden Age, the novelists following that period were mainly nonprofessional writers; and the production of the later period, comparatively speaking, was of much smaller quantity. Several of the works are exciting, many of the books are historical novels, and the typical novel again tends to be romantic—even in the category of escape reading—rather than realistic. This era was marked by an extensive use of Indiana as a setting for the stories. The best novelists were probably McCready Huston, Charles Scoggins, Margaret Weymouth Jackson, John Mellett, Robin Spencer, and Jeannette Covert Nolan.

Humor was small in quantity, and George Ade obviously dominates it with his many volumes. His best is *Fables in Slang* (1900), with which he inaugurated a style, as he would express it, that "went." Kin Hubbard, however, takes a strong second place with his famous character Abe Martin.

The short story (collected in book form) was one of the minor forms of Hoosier literature, but was strong in the Golden Age. The only early writer of note is Julia Dumont, whose romantic and sentimental *Life Sketches from Common Paths* (1856) was an important book in its day. Later collections of stories were much more numerous; and the most notable are Thompson's sensitive pieces, *Hoosier Mosaics* (1875), George Cary Eggleston's excellent portrayals of the rebel soldier in *Southern Soldier Stories* (1898), the early realistic and local-color stories of Mary Hartwell Catherwood, *The Queen of the Swamp and Other Plain Americans* (1899), Major's near-juvenile, *The Bears of Blue River* (1901), and Tarkington's *In the Arena: Stories of Political Life* (1905). These collections are all well worth the reader's time.

As in the case of the short story, the familiar essay was not a favorite form of literature in the early period, only two collections of essays being written; one of them, *Rosabower* (1855), by William Clark Larrabee, is pleasingly calm and reflective. In the Golden Age come Meredith Nicholson's several volumes, the chief being, perhaps, *The Valley of Democracy* (1918); and Elmer Davis is not too far behind Nicholson in *Not to Mention the War* (1940), which appeared after the close of the period. The latter has a lighter touch than Nicholson's books. And another collection meriting record for honors is Juliet V. Strauss's *The Ideas of a Plain Country Woman* (1906), in which by means of her shrewd common sense she pierces the fog obscuring contemporary problems.

Drama, the last category of literature, is conspicuous by its absence before 1871, the only real play being Robert Dale Owen's stilted production, *Pocahontas: A Historical Drama* (1837). But in the Golden Age drama came into a late flowering with William Vaughn Moody's philosophical verse trilogy on the subject of sin—*The Masque of Judgment* (1900), *The Fire Bringer* (1904), and the uncompleted "The Death of Eve"—which was followed by his thought-provoking studies of morals, *The Great Divide* (1909) and *The Faith Healer* (1909). Contemporary with Moody were George Ade's light, sparkling comedies and musical shows, the best being *The Sultan of Sulu* (1902), *The County Chairman* (1924), and *The College Widow* (1924). Somewhat as in the case of Ade, Tarkington's plays are light and entertaining and of about the same value, one of the best—perhaps, the best—being *The Guardian* (1904, written with Harry Leon Wilson). Consequently, we must conclude that the greatest Hoosier dramatist is Moody.

Satire, humor, the short story, the familiar essay, and drama were absent in the period following the Golden Age.

Comparing as a whole the three periods, Early Literature, the Golden Age, and Literature since the Golden Age, we should observe that sentimentality is the dominant attitude before 1871 and that it continues strongly in the poetry in the later period. Yet, in the Golden Age, which was overshadowed by the novel, and in the last period romanticism is dominant. Realism, as in Edward Eggleston, forms a minority report on the Hoosier scene. One must note, also, that whereas there were practically no professional writers in the early period and few in the third, the main figures of the Golden Age are all, to at least some degree, professional men or women of letters.

The most outstanding Indiana authors of all three periods were, in order of birth, Sarah T. Bolton, Alice Cary, Lew Wallace, Edward Eggleston, George Cary Eggleston, Maurice Thompson, Mary Hartwell Catherwood, James Whitcomb Riley, Caroline Virginia Krout, Charles

Major, Evaleen Stein, George Ade, George Barr Mc-
Cutcheon, Meredith Nicholson, Kin Hubbard, Gene
Stratton Porter, William Vaughn Moody, Booth Tarkington, Margaret Bruner, Charles Scoggins, McCready
Huston, and Marguerite Young. And the greatest Indiana
authors are Edward Eggleston, Moody, and Tarkington.
Through all these writers—and, of course, many others—
good literature has constantly gushed from the well springs
of Indiana and has been produced nearly as regularly as
corn and cut limestone.

An interesting observation can be made as to the geographical location of the writers within the state. If a line
were to be drawn across Indiana north of Lafayette, com-
partively few of the main writers—and lesser writers as
well—would be above it. Central and southern Indiana,
then, have dominated Hoosier literature. Just what reasons can be given for this phenomenon is debatable. Perhaps the fact that the northern part of the state was settled
long after the rest of it and, therefore, has had far less time
in which to think in terms of literature is the most rea-
sonable explanation. Also, the heavy industrialization in
the North may have had some connection with channeling
energy into nonliterary activities.

THE CONTRIBUTION OF INDIANA
LITERATURE TO AMERICAN LITERATURE

The earliest glimmerings of Indiana literature came
in 1821 with the sensational confession book of Reuben
Kidder, *The Life and Adventures of John Dahmen;* followed in 1823 by the first issue of poetry, Mrs. Lard's
The Banks of the Ohio; in 1826 by an emigrants' guide,
John Scott's *The Indiana Gazetteer;* and in 1839 by the
first issue of fiction, B. V. Thorn's *Miahnomah.* All of

these publications were of small literary value, if of any at all. The first book of poetry worthy of note was *The Harp of the West,* published by Dr. Joseph S. Welsh in 1839; the first novel of interest was Baynard Rush Hall's *The New Purchase,* 1843; the Cary sisters began publishing in 1849 with *Poems of Alice and Phoebe Cary;* Mrs. Henry Ward Beecher's novel, *From Dawn to Daylight,* came in 1859; and Sarah T. Bolton's first book, *Poems,* appeared in 1865. Thus, we see that Indiana literature commenced long after American literature as a whole was flourishing.

Has there ever been an Indiana school of writers, such as the local colorists or the naturalists? Have these writers cohered as a group to gain united effort toward promulgating some particular type of literature or some certain set of ideas or philosophy? Have they come to be thought of like those writers who form the so-called genteel tradition of New England?

The continuity of good writing in Indiana has given rise to the loose use of the term, "the Hoosier school," by some literary historians. For example, *The New American Literature, 1890-1930,* by Fred L. Pattee (New York, 1930), contains a chapter on "The Emergence of Indiana." The *Literary History of the United States* (New York, 1948), edited by Robert E. Spiller and others, refers more than once to such a school[14] and calls it, mistakenly, a school of realism,[15] which it certainly was not.

Still, was there a Hoosier school of literature? In the sense that these many authors were bound together by geographical ties and often by the knowledge of each other and by personal friendship—yes; in the sense that these literary figures often wrote about their home state—

[14] See, for example, Wallace Stegner, Chapter 53, "Western Record and Romance," 2:871-72.

[15] See *ibid.,* 2:862-63.

yes, for twenty-two out of thirty-five novelists in the Golden Age, for example, each wrote at least one novel that deals with Indiana, the total number of such novels being sixty-four; in the sense that because of the presence of so many writers Indiana, and particularly Indianapolis, has been a literary center of sorts since the beginning of the Golden Age—yes. (Yet, Indiana has never deluded herself into posing as the literary hub of the universe.) Also, most of these writers were bound by a tie to romanticism and often to sentimentalism, and often they celebrated directly or indirectly the Hoosier scene and glorified Midwestern and Hoosier character. Indiana literature has been a lively regional literature.

On the other hand, it should be noted that Indiana writers wrote almost entirely for national audiences, that their subjects and methods varied widely, that they usually worked independently of each other and often independently of local conditions, that they had no set of shared beliefs or philosophy to propagandize. In this latter sense, then, there was no Hoosier school.

Indiana literature has tended toward the popular book —whether in poetry, the novel, or other forms. It has not been a great literature; there has been no Shakespeare, Milton, or Melville in the halls of Hoosier literary fame. The contribution of Indiana writers has been surprisingly good, nonetheless. If Hoosier literature has not always instructed its reader, still it has usually entertained him well and has excited both interest and envy. The principal contribution of Indiana to American literature, therefore, has been the strong current of romanticism during an age when the most important American writers have tended roughly from the time of the Civil War to be more or less realistic. Lesser contributions are the truthful presentation of the Hoosier character and scene as an addition to local-color literature and, also, pure entertainment. Finally, there have been many sincere writers, such as Edward Eggleston and Tarkington, who have had much in the way of serious observation and hard thinking to communicate.

RECENT INDIANA WRITERS

Production has continued at a strong rate. Writers beginning publication since 1939 who might be mentioned as examples of the continuance of the tradition are the poets of Indiana University Samuel Yellen and David Wagoner; the dramatist and novelist Joseph Arnold Hayes, whose *The Desperate Hours* has been written both as a novel and as drama; the famous essayist of World War II Ernie Pyle; and the novelists Alfred B. Guthrie, author of *The Big Sky* (1947); Oliver Robinson, author of *Mad as the Mist and the Snow* (1957); William E. Wilson, who penned *The Raiders* (1955); and Ross Lockridge, Jr., whose masterpiece *Raintree County* (1948) took America by storm.

Indiana literature, thus, ranks high with that of other states or regions. The promise of the early writings of the state has been more than fulfilled. And Hoosier letters are still progressing without a break. Indeed, to be a Hoosier is to fall heir to a rich literary heritage.

This, then, is the history of the literature of Indiana— the state where, as some say, a person is distinguished if he is *not* an author!

Early Literature

1

THE BEGINNINGS OF LITERARY
PRODUCTION IN INDIANA

THE BEGINNING of a literature often is not indicative of the type, the quantity, or the quality of the later and full production; a body of writings slowly rises and takes shape. English literature, it will be recalled, experienced a comparatively somber and martial birth in the dark brooding and battle glee of the Old English materials, with little foreshadowing of Chaucer, Shakespeare, Milton, and Dickens; and one has difficulty in finding in the works of Captain John Smith, William Bradford, the Mather dynasty, and Ann Bradstreet hints of the later flowering of the literature of the eastern seaboard of America in such people as Washington Irving, Edgar Allan Poe, Longfellow, Whitman, and Henry James. So it is with the literature of the state of Indiana. The early confessions, travel writings, poems, novels, and other types comprising its beginnings do not foretell the coming of a literary Golden Age; and often they are meager in quantity, trivial in subject, and poor in quality. Nevertheless, considering the frontier condition of the state during most of this period, some of these writings are surprisingly good.

At the outset we should make clear that certain types of literature will not be considered here.[1] Religious ma-

[1] See above, pages 18-21, for the complete list of types of material excluded from this study.

(35)

terials are beyond our purpose; yet we should, perhaps, tender an apology at this point in our progress, since during the 1820's and 1830's a veritable flood of religious tracts poured forth from the Indiana printing presses that had been established by that time. These items were an offshoot of the evangelical religion that spread like a wilderness forest fire across the frontier, and they have no literary value.   So also must we exclude a body of scientific writings produced mostly by persons resident at the New Harmony community for varying lengths of time.   The list includes such distinguished names as Thomas Say, David Dale Owen, Charles Alexandre Lesueur, Josiah Warren, John James Audubon, Constantine Samuel Rafinesque, and Alexander Philip Maximilian, Prince of Wied-Neuwied.

In addition, there are certain writers, or groups of writers, who, for one reason or another, can be only mentioned.   In Terre Haute in the late 1840's, for example, some young literati issued a manuscript magazine called the "Atlantian Journal," but this can not receive our attention, since periodicals have been excluded.   Then, two other writers likewise fall outside our province for varying reasons. Enion Kendall (?-1856), the illiterate pioneer of Cass County who dictated his poems, published two pamphlets: *A New Edition to the Narrative of Eliza Allen,* in Logansport in 1853, and *The History of Kansas, and March of the Western Army to Santa Fe and New Mexico, Thence to San Diego in California,* in Delphi, in 1854. Kendall's poetry is mere doggerel, and we cite it here only as evidence of the contemporary popularity of verse.   Mrs. Rebecca Wright Hill, of Richmond (1792?-1871), published, in Philadelphia in 1858, the first anthology ever compiled by an Indianan, *Grandmother's Scrap-Book; or, Western Gleaner,* which is hardly a "western gleaner," since it contains materials from eastern and English writers, but was undertaken in order to "instruct the young mind."

And now, having stated what we shall not cover, let us establish the procedure which we shall follow. First we shall discuss materials by types, listing each writer within the type of writing that he pursued, or in which he engaged the most, following a chronological order within each category and, also, presenting the types themselves in chronological order. Thus, in Part I we shall consider, in turn, confession literature, travel writing, poetry, the novel, the short story, and the essay; and, finally, we shall come to a few conclusions concerning this period.

CONFESSION LITERATURE

The literature of the state of Indiana begins with a peculiar type of writing. Certainly confessions are not always belles-lettres—they are far afield from poetry and fiction—yet they do have some significance in literature, as attested by the general agreement today that the Elizabethan confession writings, for instance, have literary value; and they are usually included in anthologies of Renaissance literature and often appear in anthologies of English literature in general. So it is with Indiana literature. These confessions were not composed as literary efforts; some of them were written as sensational pamphlets designed only to sell, much as some sensational newspapers or magazines are intended today; and some were bona fide attempts publicly to disavow an evil way of life and to warn others against its pitfalls.

The first writer of confessions is Reuben Kidder. Intensive research has failed to uncover more than a few facts concerning him, and he must remain for us to some extent a vague figure. Various court records show that he was a lawyer, first at Paoli, then in Springfield, in Posey County, when that town was the county seat. In 1816 he was an attorney of the Third Judicial Circuit and was admitted to practice before the state Supreme Court at its first session in Corydon in May, 1817. He brought one of the first cases to be tried before that court.[2] In addition to his legal production, however, he had had at least one contact with writing before he published his confession book, since he was credited by Edmund Dana with having prepared for the press his *Geographical Sketches on the Western Country*.[3]

Every generation has its own lurid murder trial, and Kidder capitalized on the classic trial of his day, that of John Dahmen, who was convicted on a charge of murder and hanged at New Albany, July 6, 1821. Kidder's slim book was *The Life and Adventures of John Dahmen, the Murderer of Frederick Nolte and John Jenzer; Chiefly Consisting of His Oral Confessions and Declarations, Taken Down in Prison. Also, a Brief Statement of His Trial and Execution. By Reuben Kidder, Counsellor at Law.* The volume was published at Jeffersonville in 1821 by George Smith and Nathaniel Bolton.[4]

This account is sensational literature. Kidder took advantage of the wave of excited and horrified interest that engulfed the countryside after the murders and continued

[2] Leander J. Monks, Logan Esarey, and Ernest V. Shockley (eds.), *Courts and Lawyers of Indiana* (3 vols. Indianapolis, 1916), 3:1146. Kidder is mentioned in connection with several cases cited in *ibid.*, 1:182. See also Order Book of the Indiana Supreme Court, A:2, 3; B:105, in Archives Division, Indiana State Library.

[3] Published in Cincinnati in 1819. See p. iii.

[4] Soon after publishing Kidder's book these two men moved to Indianapolis, where they founded the Indianapolis *Gazette*, the first newspaper of the new state capital. Bolton's wife was Sarah T. Bolton, one of the best poets of early Indiana.

until long after the hanging of the murderer. Since Kidder had defended Dahmen at his trial, he knew not only all the pertinent legal facts but also, through conversations with the defendant while building his defense, the story of Dahmen's entire life. All this information he utilized to the fullest degree, turning out an account that must have sold like hot cakes and must have caused shivers to run up and down spines in the Ohio Valley for years, until the copies were literally worn out. Possibly this is the reason why only two copies of the book are known to be in existence,[5] and these two copies are of the second edition.

In the *Life and Adventures* we learn that John Dahmen was born in 1791 in Cologne, Germany; from age thirteen he engaged in a life of violence, which included robbery and murder, with also mutilation of his victims evidently for the pure pleasure of it. His indulgence in almost every kind of crime soon made him wanted by the agents of several European governments. Yet, by means of his charming personality and handsome appearance he got himself admitted to a military academy in Metz, where he learned the manners of an officer and gentleman; and soon he was serving Prince Murat and adding to his previous vices an ability in dueling, forgery, and gambling. He was a member of Napoleon's forces, and in 1817, to escape arrest for forgery, he fled to the United States, where, because he could not pay for his passage, he was bound over to a plantation owner in Kentucky. Here he married and in 1820 moved to New Albany, where he immediately got into difficulty by settling on land without a title. Before this situation could be resolved, however, Frederick Nolte, a New Al-

[5] One of these copies is in the Indiana University Library; the other is in the Lane Library of the Library of Congress.

bany baker, was found murdered and his body mutilated. A charge of murder was entered against Dahmen, who lived about twenty miles out of the town. He quickly confessed to the crime and also volunteered the details of the murder of another man, John Jenzer, a few days after the first bloody deed. He was jailed, along with two horse thieves; but all three broke out, and Dahmen killed one of the thieves and then disappeared. Authorities later identified a body as that of Dahmen and considered the case closed until a letter written by the murderer from Canada to his wife in New Albany disclosed his whereabouts. A sheriff and two deputies made the long trip to the border, and, because Canadian authorities were little interested in extradition, managed to lure Dahmen over the border near Detroit on the pretext of delivering to him for the sum of fifty dollars his supposedly pregnant wife. Instead of his wife, Dahmen found a posse waiting for him; and he was rushed back to New Albany, where, after a sensational trial, he was hanged, over three thousand persons witnessing the execution.

Kidder issued his first publication on Dahmen well before the execution, and the prisoner then had printed in the New Albany *Chronicle* a "certificate" which denied the accuracy of the pamphlet. Kidder thereupon issued his second edition, to which there was attached a letter from the presiding judge at the trial, Seth Woodruff, supporting the reliability of Kidder's work.[6]

One wonders whether Kidder had read any Defoe, for his work has the air of the *Moll Flanders—Captain Singleton* type of rogue story. There is even the typical Defoe ingredient of frequent moralizing statements, the most

[6] A good account of the affair and of Kidder's book is found in an article by Kenneth R. Shafer, "Murder at New Albany; a Rare 1821 Imprint," in *Indiana Magazine of History*, 41 (1945):45-49.

significant difference between Defoe's work and Kidder's being that Kidder evidently is relating facts—but, still, in a very imaginative and lurid manner—whereas Defoe is writing fiction. And be the literary value of this book what it may, with it Kidder unwittingly began Indiana literature.

His example was soon to be followed. When a multiple Indian murder was committed in Madison County shortly thereafter, a quick-witted pioneer, who, perhaps, had read Kidder's book, capitalized on the publicity value of the horrors. James Hudson, who was born in Maryland in 1796 and had lived also in Kentucky and Ohio, had married and settled in Madison County, where he took to farming and hunting. There he fell in with a small group of neighbors that feared and hated two Indians who with their families were encamped nearby engaged in trapping. When one of the whites found that his horses were missing, the Indians were blamed, a search party was organized, and the braves and three squaws and two boys and two girls were all brutally slaughtered. All except one of the murderers were caught and incarcerated in a jail at the falls of Fall Creek. Hudson escaped, waded across a creek, and took refuge from the wintry night by crawling into a short hollow log, from which his feet protruded and froze; here he was found and hauled back to prison. The criminals were then tried and convicted, and Hudson with two others were hanged.[7]

Samuel Woodworth thereupon issued a short book, or pamphlet, about the murders and Hudson's execution.

[7] This account is authenticated in the main in Chapter XI, "The Tragedy of the Falls," in Jacob P. Dunn's *True Indian Stories* (Indianapolis, 1908), 197-212; also in J. J. Netterville (ed.), *Centennial History of Madison County, Indiana* (2 vols. Anderson, Ind., 1925), 1:70-79.

Even less information is available on this author than on Reuben Kidder. Samuel Woodworth (1785-1842), the poet and journalist who wrote the song "The Old Oaken Bucket," was evidently engaged in journalistic pursuits and the publishing of poetry in New York in 1825 and, therefore, could hardly be the author of this work. The only mention of a person of this name in Indiana contemporary records is found in the *Executive Proceedings of the State of Indiana, 1816-1836,* wherein a Samuel D. Woodworth is listed as surveyor of Hamilton County in 1823, and a footnote adds that "Woodworth had worked with William B. Laughlin and Thomas Brown making surveys in the New Purchase, and had settled in Hamilton County." The same source also lists a Samuel D. Woodworth as a justice of the peace, elected December 17, 1825, in Randolph County.[8] Inasmuch as the Hamilton County man married the daughter of a Randolph County judge in April, 1825,[9] we may assume that these two listings are of the same individual, and, lacking other evidence, we may presume that this is the author.

The complete title of his work is *The Life and Confession of James Hudson, Who was Executed on Wednesday The 12th January, 1825, At The Falls of Fall Creek, For The Murder of Logan, An Indian Chief Of The Wyandott Nation. To Which Is Added An Account Of His Execution. The Whole Written And Published At The Request Of The Deceased.* This was "Printed At The Gazette Office, For The Author" in Indianapolis in 1825, probably by George Smith and Nathaniel Bolton, the same printers who had issued Kidder's book in Jeffersonville in 1821.

[8] *Executive Proceedings of the State of Indiana, 1816-1836,* edited by Dorothy Riker *(Indiana Historical Collections,* Vol. 29, Indianapolis, 1947), 252, 576.

[9] Indianapolis *Gazette,* April 12, 1825.

Again, this is a sensational and lurid document, written to sell. And sold it must have, but there are very few copies extant today; like Kidder's book, it may simply have been read until it wore out. Writing in the first person, Woodworth follows the story already told and uses a florid, emotional, and romantic style highly unfitted to what was probably the limited vocabulary and matter-of-fact speech of James Hudson, who was evidently a rather typical uneducated, rough frontiersman. Again we are reminded of *Moll Flanders* in the sentimental style and intruding moralizings.[10]

There was still another murder to be tearfully confessed —that of Isaac Heller (Young). Heller (1809-1836) was born in Dauphin County, Pennsylvania. His book bears the following long title: *The Life And Confession of Isaac*

[10] A short historical note might be appended here. The authenticating sources (see note 7) state that after Hudson and two of the other criminals were hanged, the last convict, a youth of nineteen, was standing quaking on the scaffold with the rope around his neck when the eccentric Indiana governor, James Brown Ray, made a well-timed prearranged appearance, galloping his horse furiously through the crowd. He ascended the scaffold and addressed the youth, saying, "There are, sir, but two persons in the great universe who can save you from death; one is the great God of Heaven, and the other is James Brown Ray, governor of Indiana, who now stands before you. Here is your pardon. Go, sir, and sin no more." This dramatic appearance of the Governor saved the young man's life, but not his reason, which never returned to him completely throughout the rest of his life. Of course, the pardon could have been given long before the eleventh hour if Governor Ray had wished.

These four criminals hold the dubious distinction of being the only Hoosiers ever executed for killing Indians. This was so obviously a case of out-and-out murder that authorities felt that they had to act, particularly since leaving the killers unpunished would have aroused the tribes who still inhabited adjacent areas in great numbers. Representatives of the various tribes were invited by the authorities to attend the executions to witness the white man's justice. Sandford C. Cox, an early Indiana poet, states that as a child he stopped with his family in their wagon migration from Wayne County, Indiana, to observe the four convicted prisoners awaiting their doom.

Heller alias Isaac Young Who was executed at Liberty, Union County, Ia. on the 29th day of April, 1836 for the murder of his wife and three infant children, to which is appended a brief history of the Trial, together with the Sentence pronounced upon him by Hon. Samuel Bigger, Presiding Judge. This is a booklet of twenty-two pages, privately issued—and not too well printed—at Liberty, Indiana, in 1836, and crudely bound.

Who the real author of this work may have been is a matter of some doubt, for no name is attached to the document as author or editor, unless the printer, O. V. Duggins, could be construed as the writer. The bulk of the material consists of the "Confession," which is written, as might be expected, in the first person; but the reader suspects that the language in which it is couched springs from a more educated background than that of a person like Heller, who, according to the information given in the pamphlet, attended school altogether only about twelve months and, as stated on the first page, "never took much delight in writing and consequently wrote a poor hand." As in the case of Kidder and Woodworth, someone must simply have been attempting to turn a gruesome crime and sensational trial into money. Probably he succeeded.

In the usual style of the confession, Isaac Young tells the story of his life both in Pennsylvania and in Indiana. He shows how in his first home in Dauphin County, Pennsylvania, he early became interested in religion and how it soon became a mania with him. At times he experienced delusions of various sorts and preached, exhorting others to turn to a religious life; for he believed that he had the gift of prophecy, and that the world would soon come to an end. Yet, at night he feared that the devil was near by, and he could not sleep well. One night when he went to bed in his brother's house, he thought he was pursued by the many-headed beast spoken of in the book of Revelation; but when the beast disappeared before he could attack it, he turned his fury onto a little orphan girl sleeping in the house, beat her, and cut off her head. For this crime he was adjudged insane, was confined in chains in the poorhouse for a time, then, seeming to be again rational, he was freed. Young went immediately to Indiana, took his mother's maiden name, Heller, lived normally, married, and became the father of three children. Then his religious mania recurred; he again preached and suffered delusions, believing himself, for some time, to be the commander of a great army engaged in a righteous war. At length he yielded to a recurring impulse and murdered his wife and children with an axe. The story of his trial shows how he was judged sane and, therefore, was hanged.

The main difference between Heller's confession and the narratives of Kidder and Woodworth is that in Heller's there is considerably less moralizing. But no one interested in pleasant dreams should read this production just before going to bed.

After the blood bath of the confessions of Kidder, Woodworth, and Heller, we turn with some relief to other evils from the burden of which conscience-stricken sufferers were trying to escape. Jonathan Harrington Green (ca. 1812-?), for example, was so moved by his feeling of guilt after spending twelve years as a gambler in river towns and on Mississippi River steamboats that he issued a series of books attacking the vice. Green was born in Marietta, Ohio. In 1825, he was living with a John Bullock in Lawrenceburg, Indiana, and apparently regarded this as his headquarters. After his checkered career as a gambler, he reformed, attended Augusta College in Kentucky,

1843-44, and there wrote his first book, in which he exposed the various tricks and systems employed by gamblers; it was *An Exposure of the Arts and Miseries of Gambling; Designed Especially as a Warning to the Youthful and Inexperienced, Against the Evils of that Odious and Destructive Vice* (Cincinnati, 1843). In 1846 he married one of Bullock's granddaughters and made Lawrenceburg his home until moving in 1849 to New Haven, Connecticut. In the interest of crusading against the evils of gambling Green traveled all over the country lecturing, but financial difficulties and countercharges of gamblers against him succeeded in keeping the more critical public suspicious of him, even though he claimed endorsers such as Horace Greeley and Edgar Allan Poe.[11]

His other works, of the same general type as the first, were *The Gambler's Mirror* (Baltimore, 1844), *Gambling Unmasked* (New York, 1844), *Secret Band of Brothers* (Philadelphia, 1847), *Twelve Days in the Tombs; or, a Sketch of the Last Eight Years of the Reformed Gambler's Life* (New York, 1851), and *The Reformed Gambler; or, the History of the Later Years of the Life of Jonathan H. Green (the Reformed Gambler)* (Philadelphia, n.d. [1858]). Concerning this last book Banta remarks that "he went into such minute detail in describing the means by which the professional sharper mulcted his victims that the work became the foremost text for ambitious young men who wished to learn the lucrative trade which Mr. Green sought to destroy. The book had a remarkable sale."[12] Perhaps the same observation might be true of his first book, since it also went into great detail. Such is the fate of reformers!

[11] Biography in Banta, *Indiana Authors and Their Books*, 123.
[12] *Ibid.*, xv.

Two more confession writers remain to be covered, Luther Benson and Mason Long. Even though they published after the end of the first period of Indiana literature, in 1877 and 1878, respectively, we shall include them here in order to complete our discussion of this literary genre. After all, their dates of publication came close to the closing year of the period of early Indiana literature, which is 1870.

Following the Mexican War the tide of religious writings of the 1820's and 1830's waned somewhat; and a militant new crusade, bred in Puritan New England, roared into Indiana—based on the conviction that most of the evils of life originated in the excessive use of alcohol. Preachers, lecturers, and writers flocked to the cause of temperance.

Perhaps the answer to the temperance worker's prayer was Luther Benson (1847-1898). If anyone ever penned a soul-searing diatribe against drink, it was this converted drunkard; his *Fifteen Years in Hell* (Indianapolis, 1877) was republished in the seventies and eighties so often that it must have been a best seller in its long period of life. In a partly autobiographical, partly impressionistic, and partly incoherent manner, as though, perhaps, he were writing under the emotional stimulant of that which he sought to destroy, Benson rages and rants at alcohol.

Benson knew what he was talking about. He was born in Rush County, Indiana, and went to log schoolhouses and to Moore's Hill College, but his subsequent study of law was interrupted by the advent of his weakness, which dogged him for years. He entered, nevertheless, upon a sporadic law practice at Rushville, which he followed as much as the addiction to alcohol would permit. When he finally freed himself from this evil, he devoted most of the rest of his life to lecturing throughout Indiana and also in the East for the temperance cause.[13]

The last of the confession writers, Mason Long (1842-1903), was a reformed gambler and drunkard who took up religion and repudiated his former life. Born in Luray, Licking County, Ohio, he was orphaned at the age of ten and was reared in Medina, Ohio, by a German farmer. He served in the Union Army from 1862 to 1865, when he removed to Fort Wayne, Indiana, and let himself sink into a life of drink and professional gambling. Yet, after fifteen years of such existence, he repented of it, joined a Baptist church, and marshaled his energies as a professional reformer.[14]

Though he wrote *Fallen Women* (Fort Wayne, Indiana, 1880) and *Save the Girls* (Fort Wayne, 1883), both on the subject of why and how fallen women are to be saved, his most popular work was *The Life of Mason Long, the Converted Gambler, Being a Record of his Experience as a White Slave; a Soldier in the Union Army; a Professional Gambler; a Patron of the Turf; a Variety Theater and Minstrel Manager; and, Finally, a Convert to the Murphy Cause, and to the Gospel of Christ* (Chicago, 1878). The popularity of this book is attested by the fact that it went through at least twelve editions. The long title is sufficient to characterize the volume; a religious tone and a deep feeling of remorse are prevalent throughout.

Not much needs be said to conclude our discussion of Indiana confession literature. Images of bloody knives and axes, empty bottles, and decks of "the devil's picture cards" hang heavily over these writings. In a sense, of course, these emotional outpourings are not real literature

[13] Biography in Banta, *Indiana Authors and Their Books*, 25-26.
[14] Biography in *ibid.*, 195.

—indeed, many of the writers in a preface ask the reader to forgive their lack of literary art—yet, these are interesting documents reflecting the times.

TRAVEL WRITING

Like confession literature, travel writing, of course, does not lie within the immediate purpose of our study, for it certainly cannot be classified as belles-lettres; nevertheless, this type of writing has frequently been accorded the status of literature, as can be seen by a glance at many anthologies of English and American literature, and it is significant because it lies at the beginning of Indiana's literary production—to say nothing of its intrinsic importance in the light it sheds on the gloom of the wilderness or on the society of the pioneers. Also, some of the writing is rather well worded and polished, in spite of the obvious interest of the writer in being primarily factual. In short, this material is well worth reading.

There are two kinds of travel writing: emigrants' guides or gazetteers and Hoosier travel narratives. The first type, usually written by foreigners or residents of eastern states, arose from a desire to give information about a region the author had visited, together with an estimate of its possibilities. Many of the guides even gave detailed instructions as to how to reach the region, what equipment to bring, errors to be avoided, and what to do upon arrival. The second type of travel writing, Hoosier travel narratives, was mostly a later production, being written by Indiana residents who either journeyed within the state or else left their homes in order to travel to the Far West to find new homes or to search for gold with the "forty-niners." Some of these narratives were the result of twilight reminiscing, viewing the trip in retrospect

through the eyes of old age some forty or fifty years afterwards.

Since the emigrants' guides, naturally, appeared first,
they will occupy our immediate attention.

EMIGRANTS' GUIDES

Many of the emigrant guides were designed to attract
immigrants to the new state and to instruct them; but
inasmuch as we are concerned here with Indiana authors
only, it is necessary to eliminate all but two of the writers,
the others being nonresidents who may have traveled
briefly in the state and then wrote about the area.[15]

The Hoosier writers of this type of material are John
Scott and Henry Ellsworth. John Scott (1793-1838) was
born in Cumberland County, Pennsylvania, and became
a printer, married in 1814, and in 1816 moved with his
wife and son to Brookville, Indiana. Then followed a
career as an itinerant printer and publisher (and, also,
Methodist exhorter) in which he moved from one Indiana
town to another, being engaged mostly in newspaper editing and publishing in Brookville, Centerville, and Logansport, in which last town he died. He published the first
newspaper in northern Indiana at Logansport, *The Pota-
wattimie & Miami Times,* the first number appearing
probably August 15, 1829. At Centerville in 1826 he had
written and published with William M. Doughty, later
coroner of Wayne County, *The Indiana Gazetteer, or
Topographical Dictionary, Containing a Description of
the Several Counties, Towns, Villages, Settlements, Roads,
Lakes, Rivers, Creeks, Springs, &c. in the State of Indiana,*

---

[15] The best collection of excerpts from emigrants' guides and from
travel literature in general, at least in so far as they relate to Indiana,
is Harlow Lindley (ed.), *Indiana As Seen By Early Travelers* (Indiana
Historical Commission, Indianapolis, 1916).

Alphabetically Arranged. That this *Gazetteer* was intended, at least partly, to be used as an emigrant guide is indicated by the advertisements which were run in newspapers of the state carrying testimonials to the value of the publication to the emigrant and to those interested in the state's topography. The *Gazetteer* sold for twenty-five cents a copy or two dollars a dozen. It is marked by a quaint dignity, charm, a beauty of style, and an optimism which was typical of contemporary guides and gazetteers. Because of the lack of available information Scott had been forced to gather most of his materials at first hand in a day when mails were slow and communication difficult. Moreover, the state was in a condition of flux; towns were springing up overnight, county seats were being established, roads were being opened; yet there were large sections, mostly Indian lands, which still were not very well known. It should not astonish us, therefore, that Scott made some errors in fact, such as in the location of places and in dates and the use of statistics. In spite of these mistakes, the *Gazetteer* was, in general, surprisingly accurate and must have been very useful to the emigrant considering Indiana as a future home.[16]

A different sort of writer was Henry William Ellsworth (1814-1864). Born in Windsor, Connecticut, the son of Henry Leavitt Ellsworth, a lawyer, he was educated in Connecticut, graduating from Yale in 1834; in 1836 he migrated to Lafayette, Indiana, in the vicinity of which his father had secured large areas of land from the Federal government. He opened a law office and soon was involved in sales of lands, taking over his father's extensive

---

[16] The 1954 reissue of Scott's *Gazetteer* by the Indiana Historical Society (as Volume 18, No. 1, of its *Publications*) points up the importance of this publication and gives much interesting information about it and the author.

interests upon the latter's departure to become commissioner of patents in Washington, D. C. Soon he was engaged in politics, supporting Polk in the campaign of 1844, was a presidential elector, and was rewarded by being appointed by Polk to the position of chargé d'affaires to Norway and Sweden. He performed the duties of this position successfully until 1849, when he was charged with having attempted to smuggle British goods into Sweden. A controversy over his alleged guilt arose, which continued for years; but an investigation supported the charges, and he was dismissed. He returned to the United States in 1849 and continued his law practice until his health broke.[17]

His *Valley of the Upper Wabash, Indiana, with Hints on Its Agricultural Advantages: Plan of a Dwelling, Estimates of Cultivation, and Notices of Labor-Saving Machines* was published in New York in 1838 and was an endeavor to advertise his father's lands in the hope of stimulating immigration and making sales. The attempt was successful, for both settlers and speculators became interested; and fortunately, it was good farm land and eminently worth the purchase price.

This little book of less than two hundred pages affords some of the most interesting reading not only in its class of literature but of any type of book written in pioneer Indiana. In the introduction the author claims that he wrote "from a desire to answer numerous inquiries addressed to him by friends, and inability to effect that object, without a great expense of time and labor, in the ordinary modes of correspondence." Some of these inquiries had reference to "the purchase and sale of lands; the cost and profit of their cultivation; the products best

[17] See the biography of Ellsworth in Banta, *Indiana Authors and Their Books,* 101-2.

adapted to their soil; the income to be derived from different agricultural operations; the benefits resulting from the introduction and use of various labor-saving machines; together with the lines of communication open, or to be established, as well for travel as the exportation of produce. To impart such information is the object of this work," he says. He then praises the West for its possibilities and future greatness and states that he selected Indiana and "the rich valley of the Wabash" as his subject "partly because it was his residence" and partly because "the position of that valley, the extraordinary productiveness of its soil, its delightful climate, and its means of rapid communication with the markets of the northern and southern States, seem to designate it as a region better adapted than any other as the field of agricultural experiment, and the home of the enterprising settler."[18]

The reader must certainly agree that this is one of the most optimistic accounts ever penned! Ellsworth gives detail after detail relative to such subjects as the geographical position of the Wabash Valley; the fertility of the soil; railroads, canals, and towns in northern Indiana; errors for emigrants to avoid, like suffering from exposure because of moving onto land before a cabin has been built; crops which could be grown; the cost of various farm operations; estimates of costs in preparing various acreages for farming, up to one thousand acres; and he adds a plan for a frame house and sketches of various sorts of farm machinery (all horse-operated). All these items are presented in the most glowing terms, and the author even remarked that the profits of one year's work on a prairie farm were sufficient to pay for the cost and the usual expenditures!

[18] Ellsworth, *Valley of the Upper Wabash,* iii, viii.

Here, then, was Utopia for the grasping! How could the non-Hoosier with an itching foot, considering a new home, resist this invitation?

HOOSIER TRAVEL NARRATIVES

The first division of Hoosier travel narratives is the smaller of the two; it is concerned with Indiana residents who wrote about travels in their state, and it contains only two names, Isaac Reed and George Winter.

Isaac Reed (1787-1858), a pioneer Presbyterian minister and circuit rider, was born in Granville, New York, was graduated in 1812 from Middlebury College, Vermont, taught school and studied law for a time, then decided upon the ministry and, in search of a climate more beneficial to his health, came to Kentucky in 1816 as an agent of the Presbyterian societies of New England. After a short period spent preaching on a circuit in Kentucky, he visited Indiana in 1818 and became that year pastor of a church in the newly created town of New Albany, also making many trips to preach throughout southern Indiana. He founded the first Sunday School in the state. Until 1827, when he returned to the East, he traveled and preached for the Missionary Society of Connecticut in many sections of Kentucky and Indiana, founding and helping to organize many churches and also serving pastorates in Indianapolis, Bloomington, and Owen County, in which latter place he built a log cabin. His wife was Elinor Young, a sister of Mrs. Baynard Rush Hall, whose husband was the first professor of the school that became Indiana University. It was Hall who wrote *The New Purchase*.[19]

[19] See below, 153-56. For further details of Reed's life, see Banta, *Indiana Authors and Their Books*, 265.

Reed's narrative, *The Christian Traveller. In Five Parts. Including Nine Years, and Eighteen Thousand Miles,* was published in New York in 1828, soon after his return from the West, and is a charming account of his travels and experiences while preaching in Indiana, Ohio, and Kentucky, but mostly Indiana. He traces his journey from New England to Kentucky, his residence and work at New Albany, his travels, again, in Kentucky and also Ohio, and his return to Indiana and his labor there, along with many observations on the condition of the state. Throughout the entire account there is an air of piety, of self-sacrifice, and of devotion to his lifework. No congregation in a wintry wilderness log cabin was too small or too remote, no duty too severe, no road too primitive or ford too swift and dangerous for him to exert himself to hold his services or extend his help. And throughout his narrative one catches true glimpses of the pioneer condition of the state—the backwoods diseases, the dress, customs, manner of living, and the like— all of which reveal to the reader early Indiana: on the one hand supine and faltering in its weakness, like a newly hatched bird, and, on the other hand, strong in the power and desire to grow—in the direction of a civilized society.

George Winter (1809-1876) was of a much different cast than Reed. Inasmuch as part of his journal was first printed piecemeal as a series of articles in the Logansport *Telegraph,*[20] and since part was written first in a copy-book and never saw print until the entire journal was assembled only recently, Winter hardly belongs in a literary history which maintains as one of its entrance requirements the publication on the part of the prospec-

[20] The dates of these articles are November 4, 11, 18, 25, and December 2, 1837.

tive writer of at least one book. Nevertheless, even though his is a questionable inclusion, we shall cite him in passing as an early Indiana travel writer of very interesting material.

Winter's journal was assembled from materials which he left at his death to his family and which found their way eventually to the Tippecanoe County Historical Museum. The Indiana Historical Society published the journals and representative paintings in 1948 as *The Journals and Indian Paintings of George Winter, 1837-1839*.[21]

Having been born in England and having received but little schooling, George Winter came to the United States in 1830, studied art for a short time in New York, and then let his romantic desire to paint Indians draw him to the West. Here on the banks of the Wabash in the spring of 1837 he found himself in the frontier town of Logansport, then less than ten years old, but already numbering about two thousand inhabitants. The Potawatomi and Miami tribes were still living in large numbers in this area, though soon to leave on their enforced migration to lands beyond the Mississippi. The artist came at an auspicious time. He quickly made friends, not only with white residents of Logansport and Lafayette, but also with a number of the Indians. He circulated freely among the tribes in these two years, 1837 to 1839, painting portraits of many Indians. One of his subjects was Frances Slocum, "the lost sister among the Miamis,"[22] who had been kidnaped at the age of five by Delaware Indians from her home in Pennsylvania and who, along with her Indian daughters, was found by her family only in her old age in Indiana, having lived as an Indian

[21] See this book for biographical details regarding Winter.
[22] See the book of that title by Otho Winger (Elgin, Ill., 1936).

her entire life. The many sketches and paintings by this frontier artist-writer present the Indians as they actually were, wearing sometimes, for example, a frock coat of the latest fashion and a turban, instead of being attired, according to the usual idea of an Indian, in war paint and feathers.

His journals show that he moved freely and without restraint among the Indians, frequenting their ceremonials, councils, dances, and burials; and there glows throughout the accounts a sympathy and understanding not found in many quarters in that era. He shows that these people were human beings, and fascinating ones, too, each an individual distinct in physique, features, dress, actions, and personality. No hand is raised in anger in his records; and the war whoop and scalping knife are happily absent. Instead, what the reader finds here is one of the very best accounts of the people who gave their name to the state and the condition in which they were living just before they were forced out of the state into eventual disaster.

The second division of Hoosier travel narratives consists of writers who left accounts of their journeys to the Far West. All residents of Indiana, these men were seized by a wanderlust which led them on perilous journeys, but they eventually returned to Indiana at least long enough to set down, sometimes many years later, the interesting aspects of their adventures. These persons include Overton Johnson, William Winter, Joel Palmer, James Abbey, David Leeper, Reuben Shaw, and Origen Thomson.

Overton Johnson (1820?-1849) and William Henry Winter (1819-1879) collaborated on a book and, hence, must be considered together. Johnson was born in Ohio, but by 1834 his family had moved to Indiana, residing in and around Crawfordsville, where Johnson attended the preparatory department of Wabash College, from 1834 to 1838, and the College itself, from 1838 to 1840 and part of the academic year 1840-41. While at Wabash he wore his brown hair long, letting it fall over the shoulders in the style of the plainsmen; and when the college dormitory burned in 1838, he became so flustered that from his room on the second floor he threw out of the window his water pitcher, wash basin, looking glass, and gold watch and then came down the stairs carrying a load of clothing and bedding. A fellow student was William H. Winter, and the two must have been infected with the western fever, for they evidently planned their trip to Oregon at this time. In 1843 Johnson and Winter became members of a wagon train heading west. The former returned from the journey with notes which Winter had made and in 1846 published a book as a product of their combined efforts. Johnson did not live long enough after this publication to enjoy its popularity, however, for after teaching school for a year and, evidently, planning to return to California with Winter, he died in 1849.[23]

A manuscript of William H. Winter's youngest son, De Winter, in the Wabash College Archives,[24] records that his father was born in Vigo County, Indiana, that his mother had been married before, and that one of her daughters by her first marriage was Maria Akin, who married Major Elston, of Crawfordsville. A daughter of this couple became the wife of Lew Wallace. Winter grew up in and around Crawfordsville and was a student in the preparatory department of Wabash College 1834-36 and

[23] For biographical details of Johnson, see Banta, *Indiana Authors and Their Books,* 168-69.

[24] Quoted in *ibid.,* 344-45. The Wabash College Archives also contain biographical information concerning Johnson.

1839-40. Apparently he never enrolled in the college itself, and in 1843 he and his friend Johnson joined a wagon train starting from Independence, Missouri, heading for the Pacific Coast by way of the Platte River, Fort Laramie, Fort Hall, Idaho, and into what is now Oregon. There the company divided, one group staying in Oregon and the other group, with which Johnson and Winter were associated, going south into California, later rejoining the other party. At Soda Springs Winter gave the notes he had taken on the entire trip to Johnson, who then returned to Indiana, where he published their book. Winter's later career was varied and colorful. He remained for a time in California, returned to Indiana through Mexico and New Orleans in 1846, was captain of a company leaving Missouri in 1849 bound for the gold mines of California, returned home by way of the Isthmus of Panama, married, and within a short time brought his family west, heading another company, became a wealthy California farmer and rancher, and founded the town of Fall River Mills, where he died.

The travel narrative of these two friends was entitled *Route Across the Rocky Mountains, with a Description of Oregon and California; Their Geographical Features, Their Resources, Soil, Climate, Productions, Etc. Etc.* A small edition was published by John B. Semans, the editor of the *Tippecanoe Journal and Lafayette Free Press,* being printed by the presses of this paper in Lafayette in 1846. The book is now extremely rare and still brings one of the highest prices of early Indiana imprints. It was thought important enough to be reprinted in 1932 as one of the Princeton University Press series of Narratives of the Trans-Mississippi Frontier.

This book tells part of the story of the important emigration of 1843 to Oregon when sovereignty of that area was in dispute and Canadians were in possession and when California was still a province of Mexico. This emigration, the most significant up until that time, was known as the "Great Migration" and consisted of a thousand persons traveling in 121 wagons with 694 oxen and 773 cattle. Evidently Johnson and Winter were members of a smaller group, however, but still part of the "Migration." Their narrative covers the round trip to Oregon and back, telling of the hardships and pleasures of the trail, such as the discomfort caused by bad weather, numerous brushes with Indians of several tribes, and a fight with grizzly bears, and describes various western outposts, like Fort Boise, Fort Vancouver, and Sutter's fort, fur traders, vast herds of buffalo, Mexicans dancing their fandangos, towering ranges of nearly impassable mountains, and broad rivers, vast waste lands, and rich farming areas.

If this were all that the reader got from the book, it would be eminently worth reading, in spite of the misspellings and other printing errors, which are not unusual in early printing. But the authors were sensible and were not impressed too easily; accordingly, they set down in everyday English a careful and accurate account of what they saw and experienced, neither minimizing the obstacles to travel and settlement nor exaggerating the glories and advantages of the Far West. Realizing that the readers of the book most likely would be potential emigrants, the authors found it wise to condense the material, to keep their own personalities in the background, and, in the appendix, to give information that emigrants would probably need, such as what they could expect to find in the way of climate, soil, and commercial possibilities of the country; what clothing, equipment, provisions, and animals to bring; how to treat the Indians;

how long to expect the journey to take; and how, in general, to conduct themselves to insure safety and comfort. The authors even included a "Bill of the Route" giving a list of the water courses, information about supplies of wood, grass, and water, and mileages from Independence, Missouri, to the mouth of the Columbia River. The book, thus, is partly an emigrants' guide.

Perhaps the most significant aspect of the volume is the imaginative picture given of the Pacific Coast as a part of the United States. This rosy conception must have filled many readers with a dissatisfaction and an urge to leave their homes. Of course, Johnson and Winter made errors, as in following the rather common belief that the prairie and Rocky Mountain regions were of little use to the country, and one wishes that they had recorded more of their contacts with such people as Captain Sutter; still their production was—and will remain—a fascinating one.[25]

Whether Joel Palmer (1810-1881) was influenced by whatever popularity the book of Johnson and Winter enjoyed is difficult to determine, but Palmer's travel narrative was published in 1847, a year after that of the Crawfordsville friends, and resembles theirs greatly in its overall plan. Palmer was born in Ontario, Canada, of Quaker parents, who returned to the state of New York at the outbreak of the War of 1812. At the age of nineteen he went to work as a laborer on canals and other projects in Bucks County, Pennsylvania, thereby learning canal construction. In 1836 he was residing in Laurel, Indiana, holding a contract for constructing a portion of the White-

---

[25] An interesting sidelight is that the first novel written in Oregon, *The Prairie Flower*, by Sidney Moss, was completed in 1843; and possibly it was Overton Johnson who brought the manuscript back East, to be published in Cincinnati in 1844.

water Canal; his prosperity and standing are evidenced by the fact that in 1842-43 and 1844-45 he served in the Indiana General Assembly as a representative of Franklin County. But success in business and politics could not hold Palmer long, and he soon succumbed to the western fever and made a trip to Oregon similar to that of Johnson and Winter and covering much of the same ground. In 1847 he returned to Indiana, published his book in Cincinnati, then made the trip again to Oregon, laying out the town of Dayton and building a gristmill there. He served as Superintendent of Indian Affairs for the Oregon Territory in 1853 and was a force in state politics the rest of his life, dying in Dayton in 1881.[26]

Palmer's account, like several of these early travel narratives, is a very rare book. The entire title gives a good summary of the contents: *Journal of Travels over the Rocky Mountains, to the Mouth of the Columbia River; Made During the Years 1845 and 1846; Containing Minute Descriptions of the Valleys of the Willamette, Umpqua, and Clamet; a General Description of Oregon Territory; Its Inhabitants, Climate, Soil, Productions, Etc., Etc.; a List of Necessary Outfits for Emigrants; and a Table of Distances from Camp to Camp on the Route. Also; A Letter from the Rev. H. H. Spalding, resident Missionary, for the last ten years, among the Nez Percé Tribe of Indians, on the Koos-koos-kee River; The Organic Laws of Oregon Territory; Tables of about 300 words of the Chinook Jargon, and about 200 Words of the Nez Percé Language; a Description of Mount Hood; Incidents of Travel, &c., &c.* Like the book of Johnson and Winter, Palmer's account, then, was designed to fulfill two purposes—to afford interesting reading on a subject that was attracting more and more attention through the nation

---

[26] See sketch of Palmer in Banta, *Indiana Authors and Their Books*, 250.

and to provide an emigrants' guide for the restless spirit. The book succeeded in both aims.

Palmer's narrative is better printed than that of Johnson and Winter; it is well composed, has good grammar, good spelling, and careful description. Palmer does not scruple to present the less favorable aspects of the arduous journey, showing, for example, how emigrants often came to grief through lack of food and water, the failure of their horses or oxen, unfavorable weather, and molestation or attack by Indians. Yet, there pulses through the narrative a fortitude and courage and zest for adventure that carries both the emigrants through to Oregon and the reader to the end of the book. What is lacking in Palmer is the glowing picture of the American Pacific Coast found in Johnson and Winter.

The next recorder of travels to the Far West, James Abbey (dates unknown), followed the style laid down by the team of Johnson and Winter and also by Joel Palmer, except that instead of a trip to Oregon he tells of a journey to the California gold fields; he writes in the form of a diary, with daily entries. Abbey was born in England but apparently was brought as a baby or a child to the United States by his parents. The name of his mother, Mrs. Bersheba Abbey, is listed in the city directories of New Albany from 1848 to 1868, and James Abbey is entered as boarding at the same address as that of his mother in the directory for 1859. For many years Abbey was employed as a steward on the steamboat "United States," which plied between Louisville and New Orleans. He often did reporting for the New Albany *Ledger,* supplying river notes and other items.[27] Inasmuch as in his narrative he frequently speaks in a familiar

[27] Information from Elsa Strassweg of the New Albany Public Library, in a letter to the author, July 25, 1956.

manner of fellow travelers from New Albany and is careful to include the names of all New Albany emigrants met on the trail, and since he often mentions his home, with strong implications that it was that town, we may assume that he had lived in New Albany some time before going west.

Abbey's account, entitled *California. A Trip Across the Plains, in the Spring of 1850, Being a Daily Record of Incidents of the Trip over the Plains, the Desert, and the Mountains, Sketches of the Country, Distances from Camp to Camp, Etc., and Containing Valuable Information to Emigrants, as to Where They Will Find Wood, Water, and Grass at Almost Every Step of the Journey,* was published in New Albany that same year.[28] It is a booklet of 64 pages, priced at the time of publication at 20 cents, and is very rare today. The publishers' introduction states that

> The following brief notes of a trip across the plains makes no pretensions to literary display or rhetorical flourish. Their author is a young man who lays no claim to either of these characteristics. Indeed, they were not written with a view to publication in the present form. But the first portion of the sketches (which were published in the columns of the New Albany Ledger) having attracted the attention of a large number of readers as giving life-like, and beyond question truthful descriptions of the scenes which the writer and his companions daily encountered in their arduous journey, it was believed that it would be doing the public a service to lay the sketches or diary before them in the present form.[29]

Abbey's entries date from April 24 to September 11, 1850, and record his progress from St. Joseph, Missouri,

[28] Abbey's book was published by Kent & Norman, and J. R. Nunemacher. It was republished by William Abbott in the *Magazine of History* (New York), 46 (1933):107-63.

[29] Abbey, *California,* 3.

which he and some friends had reached after a journey of eleven days from New Albany, to the California gold fields, where they arrived in the vicinity of Weaversville (evidently the modern Weaverville) on August 19. He must have sent his material back to New Albany in four parts; for the entries are so divided, bearing the following headings: "10 Miles from St. Joseph, April 24, 1850," "Indian Territory, 8 miles from Fort Kearny, May 12, 1850," "Fort Laramie, June 1, 1850," and "Weaversville, Cal., Sept. 11th, 1850." The material was published in the *Ledger* on May 8, June 21, July 15 and 16.

The reader discovers about the same things in Abbey's account as in others, except, of course, that the route covered was somewhat different, following the valley of the Platte River to Salt Lake City, then across the mountains to northern California. Also, he and his friends experienced no difficulty with the Indians, fortunately. The writer very carefully records happenings of each day, listing, for example, how many wagons there were in the various wagon trains which he saw, how many abandoned wagons and how many dead oxen and dead horses he saw on certain days, what landmarks, like Courthouse Rock, Chimney Rock, and Independence Rock, were passed, and how many emigrants turned about and headed for home, having seen "the elephant"—that is, having gotten "fed up." Abbey traveled mostly in a train consisting of seven wagons, five of which were from New Albany, covering from two to twenty-four miles a day. The men celebrated the Fourth of July when west of Salt Lake by reading the Declaration of Independence, drinking toasts, and firing salutes with their rifles. The group had the same experience that many other emigrants did, in that toward the end of the journey the oxen became so exhausted that they could no longer pull the wagons, and the men were forced to abandon their wagons and pack their most essential belongings on the backs of the oxen. From the time of their arrival in California till the last entry in his journal, Abbey and the rest of the party prospected for gold, with increasing disgust on the part of the author, who, like so many other miners, found little of the precious yellow metal to compensate for the heavy labor involved in obtaining it. The most money he ever made in one day was nine dollars. If his luck continued like this, perhaps we can understand why he eventually returned home.

What differentiates Abbey's narrative from others of the same kind is not necessarily such things as his frequent killing of rattlesnakes but rather his feeling for religion—he recorded religious sentiments in his journal and disliked to travel or work on Sundays—and also his compassion for the sick and the dead, both men and animals. He would take pains to doctor sick men and sick oxen for whatever period of time was possible. Once when he found the newly made grave of an emigrant which wolves had disturbed, he walked several miles in order to borrow a spade with which to repair the grave; and he revisited it the next morning to be sure that the wolves had not undone his work. Thus, even though the emphasis of Abbey's account is always on fact stated in a sparse style, usually of understatement, still his own character and sweetness of spirit glimmer through it. Any value that this book had as an emigrants' guide is indirect, for no instructions are given to the prospective emigrant.

The last three authors of Hoosier travel narratives wrote near the end of their lives, viewing in retrospect the hazardous journeys they had taken in their youth, the books appearing in 1894 and 1896. Even though these volumes were published long after the closing date of the first phase of Indiana literature to which this present chapter is devoted, we include the discussion of them here since they are concerned with the same period of history and because these travel narratives belong together, constituting a literary genre. Also, in at least one case the material was simply assembled, and probably rewritten, from notes jotted down at the time of the trip. Perhaps the most interesting aspect of these narratives is the fact that old age did not seem to glamourize the experiences of a half-century before, and the writers set them down as realistically as if they had written shortly after returning home. These men are David Leeper, Reuben Shaw, and Origen Thomson.

The first of these, David Rohrer Leeper (1832-1900), was born near South Bend in a log cabin and spent his boyhood on the farm near the town. When he was seventeen years old, the California gold rush began, and Leeper persuaded his father to supply him with the essentials for making the trip. Leaving the seminary in South Bend, where he was a student, he joined five other young men, the oldest being twenty-five, in starting with two covered wagons to drive to Missouri and then all the way to the California gold fields, where three of the original six finally arrived after seven months and sixteen days of adventurous struggle. After having been gone five years, Leeper returned in 1854 to South Bend, attended school, and later served in the Indiana legislature. He wrote articles on local history and in 1894 published in South Bend *The Argonauts of 'Forty-Nine. Some Recollections of the Plains and the Diggings*.[30]

This is a very readable book. It is similar to the other narratives in the story it tells, the sights described, the

[30] A brief biography of Leeper appears in Banta, *Indiana Authors and Their Books*, 189-90.

privations endured, and the adventures encountered, except that the party experienced no serious trouble from the Indians until late in the journey. The alternating of optimism and pessimism of the California miner's life is well depicted. This was a young man's journey, full of zest in the midst of monotony, hunger, thirst, discouragement, and danger—and the appetite for all of it does not diminish through being told by the young man now grown old. Leeper appends to the story a long list of St. Joseph County Argonauts who responded to the lure of California gold, and the book is made more attractive by the inclusion of sketches depicting typical scenes involving the "forty-niners."

Somewhat the same sort of book was produced by Reuben Cole Shaw (1826-1903) in his *Across the Plains in Forty Nine,* published in 1896. He was born in Boston, his father dying shortly afterward, leaving his mother with three small children to provide for. Shaw had to be put out as a "bound" boy; later he became a master carpenter and joiner. He married in 1847, and when his first-born was less than a year old, he fell victim to the California gold fever, rejoining his family after an absence of two years, but bearing wealth only in the form of experience rather than in shape of the precious glistening dust. Having noticed on his journey the advantages of life in the Middle West, he brought his family in 1853 to Ross County, Ohio; and three years later they moved to the edge of the frontier in Kossuth County, Iowa. After a profitless struggle of five years there, he determined to return to Ross County, but the family became stranded in the little town of Farmland, Indiana, near Muncie. There he found his real California. Delighted with the pleasant, friendly community, he spent the rest of his long life there, as a farmer, miller, merchant, educator, and financier, becoming one of the leaders and one of the most respected men in the community. In Farmland he wrote his California narrative, which the Farmland *Enterprise* printed in installments in 1895; it was later collected and published in a small edition, which had little circulation at the time.

The amateurish, jerky style of the volume is an obstacle to the enjoyment of the reader; and the old man has much difficulty in remembering dates, details, and the sequence of events of this trip of his youth. Often there are obvious omissions of facts which must once have been familiar to the author, and the account is never really completed. Certainly the story was written from memory. But even though the reader is not always rewarded by finding a day-by-day factual account of the long overland journey from Boston to California of Shaw and the entire Mount Washington Mining Company of fifty men, of which he was a member, still he is often charmed by the impressionistic accounts of nature and the Indians which Shaw gives in copious quantities. That the author was to some extent cognizant of his essential interest is shown by his "Introductory," in which he states:

> To those who court adventure, and love to view from lofty mountain heights the wonders of primeval things, it [his book] may prove interesting; while to those who care less for the grandeur and beauty of nature it will probably be of little interest.

Nevertheless, in spite of its defects the Lakeside Press considered this narrative interesting enough to issue a reprint of it in 1948 as one of The Lakeside Classics.

The last of the writers of Hoosier travel narratives was Origen Thomson (1829-1882). Thomson was born in Decatur County, attended the Decatur County Seminary in the 1830's, and with his brother Orville learned the printing trade. The years 1846 and 1847 were spent at Hanover College, after which he returned to the printing business. From 1850 to 1852 he studied medicine with a Dr. Moody. In 1852, together with his newly married sister Camilla and her husband, as part of a company of about a hundred emigrants mostly from Rush and Decatur counties, Indiana, he went by covered wagon to Oregon. There he stayed six years, helping to survey government lands. Following his return in 1858 he helped publish a newspaper, *The Hoosier State,* in Lawrenceburg, Indiana, engaged extensively in surveying for railroads in the Whitewater Valley and in Ohio, and from 1872 until his death was in the stone quarry business. He died in Greensburg in 1882.[31]

Origen Thomson's book was strictly a family project. It was privately printed by his brother Orville at Greensburg, together with an introduction by their sister Camilla and also other material, and was issued by subscription, evidently in a very small edition. What is more, it was published in 1896, fourteen years after Origen's death, and seems to be a printing of Origen's manuscript entitled "Field Notes of a Journey over the Plains in the Summer of 1852." These were originally notes taken in shorthand during the trip, then later written out in accordance with a parting request of his father. As in the case of many other travel narratives, the long-winded title is in itself descriptive of the contents of the book: *Crossing the Plains. Narrative of the Scenes, Incidents and Adventures Attending the Overland Journey of the Decatur and Rush County Emigrants to the "far-off" Oregon, in 1852. Printed from a Diary of Daily Events Kept by the Late*

---

[31] The biography of Thomson is from a typed account in the Indiana Biography Series (scrapbooks of newspaper clippings), 24: 57-58, in the Indiana Division, Indiana State Library.

Origen Thomson; With an Introductory Chapter by Mrs.
Camilla T. Donnell, and a Thrilling Narrative of a Buf-
falo Hunt and Battle Royal with Mountain Wolves, by
Mr. Sutherland McCoy. Here we find the same subject
matter of similar narratives; only the persons and the
events differ, and the company experienced no real difficulty with the Indians. The book is amateurish in construction and not very well printed. Still, it is another
narrative which so holds the reader that he finds much
difficulty in laying it down.

So ends our list of travel writers. Can we now summarize
the essential qualities of all this travel writing? As far as
the emigrants' guides are concerned, we should say that
there was a strong desire on the part of the authors to be
accurate in their descriptions and instructions, as in the
case of John Scott, and, likewise, in the case of those
who devoted a portion of their Hoosier travel narratives
to emigrants' guides—namely, Overton Johnson and William Winter and Joel Palmer. Still, there was always the
tendency to be overenthusiastic about the possibilities
of new lands, the worst example in this regard being
Henry Ellsworth, who, of course, had an ax to grind. The
writers of the Hoosier travel narratives, in addition, did
their best to present a true and accurate picture of what
they had seen and experienced, like Isaac Reed and George
Winter, both of whom described the Indiana scene, and
also all those others who described the Far West, to which
they journeyed. No document in all this travel writing
makes any pretense to literary style or even to being literature; but all of it is nothing short of fascinating for
the reader.

The writers of the chronicles of travels to the Far West
all present much the same sort of experiences and sights:
the drenching, chilling rains; the fording of swirling

brown streams; abandoned wagons and the ugly sight of dead cattle by the trail; the fiendish yelling of naked savages circling a few wagons drawn into a protective circle; the skin-tingling howling of wolves; the piercing cold of the snowy mountain passes, and the choking dust of the parched desert; disease, hunger, disaster—death. But on the other hand, there was the monotonous, but satisfying jogging over rolling prairies; the symmetry of long twisting lines of prairie schooners, with their white tops floating like clouds over the tall grass, following the lumbering oxen; the slowly moving herds of cattle; the thundering of black buffalo masses; the sense of the immensity of the open prairies or the towering mountains; the lonely campfires at night under the stars, enlivened by fellowship, a snatch of song or a twang of guitar; the feeling of being the makers of history; and the glowing anticipation of the "promised land"; mutual help, adventure, courage—success.

Certainly these narratives are valuable as history. The reader learns such facts as that the emigrant trains were usually made up at towns in Missouri, each year in March, April, or May, and followed much the same routes to their destinations, arriving, unless disaster overtook them, in something over five months; that the emigrants, being accustomed to a forest-water type of agriculture, uniformly regarded the Great Plains as a great desert incapable of becoming farm land; and, that the only attitude toward the plains and mountain Indians was that of careful watching against thieving and attack. Still, in spite of frequent amateurish writing, factual errors, indifferent construction, and careless printing, these documents record an overwhelmingly romantic spirit and are close to the status of literature.

2

POETRY

MRS. LARD—JOHN CAIN—DR. JOSEPH S. WELSH

AFTER THE SENSATIONALISM of the confession literature and the factual impact of the travel materials, we turn to a more pleasantly imaginative kind of writing, poetry, which began in Indiana at roughly the same time as the other two types.

The first Indiana poet is a "Mrs. Lard," who, in 1823, published privately at Windsor, Vermont, a twelve-page poem entitled *The Banks of the Ohio*. Just who this person was is a matter of some concern. Little information is to be gained from the publication itself; the "Advertisement" printed with the poem says that the author is a lady of Vermont now "amid the wilds of Ohio" and that this is a "Rejected Prize Poem."[1] An undated excerpt from the Cincinnati *Gazette* printed on the cover of the poem states that this was the next best poem in a contest in which twelve poems were entered, sponsored by the Philomathick Society of Cincinnati College, and that this poem "was written by a lady of Indiana."

With only such meager information to begin with, the problem of hunting down this Mrs. Lard is a thorny one.

[1] *The Banks of the Ohio* (Windsor, Vt., 1823), 2. The Indiana Historical Society Library has a photostatic copy of the volume, made from an original in the library of the Historical and Philosophical Society of Ohio.

A manuscript autobiography of Charles Kendall Laird (or Lard),[2] who was born in 1808 in Vermont and lived for some time in Indiana, says that he was the son of Mrs. Rebecca Lard, wife of Samuel Lard, and that the family moved to Indiana, the father in 1813 and the mother and children following in 1820. He represents his mother as being well educated and teaching schools in Madison and Vernon. The husband complained of this, and they were separated and finally divorced. In 1827 Charles accompanied his mother back to Vermont to visit relatives. Although there is no mention of the poem in this autobiography, we are led to conclude that this woman was the author and that she sent it back to Vermont to friends or relatives, who had it published. The Indiana census for 1830 offers substantiation for this account. A Rebecca H. Laird in the age bracket of forty to fifty is listed in Jennings County as the head of a family consisting of, beside herself, one male in the twenty-to-thirty age group. This may be the author of the poem, after her divorce, and one of her sons. A Samuel Lard is listed in the same source as the head of a family of three males.[3]

The Banks of the Ohio is written in heroic couplets and, with rather pompous and florid description, traces the history of the Ohio Valley from the earliest times to the composition of the poem, dealing with the Indians and their savagery, the rise of Indiana towns, like Vevay and Madison, and offering praise of the West, of Indiana, and of the progress of science in the West. The poem closes with an address to the Philomathean Society of

[2] In the Indiana Historical Society Library. It covers the years 1817 to 1859 and records Charles Laird's life in Indiana and his travels and experiences from southern Indiana to Vermont, down the Ohio and the Mississippi River to New Orleans, etc.

[3] U. S. Census of Indiana, 1830, vol. 7:271, photostatic copy in Genealogy Division, Indiana State Library.

Philadelphia, charging this group to take note of the rise of the West. There is a flavor of eighteenth-century neo-classical poetry about the production, and it is also stiff and wooden. Yet, it is Indiana's first recorded poem; and considering the fact that it was published when very early frontier conditions prevailed, only seven years after Indiana became a state, *The Banks of the Ohio* is more than satisfactory as poetry.

How interesting it would be to be able to examine the first complete book of poetry written by a Hoosier—and carrying the double distinction of being the first ever published in the state as well! But unfortunately, no copy of John Cain's *Miscellaneous Poems,* published evidently by himself in Indianapolis in 1832, is known to be in existence.[4] All that we can do is to recall the title and give a short biography of the author, expressing regret that no more can be done.

Captain John Cain (1805-1867) was born in Culpeper County, Virginia, where he later learned the book-binding business. Before he was twenty-one, he went to the West, working at his trade for a short time in Hamilton, Ohio. In 1826 he ventured farther west, to Indianapolis, which at that time had a population of only eight hundred, and opened the first book bindery in the town. He also opened the first bookstore at approximately the same time. He married; and having supported Andrew Jackson, was appointed postmaster after the latter's election to the Presidency in 1829, holding the position for many years. Later he engaged, unsuccessfully, in merchandising. About 1847 he sold the land he had acquired in Indianapolis, moved to Kentucky, and bought a mill and farm which he operated with Negro labor. In retaliation

---

[4] Miss Caroline Dunn, librarian of the Indiana Historical Society Library, thinks that no copy of Cain's book has ever been located.

for his excessive rigor in handling them, the Negroes set fire to his buildings, and following this loss he returned to Indianapolis, where he managed a hotel. Then he was appointed in 1853, by President Pierce, Indian agent for Washington Territory. He died in Indianapolis.[5]

We come next to the first Indiana poet that wrote an entire volume of verse whose work is extant, Dr. Joseph S. Welsh (?-ca. 1846). Unfortunately, there is little biographical information available, most of it coming from a county history.[6] However, it is evident that when Dr. Welsh died on Coal Creek, in Fountain County, about 1846, having lived there about sixteen or eighteen years, his death was mourned by a large circle of admiring friends. He had served faithfully as a physician in that area for some time, and he was noted also as a great conversationalist and as a teacher of "the great, the good, and ennobling principles of morality, virtue, and patriotism."[7] The only other mention in contemporary records of anyone of that name is the recording of a Joseph S. Welsh in the 1830 census as a resident of Switzerland County. He is listed as the head of a family composed of a male in the twenty-to-thirty years age bracket, a female of the same age group, and a male of ten to fifteen years; presumably this is the poet, his wife, and a son.[8] A history of Switzerland County states that the first drugstore in Vevay was opened by Dr. James Welsh, who was also a Presbyterian minister and a merchant, in conjunction with his son George, and that after the death of George, the store was

[5] Cain's biography is given in detail in John H. B. Nowland, *Sketches of Prominent Citizens of 1876* (Indianapolis, 1877), 369-71.

[6] H. W. Beckwith, *History of Fountain County, Together with Historic Notes on the Wabash Valley* . . . (Chicago, 1881), 313.

[7] *Ibid.*

[8] U. S. Census of Indiana, 1830, vol. 14:142, photostatic copy in Genealogy Division, Indiana State Library.

continued by Dr Welsh and another son, Joseph S. Welsh. The death of the father terminated the business in 1826;[9] and if the son Joseph is our poet, it is possible that he moved to Fountain County a few years later, about 1830.

Dr. Joseph S. Welsh, the poet, fared surprisingly well in his literary endeavors considering that the date of his volume, *Harp of the West: A Volume of Poems,* was 1839. The book was published in Cincinnati and is considered rare. In many ways it is a remarkable collection. Welsh uses several verse forms, but usually the heroic couplet and blank verse—and often rather dexterously. He treats many subjects, mostly of the West and the United States in general, dwelling upon battles with the Indians, patriotic deeds, and religion. He also shows concern with less grandiose subjects, as in the poems entitled "The Mother" and "The Victim of Seduction," and an interest in subjects outside the United States, as in "Greece, to Arms!" "The Pirate Ship," and "Bonaparte's Retreat from Russia." Still, he is essentially Midwestern and Hoosier in flavor and sympathy, and pens with pride poems of Indiana interest, like the "Expedition of Col. George Rogers Clark" and "Death of Tecumseh." In "Description of the Grand Prairie," he gives, in heroic couplets, a good picture of a prairie with the elements of nature playing upon it—the wind, storm, sun, the snow and the freezing cold, the drought, the terrible prairie fires, and even the harassing forces of mosquitoes, wolves, and Indians.

A very interesting poem is "The Indian Warrior's Reflections, on the Banks of Coal Creek, and His Description of the Combat at Tippecanoe." One of the surprising facts about the poem is that it is told from the Indian

[9] Perret Dufour, *The Swiss Settlement of Switzerland County Indiana* (*Indiana Historical Collections,* vol. 13, Indianapolis, 1925), 186, 392.

point of view, an attitude not often found in that day—
portraying an idyllic life for the Indians around Coal
Creek before they went to the Battle of Tippecanoe to
protect their freedom and their homes. The Indian narrator relates that after their defeat and removal to the West
he, as an old man, returned to his former home and to the
graves of his fathers on Coal Creek and found all the region inhabited by the whites, the game driven away, and
the forest disappearing before the magic of ax and plow.
Sadly he departs. A good passage describing the battle is
the following:

> Our leader's mandate rung upon our ears.
> "On! warriors, on! your fathers' spirits ride
> Upon the murky clouds, and loudly call
> On you to do your duty! Now their frowns
> Descend upon you, darker than the hour
> Of midnight blackness! Onward! warriors, then;
> Strike for your freedom, for your lives, your homes—
> Your lovely homes—where sleeps the honor'd clay
> Of your departed sires, who never felt
> The degradation of defeat, and look
> For you to shield from sacrilegious tread,
> The spot that long has held their mould'ring bones!
> On, then, my warriors, on! Firm be the stroke
> Of the deep plunging tomahawk! Use well the knife,
> And let the mouths of all your rifles pour
> Incessantly the storms of leaden death!"[10]

Probably Welsh will always be known best for his two
poems "Indiana Georgicks" and "The Valley of the Mississippi, One Hundred Years Hence." The former poem
praises Indiana and its prosperity and the abundant farm
life with its joys, as in the following passage:

> Hail! Indiana, garden of the West,
> Thy lovely plains with teeming harvests bless'd,

[10] Welsh, *Harp of the West* . . . (Cincinnati, 1839), 40.

Pours forth for man and beast a rich supply
Of luscious food, beneath thy smiling sky.
Here corn and wheat luxuriantly grow,
And the potato's modest flow'rets blow;
Tall stately oats here hang the heavy head,
And clover fields their fragrant odors shed.
From the rich meadows, waving in the wind,
Thy lowing herds abundant plenty find.
The orchards stand in beautious [sic] garb array'd,
With blooming foliage and sweet fruits display'd
While rippling streamlets kiss their grassy shore,
As through the vales their little billows pour.
Who would not think that here is earthly bliss,
And love to wander through a scene like this;
He who could not upon those vallies [sic] live,
Nature her choicest blessings should not give;
For if his plough but scrapes along the ground,
Plenty soon rising, smiles and laughs around.

Hail! Indiana! may the glowing light
Of virtuous science, lead thy sons aright;
O'er thy fair vales the torch of freedom burn,
Whose sod thy martyr'd heroes' bones inurn;
Who firm and steady as the Alpine rock,
Met the red foeman in the battle's shock,
When far from home, unus'd to martial toil,
Freely their blood they pour'd upon thy soil.
No despot's foot upon their couch shall tread,
Where peaceful sleep the brave and noble dead,
But high enroll'd on glory's shining page,
Their valorous actions live from age to age.[11]

But it is in "The Valley of the Mississippi, One Hundred Years Hence" that Welsh's idealism and majestic sweep of verse approach sublimity in his prophecy of the future greatness of the Middle West, coupled with a strong warning to seek the paths of virtue. So important

[11] *Ibid.*, 85, 92.

will the Midwest become, he asserts, that the nation's
capital will be relocated there:

And what has forty years accomplish'd now,
Within the West? Great forests have been swept,
As by a giant's arm, from off the face
Of the broad land; millions of citizens
Do now exist upon its fertile soil.
An empire wide of cities, and of towns,
Has been rear'd up. Full thirty thousand miles
Its navigation spreads, to every point,
Bearing its blessings through a space of earth,
Larger than half of Europe, and four times
As large as the Atlantic states, that lie
Along that ocean's border. In this land
Of yesterday, the sciences and arts
Are shining forth, and spreading far and wide
Their dazzling beams around the lonely throne
Of Solitude, where yet the savage strays.
Then, if the space of forty years hath done
Such wondrous things, what will one century do?
Millions on millions yet will roll along,
And spread like ocean waves, across the land
Of the fair fertile west, while millions more
Will claim it as their lov'd and natal home.
Cities innumerable here will rise,
Whose massive domes and towers uplifted far
In the mid heaven, will catch the wand'ring eye
Of the astonish'd traveller, as he wends
His way through this dense mass of living souls.
Soon the great central power of the United States
Will here be fix'd, secure and far remov'd
From all invasion, by the boldest foe
Upon the face of earth. . . .[12]

The poet says that the fame and power of the United
States will be world-wide, and she will stand for freedom
and truth. He closes with a moving appeal:

[12] Welsh, *Harp of the West,* 94-95.

O patriots, rise! Let the clear sacred light,
Of moral purity, in lustre beam,
Upon your institutions. Let your land,
Be dotted o'er with colleges and schools,
To rear the tender mind, deeply engraft,
The principles of Virtue, and of truth:
Then you'r [sic] secure, and as the stream of time,
Unceasing flows, it still will find you safe.
Remember, He, that quickly plucketh up,
And planteth down a nation, at his will,
Now looks upon you. Humbly then obey,
His JUST COMMANDMENTS and His Mighty arm,
OMNIPOTENT, will be a wall of fire,
To shield, and guard Columbia's happy land.[13]

What shall we say, then, in conclusion concerning Dr. Welsh? Since he stands so early among the Indiana poets, we have quoted him at some length in order to provide good samples of his work. Certainly we must observe that some of his verse is amateurish and labored, but in spite of some typographical errors and what we would call to-day errors in grammar and punctuation, he displays much poetic talent and writes surprisingly good poetry considering the times. He is the first Hoosier who is really entitled to the name of poet. He has been too long neglected and has been lost amid the sounds of the pioneer ax, the smoke from factory chimneys, and the harangues and debates of Hoosier politics.

GEORGE W. CUTTER—JOHN S. REID

George Washington Cutter (1801?-1865) is a poet of nearly the same stature as Welsh, although he did not develop his talent well. To Cutter goes the honor of having published in Indiana the first book of poetry which is

[13] Ibid., 103.

extant; for John Cain's volume, as before remarked, has disappeared, and Joseph Welsh's collection was published in Cincinnati. Cutter's first volume of verse was *Elskwatawa, or the Moving Fires; and Other Poems,* published in Indianapolis in 1840,[14] one year after Welsh's book.

George Washington Cutter was born, evidently, in Kentucky[15] and later appeared in Indiana in the role of lawyer, orator, leading citizen, and politician, serving for a time as an ardent Whig member of the legislature from Terre Haute. He was one of the group of eloquent orators who contributed so much to the unusual success of the "hard cider campaign" of 1840. A captain during the Mexican War, he wrote most of the poem "Buena Vista" after the battle, on a cartridge keg in his tent on the battlefield, and it soon became famous throughout the country. He was considered by some of his contemporaries the state's leading literary figure of his time. He was twice married, his first wife having been the tragic actress, Mrs. Alexander Drake, a woman much older than Cutter, about whom he acted very foolishly. After his second marriage he sank into sporadic idleness, worked a little on Cincinnati newspapers, and late in his life moved to Washington, D. C., where he had employment in a government department and where his declining years were clouded by loss of health, both mental and physical.

His first volume of poetry, *Elskwatawa, or the Moving Fires* (1840), is composed mostly of the fifty-page title poem, "Elskwatawa," in which he expresses a feeling,

[14] By Stacy and Williams.

[15] An undated clipping from the Indianapolis *Sentinel,* entitled "Early Hoosier Literature" (written evidently about 1885), found in a scrapbook of the well-known Indiana historian, Jacob Piatt Dunn, says that he was born in Canada but came as a boy or young man to Indiana. The scrapbook is now in the Indiana Historical Society Library.

rather unusual for its day, of sympathy for the Indians oppressed by the faithless, treaty-breaking whites, who despoil the Indians' land. He recommends that the Indian tribes all unite in peace under one chief, withdraw from the whites, and live according to their time-honored customs. A slender narrative is mingled with the description of the Indians as noble, fearless, and savage. Although unfinished, it is, all told, a rather majestic poem, somewhat rough and rambling in spots but still surprisingly good for a period which was very close to actual frontier life. At times Cutter rises to poetic heights, as in the following passage early in the poem, which is reminiscent of the old Calvinist hymn, "From Greenland's Icy Mountain":

> From Labrador's eternal snows
> To Patagonia's frigid strand;
> From where the blue Atlantic flows,
> To where Kiomi's forests stand;
> Of stream, or forest, field or flood,
> There's not a foot their conqueror owns,
> But has been color'd with their blood,
> Or whitened with their bleaching bones!—
> And when the awful trump of God,
> (Dissolving death's mysterious chain,)
> Shall rend the marble and the sod,
> To give each form its soul again,—
> There's not within this broad domain
> A single rood, of sea or earth,
> But dyed with many a murderous strain,
> Will give a slaughter'd Indian birth.[16]

Several short poems, lyrical in nature, such as "To My Mother," a beautiful tribute; "The Burning Boat," a description of a burning steamboat; and some love poetry, make up the rest of the volume.

Cutter's second collection of poems, *Buena Vista: and*

[16] Cutter, *Elskwatawa, or the Moving Fires* (Indianapolis, 1840), 12-13.

Other Poems (Cincinnati, 1848), reprints several of the poems of his first volume but includes the title poem "Buena Vista," which is a long piece in praise of the American valor shown in that battle; "The Song of Steam," a personification of the driving force of engines; and "E Pluribus Unum," another well-known poem of the day, popular because of the patriotic appeal, as the stirring last stanza reveals:

> Then up with our flag—let it stream on the air—
>   Tho' our fathers are cold in their graves;
> They had hands that could strike—they had souls that
>   could dare,
> And their sons were not born to be slaves.
>
> Up, up with that banner—where'er it may call,
>   Our millions shall rally around;
> And a nation of freemen that moment shall fall,
>   When its stars shall be trailed on the ground.[17]

His last volume, *Poems and Fugitive Pieces* (Cincinnati, 1857), is the least distinguished of the three books, for in addition to some new lyric poetry, such as the brilliant "The Song of Lightning," he reprints many pieces from the other collections and includes "The Captive," which is the same poem as that entitled "The White Chief" in his second volume, the material of which, in turn, had been drawn originally from "Elskwatawa."

Cutter was important enough to be included by William T. Coggeshall in his *The Poets and Poetry of the West*, published in Columbus, Ohio, in 1860. Coggeshall criticizes "The Captive" severely and generalizes from this observation to a criticism of Cutter as a poet:

... Mr. Cutter is not a poet of art, but a poet born. It is not his business, any more than it is the bobolink's to construct

[17] Cutter, *Buena Vista*, 40.

sweet tones into consistent tunes. The tones may come of themselves, and link themselves together, and sing themselves, if they will; but they get little help from Mr. Cutter, that is clear. The poetic spirit with which he is possessed, takes him and does with him whatsoever it will. He *feels* more poetry than he writes. Now and then the pent lightning within him flashes forth full into the dark of language, and dazzles all; but for the most part he has not half told himself, because he has never *studied* expression.[18]

Coggeshall continues, saying that if Cutter had only applied himself he could have become an outstanding poet; yet, he lists as Cutter's chief redeeming qualities sublimity and perspicuity and praises his patriotic poetry.

On the whole, we must admit the truth of this criticism.[19] With more training and effort on his part probably Cutter could have blossomed into a much better poet; and although he often comes close to the quality of Sarah T. Bolton, who published somewhat later, he must be thought of as an inferior poet in many ways, but one who left a few pieces well worth remembering. Of course, the type of instruction by which Cutter could have benefited the most was not nearly so available in the Midwest in his day as in our own; nevertheless, more effort on his part would undoubtedly have yielded happier results.

The next name in the devolment of Hoosier poetry is that of John S. Reid (1815?-1879), whose volume of poetry is a strangely exotic flower to bloom in the Indiana forests and fields. If Reid owed anything to his predecessors, Welsh and Cutter, his debt is in no way apparent, unless it be the inspiration of their example in publishing

[18] Coggeshall, *Poets and Poetry of the West*, 303-4.
[19] The article in the Indianapolis *Sentinel,* referred to in note 15, above, offers criticism similar to Coggeshall, saying that Cutter "was the most striking example of wasted talents and apt opportunities in the literary history of the State. He could have been 'facile princeps,' and ended in nothing."

their poetry. Reid's *Gulzar; or, The Rose-Bower: a Tale of Persia* was published in Indianapolis and Cincinnati in 1845,[20] five years after the appearance of Cutter's first volume.

In one sense Reid was hardly a Hoosier, for he was born in Scotland[21] and may have obtained whatever knowledge of Persian language and literature he had and developed an interest in orientalism from residence in England, where he was educated at Oxford. Nevertheless, coming to the United States in 1839, he spent most of his life in Indiana. He was granted a degree from Miami University, in Ohio, and taught school and also practiced law, in Liberty, Indiana, from 1840 to 1851, practiced law in Connersville from 1851 to 1876, then moved to Indianapolis, where he lived the last two years of his life, dying September 5, 1879. When he was practicing in Connersville, a young law student, Luther Benson,[22] read law in his office. Reid was common pleas judge at Connersville from 1852 to 1860, was a member of the state senate from 1849 to 1852, and a member of the Constitutional Convention of 1850.[23] Thus we may conclude that Reid became well "Hoosierized." According to a history of Fayette County, Indiana, "he was considered one of the best poets of the state during his generation. . . ."[24]

[20] By Samuel Turner, Charles B. Davis, and G. A. & J. P. Chapman.

[21] An unsigned penciled note dated 1877 in the back of the copy of Reid's *Gulzar; or, The Rose-Bower* which is in the Indiana Division of the Indiana State Library says that Reid was born in Perth, Scotland, April 1, 1815. This has not been confirmed other than that the place of birth was somewhere in Scotland, nor has the identity of the writer of the note been determined.

[22] See above 47-48.

[23] Frederic I. Barrows (ed.), *History of Fayette County Indiana . .* (Indianapolis, 1917), 324-25.

[24] *Ibid.*, 325.

Whether Judge Reid knew the Persian language and translated from it is a matter of question; nowhere does he make any claim to having translated *Gulzar* from a Persian source. Indeed, there is no definite source for the story ascertainable, and the tale may be a product of his own imagination, suggested, perhaps, by his reading of Persian history and literature—and, also, by the example of Thomas Moore's *Lalla Rookh,* which was published in 1817. The poet's notes at the end of each of the seven cantos give evidence of some personal knowledge of Persian materials; and the "Gazels, or Love-Songs" printed after the main poem, "Gulzar," are "versified by the Author, from prose translations made by eminent Persian scholars."[25] *Gulzar,* then, is a manifestation, transplanted to Indiana, of the interest in orientalism which flourished in England from the eighteenth century, as seen in Joseph Addison's tale, "The Vision of Mirzah," beginning in *The Spectator,* No. 159 (September 1, 1711), Samuel Johnson's *Rasselas* (1759), and William Beckford's short novel, *Vathek* (1786), through the early nineteenth century—for example, *Lalla Rookh*—and continuing later into the century, as in Edward Fitzgerald's *The Rubáiyát of Omar Khayyám* (1859).

Gulzar is indeed an exotic poem. Written in iambic tetrameter couplets, much as in the manner of *Lalla Rookh,* it is a long poem interspersed with episodes of the main story, which is given in prose; or perhaps it may be considered to be a story told in prose interspersed with long poems, in seven cantos, which are the stories sung by Humza, the Dervise.

Toward the close of the reign of Aga Mohammed, Shah of Persia, his favorite daughter, the Princess Gulzar, lay

---

[25] *Gulzar; or, The Rose-Bower: a Tale of Persia* (Indianapolis, 1845), 184.

very dangerously sick in the palace, baffling the skill of the greatest physicians to heal her. Her lover, the Abbas Mirza, had offended her father, the Shah, by aspiring to her hand; and the Shah had spirited off and imprisoned Mirza, with the result that Gulzar was now pining away for him. The sorrowing Shah published a proclamation that any one who healed Gulzar could either have her as his bride or claim a prince's ransom.

At length Humza, a Dervise, came to the palace and asked permission to try to heal Gulzar. By means of a magic potion he did so, and she was restored to health. Great rejoicing ensued, and the court and the Shah made merry for several days. Each night Humza, besting all the other bards, took a harp and sang a wonderful story about great heroes. Finally Humza claimed Gulzar as his bride, according to the terms of the proclamation. She and the Shah and all the court objected because Humza was old, but Humza stood firm. He was questioned by wise men and answered them well. Suddenly he was attacked by a rival prince, and he defended himself successfully; then throwing off his disguise as Humza, he stood revealed as the Abbas Mirza himself. The Shah then bestowed his daughter upon him.

At times the poetry is rather good. Here are the opening lines:

> O! who has gaz'd on Babylon,
>   The city of the brazen gates—
> And seen, bright gleaming in the sun,
>   Her gilded domes and minarets?
> And heard the camel's tinkling bell
> Come softly on the ev'ning gale;
> And breathed the sweet and scented air,
> The perfum'd breath of Diarbekir;
> And swept his eye across that land,
> From Syria to Samaracand [sic],—

Drank of the famed Euphrates' stream,
And seen the pale moon's silv'ry beam
  Play over its translucent wave,
Could ever dream so fair a scene
  Would be one lone and matchless grave,
And be as if it ne'er had been?[26]

The "Gazels, or Love-Songs, from the Persian of Hafiz," which make up the rest of the volume, include twelve short poems, sweetly and beautifully formed. Also, there is "Dunallen: a Tale of the Isles," which is a Scottish story, reflecting, perhaps, Reid's own Scottish background.

That Reid's poetry is almost remarkable for the Indiana of 1843 is well illustrated by his "Gazel II":

The rose unfolds its velvet leaf,
  The leaf the bulbul loves so well,
And woos, with sweet and balmy breath,
  Young love, within her bower to dwell:
Then, LEILA, let us seek the bower
Where blooms that love-diffusing flower,
And drink from Lethe's bubbling stream,
  And drown the past in rosy wine;
'Midst roses toy, 'till morning bright
  Illumes the curtains of the sky,
And wakes to life love's witching light,
  That now is in thy dreamy eye:
For it is sweet with one we love,
To seek the fragrant jasmine grove,
And breathe afresh love's ardent vows,
  And nectar sip from dewy lips,
Far sweeter, redder, than the rose
  From which the bee its honey sips.
Then haste, my LEILA! e'er the bloom
  Has from the cheek of summer fled!
Haste to the bower of sweet perfume,
  And wreathe with am'rous flow'rs thy head:
And while we quaff the ruby wine,

[26] Reid, *Gulzar; or, The Rose-Bower*, 21.

Let Hafiz sing his melting lay,
Reclining on that breast of thine,
Breathing his heart and soul away.[27]

In its ardent romanticism and orientalism, Reid's poetry is so far removed from the contemporary prosaic tasks involved in building the modern state that the author is seen as not only unique but almost unbelievable.[28]

HORACE P. BIDDLE

We move now to the consideration of a man whose name assumes importance in the legal and cultural history of Indiana and whose poetic accomplishment is large in quantity but uneven in quality. During his life in the state Horace Peters Biddle (1811-1900) was not only a leading lawyer and judge but was also an outstanding apostle of culture, a sort of Hoosier Matthew Arnold.

Biddle was born on March 24, 1811, in Hocking County, Ohio, of parents who had come from New England. Having received an elementary education from subscription schools, he read law and in 1839 was admitted to the bar in his home state. Almost immediately, however, he removed to Logansport, Indiana, where he soon acquired a very profitable practice, becoming, by the time he reached middle age, one of the wealthiest citizens in town. He advanced rapidly in his profession, being elected in 1846 presiding judge of the Eighth Judicial Circuit and serving, from 1874 to 1881, as a judge of the Indiana Supreme Court. Biddle was a member of the Constitutional Convention of 1850. From his retirement in 1881

---

[27] Reid, *Gulzar; or, The Rose-Bower*, 186-87.

[28] As a matter of fact, *Gulzar* actually proved an annoyance to Judge Reid in the courtroom, for lawyers quoted from it until he disavowed authorship and attempted to buy up and destroy all copies. He was unsuccessful.

until his death, May 13, 1900, he intensified the role which he had been playing during his active career and for which he is best remembered in the state—that of a very versatile scholar in the fields of science, music, philosophy, and literature, and a patron of the arts. A knowledge of French, German, Spanish, Italian, Portuguese, and Latin was part of his vast storehouse of information; and he made translations from German and French poetry. Even while young he was a contributor to several periodicals, such as *The Ladies' Repository* and the *Southern Literary Messenger,* for which latter periodical he began writing in 1842. In his beautiful rambling home on what was named Biddle's Island in the Wabash River near Logansport he collected a library of eight thousand volumes plus many rare manuscripts and relics—one of the most valuable collections in the Midwest—and there lived a retired life, doing as he wished, an object of envy and awe of the many Indiana writers who visited him.[29]

To recount the many-sided writings of Judge Biddle is not easy; nor does it enter within our present purpose. We might remark, however, that he described to the public through his publications two musical instruments which he had invented and named the "tetrachord" and the "euraka"; he composed a dictionary of music; he wrote some literary criticism, which is so slight as not to merit our attention; he produced a biographical sketch of John B. Dillon and some essays on logic; and he gave and later published a *Discourse on Art, Delivered on the Occasion of George Winter's Annual Distribution of Oil*

[29] Biographies of Judge Biddle abound in Indiana historical, biographical, and legal materials. Probably the most readily available short biography is in Banta, *Indiana Authors and Their Books,* 28-29. A good newspaper account is by George S. Cottman, "Biddle's Versatility," in Indianapolis *News,* February 23, 1926, p. 6.

Paintings, at the Melodeon Hall, Lafayette, Dec. 30, 1854.[30]

His first book, entitled *A Few Poems,* was issued in 1849, but, apparently, no copy is extant. According to Coggeshall,[31] this collection was in pamphlet form. A second edition was issued in 1852. It was about this volume that Washington Irving said, in a letter to Biddle, "I have read your poems with great relish: they are full of sensibility and beauty, and bespeak a talent well worthy of cultivation. Such blossoms should produce fine fruit."[32] His volume of 1858, also entitled *A Few Poems,* published in Cincinnati, was enlarged, apparently, from the first edition and includes an essay, "What is Poetry?" in which he carefully builds a case for his definition that "Poetry is beautiful thought, expressed in appropriate language—having no reference to the useful."[33] The essay is full of references to European writers and literary critics. The most usual subjects of his poems here are love, nature, death, philosophy, and religion. The verse is sometimes rough, containing artificialities of diction which do not always fall pleasantly on the ear today, as in the first poem of the book:

The Cottage

The day din was past, night had hushed the soft breeze,
    Afar o'er the hills the church-bells were chiming;
I found a lone cottage, 'twas hid in the trees,
    And the wild rose and vine o'er its lattice were climbing.

[30] See the discussion of George Winter, above, 55-57.

[31] Coggeshall, *Poets and Poetry of the West,* 332.

[32] Quoted in *ibid.,* 332. It is interesting to see, however, that Biddle printed this quotation from Irving on the fly leaf of the 1858 edition of his poems, but deleted the part following the word "beauty." Perhaps Biddle felt that his talent had already been cultivated.

[33] Biddle, *A Few Poems* (Cincinnati, 1858), 35.

Methought, as I gazed on the flowers so fair,
If earth has a spot that is lovely, 'tis there!

. . . .

Time's wing flew so softly I knew not it stirred,
  But the moon was on high and the dewdrop did glisten,
Though Time, too, had tarried, I'm sure had he heard,
  For the stars of the azure seemed pausing to listen.
Methought, for this cot was no home for old care.
If there's love on this earth, it is surely *there*![34]

But there are many poems that contain redeeming features. Some are fanciful and highly imaginative, like
"Love, Venus, and Hymen" and "The Bath," which latter
poem in a sensuous story of a shy maiden observed by an
equally shy but amorous youth while she was bathing in a
stream. "The Soul's Soliloquy" is heavy with philosophy.
Perhaps one of the most beautiful poems, filled with a
sensuousness that is surprising for his day, but still somewhat singsong in style, is "Wedded Love."

Wedded Love

The lattice opened to the sky,
  The gentle moon, with soft approach,
Stole from a fleecy cloud on high,
  And shone upon the bridal couch.

His virgin wife slept by his side,
  Encircled fondly in his arms;
He gazed upon the lovely bride,
  And counted o'er and o'er her charms.

Her head his glowing bosom prest,
  Her neck was hid in streaming tresses;
The vesture half disclosed a breast
  That all a woman's charms confesses.

[34] *Ibid.,* 47.

The moonlight softly kissed her brow,
  So clear it seemed to pierce it through,
As white and pure as unprest snow,
  Save little traces tinged with blue.

His hand just touched her swelling breast,
  A treasury of virgin love,
And as she breathed it gently prest
  Against it, like a nestling dove.

Her eyes, whose bright soul-beaming flashes
  Their lids so soft could scarcely shroud
A little shown betwixt their lashes,
  Like stars that twinkle through a cloud.

At dreams of love's delicious blisses
  Her modest cheek in sleep e'en blushed;
Her tempting mouth, the home of kisses,
  Told tales of love, although 'twas hushed.

Her blushing cheek was turned away
  As if at some sweet fear she started,
And those ripe lips where raptures play,
  So full of sweets were slightly parted.

Formed in the sweetest mold of love,
  Chaste as a rose just washed with dew,
Pure as a spirit from above,
  Fair as an angel and as true.

While gazing thus with thrilling pleasure,
  His kindling heart burst in a flame,
Unconsciously he clasped his treasure,
  She, waking, softly lisped his name.[35]

Judge Biddle's third volume, *Poems* (New York, 1868), contains much of the material of his previous volumes but includes also additional verses. It is, in a sense, a revised

[35] Biddle, *A Few Poems*, 116-18.

edition of *A Few Poems*. He utilizes the same subjects, in general, and the same criticisms may be applied to this edition. A good poem found in the volume is "The Soldier's Burial," referring, evidently, to the death of a Union soldier in the Civil War. Two or three other poems here were inspired by the War. The book was reissued in 1872.

The fourth volume of poetry, *Glances at the World*, discloses Biddle's playful eccentricity, for it is "By Hieronymous Anonymous." It must have been published privately, for the facts of publication read "Mundus: Published by Cadmus Faustus, 5878"—the date being, in reality, 1873. The subject matter of this book is tremendous in scope; it contains twelve "Glances," written in octava rima, covering Creation, America, Heroes, Authors, Poets, Lovers, Critics, Priests, Politicians, Shams, Explanation, and Conclusion. Of course, nearly anything can be included under such titles—and it is. There is much rambling far afield, often in rather rough verse, bad rhymes, and awkward diction.

Biddle's next publication, *My Scrap Book* (Logansport, 1874), also was privately printed; as a matter of fact, a statement on the verso of the title page is "This book is not published." Many of the same subjects dealt with in previous volumes are continued here, and there is much on the subject of death. A few of his earliest verses are included and also some of his previously published poems. Most of the poems are short and are sometimes singsong.

American Boyhood, privately published in Philadelphia in 1876 and reprinted in 1881, carries this statement in its preface: "The following poem is an attempt to portray American Boyhood, with its surroundings, as it was in the early part of the nineteenth century. It is mainly a picture of country boyhood. . . . It is an effort to represent *National* Boyhood—the boyhood of all sections and of every class—blended into the unity—AMERICAN."[36] This long poem of over two hundred pages in eight-line stanzas (rhyming a b a b c d c d) has many good passages and presents a nostalgic, but clear, view of boyhood. Yet it is often marred by Biddle's usual flaws.

Amatories—By an Amateur, "Mundus: Eros and Anteros, Aphrodite and Psyche, Venus, Cupid, and Hymen. Anno Mundi 5883" is another example of the poet's learned playfulness. It was privately printed, probably in 1878, in an edition of ten copies. It contains love poetry alone. One of the pieces, "Love's Excuse," was reprinted in 1895, under its own title.

Except for the last-mentioned publication, *Last Poems* (Cincinnati, 1882) is the final issue of Biddle's poetry. The poems included were written mostly after 1872, and the book contains no reprinting of earlier poems. The same observations concerning the verse given for other volumes apply here; the range of subject matter is very large. It is the longest of his books, 435 pages.

Our conclusion concerning Biddle is now obvious. That he was a talented, versatile person and a very prolific writer is certainly true; but as a poet he often fell far short of what, by means of more study and application—and a much more liberal use of the wastebasket—he could probably have achieved.

ALICE AND PHOEBE CARY

It is a pleasure to discuss next two rather well-known minor American poets, the sisters Alice Cary (1820-1871) and Phoebe Cary (1824-1871), whose work was very

[36] Biddle, *American Boyhood* (Philadelphia, 1876), 7.

popular in its day. These two sisters must be considered together, for not only did they live together most of their lives, but they published much of their poetry in the same volumes and, in general, participated in a common intellectual and spiritual life. Also, they must be shared with Ohio and New York, since they spent part of their lives there.

The two poets were born on a farm called Clovernook (later to be made famous by Alice's volume of the name) eight miles north of Cincinnati—Alice on April 26, 1820, and Phoebe on September 4, 1824. Their father, Robert Cary, claimed descent from Thomas Cary, a cousin of Queen Elizabeth, and from John Cary, who taught Latin as early as 1630 in Plymouth, Massachusetts. Robert Cary was a farmer of undeveloped poetic temperament, and his wife, Elizabeth Jessup, was devoted to culture. Their nine children, of whom Alice was the fourth and Phoebe the sixth, were reared in somewhat primitive rural conditions which necessitated hard work on the part of everyone with few opportunities for education and intellectual development. Yet in spite of these difficulties Alice began publishing poems in a Cincinnati newspaper when she was eighteen. Before this time, however, tragedy had already struck in the family, and sorrow had been established as the ruling motif of the poet sisters' lives—at least that of Alice. In 1833, after a new house had been built, some of the family, including Alice, thought that they saw in front of the new house an apparition strongly resembling two of the children: Rhoda, holding Lucy in her arms; and then the ghosts appeared to sink into the ground. In a few months Rhoda and Lucy were dead, and the mother followed them in death in 1835. Alice was particularly struck by this tragedy and with one sorrow and disappointment following another throughout much of her life, she remained to the end a melancholy and brooding person, still retaining, nonetheless, a sweetness of spirit and disposition.

The woman that the father married two years after Alice and Phoebe's mother died had no sympathy with culture and writing and forced the girls to work hard all day, even denying them a candle at night. But the inimitable seventeen-year-old Alice and thirteen-year-old Phoebe spirited a saucer of lard up to their room which, with a rag wick, gave sufficient light for reading and the writing of verse.

Unable to get along with their stepmother, the sisters eventually moved to Oxford, in Benton County, Indiana, to live with an older sister, Susan, who was married to Alexander Swift. Alice and Phoebe lived in Oxford in 1848, 1849, probably in 1850, and also during the summers of 1851 and 1852; they were well liked by the townspeople, many of whom were proud of their acquaintance with the sisters after they had become well-known authors living in New York City. Alice and Phoebe always considered Oxford their home.[37] Many of their poems of nature and rural life were either inspired by residence in Oxford and the near-by countryside or were actually

[37] The Indiana residence of Alice and Phoebe Cary is not a well-known fact and is often omitted from their biographies. It is authenticated by Jesse S. Birch, "The Cary Sisters in Oxford," in *Indiana Magazine of History*, 20(1924):187-93, and by an article by Ralph L. Brooks, "Hoosier Poets by Choice," in Indianapolis *Star Magazine,* October 19, 1952, pp. 32-33. Both articles give interesting details of the sisters' life in Oxford. Birch says that they lived there from "1849 to 1850 and part of 1851 and 1852," and that he personally had known some of the Oxford residents who were acquainted with them. He adds that a few distant cousins of the poets still were living in Oxford [in 1924]. The article by Brooks carries a photograph of the house in which the sisters lived with the Swifts; the house, of course, is now much remodeled. L. A. McKnight in *Progress of Education in Benton County* (Indianapolis, 1906), 131-32, attests also to the facts of the residence in Oxford.

written in the Swifts' home—such poems as Alice's "The
West Country" and "Pictures of Memory" and Phoebe's
"Field Preaching," "The Lamp on the Prairie," "The
Maize," "The Prairie Fire," "Our Homestead," and a
beloved hymn, "Nearer Home."[38] Alice's famous poem,
"Pictures of Memory," was inspired by the Swifts' loss of
a child, a little boy who died after his nurse let him fall
from a horse; and the picture of the "gnarled oaks olden"
was suggested by a forest of oaks across the road from the
home of the Swifts. Edgar Allan Poe judged this poem
to be "one of the most musically perfect lyrics in the
English language."[39] It bears repeating here:

Pictures of Memory
Among the beautiful pictures
    That hang on Memory's wall,
Is one of a dim old forest,
    That seemeth best of all:
Not for its gnarled oaks olden,
    Dark with the mistletoe;
Not for the violets golden
    That sprinkle the vale below;
Not for the milk-white lilies
    That lean from the fragrant hedge,
Coqueting all day with the sunbeams,
    And stealing their shining edge;
Not for the vines on the upland
    Where the bright red berries be,
Nor the pinks, nor the pale, sweet cowslip,
    It seemeth the best to me.

I once had a little brother,
    With eyes that were dark and deep—
In the lap of that old dim forest
    He lieth in peace asleep:

[38] See citations to Birch, Brooks, and McKnight in preceding note.
[39] Quoted in Birch, "The Cary Sisters in Oxford," in *Indiana Magazine of History*, 20:193.

Light as the down of the thistle,
  Free as the winds that blow,
We roved there the beautiful summers,
  The summers of long ago;
But his feet on the hills grew weary,
  And, one of the autumn eves,
I made for my little brother
  A bed of the yellow leaves.

Sweetly his pale arms folded
  My neck in a meek embrace,
As the light of immortal beauty
  Silently covered his face:
And when the arrows of sunset
  Lodged in the tree-tops bright,
He fell, in his saint-like beauty,
  Asleep by the gates of light.
Therefore, of all the pictures
  That hang on Memory's wall,
That one of the old dim forest
  Seemeth best of all.[40]

In 1849 their first volume appeared, *Poems of Alice and Phoebe Cary*, published in Philadelphia. That same year they became acquainted with Horace Greeley and corresponded with John Greenleaf Whittier, whom they met the next year. Whittier recorded their visit to his home in his poem "The Singer." Alice, in poor health and saddened still more by the death of a favorite brother, decided to seek her literary fame and fortune in New York City and went there to live, being joined soon by Phoebe and a younger sister.

Here Alice made up a collection of her short stories and studies of the country life which she knew so well and issued them as *Clovernook or Recollections of Our Neighborhood in the West* (New York, 1852). The book's

---

[40] Alice Cary, *Poems* (Boston, 1855), 29-30.

truthfulness and faithfulness to local coloring in its presentations of farm life of the Ohio Valley are very evident, but the fault in these well-turned stories is the same one that pervades Alice's poetry—the prevailing sentimentality of its sad themes. No matter how idyllic the presentation of the health, simplicity, and happiness of farm life, there is sure to be a deathbed or tombstone at the end of the story. Yet, despite the depressing tone, the book was popular; a second edition was issued in 1853 and *Clovernook Children* (Boston), a charming book for children, in 1855. *Hagar, A Story of To-day,* a long narrative, which had been published serially in a Cincinnati newspaper, was issued as a book in New York in 1852; and in the same year came *Lyra and Other Poems* (New York), a book of sadness containing poems like "Lyra: A Lament," "Written in Illness," and "Hymn to the Night," which were pronounced by many critics as not inferior to any American poetry in beauty of imagery, pattern, and grace.[41] *Poems* (Boston, 1855) included all of Alice's poems published up till that time and met with general approval, although a review in *Putnam's Monthly* said: "It is a sob in three hundred and ninety-nine parts. Such terrific mortality never raged in a volume of the same size before. It is a parish register of funerals rendered into doleful rhyme."[42] Since styles in poetry have changed, the modern reader will probably agree with this opinion, although he should realize that the grief abounding in the verse was genuine with Alice, deriving from her state of health, the frequent deaths in her family, and also the memory of the loss of a lover, who, under pressure from his family, had married another. And at the same time

[41] Coggeshall, *Poets and Poetry of the West*, 345.

[42] Quoted in W. H. Venable, *Beginnings of Literary Culture in the Ohio Valley* (Cincinnati, 1891), 494.

that some reviewers were pungently vivisecting her poetry, others were acclaiming Alice the foremost woman poet of the day.

In the meantime Phoebe issued her *Poems and Parodies* (Boston, 1854), which displayed the happier, gayer spirit of the younger sister. Later came her *Poems of Faith, Hope, and Love* (New York, 1868), a collection showing independent thought, a happy faith, and an optimistic philosophy. *Hymns for All Christians* (1869) was edited with Alice.

Two samples from *Poems and Parodies* will provide the reader with an insight into Phoebe's work. The first is an excerpt from a well-known hymn.

Nearer Home

One sweetly solemn thought
   Comes to me o'er and o'er,—
I am nearer home to-day
   Than I ever have been before;—

Nearer my Father's house
   Where the many mansions be;
Nearer the great white throne,
   Nearer the jasper sea;—

Nearer the bound of life
   Where we lay our burdens down;
Nearer leaving the cross,
   Nearer gaining the crown.

But lying darkly between,
   Winding down through the night,
Is the dim and unknown stream
   That leads at last to the light.[43]

Yet, though Phoebe could be solemn and religious, her characteristic spirit is much better evidenced by the following devastating parody of Longfellow:

[43] Phoebe Cary, *Poems and Parodies* (Boston, 1854), 101-2.

A Psalm of Life

What the Heart of the Young Woman
Said to the Old Man

Tell me not, in idle jingle,
    Marriage is an empty dream,
For the girl is dead that's single,
    And things are not what they seem.

Married life is real, earnest;
    Single blessedness a fib;
Taken from man, to man returnest,
    Has been spoken of the rib.

Not enjoyment, and not sorrow,
    Is our destined end or way;
But to act, that each to-morrow
    Nearer brings the wedding-day.

Life is long, and youth is fleeting,
    And our hearts, if there we search,
Still like steady drums are beating
    Anxious marches to the church.

In the world's broad field of battle,
    In the bivouac of life,
Be not like dumb, driven cattle!
    Be a woman, be a wife!

Trust no Future, howe'er pleasant!
    Let the dead Past bury its dead!
Act,—act in the living Present;
    Heart within, and MAN ahead!

Lives of married folks remind us
    We can live our lives as well,
And, departing, leave behind us
    Such examples as will tell;—

Such examples, that another,
  Sailing far from Hymen's port,
A forlorn, unmarried brother,
  Seeing, shall take heart, and court.

Let us then be up and doing,
  With the heart and head begin;
Still achieving, still pursuing,
  Learn to labor, and to win![44]

Within a few years after the sisters established themselves in New York, their home became the center of a social and literary group, meeting mostly on Sunday evenings and including such notables as Bayard Taylor, John Greenleaf Whittier, R. H. Stoddard, Thomas Bailey Aldrich, Robert Dale Owen, and Horace Greeley. For years Alice had the patronage of Horace Greeley and Rufus Griswold. The poet sisters were popular with their guests not only on account of their writings but also because of their social graces. Phoebe soon gained the reputation of being one of the wittiest women in the country.

Alice's second novel, *Married, not Mated; or, How They Lived at Woodside and Throckmorton Hall* (New York, 1856), followed her *Clovernook Children;* and *Pictures of Country Life* (New York, 1859) proved to be one of her best attempts, much like *Clovernook* in materials used. The poet was trying desperately both to earn a living and to make her place in the literary world. Several volumes of poetry appeared: *Ballads, Lyrics, and Hymns* (New York, 1866), *Snow-Berries, A Book for Young Folks* (Boston, 1867), a delightful book of children's verse, and *A Lover's Diary* (Boston, 1868), which was a beautifully poignant recording of her love for a dead sister. A last novel, *The Bishop's Son* (New York,

[44] Phoebe Cary, *Poems and Paradies*, 193-95.

1867), had first seen print as a newspaper serial. She was working on another novel, "The Born Thrall," in which she had hoped to express her convictions concerning the wrongs and sorrows of women, at the time of her death.

Alice died February 12, 1871. Phoebe died on July 31 of the same year. From 1873 with the publication of *The Last Poems of Alice and Phoebe Cary* (New York) until 1903 with *The Poems of Alice and Phoebe Cary* (New York) their poetry was edited and republished in whole or in part altogether eight times, works of both sisters being included in each volume, thus attesting to their continued popularity.

Can we now characterize and evaluate these "Singing Sisters?"[45] Their devotion to each other was touching; although each had several opportunities to marry, neither did. Each supplemented the other. Alice always drove her frail body with a fierce intensity to keep a stream of words flowing from her pen, doing this partly from economic necessity, partly from a strong ambition to reach whatever literary heights she could, and partly from a desire to let no portion of her talent remain unused. The result, of course, was that she wrote too much, and her earlier writings have a freshness and naturalness and melody about them which is often lacking in the later pieces. She never could achieve her literary ideal—whatever it was. Phoebe, on the other hand, had less command of her poetic talent and depended more upon her mood—with the result that she produced less than her sister.

That Alice Cary enjoyed a large following among the reading public is indicated by the success of her books, in England as well as in the United States. At the present time, however, she has been largely forgotten. The reason

[45] See the novel of that title by Laura Long, based on the lives of Alice and Phoebe Cary (New York, 1941).

is not difficult to discover. We must agree that she has a delightful originality and vigor when dealing with nature and rural subjects and that she writes from the fullness of her heart. Yet she suffered from a lack of complete mental discipline and too little experience with the world. In her attempts to reveal the passions and faults of people in her novels we discover her most uneven writing; in her poetry her dainty imagination and grace to some extent conceal her lack of more active participation in life. But what bothers the modern reader the most about her poetry is the tone of sad sentimentality and didacticism that dominates it. The twentieth century does not enjoy sorrow for its own sake to the extent that the nineteenth century did. And for this reason we tire before long of reading of graves overshadowed by beautiful old forests and of pure, innocent, dying maidens. We can understand the reasons for sorrow prevailing in Alice's life, but we have difficulty in comprehending why she made no greater effort to rise above it, as did her sister Phoebe, who, after all, experienced at least the same family losses. We must conclude that to a great extent Alice enjoyed her melancholy—perhaps subconsciously—and would not have done much to change it if she could. It is a pity that she made little attempt to broaden her field of vision and deal with more of the basic issues of life.

Still, we should not be too harsh with Alice. Her poetry often carries a pleasing sweetness and beauty and melody, and her sympathetic descriptions of nature are correct in detail and are effective. She has left well nigh unforgettable portraits of people—lovers like "Jessie Carroll" and "Annie Clayville"; rustic characters drawn with the vividness of Wordsworth, as "The Farmer's Daughter"; and eccentrics, such as the fiddle-playing grave digger, "Uncle

Joe." And through the large quantity of her writing the simplicity and beauty and tenderness of her womanly soul stand forth—giving her work an appeal to the masses of people that has made it last for generations.

Less need be said of the verse of Phoebe Cary. Her lighter-hearted disposition is perhaps more attractive to us today, and we enjoy her many literary parodies, written at the expense of famous poets, which her grip on reality enabled her to produce. She is the writer of several famous hymns, and much of her verse has more universal appeal than does so much of Alice's, as shown in the strong dramatic sense of her ballads and the powerful faith of her religious poetry. There is more spirit and humor in her work. It may be, then, that in spite of the smaller quantity of her production, Phoebe will be remembered longer than her intense sister Alice.

Finally, we should thank both poets for their realistic depiction of rural life in the West, then a generation or so removed from the frontier, and presented with a tender domestic touch. Alice in particular, though on the one hand a romantic sentimentalist, was enough of a realist for us to identify her as a precursor of western realism, to be seen later in the work of Edward Eggleston.[46]

Would that all Hoosier poets were as significant as the Cary sisters! Our next task is to turn to several poets of much less importance, but who still have a part in the development of early Indiana poetry.

[46] For further study of Alice and Phoebe Cary see especially citations to Birch, Brooks, and McKnight, note 37, above, and Venable, *Beginnings of Literary Culture in the Ohio Valley*, 482-503; also Mary Clemmer Ames, *A Memorial of Alice and Phoebe Cary* (New York, 1874).

SIDNEY M. DYER, PHOEBE FARMER, ORPHEUS
EVERTS, MARY LOUISA CHITWOOD

The first of these lesser lights following the Cary sisters is the Reverend Sidney M. Dyer (1814-1898). He was born February 11, 1814, in Cambridge, New York. At sixteen he was an ignorant drummer boy in the American army; then falling under the benevolent influence of a kind woman, he began to study. He was mostly self-taught and in 1836 commenced studying theology, being ordained to the ministry of the Baptist Church in 1842. He served as missionary to the Choctaw Indians, and as the secretary of the Indian Mission Board located in Louisville, then in 1852 became the pastor of the First Baptist Church in Indianapolis. After remaining there seven years, he took the position of district secretary of the American Baptist Publication Society in Philadelphia. He died in 1898.[47]

Dyer composed lyrics for many songs and is remembered both for them and for his authorship of four volumes of poetry and of several books of natural history, mostly for children, one juvenile tale, and several works on religious subjects. His first collection of poetry, *Voices of Nature, and Thoughts in Rhyme* (Louisville, 1849), is composed of verse previously published in magazines. It is dominated by light nature pieces, such as "The Snowflake," "Song of the Sunbeam," and "Morning in Summer"; but there are also some religious poems. A few poems, such as "To an Absent Wife," are of fair quality, but much of his verse is singsong. *An Olio of Love and Song* . . . (Indianapolis, 1855) was published after being delivered before a meeting of the Athenian Society of Indiana University. In end-stopped, wooden verse, it

---

[47] Banta, *Indiana Authors and Their Books,* 95, and Coggeshall, *Poets and Poetry of the West,* 378.

covers many subjects and honors this Society. *Songs and Ballads* (New York, 1857) is a book of songs, many having previously been set to music, a good example of which is "Ah! Yes, I Remember," written in memory of his little daughter. This poetry, again, is singsong and undistinguished. *The Drunkard's Child* (New York, 1865) is temperance poetry. In general, then, Dyer has little to say; and not much of his verse is worthy of remembrance.

Much the same sort of poetry is found in *The Captives and Other Poems* (La Porte, Indiana, 1856), the only verse issued by Mrs. Phoebe Farmer (1814-1895). An unfortunate fact about Mrs. Farmer is that her biography is more interesting than her literary production.

She was born Phoebe Weston on August 26, 1814, in Townsend, Massachusetts. Her mother's maiden name was Marcia Cary, and the mother's two brothers, Robert and William, had earlier migrated to an area near Cincinnati. Robert was the father of Alice and Phoebe Cary;[48] thus, Phoebe Weston was their first cousin. The glowing reports of the brothers about the new land induced the Weston family to move to Ohio, where the parents soon died, leaving Phoebe to live part of the time with the Cary families. In 1842 she married Franklin Farmer, and they lived in Wilmington, Ohio, two children being born to them, one of whom died in infancy. Mrs. Farmer now began to write verse, along with the Cary sisters, both of whom were younger than she. The Farmers moved to Nauvoo, Illinois, in 1846. Then with the decline of Mr. Farmer's health the family moved to Louisiana about 1850; but with further distress in his physical condition and the advent of pestilence in Louisiana, they returned north to Otis, in La Porte County,

---

[48] See above, 97.

Indiana, in the winter of 1854-55, where the Farmers managed a hotel.

Here Mrs. Farmer made plans to publish a selection of her poems; and with no encouragement from others (even her husband was unsympathetic), she determined to emulate the literary glory of her cousins, who had already issued several successful books. She incurred a large debt in having the verses printed privately by the firm of Millikan & Holmes in La Porte, Indiana, which issued them in a wretchedly printed edition that made the book practically unsalable. She was crushed by the disappointment.

The family now moved again, spending a year in Michigan City, about two years on a farm near Otis, finally returning to their former home in Louisiana in 1859—a most unfortunate time. With the outbreak of the Civil War this Yankee family soon found itself in danger; first the father escaped to New Orleans, then the mother and daughter followed, making their way across lakes and down the Mississippi in a dangerous skiff. Here Mrs. Farmer nursed in Federal hospitals. After the war the family returned to La Porte County, Indiana, whence Mr. Farmer set out on a prospecting trip west— but was never again heard from. In 1872 the daughter, Alice, married; and her mother lived with her and her husband in West Plains, Missouri, until her death in 1895.[49]

The Captives and Other Poems does not compare favorably with the work of the Cary cousins. That Mrs. Farmer was aware of the shortcomings of her verse is indicated by the following excerpt from her "Introduction":

[49] Biography of Phoebe Farmer from "Remarkable Life of La Porte Woman," in La Porte *Daily Herald*, November 14, 1905. This is a clipping in the Indiana Division, Indiana State Library.

Though there may be some harshness in the tone,
Be lenient, turn not in scorn away.
If thou hast sung, compare it with thine own,
When first thy harp awoke its minstrelsy.

If lofty flights, 'mid fancy's airy maze,
Alone can charm thy o'er fastidious ear,
Or polished sentence in high sounding phrase,
Lay down the book, you will not find them here.[50]

But she was a little hard on herself, for at least some of
the material is better than she intimates. The title poem,
"The Captives. A Tale of the Revolution," gives an
interesting story of how two frontier scouts, Cook and
Carey (the latter an ancestor of hers?) were captured by
Indians during the Revolutionary War and imprisoned
in Canada but later escaped and made their way home,
avoiding the dangers of death by drowning in the St.
Lawrence or starving in the wilderness. This is a good
story, but told in couplets in a rather stilted manner.

"Lena, A Legend of Lover's Leap" is another good
story, of how the daughter of a proud nobleman, exiled
from Europe, and her plebeian lover, fleeing her angry
father, choose death by jumping from a cliff rather than
capture. Several lyric poems, like "Lines Written on My
Thirty-sixth Birth Day" contain good lines and stanzas.
A portion of "The Western Land of Ours" may bear
repeating:

Fair bard! I pray thee, hither come, 'twill cheer thy
     sadden'd muse,
Come roam with me o'er grassy lawns, bright with
     the morning dews;
We'll wander by the murmuring rill and cull the
     sweet spring flowers;

[50] *The Captives and Other Poems* (La Porte, 1856), 3.

This is the land for poets' dreams, this western land
    of ours.
My home is on the distant shore of Mississippi's tide,
And many a league of hill and dale our cherished
    hearts divide;
I know thou lov'st thine own fair streams and all
    thy woodland bowers,
But they can ne'er inspire thy harp, like this bright
    land of ours.[51]

Phoebe Farmer's poetry is all cast in a conventional
vein, in conventional verse (often the closed couplet),
and says conventional things about life. Little of it would
be interesting today except for the comparatively early
date of its production. The Library of Congress lists a
book, *Louisa Williams; or, The Orphan Bound-Girl, a
Tale of the Queen City,* printed in Cincinnati in 1859,
by Mrs. P. W. Farmer; but there is insufficient evidence
to state that this is definitely the same person as our poet.

A poet who published his first book in La Porte only
a month or two after Mrs. Farmer published her volume
did not experience her miserable luck. Dr. Orpheus
Everts (1826-1903) had many opportunities in life and
lived out many years, with literature merely one of his
avocations. He was born December 18, 1826, in Liberty,
Indiana, received his education in the schools of his
county and his M.D. degree in 1846, at the early age of
nineteen, from the Indiana Medical College at La Porte.
He was of a family of doctors, his father and three brothers
all being practicing physicians. For a time he abandoned
his profession, becoming editor of the La Porte *Times,*
and in 1857 he was appointed by President Buchanan
register of the land office at Hudson, Wisconsin. Nevertheless, during the Civil War he served as surgeon in the

[51] *The Captives and Other Poems,* 121-22.

20th Regiment of Indiana Volunteers, and from 1868 to 1879 was superintendent of the Indiana Hospital for the Insane. In 1880 he was appointed superintendent of the Cincinnati Sanitarium. In addition to his professional duties, he was a writer of medical literature, a painter, and a poet.[52]

Dr. Everts is an uneven poet. If he had continued the work begun in his first two books and if he had concentrated on writing, he might have become a poet of some note. As it turned out, however, his first two volumes are his best; and since they evidently had small circulation, he never became very well known. He had ability, and he could write moving poetry when he chose.

O-na-we-quah; and Other Poems was printed privately and anonymously at the press of the La Porte *Times* in 1856. The preface tells the reader that the book was produced at the request of friends and "is not offered to the public either for sale or criticism."[53] The author goes on to say that the title poem "O-na-we-quah; a Legend of Illinois," is founded on a legend that a warlike tribe of Indians, who once inhabited the central portion of what is now Illinois, being attacked by other tribes who desired to wrest the territory from them, at length took refuge on a large rock in the Illinois River above the present city of La Salle; and here they defended themselves against a superior force but were eventually starved out, only a few escaping. This is a narrative poem of fifty-one pages, mostly in iambic tetrameter couplets, recounting the legend with the addition of a love story about the daughter of the chief of the Potawatomi and the son of

[52] Biography of Dr. Everts taken from Banta, *Indiana Authors and Their Books*, 106; Coggeshall, *Poets and Poetry of the West*, 545; and Benjamin S. Parker and Enos B. Heiney (eds.), *Poets and Poetry of Indiana . . .* (New York, 1900), 430.

[53] Everts, *O-na-we-quah . . .* (La Porte, 1856), 1.

the chief of the Illinois, who had been a captive of the Potawatomi and then released. The Indian maiden, Nee-nah, steals away from her tribe to warn her lover, called the Panther, of an impending attack on the Illinois by the Potawatomi and is thus described by Everts:

> No pallor, on her brown cheek spreading,
> Betrays the danger she is treading;
> Her feet as light as nimble deer's,
> Are winged with love's elastic fears;
> Her moccasins adorned with quills,
> Tread soft, as morning o'er the hills;
> Her glossy braids of raven hair,
> Are floating 'round her shoulders bare,
> Her swelling bosom, tinged with hue
> Of sunny brown, has felt the dew;
> And gaudy scarf of crimson dye,
> Obscured its beauty from the eye.
> About her waist, a beaded belt
> Suspends a skirt of rudest felt;
> Her rounded limbs, of tapering mould,
> Disdain protection from the cold;
> Her eye—the Eagle's on yon' peak
> Hath not the power which her's [sic] can speak![54]

Then come attack and counterattack, pursuit, the siege of the Illinois on what came later to be known as "Starved Rock," and finally the destruction of all the Illinois except the Panther, who escapes with Nee-nah. This thrilling story is well told; it has good description, emotion, and power. A few lyrics complete the volume.

Because the first book was favorably received, *The Spectral Bride and Other Poems* (La Porte, Indiana, 1857) was issued, this time with Dr. Everts' name. In a sense it is a new edition of *O-na-we-quah*, differing from the first publication only in the increased number of miscel-

[54] Everts, *O-na-we-quah*, 3-4.

laneous poems and in the addition of the title poem, "The
Spectral Bride." This is another long narrative and descriptive poem, telling of the fantastic dream of a youth
and a spectral bride. The poem is not nearly so good as
the Indian legend, but the Spenserian stanza used is often
adequate, as in this sample:

> O! wondrous world of strange reality!
> Of fiction-gilded facts—of mighty fears!
> Of magic pictures, born of phantasy—
> And truths rolled back from long forgotten years!
> In thy bright mirror, to our sight appears
> Things to be loved, and dreaded! Prophecy
> Here hath her temple—and her altar rears—
> Omens attend, inspired, with auguring eye,
> And offers sacrifice deep mystery to descry![55]

Everts' third volume, *Giles & Co., or, Views and Interviews Concerning Civilization* (Indianapolis, 1878), is
rather ineffective discussion, by means of loosely connected short stories or sketches, of various aspects of
civilization, such as money, war, justice, and capital and
labor. *Constancy, a Midsummer Night's Idyl* (Indianapolis, 1881) is a short poem on love. *Facts and Fancies
(Light and Heavy); a Metrical Melange* (Cincinnati, 1896)
tells in doggerel verse the story of a long train ride, with
philosophical observations mixed in; and *The Cliffords;
or Almost Persuaded* (Cincinnati, 1898) is an undistinguished novel. *The Lost Poet* (Cincinnati, 1901) gives in
rather good heroic couplets the obscure story of a poet
who lost his poetic force and inspiration.

Dr. Everts, therefore, had the makings of a poet—on
occasion he displays poetic feeling and poetic art—but
his unevenness and lack of concentration on his writing
lead him to fall short of real stature as a poet.

[55] Everts, *Spectral Bride* . . . (La Porte, 1857), 8.

If Mrs. Farmer, as mentioned above, had a disappointing experience with literature, a much more tragic situation is found in the life of Mary Louisa Chitwood (1832-1855), who died at the threshold of a very promising career as a poet. Miss Chitwood was born on October 29, 1832, near Mount Carmel, in Franklin County, Indiana; she attended the elementary schools and early attracted the envy of other pupils by her poetic talent. A Connersville paper published her first poem, and she soon made herself familiar to readers of poetry through the Louisville *Journal, The Temperance Wreath, The Ladies' Repository, The Genius of the West,* and several other magazines and newspapers. Her ability and youth exciting much attention, she was soon receiving magazines, books, and letters from writers with well-established reputations. She was described as beautiful—of medium height with fair complexion, rosy cheeks, rich blue eyes of a sweet and soft expression, and long flaxen-colored hair of a somewhat golden hue. She must have looked the part of a dreamy poetess. Some of her correspondence was with Alice and Phoebe Cary, and all arrangements had been completed for her to visit for a time in their home in New York and meet their literary friends when suddenly she became ill with typhoid fever. Almost before anyone knew she was sick, she died at her home on December 19, 1855—at the age of twenty-three.[56]

The many literary people who knew her, by personal acquaintance or correspondence or only through reading her poetry, were shocked by the sudden death of one so young and so promising in talent. Many authors wrote tributes to her. George D. Prentice, the editor of the

[56] Biography of Miss Chitwood taken from Banta, *Indiana Authors and Their Books,* 59; Coggeshall, *Poets and Poetry of the West,* 628-29.

Louisville *Journal,* had promised to help her prepare a
selection of her poems for publication; and he now set
out to fulfill this obligation, but without her expected aid.
In 1857 he published the book in Cincinnati, for the
benefit of Miss Chitwood's mother, entitled *Poems by M.*
Louisa Chitwood, Selected and Prefaced by George D.
Prentice. He states in the preface:

... she was our very dear, personal friend, and one of the
brightest among the young women of genius in this country. . . .
    Miss Chitwood was young; but in her brief career of life,
she knew something of sorrow, and her heart was both sof-
tened and strengthened by the stern discipline. She was kind,
and gentle, and true, and good—warm-hearted and high-
souled—diffident and shrinking, but conscious of bright and
beautiful thoughts, and of strong powers, given her by God
for useful purposes. Her whole nature was deeply and intensely poetical; and thus to her the whole world was full of
poetry. The deepest griefs of her young bosom were turned to
music—soft, sweet, and mournful music, on her lips.[57]

Mary Louisa Chitwood's poetry is highly romantic and
sentimental, full of expiring orphans, and lovers, as in
"The Dying Betrothed" and "Why Did I Weep When
Johnny Died?" and abounding in dreams, moonlight,
silver streams winding through beautiful forests, as in
"To a Favorite Stream" and "Dreaming in the Twilight."
Beauty and sorrow are everywhere present, expressed in
a poetic diction common in her day, but her phraseology
is well chosen. Probably she is not so fond of sorrow as
are Alice Cary and Sarah T. Bolton. That she is adept
at metrics is seen in such poems as "The Robin's Song,"
the first stanza of which is as follows:

[57] *Poems by M. Louisa Chitwood* . . . (Cincinnati, 1857), 11-12.

> I hear a robin singing
>   Out in the Autumn rain;
> My soul its way is winging
>   To childhood's time again;
> I hear the south winds blowing,
> The rush of the harvest mowing,
> And the voice of the river flowing,
>   Where lilies lived and died;
> I rest beneath the shadow
> Of the aspen in the meadow.
>   With no hope crucified.[58]

This poem may have been inspired by the sonorous aspect of the work of Poe. The first two stanzas of the following poem, "The Graves of the Flowers," illustrate her light touch:

> The woods are full of tiny graves,
>   The sweet graves of the flowers,
> That sprang in every sheltered nook,
>   Amid the Spring-time hours.
> The buttercup lies on the slope
>   Where first the sunlight fell;
> The violet sleeps beside the rill,
>   The daisy in the dell.
>
> Upon no stone is carved the name
>   Of April's children fair;
> They perished when the sky was bright,
>   And gentle was the air.
> To the soft kisses of the breeze
> They held, half-trembling, up,
> Full many a small transparent urn
> And honey-laden cup.[59]

It is as idle to ask ourselves what Louisa Chitwood would have written if she had had the benefit of more

[58] *Poems by M. Louisa Chitwood*, 186.
[59] *Ibid.*, 160.

education, experience, and years as it is to wonder what Keats and Shelley might have done if they had been granted more time. Miss Chitwood, of course, was not a Keats or a Shelley. But probably she would have become, at least, one of Indiana's better poets.

ALFRED J. COTTON

To proceed from Miss Chitwood to Alfred Johnson Cotton (1800-1858) is practically to go from the sublime to the ridiculous. To say the least, Cotton's book is amusing, and the author must have been an eccentric and peculiar figure. Not much biographical information can be obtained concerning the Reverend Judge (he liked the double title) Cotton other than is found in the history of his county (Dearborn) and in the autobiographical sketch contained in his own book of poetry. His personality makes itself felt forcefully, but many details of his life are omitted. His autobiographical work, *Cotton's Sketch-Book*, published in Portland, Maine, in 1874, long after his death, does not help much with biographical details. He was born April 20, 1800, in Cumberland County, Maine, the fourth in a family of nine children. He came to Dearborn County, Indiana, in 1818, built a log cabin in the forest, became a schoolteacher, and was ordained in the ministry in 1825. An excursion into politics was unsuccessful, for he was defeated several times as a candidate for various offices. He was editor of the New Castle *Banner* for a while, but returned to Dearborn County and filled the position of associate judge for six years and that of probate judge for four years. His death in 1858 must have occurred shortly after his one volume of poems was published.[60]

[60] Biography of Cotton taken from Banta, *Indiana Authors and Their Books*, 73.

The complete title of this book is as long-winded as many other titles of the day, but it is, at least, descriptive of the contents. It is *Cotton's Keepsake. Poems on Various Subjects, by Rev. Judge A. J. Cotton, Philom. To Which Is Appended a Short Autobiographical Sketch of the Life of the Author, and a Condensed History of the Early Settlements, Incidents, and Improvements of the Country, from the Early Settlers Themselves, and from Observation and Experience in It, for the Space of Forty Years Last Past* (Cincinnati, 1858). The book was published privately and is now considered rare.

To enable the reader to appreciate the eccentricity of the author, the "Advertisement" at the front of the book, signed by "The Author," is set down here:

Advertisement

Although the subject of most of my Poems, and the incidents recorded in my little book are mainly located in Dearborn county, Indiana, yet those incidents being common throughout the Great West, it is thought and intended to be a work of such a general character, as to merit a liberal patronage and a wide-spread circulation. Such a picture of human life, *as it is,* has never before been presented to the public, from Adam down to this time. Read it and see.

Accidents and sudden deaths, suicides and murders, turkey, deer and moose, bear, wolf and panther, rattlesnake, copperhead and Indian stories, with which the Historical portion of it will abound, are always interesting, everywhere, and to everybody—which, together with its originality, its oddity, its variety, and its truthfulness, will, it is confidently hoped and believed, make it emphatically "the book for the times," and "the book for the multitude."[61]

Excerpts from Cotton's preface to the book add to the impression of the writer's personality:

[61] *Cotton's Keepsake* . . . (Cincinnati, 1858), 3.

In this book-making age, various are the causes which in-
duce men to turn authors. Ambition, avarice, revenge and
vanity have furnished the main promptings. Now, every body
who knows me, will, of course, acquit me of all the *vanity*
incentives, because my great modesty is proverbial, even to a
fault, perchance, for one of my brilliancy of intellect and
classic and poetic fame—a weakness of my youth which I am
now too old to correct. But by a great and herculean effort,
I have on this occasion, so far mastered myself as to say, what
is really true, that it would gratify me exceedingly to leave
behind me, when "the curtain of life falls," a memorial that
I had once lived—something to be remembered by—something
to speak for me in the behalf of truth and benevolence—of
virtue and religion—that, in after times, it may be said of me,
as of one of old, "he being dead, yet speaketh." Yet *necessity,*
which is the mother of inventions, has rather forced me into
its execution at this time.[62]

Having allowed Cotton to reveal himself, we believe the
reader will agree that he must have been in some ways a
rather ludicrous figure.

The Reverend Judge's verse is mere doggerel. It is singsong and full of bad rhymes and outlandish sentiment.
The poetry of this *Keepsake* is divided into sections:
"Religious," which tells of his conversion at sixteen and
his call to the ministry; "Criminal," narrating the stories
of the executions of criminals of the day; "Temperance,"
full of weeping stories of men crazed by drink, engaging
in rum orgies, and then beating their wives; "Political,"
consisting mostly of patriotic poems; "Editorial," made
up of an "Ode to the Newcastle Banner, by the Editor";
"Literary"—about school; "Epistolary," containing letters
to his family; "Hymeneal Punnings," in which he em-
ploys puns on the names of couples he has joined in marriage; lastly, "Odes," "Elegies," "Obituaries," and "Miscellaneous."

[62] *Ibid.,* 14.

Here, then, is not simply badness; it is inspired badness. Cotton deserves no ranking as a poet; his rhymes can hardly be called poetry. But we should say in justice to him that in spite of his eccentric personality, he evidently was a sincere and generous person. His ridiculous and egotistical pose is, in one sense, refreshing.

Sarah T. Bolton

In leaving Cotton for the study of Sarah T. Bolton (1814-1893) we are again experiencing extremes, for here is one of the best known of all the Indiana poets and certainly the poet of greatest reputation in the state in this first period of literature. So well is she recognized as an outstanding Hoosier poet that in the rotunda of the state capitol building there stands a bronze plaque placed there in 1941 by the Indiana Branch of the National League of Pen Women. Prior to Riley she was thought of as *the* poet of the state, and she enjoyed for many years public acclaim as the unofficial Hoosier laureate.

Since she published her verse in periodicals until rather late in life, let us first note her biography before examining her production. Sarah Tittle Barrett was born on December 18, 1814, in Newport, Kentucky, the grand-daughter on her father's side of Lemuel Barrett, distinguished officer of the Revolutionary Army, and, on her mother's side, the granddaughter of one of the Pendletons of Virginia, a cousin of James Madison. When she was a small child, the family moved to the wilderness of Jennings County, Indiana, where they were among the earliest settlers. Though her father steadily developed his frontier farm, when Sarah was nine he reluctantly sold it and moved to Madison, Indiana, to provide educational advantages for his children. It took only two months for

Sarah to learn to read and write, and when she was
thirteen, her first poem was published in the Madison
Banner. From that time until she was married her verse
usually was printed weekly in the newspapers of Madison
or Cincinnati.

Her writing led to her acquaintance—and marriage—
in 1831 with a Madison editor, Nathaniel Bolton, who
had helped found in 1822 the first newspaper published
in Indianapolis, the *Gazette*. The couple bought a farm
west of Indianapolis, and two children were born to
them. Mr. Bolton suffered financial loss from having stood
security for debts of friends and was forced to open a
tavern on his farm, and the young Mrs. Bolton found
it necessary to take care of a public house and a large
dairy for nine years practically single-handed. While her
husband served as state librarian and also the custodian
of the statehouse, she sewed almost without help new
carpets for the building for a meeting of governors of
western states, composing while she worked, her poem
of courage despite odds, "Paddle Your Own Canoe." Mr.
Bolton also was appointed an officer of the state legislature
and was register of the land office. Mrs. Bolton became
known both for her leadership in the movement for wom-
en's rights and for her constant production of popular
poetry; and she received honors, among others the presentation to her of a silver cup as a prize because of an
ode which she wrote for the laying of the cornerstone of
the Masonic Hall in Indianapolis. In 1855 Mr. Bolton was
appointed by President Pierce United States consul at
Geneva, Switzerland, and his wife and daughter lived with
him there for some two years. He died in 1858. Mrs.
Bolton, saddened also by the loss of her daughter, plunged
into a grief from which she never fully recovered. In
1863 she married Judge Addison Reese of Missouri, but

the marriage was a failure. In 1871 she acquired "Beech Bank," a home close to Indianapolis in what is now the town of Beech Grove, where she resided until her death on August 4, 1893.[63]

Four volumes of Mrs. Bolton's verse were published during her lifetime; one, *Paddle Your Own Canoe and Other Poems* (Indianapolis, 1897), was merely a reprint of a selection of earlier poems. Except for thirty-five pieces, her first volume, *Poems by Sarah T. Bolton* (New York, 1865), was incorporated bodily into her second publication, *The Life and Poems of Sarah T. Bolton* (Indianapolis, 1880), which was then issued along with some new poetry; hence, these two volumes can be considered together.

Sarah T. Bolton is a many-sided poet, and no one generalization can easily characterize and evaluate her work. At the outset something should be said about her poetic technique. As a craftsman, she can build her rhyme and stanzas carefully and effectively, using with ease such forms as the Spenserian stanza, the ode, and intricate seven-line stanzas. The less unusual metrical feet, like the dactyl, came readily from her pen, as in "Let Us Be Glad While We May." Following the example of Poe, she can even use internal rhyme with good effect, as in the first two stanzas of the following imitation of "The Raven":

Death of Edgar A. Poe

They have laid thee down to slumber, where the sorrows that encumber
Such a wild and wayward heart as thine, can never reach thee more;
From the weariness and sadness, from the fever and the madness,

[63] Coggeshall, *Poets and Poetry of the West,* 367-70; *The Life and Poems of Sarah T. Bolton* (Indianapolis, 1880); and information supplied by Lloyd Bolton Mann, great-grandson of the poet.

Of a life that knew no gladness, to a bright and blessed
    shore,—
To the wondrous joy and beauty of the distant Aidenn shore,
        Thou art gone forever more.

Thou wert like a meteor glancing through a starry sky
    entrancing,—
Thrilling, awing rapt beholder with the wondrous light
    it wore;
But the meteor has descended, and the "Nightly" shadows
    blended;
For the fever-dream is ended, and the fearful crisis o'er,—
Yes, the wild, unresting fever-dream of human life is o'er,
        Thou art sleeping evermore.[64]

Sometimes her verse is ambiguous and contains trite
phraseology; but on the other hand, her diction can be
rather well polished.

As in the case of most poets, Mrs. Bolton's themes are
various; but usually she writes sad, sentimental stories
which give the reader a lump in the throat—unless, of
course, he finally becomes hardened to them. Title after
title can be cited as examples of this favorite turn of mind
of the poet, some of the subjects undoubtedly reflecting
her European experiences. "Legend of the Castle Mon-
netier" tells how in the absence of her betrothed, who
had gone on a crusade, the Lady Linneleid is forced to
wed a ruthless baron. Her lover returns and kills the
baron, but then Linneleid kills herself by jumping from
her castle window. In "Infanticide" a starving unwed
mother kills her child and dies in the snow, thinking
of the father of the child, whose sin is unknown and who
is marrying another. But perhaps the most sentimental
of all these verse narratives—certainly the longest—is
"Leoline," which recounts how a girl of noble birth is

[64] *The Life and Poems of Sarah T. Bolton,* 213-14.

kept by her proud and scornful father from her love, "a poor, pale artist," until she elopes with him, lives an idyllic life only a short time until he dies, and she and her baby are reduced to poverty; then, of course, the baby dies. Some stories also cover Civil War themes, and these are in many ways even harder for the reader to bear. In "Coming Home" a fond old mother waits for her two sons to come home from the war, thinking they are wounded; but men enter, carrying two coffins. Perhaps the most heart-rending of these war tales is that given in "Left on the Battlefield," which relates how two brothers on different sides in the War meet in the haze of the battlefield and unknowingly wound each other fatally, and, recognition coming too late, breathe their last in a final embrace, in which they are buried. We must say, at the least, that the poet can tell stories well, and in justice to her we should point out that a very few of the stories do end happily.

Mrs. Bolton's grief, however, is by no means confined to legend or imagination or partial fact. In poem after poem she sorrows for her beloved dead, as in "To our Tetie," "Two Graves," "My Daughter," and others. Indeed, these two books are made up largely of sorrow and despair—real, vicarious, or imagined.

Much religious verse is found also in them. Sometimes the author gropes for faith in the afterlife, as in "Going Down the Hill" and "Doubt," and at times seems more certain of it with "Dead" and "The Land Over the River." Also, her poetry displays an idealism, such as we see through her well-known poem, "Paddle Your Own Canoe," which affirms hope, courage, and resolution to accomplished something worth while in life. The first two stanzas follow:

Voyager upon life's sea,
   To yourself be true,
And where'er your lot may be,
   Paddle your own canoe.
Never, though the winds may rave,
   Falter nor look back;
But upon the darkest wave
   Leave a shining track.

Nobly dare the wildest storm,
   Stem the hardest gale;
Brave of heart and strong of arm,
   You will never fail.
When the world is cold and dark,
   Keep an aim in view,
And toward the beacon mark
   Paddle your own canoe.[65]

"Paddle Your Own Canoe" is not nearly so good a poem as some of her verse narratives, however. Neither does her piece, "Indiana," though locally famous, rank so well poetically as many other poems, as the first stanza gives evidence:

Though many laud Italia's clime,
And call Helvetia's land sublime,
Tell Gallia's praise in prose and rhyme,
   And worship old Hispania;
The winds of Heaven never fanned,
The circling sunlight never spanned
The borders of a better land
   Than our own Indiana.[66]

The last four lines of this stanza have often been quoted—in spite of the poet's attempt to make the sunlight circle and "Indiana" rhyme with "Hispania." Later in the poem "Brittania" and "cannie" are also given to rhyme with "Indiana." Mrs. Bolton's ear was not perfect.

[65] *The Life and Poems of Sarah T. Bolton*, 277.
[66] *Ibid.*, 380.

Mrs. Bolton is best in her remembrance of the dear, dead past. A portion of the poem "Colonel James P. Drake" states well this frequent theme of her verse:

> The interests of the Present pass away,
>   And that which was, but is not, seems to be;
> Dead hopes revive, old thoughts resume their sway,
>   And by the soft, uncertain light I see
> The genial faces I was wont to meet,
> When hope was new and life was fair and sweet,
> And we went down its paths with buoyant feet.[67]

In the main, Sarah T. Bolton writes fairly good verse—indeed, a little of it is better than that; in view of her background and lack of higher education she does very well. In spite of some roughness in her verse and occasional bad rhymes, she has a surprising command of many different forms of versification. Her nature, as revealed through her poetry, is sweet and refined, idealistic and religious; and she has delicate imagination and appreciation of beauty and the simple life. Yet, the greatest impact of her poetry on the reader is that of sorrow.

What has been said about *The Life and Poems* generally applies also to the volume *Songs of a Life-Time* (Indianapolis, 1892). Some of the poems from the previous volume are reprinted here. In the *Songs* we find a continuation of her sentimental verse, as, for example, in "The Miner's Story," a genuine "tear-jerker" about how a boy, not so strong as his brothers, is driven by their derision away from his home and loving mother. Unknown to her, he works for ten years in order to make enough money to enable him to return and take care of her; but just when he is ready to go, he learns that she is dead, and he arrives only in time for the funeral. So Mrs. Bolton has not changed the style of her poetry or

[67] *The Life and Poems of Sarah T. Bolton*, 234-35.

improved its quality; she still utilizes the same themes with the addition of an interest in some social problems, such as drinking and the plight of labor.

Let us conclude our study of Sarah T. Bolton, then, by saying that she is a sentimentalist, long on tears and short on clear, analytical thinking. She has little to say. Like her predecessor, Alice Cary, who wrote somewhat the same kind of verse, she loves to weep and, to at least some extent, enjoys her sorrow. We can understand how the deaths in her family gave rise to such emotions on her part, but it is difficult to see today why she permitted sorrow to be the motif of her life, tending to eclipse other subjects and thoughts. Her work, therefore, in many ways is dated and does not well stand the test of time. Still, she and the Cary sisters share the honors of being the best poets in early Indiana literature.

JOHN FINLEY

In the minds of many Mrs. Bolton is the writer of only one poem, "Paddle Your Own Canoe." So also the name of John Finley (1797-1866), when it is recognized at all, tends to be connected with a single poem, "The Hoosier's Nest," rather than with his total production. He published much less than Mrs. Bolton and does not begin to attain to her quality; yet he is significant for at least this one poem, if not several others. Some idea of his popularity is indicated by the fact that for years he was known as "The Hoosier Poet," long before the time of James Whitcomb Riley; and in 1834 the *Indiana Democrat* called him the "Poet Laureat [sic] of Hoosierland."

Finley was born on January 11, 1797, in Brownsburg, Virginia; and when he was sixteen, during the War of 1812, he was forced by his father's financial reverses to give up his formal education in a country school and rely

upon careful reading for whatever else he learned. In
the tradition that he later established for himself as a
humorist, he once said that all he learned in school was
to read, write, and cipher up to the rule of three—and
that it took him ten years to learn that much. After
serving an apprenticeship as a tanner and currier, he went
west in 1816, stopped for a short time in Cincinnati, then
settled in Richmond, Indiana, in 1820, where for the rest
of his life he was a man of note because of his activity
in public affairs. He was justice of the peace from 1824
to 1827, a member of the state legislature from 1828 to
1831, clerk of the Wayne County courts from 1837 to
1845, and mayor of Richmond from 1852 until his death
on December 23, 1866. He was editor and part owner of
the Richmond *Palladium* from 1831 to 1834.[68]

Finley first came into literary prominence with the publication of his poem, "The Hoosier's Nest," in the Indianapolis *Journal* on January 1, 1833. Although this was not
the first printed use of the word "Hoosier," it was the
first use that attracted much attention. The tremendous
popularity of this poem must have surprised the author
as much as anyone, for it was reprinted in almost every
frontier newspaper and then made its way to the East
and even to England, where it was hailed as an example
of backwoods poetry. It was the earliest poem from the
West to attract widespread attention, and in this respect
Finley was unique, standing quite alone for many years.

It is interesting that "The Hoosier's Nest" has usually
been printed in a shortened version. Originally it contained ten long stanzas and discussed, in a semihumorous
strain, the glories and future of the West, the advantages

[68] Biography of Finley taken from Banta, *Indiana Authors and Their Books*, 108; Coggeshall, *Poets and Poetry of the West*, 83; and Parker and Heiney (eds.), *Poets and Poetry of Indiana*, 430-31.

of Indiana in particular, the virtue of toil, the coming
of the emigrant to the state, the erection of his cabin,
and the growth of his family and fortunes—all this before
that latter portion of the poem which alone is most often
printed under the title, telling of the visit of a stranger
to a Hoosier cabin in the woods.[69] Perhaps the best
stanza in the poem is the following:

> Blest Indiana! in thy soil
> Are found the sure rewards of toil,
> Where honest poverty and worth
> May make a Paradise on earth.
> With feelings proud we contemplate
> The rising glory of our State;
> Nor take offense by application
> Of its good-natured appellation.
> Our hardy yeomanry can smile,
> At tourists of "the sea-girt isle,"
> Or wits who travel at the gallop,
> Like Basil Hall or Mrs. Trollope.
> 'Tis true among the crowds that roam
> To seek for fortune or a home,
> It happens often that we find
> Empiricism of every kind.[70]

The stanza is rough and ambiguous enough, but it represents about the best of published poetry that Indiana
could turn out in 1833.

John Finley finally collected some of his poetry and
published it in a single small volume entitled *The
Hoosier's Nest, and Other Poems* (Cincinnati, 1866), the
year of his death. Many types of verse are included in
the book. He can be serious, as in "What is Life?" "What

[69] The original text of "The Hoosier's Nest" may be found in Oliver H.
Smith, *Early Indiana Trials: and Sketches* (Cincinnati, 1858), 211-15, and
John Finley, *The Hoosier's Nest, and Other Poems* (Cincinnati, 1866),
11-17.

[70] Finley, *The Hoosier's Nest*, 12-13.

is Faith?" and "Lines, Written on Opening a Mound on the Bank of Whitewater, Near Richmond, Ind., Containing a Human Skeleton." These poems are of fair quality. He also has some pieces on politics, patriotism, and temperance. But what shines forth particularly in the collection is his humorous verse, and he thereby takes a position as the first Hoosier humorist. W. H. Venable thus analyzes him:

He may be described as the father of western humorous poetry. Besides him, only a very few of the early "bards" attempted the facetious. . . . Finley was a born humorist, and nearly everything he wrote is piquant and amusing. His lines "To My Old Coat," "A Wife Wanted," and the graphic piece in Irish dialect, "Bachelor's Hall," still hold their place as general favorites. The last named went the rounds of newspaperdom credited to Tom Moore.[71]

An excerpt from "Bachelor's Hall" will give a fair sample of his humor. It was reported that this poem was set to music to be sung at a banquet for members of the state legislature.

> Bachelor's Hall! What a quare-looking place it is!
>   Kape me from sich all the days of my life!
> Sure, but I think what a burnin' disgrace it is,
>   Niver at all to be gettin' a wife.
>
> See the ould bachelor, gloomy and sad enough,
>   Placing his tay-kittle over the fire;
> Soon it tips over—Saint Patrick! he's mad enough
>   (If he were present) to fight with the Squire.
>
> . . . .
>
> Late in the night then he goes to bed shiverin';
>   Niver the bit is the bed made at all;
> He crapes like a terrapin under the kiverin';
>   Bad luck to the picture of Bachelor's Hall!

[71] Venable, *Beginnings of Literary Culture in the Ohio Valley*, 278.

So Finley blazed the dialect trail in Indiana poetry which Riley would follow so well nearly half a century afterward.

It is unfortunate that he is known mostly for his "The Hoosier's Nest," for that is one of his worst poems. All told, however, his poetry tends to be singsong, with bad rhymes and odd and ineffective combinations of words that are difficult to appreciate today. Finley, therefore, is a minor writer in the intrinsic worth of his work, but is significant because of his one poem and because of his humor.

THE WILLSONS

The story of the next two poets is interesting but sad; for like Louisa Chitwood, they were cut off before their prime. Among the majestic hills and lovely valleys where the Whitewater River flows toward the Miami River and the Ohio there is a graveyard at Laurel, in Franklin County, Indiana, where side by side are buried two young poets, united in death as in life—Forceythe Willson (1837-1867) and his wife, Elizabeth Conwell Willson (1842-1864). In tribute to them and to their poetry Oliver Wendell Holmes once visited their graves. Since their stories are intertwined, we shall tell them together.

Byron Forceythe Willson was born April 10, 1837, at Little Genesee, Allegany County, New York.[72] His father, Hiram Willson, an abolitionist and a believer in liberal education, took the family west about 1846, to Maysville and then Covington, Kentucky, and, in 1852,

[72] The biographical information on Forceythe Willson was taken from Banta, *Indiana Authors and Their Books*, 341-42; Parker and Heiney (eds.) *Poets and Poetry of Indiana*, 463-64; John James Piatt, "Forceythe Willson," in *Atlantic Monthly*, 35(1875), 332-44; Venable, *Beginnings of Literary Culture in the Ohio Valley*, 285-86; and Minnie O. Williams (comp.), *Indiana Authors, a Representative Collection for Young People* (Indianapolis, 1916), 347-50.

to New Albany, Indiana, where, until he died in 1859, three years after his wife, he managed a thriving lumber business. Forceythe was the eldest of eight children thus bereaved, and he seems to have cared for the younger ones. Fortunately, their father's estate left them all well provided for. Suffering always from ill health, still Forceythe loved nature and rough out-of-door sports. He attended the colleges of Antioch, Harvard, and Oberlin, studying as much as his health permitted. When a wave of interest in spiritualism struck New Albany about 1858, he studied the matter and for a while served as a medium, but soon abandoned the practice, though retaining a belief in his own psychic powers—which he was later to demonstrate to several of the Cambridge-Boston literati. He believed in communication between the living and the dead; and it is reported that he possessed a unique faculty by which, for example, he could report the contents of a sealed letter held to his forehead, along with the age, sex, character, and sometimes, even the name of the writer.[73] After the death of his father he lived by himself, evidently in a house separate from his brothers and sisters, and pursued the life of a careful scholar and writer—quiet, reserved, and dignified.

His writings in the form of some rather peculiar and incoherent poetry soon attracted attention. When the Civil War began, he wrote editorials for the Louisville *Journal;* and in the autumn of 1862 he organized a militia company (at his own expense) to meet the threatened Confederate raid into Indiana. He was chosen captain of the unit but did not serve, evidently because of his health.

At about this time Willson made the acquaintance of Elizabeth Conwell Smith at a meeting of a literary club

[73] Piatt, "Forceythe Willson," in *Atlantic Monthly,* 35:334.

in New Albany, where they were both guests of the evening. She had been born June 26, 1842, at Laurel, Indiana, the granddaughter of the pioneer Methodist preacher, the Reverend James Conwell, founder of Laurel, and was attending the DePauw College for Women in New Albany. She is described as "a woman of very lovely and gentle character, with a poetical gift of much sweetness and tenderness, which did not attain maturity of expression."[74] Since her sixteenth year she had been publishing her poetry in the local papers. At once the two poets discovered their mutual interests.

Willson's reputation was secured by one brilliant stroke—the anonymous publication as the carrier's address in the Louisville *Journal* on January 1, 1863, of his pathetic and striking poem, "The Old Sergeant." The effect of this poem was little short of magic. In two days it was being wept over in Washington by congressmen, and it was reprinted in newspapers throughout the North. The poem was brought to the attention of President Lincoln, who read it and loved it and who inquired of Oliver Wendell Holmes if he knew who the author was. Holmes, greatly admiring it himself, did not know and started writing letters of inquiry; in the meantime he read it to many audiences as part of the lecture which he was then giving on the poetry of the War, comparing it for interest to "The Rime of the Ancient Mariner." Other readers and reciters took it up until its fame was widespread in the northern states. As we shall see, it was this poem which proved to be for Willson the key to unlock the door to the society of the New England poets.

"The Old Sergeant" is the story of the Battle of Shiloh as told by an old sergeant of the Union Army who received a fatal wound in the engagement and lies dying.

[74] *Ibid.*, 35:337.

Extremely realistic, giving the actual names of places and persons as related to Willson by a Federal assistant surgeon whom the poet knew at New Albany, still the poem "is yet so idealized and subjective that its hero becomes a vivid type of the brave soldier-martyr of every country, and its patriotism breathes a universal air."[75]
An excerpt will be interesting to the reader.[76]

"I have got my marching orders, and I'm ready
  now to go;
Doctor, did you say I fainted?—but it couldn't
  ha' been so,—
For as sure as I'm a Sergeant, and was wounded at
  Shiloh,
I've this very night been back there, on the old
  field of Shiloh!
. . . .

"There was where the gunboats opened on the dark
  rebellious host;
And where Webster semicircled his last guns upon
  the coast;
There were still the two log-houses, just the same,
  or else their ghost,—
And the same old transport came and took me
  over—or its ghost!
. . . .

"There was where Lew Wallace showed them he
  was of the canny kin,
There was where old Nelson thundered, and where
  Rousseau waded in;
There McCook sent 'em to breakfast, and we all be-
  gan to win—
There was where the grape-shot took me, just as
  we began to win.

[75] Venable, *Beginnings of Literary Culture in the Ohio Valley*, 285.
[76] Forceythe Willson, *The Old Sergeant, and Other Poems* (Boston, 1867), 10-18.

"Now, a shroud of snow and silence over everything
was spread;
And but for this old blue mantle and the old hat
on my head,
I should not have even doubted, to this moment, I
was dead,—
For my footsteps were as silent as the snow upon
the dead!

"Death and silence!—Death and silence! all around
me as I sped!
And behold, a mighty TOWER, as if builded to the
dead,—
To the Heaven of the heavens, lifted up its mighty
head,
Till the Stars and Stripes of Heaven all seemed
waving from its head!

"Round and mighty-based it towered—up into the
infinite—
And I knew no mortal mason could have built a shaft
so bright;
For it shone like solid sunshine; and a winding
stair of light,
Wound around it and around it till it wound clear
out of sight!

"And, behold, as I approached it—with a rapt and
dazzled stare,—
Thinking that I saw old comrades just ascending
the great Stair,—
Suddenly the solemn challenge broke of—'Halt,
and who goes there!'
'I'm a friend,' I said, 'if you are.'—'Then advance, sir, to the Stair!'

"I advanced!—That sentry, Doctor, was Elijah
Ballantyne!—
First of all to fall on Monday, after we had formed
the line!—

'Welcome, my old Sergeant, welcome! Welcome
  by that countersign!'
And he pointed to the scar there, under this old
  cloak of mine!

"As he grasped my hand, I shuddered, thinking only
  of the grave;
But he smiled and pointed upward with a bright and
  bloodless glaive:
'That's the way, sir, to Head-quarters.' 'What
  Head-quarters!'—'of the Brave.'
'But the great Tower?'—'That,' he answered,
  'Is the way, sir, of the Brave!'

"Then a sudden shame came o'er me at his uniform
  of light;
At my own, so old and tattered, and at his so new
  and bright;
'Ah!' said he, 'you have forgotten the new Uniform to-night,—
Hurry back, for you must be here at just twelve
  o'clock to-night!'

"And the next thing I remember, you were sitting
  there, and I—
Doctor—did you hear a footstep? Hark!—God
  bless you all! Good by!
Doctor, please to give my musket and my knap-
  sack, when I die,
To my Son—my Son that's coming,—he won't
  get here till I die!

"Tell him his old father blessed him as he never
  did before,—
And to carry that old musket"—Hark! a knock is
  at the door!—
"Till the Union—" See! it opens!—"Father!
  Father! speak once more!"—
"*Bless you!*"—gasped the old, gray Sergeant,
  And he lay and said no more!

There is little doubt that this is one of the most famous poems to come out of the Civil War.

In 1863, while Willson's fame was growing, he and Elizabeth Conwell Smith were married; and in order to provide a home for a younger brother of Willson's who was a student at Harvard, the young couple moved to Cambridge, Massachusetts, where they purchased a house near that of James Russell Lowell and opposite to that of Longfellow. In spite of their proximity, the poets made no attempt to get in touch with the select circle of Lowell, Longfellow, Emerson, Holmes, and William Dean Howells, whose stimulating society flourished practically within arm's reach. The happiness of the poet couple was ill-fated, however, for after little more than a year of marriage, Elizabeth Willson and an infant child died on October 13, 1864.[77]

Her husband collected her poems and published them privately as *The Poems of Elisabeth [sic] Conwell Willson* (Cambridge, 1866). This is a slender book of immature poetry, the meaning often being lost in beautiful imagery and verbosity arising, evidently, from a love of imagination for its own sake and a desire to effect interesting and unusual combinations of words. Yet, on the other hand, Mrs. Willson tends toward exquisiteness in some of these verbal arrangements; and her poems are beautiful, even if they have little to say about their subjects: love, memories, death, religion, and legend. Probably the piece most interesting to the modern reader is "February 27, 1861," in which by means of imagery heavy with religious symbolism she bewails what she believes to be the treachery of the South. Undoubtedly Mrs. Willson would have

[77] Biography of Elizabeth C. Willson taken from Banta, *Indiana Authors and Their Books,* 342.

improved greatly if she had lived more than her twenty-two years.

In the meantime Holmes had finally learned the name of the author of "The Old Sergeant," had traced him to Cambridge, and, to his embarrassment, discovered that Willson's home had been visible for nearly two years from his own window. Quickly Willson was brought into the fellowship of the Cambridge literati. After his death Dr. Holmes wrote about him:

He came amongst us as softly and as silently as a bird drops into his nest. His striking personal appearance had attracted the attention of the scholars and the poets who were his neighbors, long before they heard his name or condition. It was impossible to pass without noticing the tall and dark young man with long curled locks, and large, dreamy, almond-shaped eyes. . . .[78]

An interesting demonstration of Willson's psychic powers occurred at this time, as related by Meredith Nicholson:

After the death of his wife and infant child, October 13, 1864, Willson was often at [James R.] Gilmore's house, where he first saw Emerson. Gilmore relates that he returned home one day from Boston to find Lowell lying at full length on a lounge in the library, in animated conversation with Willson. On this occasion an incident occurred illustrative of Willson's gift of "second sight." Longfellow was mentioned in the conversation and Willson remarked that the poet would be there shortly. No one had an intimation of the visit, but Willson described the route that Longfellow was then following toward the house; and when the poet presently arrived, he affirmed the statement of his itinerary as Willson had given it.[79]

---

[78] Quoted in Banta, *Indiana Authors and Their Books*, 342.
[79] Meredith Nicholson, *The Hoosiers*, 263-64.

Willson was not to enjoy the friendship of these famous writers for long, for in 1866 he experienced a recurrence of an old malady, probably tuberculosis, and died on February 2, 1867, at Alfred, New York. His one small collection of verse, *The Old Sergeant, and Other Poems* (Boston, 1867), is his monument, in which his delicate genius is everywhere visible, showing promise of much greater accomplishment had he lived. The title poem, of course, overshadows the rest of the volume; and there is also a rather similar piece, "The Rhyme of the Master's Mate," in which a master's mate tells, in service slang, of the Federal capture in 1862 of Fort Henry on the Cumberland River. This feigned record was supposed to have been found on the body of the sailor after the engagement; and the poem is forceful, though not so powerful as "The Old Sergeant." Another striking poem is "The Enemy," which represents the poet's horrible midnight struggle with the ghostly figure of death, an imaginative representation that may have been inspired by the coming death of his wife. Other poems show, perhaps, the influence of Emerson in a sort of mystical quality, as seen in "To Hersa" and "The Sphere Song." Through all this verse there run an elusive grace and beauty, as in the brightest of his inclusions, "The Estray":

> "Now tell me, my merry woodman,
> Why standest so aghast?"
> "My lord!—'t was a beautiful creature
> That hath but just gone past."
>
> "A creature—what kind of a creature?"
> "Nay now, but I do not know."
> "Humph—what did it make you think of?"
> "The sunshine on the snow."

"I shall overtake my horse then:"
The woodman opened his eye:—
The gold fell all around him,
And a rainbow spanned the sky.[80]

Also, there are pathos, force, religious ecstasy, and mysticism—as well as eccentricity. It is no wonder that Emerson spoke of Willson as a poet of great promise.

The marriage of the Willsons has been compared with that of Robert Browning and Elizabeth Barrett, whom Mrs. Willson was said to resemble in appearance. Also, Byron Forceythe Willson represents the only close contact that Indiana poets had with the illustrious New England literary group.

Sandford C. Cox

In contrast to the Willsons, little romance attaches itself to the life of Sandford Cull Cox (1811-1877). He was born on July 1, 1811, near Richmond, Indiana, and about 1825 moved to Montgomery County with his parents and settled on Sugar Creek, stopping on the way at the falls of Fall Creek to view the "Indian Murderers," who were awaiting execution.[81] Shortly after their arrival at their new home a tree which was being cut down by Sandford's brother and sister fell on him, crushing his legs and making him a lifelong cripple. One leg finally had to be amputated, the entire operation, supposedly the first major surgery performed in Indiana, being effected without benefit of anaesthetic, pain killer, or drugs. In fact, the amateurs who began were forced at length to send for a physician sixteen miles away to tie up the arteries and sear the cut surface with a hot iron. Miraculously, the patient survived all this crude handling; but

[80] Willson, *The Old Sergeant, and Other Poems,* 36.
[81] See above 41-43n.

becoming despondent because of his crippled condition, he later stole away from his family, crossing the Wabash in a hog trough, and organized and taught a school on the other side. Thereafter his rise in the world tended to compensate for his disability. He was repeatedly elected Tippecanoe County recorder, serving for more than twenty-two years, and afterward enjoyed a successful career as a lawyer and businessman. He married, and to him and his wife were born seven children. Five sons were to found the Lafayette *Evening Call.* As an aboli- tionist and worker on the underground railroad, as a public speaker and wit, and as a newspaper editor, he was energetic and popular. He died October 4, 1877.[82]

Cox is known for two books: a book of reminiscences entitled *Recollections of the Early Settlement of the Wabash Valley* (Lafayette, 1860) and *The Evangelist, and Other Poems,* privately published in Cincinnati in 1867. The material composing the *Recollections* was first printed in the Lafayette *Daily Courier* in the fall of 1859 with the signature "In cog." and was popular enough to encourage Cox to collect it in a small edition the next year. This is a well-written book, which has been for some years a collector's item. It deals with many sub- jects, all written in a very readable style with plenty of detail: the Indian murderers; a thrilling, gory tale of Indian captivity told to Cox by his grandfather;[83] the land sales at Crawfordsville; the settling of Tippecanoe County; the Battle of Tippecanoe; the organization of Fountain County; pioneer schools; settlers of Williams-

[82] Biography of Cox from Banta, *Indiana Authors and Their Books,* 76-77, and *Biographical Record and Portrait Album of Tippecanoe County* (Chicago, 1888), 707-10.

[83] The account of the Indian captivity given by Cox was reprinted by Richard E. Banta in his *Hoosier Caravan. A Treasury of Indiana Life and Lore* (Bloomington, Ind., 1951), 61-77.

port and Clinton County; the Black Hawk War; early churches and physicians; the serpent reputed to dwell in Lake Manitou; steamboat trips to Logansport and Peru; and the organization of Wabash College and Indiana Asbury (now DePauw) University. Of course, reminiscences do not fall within the province of our study, but we might remark that this volume deserves much more attention than it has ever received, both for its literary style and its historical content.

We are more interested here in Cox's *The Evangelist, and Other Poems,* even though his *Recollections* is better known. The poems, written mostly as early as 1833, are rather good, but do not equal his prose in quality. Cox excels in blank verse and good diction and displays strong poetic imagination. A flavor of religion is found throughout the volume, as seen in "The Evangelist," which is a description of an evangelist and his sermon, given by the poet in very passable blank verse, reflecting his confirmed Methodist beliefs. Likewise, "The First Sabbath" describes Adam and Eve in the Garden, again in the same sort of verse. Other subjects touched on include nature, his childhood, friends, and slavery, such as the following excerpt:

Slavery

What a foul stain of deep disgrace,
Now rests upon our country's face;
The hapless African may mourn,
And bow, degraded and forlorn,
To his rough task, and daily feel
The driver's lash—entreat and kneel;
But all is vain; he still must bear
The scourge, and chains of slavery wear!

Ah! will not JUSTICE yet unsheath
His slumbering blade, and vengeance breathe?
Alas! the terrors of that day,
When retribution gains the sway,
And with the trumpet-voice of wrath,
Strews desolation in his path:
The captive then will snap his chain—
No more in bondage to complain;
The cup of worm-wood and of gall,
Will on the proud oppressor fall.[84]

"Lays of the Year" contains very patriotic poetry in support of the North during the Civil War; "The Wampum Returned" narrates an Indian love story, and "The Antediluvians" ambitiously attempts to trace the history of the world as far as the Flood. Cox's poetry is worth reading, but far from being great. If he had concentrated more on it instead of spreading his talents, probably he would have done better.

PETER FISHE REED

Peter Fishe Reed (1817-1887) is the last poet of this period. Since he also wrote a novel, he represents a good transition to the next chapter, which discusses the novelists. Reed was born in Boston, May 5, 1819; his father having entered the army and his mother having died, he was left at an early age to make his own way in the world. He soon showed affection for music and poetry and drifted from one vocation to another, following at various times the work of a farmer, shoemaker, sign and house painter, doctor, editor, music teacher, photographer, and artist. Around 1850 he was residing in Vernon, Indiana, and from 1850 to 1863 he lived in Indianapolis; certainly a large portion of his poetry was written in Indiana. Later

[84] Cox, *The Evangelist, and Other Poems* (Cincinnati, 1867), 30.

he moved to Ohio; he died in Burlington, Iowa, at his son's home.[85]

Although there is no information available about Reed's success in his various occupations, it may be that he was a "jack of all trades but master of none," for as far as his poetry is concerned, he did not scintillate. His *The Voices of the Wind, and Other Poems* (Chicago, 1868) is rather nondescript verse, full of bad rhymes, and artificial and faulty diction. Fortunately, now and then there are better touches, as in his use of the Spenserian stanza and in some of the lighter verse. One of the best things he can do is lamely to imitate Poe, as in "The Picture that Hangs on the Wall":

> Our Lily was fair as a fairy,
>   As modest and meek as a dove,
> As placid and pure as a peri,
>   But her heart it was fuller of love.
> Ah! merry was she as a swallow,
>   And her smile it was sweeter than all
> The smiles that the painter Apollo
>   Ever pencilled to hang on the wall.[86]

Reed's novel, happily, is more interesting. It is entitled *Beyond the Snow; Being a History of Trim's Adventures in Nordlichtschein* (Chicago, 1872). This is a series of tales told by a witty young Alabama slave named List to his idle and bored master in order to win the master's promise of liberation if he tells, as the master says, "a more wonderful TRUE story than I have ever heard." The resulting stories are of the strange land of Nordlichtschein

[85] Biography of Peter F. Reed taken from Mary Q. Burnet, *Art and Artists of Indiana* (New York, 1921), 388; Coggeshall, *Poets and Poetry of the West*, 413; Parker and Heiney (eds.), *Poets and Poetry of Indiana*, 452.

[86] Reed, *The Voices of the Wind, and Other Poems* (Chicago, 1868), 192.

near the North Pole, where on a large, strangely warmed island, bathed in an eerie half-light, lived a very thin white-skinned race some twenty feet tall, ruled over by the King Kritikoballo. This people fancy their island to be the whole world and are a strange combination of stupidity and cleverness, of truth and falsehood, superstition and skepticism. The head of anyone who lies is immediately cut off, and if anyone utters a fact which the king does not understand, off comes that unfortunate's head also. To the land comes Trim, the cabin boy and last survivor of the crew of a Yankee ship that has been caught in the northern ice. Although at great peril of his life, he is honest and courageous. Through his eyes the reader sees this strange land; and the author uses him as a device to comment upon and to display the perversities, contradictions, baseness, and injustice implicit in human nature and the ridiculous aspects of our beliefs. These stories at last win for the slave, List, his freedom, and the whole has a very curious effect. It is somewhat in the manner of Swift's *Gulliver's Travels*.

Having completed our discussion of the Indiana poets of this early period, it would be fitting to attempt some sort of summary of their work. We have seen that good biographical information is not always available and also that the biography of some of these poets is as interesting as their poetry. In poetic technique we have found that there was some influence of the heroic couplet, perhaps demonstrating a sort of cultural lag in the West; nevertheless, the greatest single influence came from Poe; and several poets, like Alice Cary, Louisa Chitwood, Sarah T. Bolton, and Peter F. Reed, made particular attempts to imitate this American craftsman. While the subject matter of all this production is extremely varied, we note the strong influence of the frontier in several of the writers, particularly in Mrs. Lard, Welsh, and Cutter. Through all this early verse there also run the subjects of temperance, abolition, and in several cases, as with Biddle, Bolton, and Forceythe Willson, the Civil War. Finally, three poets—Alice Cary, Louisa Chitwood, and Mrs. Bolton—are so bowed down with sorrow that much of their verse tends to be distasteful to moderns. Yet, there is little doubt that the best poets of the period were Alice and Phoebe Cary and Sarah T. Bolton.

3

THE NOVEL, SHORT STORY, AND ESSAY

THE NOVEL

IN THE EARLY PERIOD of Indiana literature the novel, as a literary form, does not assume the importance that poetry enjoys. There are fewer novelists than poets, they wrote only a relatively small number of novels, and most of these productions are of the nature of propaganda of one type or another. There is very little "pure" fiction. And most of this material was produced during the 1850's. Still, some of the novels were popular in their own era and also make interesting reading today.

Holman—Thorn—Hall—Jeffries—Collins—Hayden

The first name to be mentioned is that of Jesse Lynch Holman (1784-1842). Holman is a peripheral figure, since he published his one novel in Kentucky before he came to Indiana; yet he lived most of his life in Indiana. Apparently, therefore, he was the first novelist resident in the state.

Holman was born in 1784 near Danville, Kentucky, the son of Henry Holeman (the son dropped the "e" from the family name), a Virginian who emigrated to Kentucky in 1776 and for years took part in the vicious Indian warfare. While a mere boy, Jesse taught subscription schools and also began to preach. One report says that he read law in Lexington under the sponsorship of Henry Clay; at any rate, in 1805 he was admitted to the bar in his home state and practiced law in several Kentucky towns. He married in 1810, the same year that his novel was published. The couple came to Indiana the next year and built a cabin and later a brick house on a beautiful site overlooking the Ohio near the present town of Aurora. After the custom observed in Virginia and Kentucky, they named their home with a Latin compound, Veraestau—"ver" from the word meaning spring, "aest" for summer, and "au" for autumn. Now followed Holman's remarkable career in public service, which was almost completely by appointment, since his staunch character would not allow him to make the concession so often necessary to win elective offices. He was successively prosecuting attorney for Dearborn County, a member of the territorial legislature in 1814, presiding judge of the Second and Third Judicial circuits, a presidential elector, and judge of the state Supreme Court. Then he served as a county superintendent of schools, was a founder of Franklin College and of the Indiana Historical Society, and, finally, Federal District Judge of Indiana. He died at Veraestau on March 28, 1842, with a reputation for integrity seldom equaled in his day—or, in any other generation.[1]

Perhaps it is not to be wondered at, therefore, that Judge Holman attempted, sometime after the publication of his novel, to destroy the entire edition, thinking it a frivolous product of his youth, of doubtful moral value. The title was *The Prisoners of Niagara, or, Errors of Education. A New Novel, Founded on Fact. By Jessee [sic] L. Holman, a Native of Kentucky* (Frankfort, Ken-

[1] Information on Holman taken mostly from Banta, *Indiana Authors and Their Books,* 151-53.

tucky, 1810). In a preface Holman apologizes for the errors in the printing of the book—as well he might, for the printer, William Gerard, did an unusually poor job, even misspelling the name of the author. According to I. George Blake in his work, *The Holmans of Veraestau,*[2]

The book deals much with Virginia and the western country during the time of the American Revolution, with Indians, hairbreadth escapes and other dramatic incidents. "The Errors of Education" portion of the title is accounted for by the training of the hero in Richmond, Virginia; "The Prisoners of Niagara" is explained by the fact that Fort Niagara plays an important part in the story. The entire novel is told by the hero in the first person. . . . Perhaps the actual episodes are from his father's life as he was a Virginian who migrated to Kentucky. The style of the novel is somewhat Byronic—very intense, passionate, often extremely sentimental. The spirit is that of adventure, love of freedom, hatred of slavery, and opposition to drunkenness and all forms of immorality.

Only two copies of the novel are known to be extant.[3]

In addition to his novel, Holman wrote much poetry for the Indiana newspapers, also two lengthy unpublished narrative poems on the subject of Indians and their legends. The judge, then, is a figure more of historical significance than of literary importance in early Indiana. Still, he was, perhaps, the first literary figure of the state.[4]

[2] Israel George Blake, *The Holmans of Veraestau* (Oxford, Ohio, 1943), 5-6.

[3] In 1943 one copy was owned by Professor William I. Bartlett of Roanoke, Virginia, and the other was in the Howard Memorial Library in New Orleans.

[4] For further information on Judge Holman, see Blake, *The Holmans;* an article by Blake, "Jesse Lynch Holman, Pioneer Hoosier," in *Indiana Magazine of History,* 39(1943):25-51; and Orah Cole Briscoe, The Hoosier School of Fiction. Part I: Indiana Fiction Before 1870 (unpublished M.A. thesis, Indiana University, 1934), 8-10.

From Holman's novel of 1810 there is a jump of fully twenty-nine years to the next item in Indiana fiction—and that is a doubtful one. It is a pamphlet of twenty-four pages entitled *Miahnomah; a Legend of the "Dark and Bloody Ground." Compiled from the Most Authentic Sources, by B. V. Thorn. Printed by Elihu Stout & Son, Vincennes, Indiana, 1839.*[5]

According to the histories of Knox County, a B. V. Thorn was coroner of that county from 1864 to 1866.

We would not be moved to consider him as a probable Indiana author, except for the fact that *Miahnomah*, though purported to be a legend of Kentucky, was printed by Elihu Stout, the first printer in Indiana, at Vincennes. Vincennes is so far up the Wabash from Kentucky that the chances are strongly against a Kentuckian's publishing something there rather than in his home state, where many more, and much better, presses were available.

Miahnomah is hardly more than a long story. It is a highly romantic tale set amid the idyllic forests of the knobs region, evidently of Kentucky, of an Indian girl of seventeen named Miahnomah, who falls in love with a white hunter who has been living peacefully in the tribe, enjoying the respect and friendship of the warriors. But in a dispute over a fawn he makes an enemy of a brave, Worangah, who then tries to kill the white man and, failing, turns the tribe against the hunter. The latter is tied to a stake to be burned. Miahnomah, however, cuts her lover loose, they escape together, and he kills Worangah. A year later, after a battle with the whites in which all of the tribe are killed except the old chief, the girl's father, the white hunter saves the chief from being killed by a wounded buffalo. The old man, dying, forgives Miahnomah for marrying the white man.

[5] The Indiana Historical Society Library in Indianapolis has a copy.

How much of this sentimental story is legend and how much invention on the part of the writer can not be told. The only saving aspect of the work is its date.

It is, perhaps, welcome relief from the high-flown tenor of romance to consider next a controversial novel which so infuriated the citizens of the pioneer town of Bloomington and their descendants that their angry protests have scarcely yet died away. Probably, this was one of the most widely read early books in Hoosier literature, rivaling in notoriety Mrs. Henry Ward Beecher's book of a few years later.[6] It is *The New Purchase: or, Seven and a Half Years in the Far West. By Robert Carlton, Esq.,* published first in New York in 1843 in two volumes, then revised and reprinted in one volume in New Albany, Indiana, in 1855 under the title of *The New Purchase: or Early Years in the Far West.* It was reissued under the original title in an Indiana centennial edition by the Princeton University Press in 1916. To put it mildly, this book was an eye opener.

It was written by Baynard Rush Hall (1798-1863), who used Robert Carlton as a pen name. And he did well to use a pen name and to write the book in the East, considering the things he said about Indiana—and Bloomington in particular! But we must not get ahead of the story; we should first see who the author was and what he was doing in Indiana.

Hall was born January 28, 1798, in Philadelphia, the son of Dr. John Hall, who had been a surgeon on the staff of General Washington. Left an orphan as a young child, he obtained his education partly by working as a printer and in 1820 was graduated from Union College and in 1823 from Princeton Theological Seminary. In 1821 he went to Danville, Kentucky, to marry a Miss

[6] See below, 168-71n.

Young, whose family had been forced to move there because of financial reverses. The Halls returned to the West in 1823, partly to visit Mrs. Hall's family but also because Mr. Hall had his eye on a possible position—which materialized when the Indiana State Seminary, created by the legislature in 1820, opened four or five years later in Bloomington, a town of less than three hundred people in what was called the New Purchase. This was the area composing the central part of the state, which was obtained from the Indians by a treaty in 1818. Hall was appointed principal of the Seminary with the salary of $250 a year, which he later supplemented by $150 a year as pastor of the Presbyterian Church of Bloomington, the salary being paid in items of trade. In 1825 he was ordained a Presbyterian minister, and he and two other ministers, one of them Isaac Reed,[7] organized the Wabash Presbytery. Reed's wife was a sister of Mrs. Hall, and it was Reed who had influenced Hall to come to Indiana.

Ten backwoods boys formed the first class at the Seminary, and for three years Hall was not only principal but was himself the entire faculty. In the fourth year a teacher of mathematics was added. Enough students having been prepared in Latin, Greek, and mathematics (the necessary qualifications), in 1828 by act of the legislature the Indiana State Seminary became the Indiana State College;[8] from then until 1831 Hall was the professor of ancient languages. After the first president, Dr. Andrew Wylie, came to the college, quarrels arose which led to Hall's departure in 1831. He went back east, founding an academy in Bedford, Pennsylvania, where he taught

[7] See above, 54-55, for a discussion of Reed.

[8] The first class was graduated from the Indiana State College in 1830. In 1838 the name of the institution was changed to Indiana University. Two of the first trustees were Indiana authors—Jesse L. Holman and Robert Dale Owen.

and preached seven years, then preached and taught in academies at several places in New Jersey and New York. From 1852 until his death on January 23, 1863, he was principal of Park Institute and pastor of the Dutch Reformed Church in Brooklyn, New York.[9]

The New Purchase is now valuable source material on the pioneer life of the state and of south-central Indiana in particular, for the book pictures the roads and manner of traveling, the inns and log cabin homes, the pioneer weddings, games, rifle matches, barbecues, stump speeches, log rollings (the real thing, not the political variety), the court trials, and college exhibitions. But it was not this aspect of the novel that the good Bloomington folk objected to; it was Hall's tone of ill will and conceit, his lack of recognition of good intentions, his evident attempt to be cute, as in the addresses to the "Dear Reader," his rather clumsy playfulness, and his downright snobbishness and scorn.

In the narrative, Woodville, Spiceburgh, Sugartown, Sproutsburgh, and Timberopolis stand respectively for Bloomington, Spencer, Crawfordsville, Lafayette, and Indianapolis; and the author gives his unfavorable opinion of Bloomington especially, his friends and enemies, and the Seminary. Hall disguises himself in the narrative as "Carlton" and "Mr. Clarence," and the Reverend James Hilsbury is the Reverend Isaac Reed. He displays to the disadvantage of the townspeople their dissatisfaction with his teaching the students Latin and Greek when the boys had asked instead for instruction in more practical lines, such as in "book-keepin' and surveyin' "; furthermore, he shows how local politicians, considering the Seminary

[9] Information on the Reverend Mr. Hall was taken mostly from an article by James A. Woodburn in *Dictionary of American Biography, Authors Edition* (20 vols. and Index. New York, 1928-36), 8:118-19.

as something effete and aristocratic, complained that "it was a right smart chance better to have no college nohow, if all folks hadn't equal right to larn what they most like best." Hall represents himself as the only qualified applicant for the position of principal, the others being ridiculous ignoramuses, and heaps ridicule upon the boys who came to class coatless and shoeless.

As Banta says in his introduction to an excerpt from the volume printed in his *Hoosier Caravan,* some Bloomingtonians did not like the Reverend Mr. Hall from the very first, considering him a "smart aleck." When he left and returned East, many of the people still considered him a "smart aleck." But when his book was imported into the town and read, its author was easily identified, and there was then no lack of agreement: the Reverend Mr. Hall *was* a "smart aleck!"[10] Pioneer spirit being what it was, it was probably a good thing for the author that he made his home in the East for the rest of his life!

The New Purchase, thus, is in many ways hardly a novel at all; it is thinly disguised autobiography. Hall published other items, such as expository material, a Latin grammar, a book of homilies on morals and customs, and *Frank Freeman's Barber Shop. A Tale* (New York, 1852); but it will always be as the author of this caustic book that he will be known.

From Hall's interesting book we return to the realm of romance with the rather doubtful inclusion of *The Novice; a Tale of Indiana. Illustrating the advantages of Educated and Civilized Life,* by an unknown author,[11] printed

[10] Banta (ed.) , *Hoosier Caravan,* 153-54.

[11] The title page of the copy of this booklet in the Indiana Division of the Indiana State Library is mutilated, having a hole where the name of the author could have been printed. This is the only copy discovered. Solon Robinson has been suggested as the possible author. See below, 175.

in Brookville, Indiana, by C. F. Clarkson in 1845. This story was first published in the Brookville *Indiana American* in the issues of November 7, 14, and 21, 1845, with no identification of the author and simply with the remark that the publisher had copyrighted the story. Evidently owing to the popularity of the work, the story was reprinted with the addition of a title page, stitched in paper covers, and sold at fifteen cents a copy, according to an announcement in the issue of the newspaper of November 28.

The Novice is another highly romantic narrative, which, although carelessly printed, holds the reader to the very end. It is the story of how a young man, traveling through the northern Indiana wilderness to the shores of Lake Michigan just before the expulsion of the Potawatomi Indians from the state in 1838, meets on the shores of the Lake a beautiful, innocent girl, the adopted daughter of an old French trader, who had found her as a child after her parents had been murdered by the Indians. The foster father tries to marry her off to an old Indian chief, but eventually the young man is permitted to take the girl back to civilization, where she is educated, finds a long-lost brother, and finally marries her young liberator. Idyllic descriptions of the wilderness abound in the tale, and a quiet spirit of sentimentalized romance infuses the work. Included in it also is some preaching against the evils of liquor.

A tale something like *The Novice* was written by C. Jeffries (dates unknown) and published privately in 1846 in Lafayette. It bears the title *Wabash Captives; Or, the Awful Sentence: Thrilling Narrative of Crime and Death, and Wonderful Adventures of James Brady and Others, among the Indians on the Wabash, 60 Years Ago, near the Spot Where Lafayette Now Stands; Founded on Facts.*

Just who the author was is a mystery which may never be solved. A search of early records has revealed that there was a John Jeffries buried in Tippecanoe County, who at the age of 72 applied in Fairfield Township for a pension on October 11, 1832, evidently claiming service in the Revolutionary War.

The only Jeffries (spelled Jeffris) listed in the Census of 1830 for Tippecanoe County is a John who was in the 20- to 30-year age bracket and had a wife and small child living with him. Contemporary marriage records of Tippecanoe County disclose that a Cyrus Jeffries, M. G. (Minister of the Gospel) performed the marriage of Henry Messer and Celia Ann Jeffries in 1846. He would seem to be a likely candidate for the author of *Wabash Captives*. At any rate, the writer of the book seems to have been closely associated with Lafayette, for the name of the town and environs appears frequently in the story.

Wabash Captives is a very rare book; the only known copy is in the library of the Wisconsin State Historical Society. The Indiana Historical Society Library has a photostatic copy. It is a horrifying story of James Brady, his sister Matilda, their half-brother Ralph, and a beautiful neighbor girl Miranda who are captured by Indians at the same time that the Brady parents and others of the family were massacred in a lonely cabin on the bank of the Allegheny River in Pennsylvania. Many times the captives face cruelty and death but are eventually taken to the large Wea Indian town stretching for nearly six miles along the Wabash just south of what is now Lafayette, where they are adopted into Indian tribes. The half-brother turns traitor and tries to kill the others, who attempt to escape frequently but each time are caught. A rascally priest tries to put Miranda in a convent; eventually he is killed, evidently by an Indian. The perfidy of

Ralph at length is discovered by the Indians, who then cut him to pieces. James and Matilda eventually escape to Vincennes, whence they find their way back to Pennsylvania, the narrative closing in 1786. The tale is not well told from the point of view of fiction or grammar, yet its bloody incidents hold the reader to the end. The booklet was poorly printed.

Inveighing against drink is the main burden of the next novel, *Mrs. Ben Darby: or the Weal and Woe of Social Life,* published in Cincinnati in 1853 by Mrs. Angelina Maria Lorraine Collins (1805-1885). It is sheer propaganda.

Mrs. Collins was born in Virginia near Cumberland Gap, and in 1830 married James Collins, who was born in Virginia in 1802, was reared in Kentucky, and had studied law in Charlestown, Indiana. The couple lived for three years at Paoli, Indiana, where Mr. Collins practiced law; then they moved to New Albany in 1833 and resided there for about thirty years. Mr. Collins was one of the best-known lawyers in the town, was a presidential elector in 1844, and served four terms in the state Senate and one in the House of Representatives. After his death in 1869 Mrs. Collins lived with a son at Salem, Indiana, and died there.[12]

This is a terrible—and, in a sense, a rather absurdly exaggerated—novel. Mrs. Collins considers "social life" to be the drinking of tremendous quantities of alcoholic

---

[12] Biography of Mrs. Collins obtained mostly from Briscoe, The Hoosier School of Fiction, 32-33; from *Biographical and Historical Souvenir for the Counties of Clark, Crawford, Harrison, Floyd, Jefferson, Jennings, Scott and Washington, Indiana* (John M. Gresham & Company, Chicago, 1889), Part 1:277-78; and from New Albany *Ledger* (daily), September 29, 1885. See also the index to the Washington County Death Records, Genealogy Division, Indiana State Library. Mrs. Collins also compiled a cookbook, entitled *Mrs. Collins' Table Receipts; adapted to Western Housewifery,* which was published at New Albany in 1851.

beverages; and she desires to prove that imbibing is sinful, very dangerous to health, and hazardous to society. To do this she selects as the chief sinner a woman, Mrs. Ben Darby, thus deviating from what was, in that day, the rather conventional plot formula in the temperance story, which presented a man as the chief offender.[13] The setting is mostly in the mountains of Virginia, but the close of the action takes place in Hap-Hazard, Indiana—which is evidently New Albany. It is difficult to enumerate the habitual drunkards who reel and rage their way through the pages of this novel, leaving numberless innocent victims along the way.

Mrs. Sarah Marshall Hayden (1825-1899) published a different kind of propaganda novel, this one about the dangers of a girl's engaging her affections too early in life. Sarah Marshall was born July 5, 1825, evidently in Shaw neetown, Illinois; certainly she was living in Shawnee-town at the time of her marriage to John James Hayden, who was born in Rising Sun, Indiana, in 1820, and had attended Harvard University. The couple possibly lived for a time at Shawneetown, but for many years at Rising Sun, where Mr. Hayden held several public offices. From about 1862 to 1875 the family lived in Indianapolis, where Mr. Hayden was engaged in business, and from 1875 until about 1900 he was in the U. S. Treasury De-partment and then in the Post Office Department. He died in 1901, two years after his wife's death in Washing-ton, November 20, 1899.[14]

Mrs. Hayden's main novel, *Early Engagements* (Cincin-nati, 1854), written in Shawneetown when she had just turned seventeen, but published—and perhaps revised—

[13] For other temperance literature, see that heading in Index.

[14] Information about Mrs. Hayden was taken from material gathered by Miss Caroline Dunn for the Indiana Biography Series, 22:90-91, in the Indiana Division of the State Library.

later, sets out to demonstrate that a girl who becomes betrothed before she has reached maturity of judgment may meet, only too late, her "true affinity." Implicit in this novel, then, is the belief in one affinity—that for every man and woman there is only one chosen mate and that she who does not allow sufficient time for her affinity to appear may marry the wrong man and thus experience tragedy. The heroine, Florence Delisle, a southern girl visiting in Ohio for her health (goodness only knows why she chooses Ohio!) is engaged to Henri Soulé, who, with her father, is awaiting the termination of her two-year convalescence in the West. Florence, however, falls in love at first sight with the Reverend Theodore Neville and unsuccessfully resists her heart, being "the betrothed of one, the beloved of another"; for he, too, is smitten before he knows she is engaged and can not then overcome his love. The story ends in tragedy. Florence, true to her word—though not to her heart—marries her fiancé, who discovers too late that his wife does not love him; and everyone is miserable. No solution of the intolerable situation is provided.

But perhaps Mrs. Hayden was herself left too miserable by her own book; somehow, at least, she decided to alleviate the starkness of the tragedy and provided at once a sequel, *Florence,* appended to the 1854 edition of *Early Engagements* and evidently printed with it in subsequent editions. Here, after much suffering on the part of the lovers, the two are united after Henri and a baby boy have conveniently bowed their way out of the picture and into the grave; and a mutual friend brings Florence and her true affinity together again. All this is the stuff of romance.

Mrs. Hayden's third novel, *Mr. Langdon's Mistake,* published by her husband in Washington in 1901 after her death, from a manuscript written forty years before, is another romantic novel. A dignified, cultured man, Edward Langdon, falls in love with a beautiful, uneducated country girl, marries her, and takes her away to his large house in the city. She does not fit in with her husband's life, and, after the birth of a daughter, leaves him. Eventually the two are reunited happily in Europe. This novel is not at all distinguished.

In leaving Mrs. Hayden we might note that her *Early Engagements* was proclaimed at the Illinois Women's Exhibit at the 1893 World's Fair as the first novel written by an Illinois woman.[15] Indiana thus shares her with Illinois.

Kelso—Hervey—Rose—Beecher—Hiatt

The propaganda novel continued with Isaac Kelso (dates unknown), who gave it a new—and short-lived—direction, in a diatribe against the Catholic Church. Little information can be uncovered about Kelso. At the time that he wrote *Light, More Light; or Danger in the Dark* (Cincinnati, 1855) he was supposed to be living in Prairie City, Indiana, which was probably in Vigo County, in the vicinity of Terre Haute.[16] He was the joint owner of some Vigo County land, which was sold in 1855 when he was living in Kenton County, Kentucky. At the time of publication of another novel, *The Stars and Bars; or, The Reign of Terror in Missouri* (Boston, 1863), his residence was in Platte City, Missouri.

A third volume is listed under his name in the Indiana State Library: *The Winged Chariot: An Allegory* (Cincinnati, 1858), by Ben Boaz, which is evidently a pseudo-

[15] Clipping from Chicago *Inter-Ocean,* July 12, 1893, p. 5, c. 2, in Indiana Biography Series, 20:42-43.
[16] Briscoe, The Hoosier School of Fiction, 49.

nym. Herein is contained an "Autobiography of Ben Boaz," in which the author vaguely traces the facts of his life; but he seems careful to give a rosy coloring to many spots in his career which the world may have considered very dark. He says he was born in a picturesque district in western Indiana, decided as a boy to enter the ministry, went to Wabash College at seventeen, but did not stay long, and then entered the Indiana Conference of the Methodist Church. He served pastorates at Brookville, at Franklin, and finally Indianapolis, where he fell victim to what must have been a form of madness, which made him wander about the Midwest, preaching in various places and behaving at times rather strangely, with the result that newspapers published unfavorable articles about him. He sued one of the papers, but lost the suit, claiming suppression by the court of evidence in his favor. Of everything that he says, the only confirmation discovered in the records is that Isaac Kelso is listed in the 1836 catalogue of Wabash College as a student from Terre Haute. Kelso was one of those persons who excite a little interest during their lives but are not important enough for anyone to bother much about recording biographical facts.

Certainly his propaganda novel, *Light, More Light,* is merely sensational. It is a bitter and wild indictment of the Catholic Church and claims to reveal the secret sins committed in convents. The author says, "The danger is in the dark,"[17] and he locates the action mostly at the convent of St. Mary-of-the-Woods near Terre Haute. Isadora, an unwilling novice at St. Mary's sees her friend Josephine, who is engaged to Charles Clinton, Isadora's Protestant cousin, tricked by the villainous priest Dupée into believing her lover false and therefore is lured into

[17] *Light, More Light,* 47.

becoming a novice like Isadora. An insurgent nun, Fannie, however, sets Josephine right about Charles and helps him rescue Josephine; Isadora becomes insane and escapes also; another priest, by the name of Remington, falls in love with Fannie and leaves the Church. All the sins generally charged aginst the Catholic Church are here given embodiment.

An advance notice of the book appeared in the New Albany *Daily Morning Herald* of September 5, 1854, the year prior to its publication in Cincinnati, which would indicate it was perhaps first privately printed[18] or else it was being advertised in advance by the author. That the book was popular is shown by the fact that it went through at least ten editions, the title sometimes being slightly altered.

Kelso's next book—if, indeed, he is to be identified with Ben Boaz—*The Winged Chariot,* is a group of long moral stories of sentimental and romantic nature, with the autobiography before cited. His last novel is *The Stars and Bars,* which features the activities of the Knights of the Golden Circle in guerrilla warfare in Missouri before order is restored by the arrival of Union troops. It is filled with violent action, portraying the rebels as villains; the story seems very close to the actual history of Missouri in the earlier period of the Civil War. It is wild and patriotic. As a matter of fact, we may have reason to believe that much about Kelso is wild.

Somewhat more restrained is the romantic temperance novel of Dr. James Walter Hervey (1819-1905), and the author enjoyed a much happier reputation. Dr. Hervey was born, of Scotch-Irish ancestry, April 5, 1819, near Brookville, Indiana; and following the death of his father, his family moved to Hamilton, Ohio, where James went to

---

[18] No other evidence of a private printing has been discovered, however.

school. He then studied medicine in the office of an Ohio physician. Wishing to obtain better opportunities for medical study, he borrowed fifty dollars, purchased equipment, and on a pony, the gift of a friend, headed for Chicago. His small purse gave out by the time he reached Indianapolis, however, and he found himself obliged to set himself up in 1843 as a physician in Hancock County, where he remained seven years, building a reputation as a very conscientious and reliable doctor. Here he created a stir in the medical world by treating malaria victims with quinine, an almost unknown practice at the time— and a very successful one, too—and by using tincture of iodine and nitrate of silver to prevent pitting in smallpox. In 1850, still desiring further medical knowledge, he entered the medical school of Indiana Asbury (now DePauw) University; and after graduation he was induced by his former patients to return to them, setting up his office in Oaklandon, not far from his former district. Here he became an ardent temperance worker and wrote his novel, *The Scroll and Locket, or, The Maniac of the Mound,* published in Indianapolis in 1858. He served in the legislature of 1855 and, as a Republican, took an active part in politics. When the Civil War broke out, he was appointed first assistant surgeon of the Fiftieth Indiana Volunteer Infantry. At the close of the War, he took up his practice in Indianapolis and engaged in many beneficial medical and public health activities, such as getting a state board of health established. He died in Indianapolis on January 5, 1905.[19]

Dr. Hervey's novel, though containing temperance propaganda, still is a romance in a sense different from

[19] *Pictorial and Biographical Memoirs of Indianapolis and Marion County Indiana* . . . (Chicago, 1893), 129-32.

Mrs. Ben Darby, by Mrs. Collins,[20] or *Nora Wilmot,* by Mrs. Henrietta Rose.[21] The main interest lies in the love story of Alice Lovel, but there are also the figures somewhat standard in temperance novels, of the drunken father, the starving children, and the young but talented heroine who gives music lessons to support her family. The setting is mostly the town of F———, Indiana, which is undoubtedly Fairfield. The title, *The Scroll and Locket, or, The Maniac of the Mound,* arises from two objects which figure in the story—a scroll containing a will and a locket enclosing a picture of Alice—and "the maniac of the mound" is Alice's sister Laura, whose mental breakdown has been caused presumably by the father's intemperance. Alice's family is forced by the father's love of liquor to live in poverty. The story opens with an attempted seduction and kidnaping and closes with four deaths, three of them of sinners and the fourth owing to grief. This is rather strong stuff! Yet, the love of Alice and a typical romantic hero, Charles Worthington, succeeds in dominating the story, triumphing over all these gruesome facts and the kidnaping and slander of Alice. Of the three temperance novels, *Mrs. Ben Darby* presents the strongest picture of the evils of drink, *Nora Wilmot* is the best novel of propaganda, but *The Scroll and Locket* has the most attractive story.

We move then to a consideration of *Nora Wilmot: A Tale of Temperance and Woman's Rights* (Columbus, Indiana, 1858). It was written by Henrietta (Mrs. Hamilton) Rose (dates unknown), about whom very little is available. She was born in Ohio and lived for a long time in Centerville, Indiana, where she taught school before her marriage. Both before and after she was married she

---

[20] See above, 159-60.
[21] See below.

took part in the movement for temperance and women's rights. She died some time before 1889.[22]

Mrs. Rose goes further than Mrs. Collins into possible solutions of the problem of liquor, yet her plot includes the same type of incidents as in *Mrs. Ben Darby*. At the beginning of the story the heroine, Nora Wilmot, engages in a friendly argument with her cousin, Susie Grey, about drinking. Nora speaks passionately against liquor, for her father was a drunkard, her mother died of heartbreak, and she had been saved from being cast away on the world only by the kindness of an uncle. Susie, on the other hand, believes in overlooking the shortcomings of others. This attitude of Susie's is implemented by her marriage to Alfred Rayburn, who drinks occasionally; but his drinking develops into an addiction to alcohol until he becomes a raging maniac who murders Susie's brother. In contrast to Susie, Nora will not marry her own suitor until he submits to the temperance pledge, and this couple then enjoy a happy married life. The moral is thus obvious—too obvious, as a matter of fact. There are several other plot threads that reinforce the central theme, all incidents illustrating the evils of drink; poverty, slums, starving women and children, and delirium tremens are horribly and nauseatingly depicted. Yet Mrs. Rose does not stop at all this; instead she shows how Nora, in contrast to the placid Susie, engages actively in opposing social evils. Nora relieves the poor and downtrodden, works in the Woman's Rights movement, joins the ladies who spend the day knitting in the local saloon in order to discourage drinking. Having pointed the way toward the solution of the evils, Mrs. Rose closes her story with a feeling of optimism.

[22] Banta, *Indiana Authors and Their Books*, 276; Briscoe, The Hoosier School of Fiction, 39.

So ends the list of propaganda novels. They are all intense, somewhat labored, and heavily burdened with a message. An entirely different sort of novel was written by Mrs. Henry Ward Beecher (1812-1897), the wife of the famous preacher, in presenting her stinging criticism of early Indianapolis and its people. It is a novel of strong personal protest, not unlike Baynard Rush Hall's *The New Purchase* in its origin and tone, and it was regarded by the citizens of Indianapolis as an outrage and an insult.

Mrs. Beecher has been so overshadowed by her famous husband, who, in addition to his own fame, was known as the brother of Harriet Beecher Stowe, the author of *Uncle Tom's Cabin,* that it is very difficult to obtain much information about her alone; for facts touching upon her seem always to have been absorbed into the mass of materials relating to the Reverend Mr. Beecher. She is known simply as his wife, as though she never had a life of her own before her marriage or much personal identity afterward. Indeed, one of the few purely individual features of her life is her novel. She was born Eunice White Bullard, August 12, 1812, in West Sutton, Massachusetts and became acquainted with Henry Ward Beecher through her brother Ebenezer, who was his classmate at Amherst College and who brought him to the Bullard home for a visit. Eunice and Beecher became engaged and were married just before Beecher was to go to Lawrenceburg, Indiana, to accept his first pastorate in the Presbyterian Church there in 1837. There they made the best of a small salary and poor living accommodations.

In 1839 the Reverend Mr. Beecher was called to the pastorate of the Second Presbyterian Church in Indianapolis, then located on the Circle in the very center of the town; the Beechers stayed in Indianapolis until 1847, when they moved to Brooklyn, New York. They remained in the East for the rest of their lives. While in Indianapolis Beecher edited the *Indiana Farmer and Gardener* and attracted widespread attention by his preaching. Mrs Beecher died in Stamford, Connecticut, March 8, 1897, ten years after the death of her husband.[23]

Where Mrs. Beecher's book, *From Dawn to Daylight; or, The Simple Story of a Western Home. By a Minister's Wife* (New York, 1859), was written, whether in Indianapolis or in the East, is not known; but it was published anonymously twelve years after the Beechers had left Indiana and was obviously a fictional representation of their life in the state, particularly in Indianapolis. Although cast in the form of a novel, nearly all the characters, while bearing fictitious names, are real Hoosiers, some of the best-known people of the town, including Mr. and Mrs. Daniel Yandes and Stoughton A. Fletcher. Even Harriet Beecher Stowe appears in the cast of characters, under another name, of course. George Herbert represents Henry Ward Beecher, and Mary Leighton stands for the author; Glenville is certainly Lawrenceburg, and Norton is Indianapolis. Although the author does say some kind things about some of her characters and though she is nowhere really vicious, still her character portrayals are far from flattering; and the tone of the book is that of satire of the Western people, criticism of the hard lot of a

[23] Biographical information about Henry Ward Beecher and what little there is pertaining to Mrs. Beecher is readily available in a number of sources among Indiana and general reference materials, both books and magazine articles. Full biographies are Joseph Howard, Jr., *Life of Henry Ward Beecher* . . . (Philadelphia, 1887); William C. Beecher and Samuel Scoville, *A Biography of Rev. Henry Ward Beecher* (New York, 1888); and Paxton Hibben, *Henry Ward Beecher: An American Portrait* (New York, 1927). The house in which the Beechers lived while in Indianapolis is reported to have stood on the south side of East Ohio Street between Alabama and New Jersey streets, opposite what is now the Cadle Tabernacle.

minister and his family in the West, self-complacency, and bitterness. A great complaint is the "ague" which she represents as plaguing Indianapolis and from which the Herberts' little son Harry died. Frequent reference is made to the meager salary, $600 a year, of Mr. Herbert and the tardiness and evident reluctance of the congregation in paying even such a small amount. This financial difficulty is given as the main cause of the Herberts' leaving Norton.

There is no evidence that Beecher ever gave his slim salary as the reason for leaving Indianapolis; rather, several times he stated that concern for his wife's declining health was the only consideration and that he hoped that in a few years they might return, for he believed here was a field for service as important and useful as any in the East.[24] There is no record of what he thought of his wife's book.

Since the author was more interested in dramatizing her views concerning her Indianapolis experience than she was in producing a good story, the book has little value as a novel. It contains some local history, but it is interesting primarily to Indianapolis residents. When the book was published, the identity of the anonymous author, the setting and the characters were all immediately recognized in Indianapolis; such a hue and cry were raised that nearly all kindly recollections of Mrs. Beecher were killed. Her reputation, both personal and literary, sank at once, as the Hoosiers might characteristically have put it, "lower than a snake's belly."[25]

[24] See the letter which Beecher wrote September 6, 1847, from Indianapolis to his friend, C. F. Clarkson, editor of the Brookville *American,* quoted in "Book That Was Once Under Ban," in Indianapolis *News,* November 10, 1906, pp. 15, 17.

[25] We might finish this sorry story. Feeling ran high for about ten years; and even in 1872 when the City Library was established and a

From this novel of domestic unhappiness we move forward several years to 1864, when a novel of civil strife, *The Test of Loyalty*, was published in Indianapolis by James M. Hiatt (dates unknown). Search has failed to reveal information about him other than that he lived in Indianapolis at least from 1864 to 1878 and that he was

copy of the book was placed on the shelves, two enraged citizens presented themselves before the School Board, representing the book as a libel and an insult and demanding that it be withdrawn from circulation. The Board so ruled. These two need not have appeared, however, for in the meantime a white-lipped solid citizen marched into the library and boldly stole the volume from the shelf. In 1884 a new librarian, knowing nothing of this furor, bought three copies of the book at an auction and proudly displayed them for circulation, whereupon general indignation again broke forth in the city; and a group of irate persons invaded the library and openly carried off the offending books. When they were summoned to appear before the Board, they cited for their vindication the old order suppressing the publication.

In 1891, after her husband's death and thirty-two years after the book was issued and forty-four years after the Beechers had left Indianapolis, Mrs. Beecher again burst into print concerning what she still considered to be the raw deal that Indianapolis had given them. In an article in the *Ladies Home Journal* she once more criticized the Second Presbyterian Church for the small salary paid her husband. This was too much for the long-suffering congregation of that church. At once they dug into the church records and claimed that they discovered that instead of a salary of $600, Mr. Beecher had been paid $1,000, and, what was more, he received every penny of it. They found also that at that time the governor of the state was getting only $1,300, out of which he paid the salary of a private secretary. Also, when Beecher left, the church had made him a present of a watch which cost $125. The church people sent all these facts in a letter to Mrs. Beecher in December, 1891, requesting that she set the record straight; however, this elderly lady was content to nurse her old grudge to the last.

The controversy has long since died away, however, and this church now points proudly to the fact that Beecher was once its minister. And copies of *From Dawn to Daylight* for many years have been gathering dust on the circulation shelves of the Indianapolis Public Library!

Accounts of this controversy can be found in several sources. Two good accounts are given in Anton Scherrer's column, "Our Town," in the Indianapolis *Times* of December 9, 1936, and August 3, 1945.

a reformer and newspaperman. In addition to his novel he published books on politics and social questions, such as *The Ribbon Workers* (Chicago, 1878), issued with Luther Benson,[26] which is composed of biographical sketches of reformed drunkards.[27]

The Test of Loyalty is a Civil War novel, but it deals with the question of loyalty, both of soldiers and civilians in Indiana, rather than battles or antislavery propaganda. This is a dramatization of the problem which arose forcefully in 1862 with the growth of discontent in the Federal Army and the desertion of a number of soldiers who returned home and were concealed by sympathizers. The setting is mostly near Indianapolis, on the farm of the Clinton family, who are Democrats in politics but who, though unsympathetic with Lincoln, still believe that the Union must be saved. Over the opposition of neighbors who are Southern sympathizers and who bear such Dickensian names as Mrs. Venom and Mr. Hardhead, the son, George Clinton, joins the Union Army. Shortly afterward, however, his conflict in loyalties reaches such a state of indecision that he falls prey to political malcontents; and listening to them and reading over letters from his rebellious Indiana neighbors, he deserts from Vicksburg and heads home. His sister Dora learns of his defection and hastens to Evansville to intercept him and implore him to return to the Army and to his duty, but George is arrested in her presence. Nevertheless, Dora obtains the incriminating letters which Hardhead wrote to George, reveals them to the magistrates and her brother is freed, pardoned by President Lincoln. The problem of his loyalty now dissolved, he returns to the Army and gives distinguished service. In this way the author attempted

[26] For Luther Benson see above, 47-48.
[27] Banta, *Indiana Authors and Their Books,* 147.

to convince the public that everything must be sacrificed in the interests of freedom—property, party, and even life.[28]

SOLON ROBINSON

Only two novelists remain to be considered, Solon Robinson and Robert Dale Owen.

Solon Robinson (1803-1880) was one of the most famous Hoosiers of his day, known particularly for his agricultural writings. His life was an interesting one. Born October 21, 1803, at Tolland, Connecticut, a descendant of the Reverend John Robinson, who was pastor of the Pilgrims while at Leyden, he was orphaned when he was ten years old, was a carpenter's apprentice at fourteen, a Yankee peddler at eighteen, and a cashier for a Cincinnati theater at twenty-five, at which time he married Mariah Evans of Bucks County, Pennsylvania. In 1830 he was writing for local papers at Madison, Indiana, and was selling land near North Vernon. Buyers being few, he moved in 1834 to what is now Lake County in northern Indiana and here opened a general store in the wilderness and built a large trade with incoming settlers and also with the Potawatomi Indians, who had not yet been evicted from the state. This area became known as Robinson's Prairie; and in order to protect his own land and that of others from speculators he formed in 1836 a Squatters' Union of five hundred members and thus secured land at government prices. Thereafter he was known as "King of the Squatters." Following the organization of Lake County in 1837 he filled various county offices and published a news sheet at Crown Point, the county seat. He was active in the field of politics and took part in the Log Cabin Convention held in 1840 at Lafayette.

---

[28] See particularly page 6 of the novel.

His literary reputation dates from 1837, when he began contributing articles on subjects of interest to the frontier to agricultural periodicals. These simple and humorous essays, signed "Solon Robinson of Indiana," won an enthusiastic following. Along with Henry W. Ellsworth and others he attempted to form a national agricultural society, and the activities of this group led to the establishment in 1852 of the United States Agricultural Society and were influential in the foundation of the Department of Agriculture ten years later. In connection with his activities in behalf of agriculture, Robinson toured the country, sending many travel sketches to agricultural publications, such as the *Prairie Farmer* and *American Agriculturalist*. He published a periodical entitled *The Plow* in New York City in 1852 and the next year was made agricultural editor of the New York *Tribune*. When tuberculosis forced his retirement to Florida in 1868, he published the Florida *Republican* and did other literary work. He died November 3, 1880, in Jacksonville.[29]

In addition to his editorial and agricultural writings, Robinson produced two imaginative works: *Hot Corn: Life Scenes in New York Illustrated* (New York, 1854) and *Me-Won-I-Toc. A Tale of Frontier Life and Indian Character* ... (New York, 1867). These volumes are not of much moment. *Me-Won-I-Toc* is a short novel, expanded and revised from a tale entitled *The Will,* published in 1841,[30] and is in the Cooper tradition. The subtitle, *A Tale of Frontier Life and Indian Character; Exhibiting Traditions, Superstitions, and Character of a Race That is Passing Away; A Romance of the Frontier,* shows well the sort of book this is. The scene is Indiana in the fron-

[29] Article by Herbert A. Kellar in *Dictionary of American Biography, Author's Edition,* 16:50-52.

[30] No other record of this story has been found, not even in the Library of Congress. It was probably little more than a short story.

tier era, presented with careful descriptions of the prairie; and Tecumseh and the Battle of Tippecanoe are featured. All this is simply a weak imitation of Cooper.

More originality is evident in *Hot Corn,* a series of short stories first published in the New York *Tribune,* presenting the horrors of slum life in New York City. Dedicated to Horace Greeley and his co-laborers, "The friends of the working man; the advocates of lifting up poor down-trodden humanity," the book takes its title from the cry of peddlers on the New York streets. These are very realistic stories of New York life, with the demon rum as the cause of much of the misfortune here exposed. The stories abound in the pathetic figures of drunken men and women, starving women and children, rum, fires, and scenes wherein crowds of the rich in fine suits and gowns turn their eyes away while sweeping grandly past the poor and miserable. The pathos and the stark realism in description and conversation gave the book a sale of fifty thousand copies in six months.[31] And Robinson shows himself here to be both a realist and a sentimentalist—also a sensationalist. To some extent the stories form a part of the temperance literature of the time.

Solon Robinson, then, is not much of a figure from the point of view of literature, not even if the anonymous story, *The Novice,* is ascribed to him.[32] His biography and his agricultural activities far overshadow his literary work.

[31] Herbert A. Kellar (ed.), *Solon Robinson. Pioneer and Agriculturist . . .* (2 vols. *Indiana Historical Collections,* vols. 21 and 22, Indianapolis, 1936), 1:34.

[32] Robinson would be a good possibility as the author, for *The Novice* deals with the northern part of the state when it was in its primitive condition, and this area was familiar to Robinson.

ROBERT DALE OWEN

The last novelist of this period is a man who, like Robinson, was known primarily for his public life rather than for his literary pursuits. To attempt to provide in a small space anything like an adequate summary of the life of the famous Robert Dale Owen (1801-1877), who is so closely connected not only with the New Harmony experiment but also with other aspects of Indiana history, is almost futile. Here is a writer whose fame from other facets of his life greatly outshines his small output of imaginative literature.

Some family background must be sketched in order to present the writer in his proper perspective. His father, Robert Owen, was the wealthy cotton processor of New Lanark, Scotland, who astonished and angered other manufacturers by his successful experiments showing that mill workers who were well fed, well housed, and well clothed, and whose children were well educated in good common schools produced more goods than if they were starved and ill-treated. This talented, starry-eyed idealist and deist, who had everything he needed to get along in the world—except an oversupply of common sense—experienced much opposition to his economic and social ideas. Opportunely, the land on which George Rapp's communistic colony called Harmony was located was then for sale; and Robert Owen, seeing a possibility of still further realization of his Utopian schemes in a new land where there were few neighbors to object, promptly bought the land, renamed it New Harmony, and attempted to create there an earthly paradise. We cannot here go into the complicated and interesting story of how New Harmony attracted all sorts of intellectuals, scientists, reformers, and indolent eccentrics; let us observe simply that the project soon collapsed and Robert Owen returned to Scotland.[33]

Robert Dale Owen, the writer who figures in Indiana literature, was born November 9, 1801, in Scotland, attended the good model schools provided by his father at New Lanark for the children of the mill workers, and was further educated by private tutors and in the Pestalozzian school of Phillip Emmanuel von Fellenberg at Hofwyl, Switzerland. He accompanied his father to America in 1825, joined the party of scientists, artists, and idealists in Philadelphia who were starting for their supposed Utopia in New Harmony and who sailed down the Ohio on the "boatload of knowledge," as it was later called. In New Harmony he taught in the school and edited the newspaper. Here he became acquainted with the talented and beautiful, but very unorthodox, Frances Wright; and after the New Harmony experiment failed, he became her devoted follower, lecturing, lobbying, and editing a paper with her. When her marriage to Phiquepal d'Arusmont put an end to this relationship, he paid a brief visit to England in 1832 and then returned to Indiana. Here his public career began in 1836 when he was elected to the

[33] The elder Owen's four sons were associated with him, in one way or another, in the venture. Two of them, besides Robert Dale Owen, later were well known in Indiana. David Dale Owen (1807-1860) became Indiana state geologist in 1837, Kentucky state geologist in 1854, and United States geologist in 1847. Before he died, at New Harmony, he was regarded as one of the foremost in this field in the United States. Richard Owen (1810-1890) was a captain in the Mexican War, and a scientist, was the commandant of the Confederate prisoners of war at Camp Morton, Indianapolis, where his humanitarian methods earned him the affection of the prisoners, taught at Indiana University, was appointed the first president of the new Purdue University but did not serve because of opposition to his advanced ideas, and taught again at Indiana University almost up to the time of death. Both of these brothers produced much scientific writing. Good accounts of the New Harmony experiment abound in the histories of Indiana.

state legislature; then he was a member of Congress from 1843 to 1847 and a member of the Indiana Constitutional Convention of 1850, where he succeeded in getting adopted liberal views concerning women's property rights and divorce.[34] He was the chargé d'affaires in 1853 at Naples and was appointed minister there in 1855. During the Civil War he served as purchasing agent in obtaining equipment and arms for Indiana troops. Later, his interests in spiritualism became so strong that he experienced a mental breakdown and died June 24, 1877.[35]

Though Robert Dale Owen wrote much on social, philosophical, religious, political, educational, and scientific subjects, he penned only two imaginative works: *Pocahontas: A Historical Drama* (New York, 1837) and a novel, *Beyond the Breakers. A Story of the Present Day* (Philadelphia, 1870). *Pocahontas,* published anonymously "By a Citizen of the West," is the first play written by a Hoosier of which there is any record. It was not an auspicious beginning for Indiana drama. In spite of some contemporary praise lavished on the work, the reader sees that its five acts present a didactic theme in mediocre blank verse and a stilted movement of characters who are only moderately well delineated; such close attention is paid to historical accuracy that practically nothing is invented and no emotional height or dramatic effect is attained. Owen states in an "Introductory Essay" his fear that *Pocahontas* will be a failure as acted drama because "its scenes embody little deep tragedy, and less broad

[34] A bust of Robert Dale Owen standing in front of the south door of the Indiana State Capitol bears the following inscription: "An Appreciation. Erected in honor of ROBERT DALE OWEN by the women of Indiana in recognition of his efforts to obtain for them educational privileges and legal rights. Author, statesman, politician, philanthropist."

[35] Banta, *Indiana Authors and Their Books,* 243-48; Richard W. Leopold, *Robert Dale Owen. A Biography* (Cambridge, Mass., 1940).

humor. I feel it to be deficient in that bold, startling style of finish, which shows so much better than it reads. . . . In its present form, if no other objection lay against it, it is too long for representation."[36] Owen was, in fact, a better dramatic critic than dramatist.

Beyond the Breakers is no better as literature. Owen's inexperienced hand is only too evident in the weak plot, the nearly sickening sentimentality, and the use of the novel as the vehicle for his ideas on the property rights of married women, prison reform, and spiritualism. Still, the book is interesting in its presentation of Indiana as less startling and less crude than that provided by Edward Eggleston in *The Hoosier School-Master* the next year. New Harmony is idealized into the fictitious Chicksanga; and the hero, Franklin Sydenham, an urbane, cultured intellectual, the benefactor of his town, is the person Owen wished he might have been—or perhaps thought he actually had been. Several persons of Owen's day are placed in the story bearing fictitious names. Altogether, then, we can only wish that Owen had put as much effort into imaginative writing as he did into the other aspects of his interesting and useful career.

In closing our discussion of the early Indiana novel little need be added to the observations made at the beginning of this chapter. It might be reiterated that a large number of these novels were purely propaganda of some sort, with temperance being the most popular torch to carry. There is a strong tendency toward romanticism and sentiment, ranging from the *Miahnomah* of Thorn through *The Novice*, Mrs. Hayden's romantic and propaganda works, to Robinson's *Me-Won-I-Toc* and Owen's *Beyond the Breakers*. Surprisingly, the Civil War influ-

[36] *Pocahontas: A Historical Drama,* 23-24.

enced the body of contemporary fiction less than it did poetry, for only Isaac Kelso and James Hiatt wrote about this subject which later became so popular in fiction. Two of the novels—*The New Purchase,* by Hall, and *From Dawn to Daylight,* by Mrs. Beecher—were records of personal dissatisfaction with Indiana and Hoosiers, and, strangely, were so notorious that they became the most widely read and the best known of all this fiction. Solon Robinson's book of stories, *Hot Corn,* reflects an early realism later to be exploited by Edward Eggleston. As in the case of the poets, the biographies of the novelists are sometimes more interesting than the novels themselves, which, as a group, do not offer much of literary value. And, no one was a professional novelist; with all these writers fiction was only a sideline.

THE SHORT STORY

The short story, published in the quantity of at least one book of collected pieces, did not develop during the period of early Indiana literature as did poetry and the novel. Only three authors can be included in this category; and two of these have already been treated in the section on the novel: Solon Robinson and his book of stories entitled *Hot Corn: Life Scenes in New York Illustrated* (New York, 1854) and Isaac Kelso and his *The Winged Chariot: An Allegory* (Cincinnati, 1858). The remaining writer is Julia Dumont, who is of special significance in Indiana Literature.

Mrs. Julia Louisa Cory (also spelled "Corey" and "Carey") Dumont (1794-1857) was the first Indiana author to achieve a reputation throughout the entire Midwest— if not also the East—for her writings. Her stories and poems were published separately in various Midwestern newspapers and literary periodicals long before some of the stories were collected and issued as her one book-length publication, *Life Sketches from Common Paths: A Series of American Tales* (New York, 1856). She was one of the best-known authors of her day and was the first woman to attain literary prominence throughout the Ohio Valley. Not only is she significant from the point of view of literature, however; her life and her association with others make interesting consideration.

Mrs. Dumont's parents, Ebenezer and Martha D. Cory, came with the Ohio Company from Rhode Island to Marietta, Ohio, where they were among the earliest settlers; and it was there in October, 1794, that Julia was born.[37] A few months before her birth her father was found murdered, presumably by Indians. The next spring her mother, evidently having experienced enough of the hardships of the West, packed her infant daughter into a saddle bag and made the hazardous trip back to the East, where she supported herself and her daughter in Greenfield, New York, by tailoring. Here she remarried, and Julia grew up, attended Milton Academy, then taught school for two years before she was married in 1812 to John Dumont, whom she had first met because he had admired a poem of hers. The couple moved to Cincinnati, where Mr. Dumont became a land agent under William Henry Harrison. In 1814 they made a second and final move to Vevay, Indiana, beautifully situated on the Ohio River; here their eleven children were born. Several of them died in childhood, and Mrs. Dumont sorrowed for these lost ones the rest of her life. Her husband, in addition to following his profession as a lawyer, served in

[37] Banta, *Indiana Authors and Their Books,* 93. Coggeshall *(Poets and Poetry of the West,* 43-45) and Briscoe (The Hoosier School of Fiction, 11) give her birthplace as Waterford, Ohio.

various local offices in Vevay, represented Switzerland
County in the eleventh session of the legislature, and in
1837 ran for governor against David Wallace, but was
defeated. In the meantime, Julia Dumont had resumed
her school teaching about 1820 and from then until her
death on January 2, 1857, managed somehow to combine
homemaking and child rearing with teaching and writing.

She was a woman of extraordinary character and offered
a strong contrast in her excellent teaching to the usual
frontier pedagogues, whose qualifications were often ridiculously inadequate and who sometimes had a reputation for being more attracted to the bottle than to their
pupils. Two of Mrs. Dumont's students, later to become
famous Indiana authors, were the brothers, Edward and
George C. Eggleston, both of whom wrote glowing tributes
years afterward to the strong influence she had wielded
over the lives of her students. Edward Eggleston had this
to say about her, relative to her teaching in the Vevay
High School after she was sixty years of age:

I can see the wonderful old lady now, as she was then, with
her cape pinned awry, rocking her splint-bottom chair ner-
vously while she talked. Full of all manner of knowledge,
gifted with something very like eloquence in speech, abounding in affection for her pupils and enthusiasm in teaching, she
moved us strangely. Being infatuated with her, we became
fanatic in our pursuit of knowledge, so that the school hours
were not enough, and we had a "lyceum" in the evening for
reading "compositions," and a club for the study of history.
If a recitation became very interesting, the entire school
would sometimes be drawn into the discussion of the subject;
all other lessons went to the wall; books of reference were
brought out of her library; hours were consumed, and many a
time the school session was prolonged until darkness forced
us reluctantly to adjourn.

Mrs. Dumont was the ideal of a teacher because she succeeded in forming character. She gave her pupils unstinted

praise, not hypocritically, but because she lovingly saw the best in every one. We worked in the sunshine. A dull but industrious pupil was praised for diligence, a bright pupil for ability, a good one for general excellence. The dullards got more than their share, for knowing how easily such an one is disheartened, Mrs. Dumont went out of her way to praise the first show of success in a slow scholar. She treated no two alike. She was full of all sorts of knack and tact, a person of infinite resource for calling out the human spirit.[38]

Combating ill health during most of her life, she finally developed tuberculosis and put together her book only when she saw the shades of death closing about her. She had published her stories in such western newspapers and periodicals, beginning in 1824, as *The Cincinnati Mirror, The Cincinnati Literary Gazette, The Ladies' Repository, The Western Gem and Cabinet of Literature,* and *The Southwestern Journal and Monthly Review;* she now collected some of them for her *Life Sketches from Common Paths.*

The preface of the book sets forth her didactic aim, to be a good moral influence, particularly on young readers. She states that the book was designed originally for her children, and she now issued it "to strengthen by illustration the belief so salutary to the inexperienced heart, of the existence and reality of goodness in our bad world."[39] All the stories are designed to follow these precepts laid down in the preface.

The book is curiously organized around a central situation, like Chaucer's *Canterbury Tales* and Boccaccio's *Decameron.* In two introductory sketches the author introduces first a Fourth of July celebration of sixty years before, with a group of carefree boys disporting themselves

[38] "Some Western School-Masters," in *Scribner's Monthly,* 17: no. 5:-750-51 (March, 1879).

[39] *Life Sketches from Common Paths,* 9.

in a meadow near Philadelphia; and she hints mysteriously about their impending fates. Then in the second sketch she reveals the same boys as they are thirty-eight years later when as middle-aged men they attend a sumptuous dinner given by one of the more fortunate of the group. On this occasion, Harley Ives, a cripple, through whose eyes the reader glimpsed all the boys in the first sketch, sees again the condition of each. Ives then tells stories about them, one by one. Aunt Quiet, an old woman of the village, tells a few of the tales. Except for "Ashton Grey," these stories make up the body of the book.

One of the stories, "The Brothers," presents the brotherly love of George and William Branham. George married and had a large family, being forced at times to borrow money from his bachelor brother William and despairing of ever being able to repay the loans. At length William brings news that one of George's sons, Henry, who was learning a trade in a distant town, is dead and the parents are grief-stricken. Then, years later William produces Henry, with the explanation that Henry, instead of being dead, has been all this time in college, with his uncle footing the bills. In their joy the parents give William no word of reproach for his cruel way of extending his philanthropy. Other stories in the collection deal with the evils of gambling and the rewards of virtue, the author making full use of the devices of coincidence, unexpected recognition, and the pathos produced by misfortune and sin.

The last story, "Ashton Grey," is a very romantic tale of an Ohio River boatman, a traditional hero of romance, "whose innate delicacy was refinement, and whose generous impulses, chivalry" and "extreme beauty" attracted feminine admiration, and of sixteen-year-old Annabel, "the

dreamy, the impressible, the desolate Annabel." That
Mrs. Dumont thought she was writing a realistic tale is
indicated by the fact that Annabel finds this sentimentalized Ashton "her beau-ideal of the distinctive characteristics of the fearless and self-sustained backwoodsman."

Ashton, behaving in accordance with the romantic tradition, rescues three children from a burning cabin (using
a ladder, of course), and, being injured in the act, is
nursed back to health by Annabel; the two fall in love
and secretly marry, over the opposition of her guardian,
Colonel Ainsworth. Ashton is then accused of the murder
of another boatman; but his supposed father, dying, confesses to the crime, and an old Indian is opportunely
drawn into the picture to reveal that Ashton is really the
son of Ainsworth, having been stolen by Indians as a child.
Thus, the story, instead of being realistic, is the very es-
sence of romance and sentimentality. It is almost melodrama. And the action and dialogue, not only in this
story but throughout the entire book, are summarized
rather than dramatized, giving the tale still greater appearance of being a step removed from reality.

These stories provide a good sample of the work of Mrs.
Dumont. That her fiction is partly realistic is evident from
her use at times of Western scenes, such as the Ohio River,
and her occasional attempt to present Western character
and problems. Essentially, however, she is a romantic and
a sentimentalist, peopling her stories with handsome,
noble heroes and beautiful china-doll heroines, who are
ludicrous when uprooted from the drawing room and
placed against the background of frontier crudity. Their
stilted and florid language, with elaborate metaphors and
similes, and the fact that good always triumphs in the end
give additional evidence of her romanticism. Scott and
Irving were the inspiration of this type of fiction. Yet, we

should note that Mrs. Dumont's skill was greater than that of her western contemporaries, and her tales were avidly read by Westerners, who loved this style of writing. Her influence was all to the good, both in her personal life and teaching and in the impetus she gave to Western literature. Except for the early work of Alice and Phoebe Cary, her book was the first Western publication to receive favorable notice in the East, and her stories had made her famous long before. Her influence is still to be noted in Vevay.

THE ESSAY

There was only a very small production of the familiar essay[40] in this period of Indiana literature; and two writers, who produced one collection each, are all that present themselves. Both of these books are interesting, but they are hardly significant.

The first writer was a somewhat romantic figure in the annals of early Hoosier education. William Clark Larrabee (1802-1859), Methodist minister and educator, was born December 23, 1802, at Cape Elizabeth, Maine. His father, a sea captain, died soon after his son's birth; and William lived with his uncle and his grandparents until he experienced conversion in a Methodist meeting, was licensed to preach, and attended academies in Maine and New Hampshire. He went to Bowdoin College, from which he was graduated in 1828 in the same class with Longfellow and Hawthorne. He filled various educational positions in the East, including acting as principal of Alfred Academy in Maine, from 1828 to 1830, and as principal of Oneida Conference Seminary in Cazenovia, New York, from 1830 to 1834, and then became principal of Maine Wesleyan Seminary. As a delegate to the Gen-

[40] In the minimum quantity of one book, as stated previously.

eral Conference of the Methodist Episcopal Church at Baltimore in 1840 he met a young man, Matthew Simpson, the president of a new Methodist college, Indiana Asbury (now DePauw) University, founded only three years before in Greencastle, Indiana. Simpson influenced Larrabee to become professor of mathematics and natural science at Asbury, a position he held from 1841 to 1852; in addition he was acting president from 1848 to 1849. In the little town of five hundred he built a beautiful home on a large tract of land, exquisitely landscaped, filled with flowers, and complete with an artificial lake, which he named Rosabower; and it was in this home that his wife, Mrs. Harriet Larrabee, founded and conducted the well-known Greencastle Female Collegiate Seminary, which existed from 1844 until Asbury became coeducational in 1867.[41] The Reverend Mr. Larrabee was offered the presidency of both Indiana and Iowa universities but declined the offers. In 1852 he was editor of *The Ladies' Repository,* published in Cincinnati, and served as the first state superintendent of public instruction in Indiana, 1852 to 1854, laboring against ignorance and prejudice to lay the foundations of the present school system. He served another term, 1857 to 1859, and died a few months later. He, his wife, and a baby girl were all buried on the grounds near Rosabower; and for generations the place remained a romantic mecca for college students and Greencastle residents alike.[42]

In addition to religious books, Larrabee wrote *Rosabower: A Collection of Essays and Miscellanies* (Cincin-

[41] The site of this home and seminary is now occupied by Longden Hall, a men's dormitory of DePauw University.

[42] Article by W. W. Sweet in *Dictionary of American Biography, Author's Edition,* 11:7; Worth M. Tippy, "Rosabower and Mrs. Larrabee's Greencastle Female Collegiate Seminary," in *DePauw Alumnus,* April, 1948, pp. 2-3, 18.

nati, 1855), a title inspired by his Greencastle home. Beginning with the first essay, "The Bower," a delightful piece full of tender playfulness and of sorrow for his little daughter, near whose grave in his lovely garden he writes, Larrabee treats many subjects, such as friends, death, philosophy, the past, immigration to the West, science, history, the vanity of human desires, religion, camp meetings; and he even includes a tribute to Sarah T. Bolton. Elements of autobiography figure here and there. The essays are very attractive to the reader because of the excellent diction and the balanced phraseology, but particularly on account of the sense of peace and serenity and the calm moral tone, which is not overdone. A delicacy, a tenderness, a universality, and a sure control over both the subject and the medium pervade the various pieces. The feeling of Larrabee's strong personality is evident throughout. In this hurried age of rush between work and play one could do much worse in selecting a book to read than to rediscover *Rosabower*.

Following Larrabee's book by only four years was *First Quarrels and Discords in Married Life* . . . (Cincinnati, 1859), by James H. Burk (1835-1864). He was born in Decatur County, Indiana, the son of John and Susannah (Smith) Burk, and married Elizabeth Shopp of New Castle. He died of battle wounds at Nashville, Tennessee, July 9, 1864, while serving as captain in the Thirty-seventh Regiment, Indiana Infantry.[43]

First Quarrels almost resists classification as to type. One section is devoted to short essays on the subject of married life, but the greater portion of the book is made up of incidents and sketches, often with a statement of opinion

[43] George Hazzard, *Hazzard's History of Henry County, Indiana, 1822-1906* (2 vols. New Castle, Ind., 1906), 1:541, and information on the Burk family in the pamphlet file, Genealogy Division, Indiana State Library.

and some sermonizing at the end. In spite of the fact that the title page lists Burk as the editor, he evidently wrote the entire book, except for a few quotations from others; but he must have collected many of the incidents from his friends, as the preface implies. The point which Burk illustrates in his sketches and incidents, and which he brings out forcefully in the "morals" to the stories and in his short essays, is that toleration, kindness, and understanding must always be utilized by both partners in the marriage relationship. The unkind remark, the sharp retort, hurt pride, and the flaring temper are all out of place and lead to nothing but heartache and matrimonial disaster. Included with these contentions is also some advice to wives to beware of small faults in men, like occasional intemperance, which may lead to eventual misery and death. The book is written in a very readable style, with many highlights of humor to vary the didactic intent. In our present era of a high divorce rate it could well be read; for the situations it presents tap the universal in human character, and there is good sound advice aplenty. At least, the reading public of that time must have thought so, for new editions were issued in 1864 and 1869.

Can we now draw a few conclusions from the study of this early Indiana literature?

Considering the pioneer condition of the state, we see that the early literature is a voluminous output of many different types of writing. The quality was often low or at times mediocre; yet here we find testimony to the fact that in most conditions of society, however trying they may be, the creative impulse always tends to rise to the top. That the Hoosiers came primarily of good stock was a factor which aided tremendously the rise of letters. And some aspects of this body of literature were of surprisingly high quality, as seen particularly in the poetry.

The lives of the authors are often as interesting as their writings—sometimes more so—for this was the era of the formation of modern Indiana; though the men and women often led lives of labor and danger, they had high hopes for the future. Though some died young, the collective energy of the writers appears unlimited. Also, we must hasten to add to the roster of early Indiana authors the name of Abraham Lincoln, who spent his formative years, from ages seven to twenty-one, in southern Indiana. Without attempting in any way to enter into the complexity of a detailed discussion of his life and the influences brought to bear upon him, we should observe that the ruggedness of his pioneer Indiana environment helped to shape the personality and character which were to express themselves so simply, yet powerfully, years later in the "Gettysburg Address" and the "Second Inaugural Address," both of which, though originally thought of only as speeches, have since become classics in American literature.

Literature in this period was almost entirely an avocation to the creators of it; all except the Cary sisters obtained their livelihoods by other means. The Carys are Indiana's only professional authors before the Golden Age. The personalities and figures which dominate the era are those of Alice and Phoebe Cary, Sarah T. Bolton, and perhaps Forceythe Willson—all in poetry—and Julia Dumont in the short story. The period was dominated by poetry; the novel was mostly confounded in propaganda, and all the other types of literature were relatively slight. The travel writing, however, and also the confession literature, though lurid, are fascinating and are significant historically.

The prevailing motif thus far in the development of Indiana literature was sentimentality, with, as previously noted, a strong element of propaganda, seen chiefly in the novel. Yet the realism of the confession and travel literature, observed, in addition, here and there in the short story, was a leveling influence.

Early Indiana literature, therefore, had an auspicious beginning; even so, however, it hardly heralded the greatness of the era to come. Yet, the groundwork had now been laid. The Golden Age of Indiana literature was ready to be born.

The Golden Age

4

POETRY

THE GOLDEN AGE of Indiana literature, the fifty-year period from 1871 through 1921, was the era during which the most significant writing was produced, the writing for which Hoosier literature is best known and remembered. Although some authors of the early period are still more or less familiar today—such as Sarah T. Bolton and Alice and Phoebe Cary—the great bulk of them have been forgotten; and many of these had little claim to literary remembrance. Not so with the writers of the Golden Age. For in this second grouping are such well-known figures as Edward Eggleston, George C. Eggleston, Lew Wallace, Mary H. Catherwood, Maurice Thompson, Meredith Nicholson, Charles Major, Booth Tarkington, Caroline Krout, George Barr McCutcheon, Gene Stratton Porter, Kin Hubbard, George Ade, Evaleen Stein, William Vaughn Moody, and even "Mr. Indiana"—by name, James Whitcomb Riley. Any era dominated by writers of such stature or popularity is bound to be significant.

This period begins with the publication in 1871 by Edward Eggleston of his famous novel, *The Hoosier School-Master,* which brought national fame not only to the author but also to the state, and includes many celebrated books—Lew Wallace's *Ben-Hur,* Maurice Thompson's *Alice of Old Vincennes,* Meredith Nicholson's *The House of a Thousand Candles,* Charles Major's *When Knighthood Was in Flower,* George Barr McCutcheon's

(195)

Graustark, Gene Stratton Porter's *A Girl of the Limberlost,* Riley's poems, William Vaughn Moody's *The Great
Divide,* George Ade's *Fables in Slang,* and Booth Tarkington's *The Magnificent Ambersons.*

These books and their authors possess today various
degrees of fame, and the period they represent was truly
a remarkable era of literary production in the state. Although the Golden Age took a little time in which to
gain momentum, Eggleston's fame requires the dating
of the age from his masterpiece of 1871; and there is a
rather orderly progression from that date until the age
reached its height around the turn of the century with
best sellers and important books blossoming by the bouquet each year. Probably the most important decade was
that of 1900 to 1910, followed by a slight decline until
the publication of Tarkington's *Alice Adams* in 1921,
with which date the Golden Age closes. For even though
Tarkington and others continued to publish, and in spite
of the fact that newer writers replaced many of the older
ones, still no book of the quality of *Alice Adams* or of
the great host of significant publications of this era was
issued for many years. If, then, *The Hoosier School-
Master* ushered in the rosy glow of the sunrise of the
Golden Age, *Alice Adams* marked the beautiful waning
of its sunset. Consequently, this was the period which
gave Indiana literature its great renown. It was the
age of famous men and their famous books. In it Indiana,
and particularly Indianapolis, became a literary center
which in many ways rivaled the East.

Although poetry remained very important, the era,
nevertheless, was dominated by the novel. Throughout
most of the productions of the time there is a strong
romantic tendency blended with an important flavor of
sentimentalism, seen in its greatest development in Riley.

Realism, as in Edward Eggleston, is definitely a minor theme.

The types of material included in this age are poetry, the novel, humor, the short story, the familiar essay, and drama. Following the procedure of the preceding section, for the sake of consistency, these types will be covered in the order named. It should be noted, however, that many of these authors wrote in more than one category, and in such cases we have placed each person in the type for which he is best known.

Poetry, then, receives our first attention.

At the outset it should again be pointed out that we can not here consider individual poems and their authors, since, as before stated, we are limiting ourselves to poetry published in the minimum quantity of one volume. It is with some reluctance, therefore, that we give only passing notice to Will Henry Thompson (1846-1918), whose record of book publication consists only of a book on archery which he wrote in conjunction with his brother Maurice Thompson:[1] *How to Train in Archery: Being a Complete Study of the York Round* (New York, 1879). This was revised by Will Thompson in 1905. In 1928 Will added a chapter to the revised edition of his brother's volume, *The Witchery of Archery,* originally published in 1878. These books created a tremendous interest across the nation in archery as a sport. But it is as the writer of two well-known poems that we take note of Will H. Thompson here: his "High Tide at Gettysburg," first published in *The Century Magazine* in July, 1888, and "The Bond of Blood," published in the same magazine in March, 1899. They presented the Civil War from the point of view of the Southern soldier and yet gave expression to a desire for reconciliation of the two

[1] See below, 315.

sides and for a revival of patriotism for the Union. These poems, particularly the former, became famous. It is regrettable that Thompson did not concentrate more on poetry. He wrote the two poems out of the fullness of his own experience, however, for he was born March 10, 1846, in Georgia, spent his youth in that state, and served in the Confederate Army, in the Fourth Georgia Infantry. He and his brother Maurice came to Crawfordsville, Indiana, in 1868, where he married and worked as a civil engineer, helping to build railroads, then became an attorney in partnership with his brother. In 1889 he moved to Seattle, Washington, where he continued the practice of law until his death on August 10, 1918.[2]

Also, we should note that seven persons who wrote verse made their main contributions in the form of the novel and so are discussed in that section. These are Lew Wallace, Maurice Thompson, Maurice F. Egan, Meredith Nicholson, Otto Stechhan, George W. Louttit, and Gene Stratton Porter.

Benjamin S. Parker

Now the first poet of the Golden Age is Benjamin Strattan Parker (1833-1911). Born on February 10, 1833, in a log cabin in Henry County of parents of intelligence and of some education, he was accustomed to the hardest kind of farm labor, which was somewhat relieved by attending a school taught by his father. His interest in literature arose from his parents' habit of reading aloud

---

[2] Biography of Will H. Thompson taken from Banta, *Indiana Authors and Their Books*, 320-21, and from Dorothy R. Russo and Thelma L. Sullivan, *Bibliographical Studies of Seven Authors of Crawfordsville, Indiana* (Indianapolis, 1952), 285-88. The latter contains much detailed material on the Thompson brothers.

before the open fireplace from Scott, Burns, Byron, and
other authors. Parker became a teacher himself and was
also a businessman, publisher of the New Castle *Mercury*,
a holder of various county and state offices, and a con-
sular office in Canada. In 1869 he married Huldah Wick-
ersham; he died in New Castle, March 14, 1911.[3] Parker
was the second president of The Western Association of
Writers.[4]

It is a pity that Parker did not have more education,
for his talent might have been developed into a clear
and sweet poetic utterance; as it was, however, all that
he could do was to grind out mediocre verse of a sentimental nature with an often monotonous repetition of a
few themes. Like Alice Cary and Sarah T. Bolton, he
longs frequently for a dear dead past, when life was rosy
and his wife and children and friends moved in the routine of a simple but happy rural life. Much of his thinking is religious. He has a genuine feeling for nature, and
his appreciation at times bids fair to reach eloquence—
but always stops short of it. Yet with all his nostalgia, he
is not so shortsighted as to be a pessimist; and he can
write humorous pieces with some effect. All his verse
tends to be singsong with end-stopped lines, occasional
awkward constructions, and much poetic diction of a
highly artificial nature.

An appealing quality is to be found in his work. The
title poem of his first volume, *The Lesson; and Other
Poems* (New Castle, Indiana, 1871) is a sentimental treatment of childhood, age, and death in the example of a

[3] Biography of Parker taken mostly from Banta, *Indiana Authors and
Their Books,* 250; Nicholson, *The Hoosiers,* 254-56; and the anthology
which Parker helped to edit: Parker and Heiney (eds.), *Poets and Poetry
of Indiana,* 448-49.

[4] For a discussion of the Western Association of Writers, see above, 14.

little boy playing by a brook, who returns to the brook as a middle-aged man, then as an old man, and finally dies. Likewise, the title poem of *The Cabin in the Clearing, and Other Poems* (Chicago, 1887) is effective in its view of the author's former life of labor with his wife and family in a pioneer cabin, including the death of a child. *Hoosier Bards with Sundry Wildwood and Other Rhymes* (Chicago, 1891) contains what must in his own day have been a well-known poem, "The Building of the Monument," a piece which was originally read at the laying of the cornerstone of the Indiana State Soldiers' and Sailors' Monument in the Circle in downtown Indianapolis on August 22, 1889. *Rhymes of Our Neighborhood* (New Castle, Indiana, 1895) contains his usual themes and some verse inspired by the Civil War; and his last volume, *After Noontide. A Volume of Verse in Various Keys* (Richmond, Indiana, 1905), illustrated by the Indiana poet Evaleen Stein, is probably his best. Although the same subjects have now grown monotonous to the reader, he sees that a serenity and resolution pervade this collection more than the others. Benjamin Parker, thus, is a sentimental rhymer with his eyes turned nostalgically toward the past but is also an interpreter of nature and the pioneer life.

The collection of Indiana poetry which he compiled with Enos Boyd Heiney, entitled *Poets and Poetry of Indiana* (New York, 1900), performed a signal service in being the first of many anthologies of Indiana literature; but the book is badly warped by the compilers' praise—often extravagant laudation—of every poet included, most of whom were known only locally and have been rather quickly forgotten. One looks in vain through the biographies at the end of the book for careful judgments or even a word of adverse criticism.

Dulcina Mason Jordan

Dulcina Mason (Mrs. James J.) Jordan (1833-1895), whose one book, *Rosemary Leaves* (Cincinnati, 1873), followed the first publication of Parker by only two years, is somewhat the same sort of poet as Parker; for, although she has sincerity, poetic fancy, and poetic spirit, these qualities are not sufficient to cause her to be remembered as a poet. Her lines tend to be wooden and lifeless; her subject matter is much like Parker's, although a scattering of better poems, like "Home to the Village," is to be found.

Mrs. Jordan was born July 21, 1833, at Marathon, New York, came to Indiana at the age of ten, and educated herself. In Richmond, Indiana, she married at an early age and reared a large family, still finding sufficient time to write and do newspaper work in Indiana and Ohio. She died at Richmond on April 25, 1895.[5]

Lee O. Harris

Another figure of quite modest literary attainments is Lee O. Harris (1839-1909), who can claim distinction only in having been one of the early teachers of James Whitcomb Riley and in having stimulated Riley's interest in poetry. Born in Chester County, Pennsylvania, January 30, 1839, young Harris was taken by his family first to Washington County, Pennsylvania, and then to Andersonville, Indiana, where he was educated, later adding to his education by travels in Canada and the United States, including a trip overland in 1856-57 to Washington and Oregon territories. After studying medicine for a time, he became a teacher and newspaper editor. In 1860 he

[5] Biography of Mrs. Jordan taken from Parker and Heiney (eds.), *Poets and Poetry of Indiana*, 438-39.

was publishing the Greenfield (Indiana) *Constitution and Union;* he married America Foster in 1861 and, except for a period of sickness, served in the Indiana infantry and cavalry during the Civil War. After the war he resumed his teaching in Greenfield and died December 23, 1909.[6]

Harris published one novel and one book of poetry. His novel, *The Man Who Tramps. A Story of To-day* (Indianapolis, 1878) is a sort of Horatio Alger story of a hard-working, misunderstood orphan who makes good; and the collection of poetry, *Interludes* (Indianapolis, 1893), moves slowly, and sometimes falteringly, in sing-song, end-stopped lines. There is much nature poetry and reminiscing about the past, the dead, and the war. His poem, "What Shall It Teach?" like Parker's "The Building of the Monument," was read at the laying of the cornerstone of the Soldiers' and Sailors' Monument in Indianapolis. "The Old Schoolmaster" is tender in its delineation of an old teacher who dies in his classroom after school is out.

It is difficult to see in the work of Harris much trace of the inspiration which, perhaps, helped produce Riley. Harris has no dialect verse, no particular interest in rural folk or in children as subjects of poetry, and his volume of verse was published after Riley had many volumes of poetry in print and had established his own fame.

JAMES WHITCOMB RILEY

Thus, the precursors of Riley in the Golden Age were of little consequence. They hardly did much more than keep poetry alive in the state and retain its sentimentality

[6] Biography of Harris is from Banta, *Indiana Authors and Their Books,* 135.

of tone. No one was a harbinger of the outpouring and popularity to come.

James Whitcomb Riley (1849-1916), then, burst dazzlingly upon the literary—and popular—world. At first he was known in Indiana only, but soon he became famous over all the nation. He was the first Indiana poet to attract widespread and continuing attention and love, and no other Hoosier man of letters has ever enjoyed such an enthusiastic following during his lifetime nor left behind him such an enduring memory. Indeed, no American poet, except, perhaps, Longfellow, has ever received similar nationwide acclaim.

Readers tend not to take any middle ground on Riley. Either they accept him for what he is, ignore what he is not, enjoy his verse, and, in the poet's rosy atmosphere of remembered childhood, with its circus parades, white clapboard cottages shaded by huge leafy trees, and splashing boyhood swimming holes, love him; or they condemn him at once for his lack of penetration of life and reality, for his endless sentimentalizing over a type of life that never really was, and his folksy dialect verse, and cast him into outer darkness as subliterary. Hoosiers, of course, as well as the general reading public across the country, tend to the former point of view, whereas many literary critics take a definite stand in the latter. Perhaps, however, the truth lies somewhere between the two extremes.

Riley was born on October 7, 1849, in the little town of Greenfield, the seat of Hancock County, on the National Road in eastern Indiana, the third of six children of Reuben A. and Elizabeth (Marine) Riley. Of Dutch ancestry, the father, a native of Pennsylvania, served as a captain of cavalry in the Federal Army during the Civil War and was a lawyer and political orator. The mother was a sympathetic and kindly person in whose family skill in rhyming had been prominent and whose death, when the poet was twenty, made a deep impression which influenced his later life and writing.

Riley attended the Greenfield schools, where, fortunately, a teacher, Lee O. Harris,[7] who himself wrote verse, gave up hope of teaching his pupil mathematics and interested him instead in literature. Riley frequently accompanied his father to the courthouse, carefully observing the Indiana country folk and their manner of speech and thus acquiring much valuable material, of which he later was to make full use. After leaving school at the age of sixteen, Riley read law for a time in his father's office, then drifted about, first as a sign, house, and ornamental painter and next as advance agent for a wagon show, painting advertisements on barns and fences about the countryside. His talent for versifying coming to the fore, he graduated to writing lyrics for the songs presented by the show; and probably it was here that he developed his acting ability, which he later utilized so cleverly in countless readings of his poetry across the country. His first poem to be published appeared in the Greenfield *Commercial* in the fall of 1870. He sent, in 1872, several poems to a literary weekly, the Indianapolis *Saturday Mirror,* which were published over the signature of "Jay Whit."

In 1873, at the age of twenty-four, he returned, much traveled and experienced, to Greenfield; and after serving briefly as editor of the town paper and seeing some of his verse published by various newspapers, he took employment in 1877 with the Anderson *Democrat.* It was at this time that he broke into the literary world— rather ingloriously, to be sure. To prove his theory that

[7] See above, 201-2.

in order for a poem to be popular and successful it need be known only as having been written by "a genius known to fame," he wrote a poem, "Leonainie," in the manner of Edgar Allan Poe and sent it, signed with Poe's initials, to the Kokomo *Dispatch,* saying that it had been found on the flyleaf of an old dictionary. The *Dispatch* published it, and the poem was accepted by many critics as an authentic poem of Poe,[8] several maintaining their opinions even after Riley finally admitted the hoax, of which he soon came to be ashamed. The Anderson *Democrat,* shocked, according to tradition, at its employee's lack of integrity, then cast him forth; but this unfortunate occurrence was actually advantageous for him, for he was hired promptly by the Indianapolis *Journal,* where he remained from 1877 to 1885.

On the *Journal* he did routine assignments; but he came more and more to write verse for its columns, at length organizing his contributions into a series, signed "Benj. F. Johnson, of Boone," which included one of his famous poems, "When the Frost Is on the Punkin." Riley gave the impression that the series was really written by a farmer; to add to the air of authenticity, he introduced letters as a preface, somewhat as Lowell had begun the "Biglow Papers." From these poems the figure of a lovable, whimsical character, recording his own joys and sorrows, emerged.

Riley's popularity began when he started working on the *Journal,* and his greatest production commenced in 1878. His first book was a paper-backed collection of fifty pages of the *Journal* series and was entitled *"The Old Swimmin'-Hole," and 'Leven More Poems, by Benj. F.*

[8] Louise P. Richards, "James Whitcomb Riley on a Country Newspaper," in *The Bookman,* September, 1904, pp. 18-24, and reprinted in the issue of September, 1916, pp. 79-87.

Johnson, of Boone (Indianapolis, 1883). Since no publisher had accepted it, the book was financed by Riley
himself and by George C. Hitt, the business manager of
the *Journal*. The edition of a thousand copies was speedily sold, the amount of profit being $166.40. (Any origi-
nal copy of that edition would sell today at many times
that price.) A second edition was issued by Merrill, Meigs
& Company, Indianapolis; and this company and its suc-
cessors, the Bowen-Merrill Company and the Bobbs-Merrill Company, became, fortunately both for them and for
Riley, his regular publishers.

Soon his poetry was being issued, usually annually, in
small booklets, often in Christmas dress. Leaving the
Journal, Riley settled down to becoming first a curiosity
and celebrity, then an accepted, loved, and famous writer
and entertainer, and finally an institution, a tradition,
and practically a myth. The poet showed himself to be
one of those to whom education is only incidental in
their careers and who learn, perhaps intuitively, as they
pass through life with their eyes and ears open. He had
begun to write rather casually, somewhat as he had
learned to play the guitar, simply because he felt a need
for self-expression and not because of his contact with a
literary atmosphere of any kind or because he had decided
on a literary career. Indeed, he was the literary heir of
Robert Burns in his closeness to the common people and
his use of them as subjects and the literary heir also, in
one sense, of Crabbe in his realistic approach to them—
though certainly without Crabbe's unflinching portrayal
of the less favorable aspects of life.

Riley was, then, a natural poet. He had a good ear and
reproduced much of what he had heard and experienced
as a boy; he had a natural appreciation of what is good in
literature, a nice sense of proportion, a sure feeling of

situation and character, and a delight in forming odd and amusing combinations of words. He read widely, but still did not allow his originality to be unduly influenced. As his public increased and became more demanding of him, his touch grew firmer; and while continuing his dialect poems, he also strove for excellence in using literary English.

His most popular poems are probably "Little Orphant Annie," "The Old Swimmin'-Hole," "The Old Man and Jim," "When the Frost Is on the Punkin," "Knee-Deep in June," "The Raggedy Man," "The Object Lesson," and "Out to Old Aunt Mary's." For most readers it is an emotional experience simply to hear these titles and many others—let alone to call the verses themselves to mind. Among his long list of books the most popular were *Afterwhiles* (Indianapolis, 1888), *Old-Fashioned Roses* (London, 1888), *Pipes o' Pan at Zekesbury* (Indianapolis, 1889), *Rhymes of Childhood* (Indianapolis, 1891), *Green Fields and Running Brooks* (Indianapolis, 1893), *Poems Here at Home* (New York, 1893), *Riley Child-Rhymes* (Indianapolis, 1899), *The Book of Joyous Children* (New York, 1902), and *An Old Sweetheart of Mine* (Indianapolis, 1902).

Other than the above-mentioned books, his published volumes include: *Character Sketches, The Boss Girl, A Christmas Story and Other Sketches* (Indianapolis, 1886), *Nye and Riley's Railway Guide* (with Edgar W. Nye, Chicago, 1888), *"The Old Swimmin'-Hole" and 'Leven More Poems. Neghborly* [sic.] *Poems on Friendship Grief and Farm-Life by Benj. F. Johnson, of Boone* (Indianapolis, 1891), *The Flying Islands of the Night* (Indianapolis, 1892), *Armazindy* (Indianapolis, 1894), *The Days Gone By and Other Poems* (Chicago, 1895), *A Tinkle of Bells and Other Poems* (Chicago, 1895), *A*

Child-World (Indianapolis, 1897), *Rubáiyát of Doc Sifers* (New York, 1897), *The Golden Year from the Verse and Prose of James Whitcomb Riley* (London, 1898), *Riley Love-Lyrics* (Indianapolis, [1899]), *Home-Folks* (Indianapolis, 1900), *His Pa's Romance* (Indianapolis, 1903), *Out to Old Aunt Mary's* (Indianapolis, 1904), *A Defective Santa Claus* (Indianapolis, 1904), *Riley Songs O'Cheer* (Indianapolis, [1905]), *While the Heart Beats Young* (Indianapolis, [1906]), *Morning* (Indianapolis, [1907]), *The Raggedy Man* (Indianapolis, [1907]), *The Boys of the Old Glee Club* (Indianapolis, 1907), *The Orphant Annie Book* (Indianapolis, [1908]), *Riley Songs of Summer* (Indianapolis, [1908]), *The Lockerbie Book* (Indianapolis, 1911), *The Riley Baby Book* (Indianapolis, 1913), *Riley Songs of Friendship* (Indianapolis, [1915]), *The Old Soldier's Story* (Indianapolis, [1915]), and *The Hoosier Book* (Indianapolis,1916). In addition to all these publications, many collections of poems previously published or of single poems beautifully illustrated and selected from previous collections were issued. Also, several editions of collected works appeared. The three which include materials not previously published are *The Homestead Edition: The Poems and Prose Sketches of James Whitcomb Riley* (16 volumes. New York, 1897-1914); *The Complete Works of James Whitcomb Riley . . . Biographical Edition* (6 volumes. Indianapolis, 1913); and *Memorial Edition, James Whitcomb Riley's Complete Works . . .* (10 volumes. Indianapolis, 1916).[9]

[9] For a complete listing of Riley's writings, including ephemeral pieces, together with much information concerning each publication, such as the changing titles and contents of poems, pseudonyms, songs based on Riley's poems, periodicals, and collected works, see Anthony J. Russo and Dorothy R. Russo, *A Bibliography of James Whitcomb Riley* (Indianapolis, 1944).

Early in his career as a poet Riley joined Edgar W. (Bill) Nye to form a team for the purpose of giving entertainments, and the broad humor of Nye was complemented by Riley's sentimentality. Part of the poet's fame arose from these reading and reciting tours, and there are many apochryphal stories surrounding them which still survive. He also appeared on the same platforms with Samuel L. Clemens (Mark Twain), Eugene Field, and Robert J. Burdette. Riley became a very popular lecturer in his own right, however; and audiences which thronged to see what they thought would turn out to be an uncouth rustic who had penned bucolic nature poetry were astonished to find instead a dapper little man, immaculately dressed, wearing a white waistcoat and a huge gold watch chain, who was urbanity personified and who held his audience in the palm of his hand as he recited his poetry, making them laugh or weep at will. His stage presence, his facial expression, and his acting ability made a Riley "lecture" one to be remembered a lifetime. He performed over all the nation, except in the Far West, and for about twenty-five years he was the guest at the White House of each succeeding president.

Much of the charm of his verse lies in its subject matter, which so often concerns children—or adults so simple in make-up as to be childlike, such as rustic philosophers. Yet, while recording the drolleries of childhood, he is careful to reject the conventional representation of children found in literature, which he calls that of "the refined children—the very proper children—the studiously thoughtful, poetic children"; he records instead "the rough-and-tumble little fellows in 'hodden gray,' with frowzy heads, begrimed but laughing faces, and such awful, awful vulgarities of naturalness, and crimes of simplicity, and brazen faith and trust, and love of life and every-

body in it!"[10]   In this spirit he presents many types of
children—the naïve, the elfish, the erring child, the child
wide-eyed with wonder at ordinary phenomena; and he
recreates, for children and adults alike, the imagination
and enchantment of childhood. There is nothing patron-
izing in his writings; he listens to childhood and becomes,
as it were, an amanuensis, transcribing the child's mind
and legends. Thus the Raggedy Man, the shabby, uneducated worker at odd jobs for the well-to-do, is transformed through Riley into a boy's oracle, full of all sorts
of wisdom because he

> Knows 'bout Giunts, an' Griffins, an' Elves,
> An' the Squidgicum-Squees 'at swallers the'rselves![11]

Orphant Annie, likewise, is versed in the knowledge of
goblins that "'ll git you ef you don't watch out!" He can
reproduce vividly the child's breathless manner of eager
speech as he excitedly attempts to tell a thrilling story or
experience. As Edgar Lee Masters says,

. . . his work of incomparable merit, of unmatched excellence was in the field of childhood delineation. Here he has no
equal, and no one to be mentioned in the same breath with
him. Here he was pure genius. The work of other poets in
this domain is artificial compared to Riley's. It is but tin
toys prettily made and brightly painted and varnished when
placed by the side of Riley's flesh and blood creations, native
to a spot and a life of America—now vanished! His success
with poems of children was largely due to the fact that he

[10] James Whitcomb Riley, *Dialect in Literature* (Indianapolis, 1896),
17-18. This is a reprint of an article originally published in *The Forum*,
December, 1892, pp. 465-73.

[11] Quoted from "The Raggedy Man," in *Joyful Poems for Children*
(copyright 1946-1960 by The Bobbs-Merrill Company, Inc.) by special
permission of the publisher.

really loved them, and by reason of his child-like heart entered into their secrets.[12]

Yet it must not be supposed that Riley's poetry is effeminate, for he likes rugged manhood everywhere, as in the touching lyric, "Away," whose subject is an Indiana soldier of the Civil War:

> I cannot say, and I will not say
> That he is dead—He is just away![13]

Riley's poetry, then, is not bookish. Even though he penned some imitations of the poems of Longfellow and Tennyson and of the prose of Dickens and Scott and although at times he has imagined Pan as piping in Indiana settings, he is still pre-eminently natural, so much so that he has often been read and quoted by people who would blush to be surprised in the act of reading a poem. That Riley succeeds with this type of reader is due to the fact that he makes sentiment appear perfectly natural and real, and through many devices he entraps the reader into the emotion of the poem, as in "Nothin' to Say," in which the subject is the isolation and loneliness of the father, who suddenly realizes that his daughter is about to marry and who reacts clumsily, as do all fathers in such a situation, and thinks, naturally, of his dead wife.

His verse has been appreciated by such a large body of readers of all tastes because it represents wholesomeness, instead of sensuality; common sense, cheerfulness, rather than cynicism and dejection; and humor and pathos, often inextricably intertwined. He never denounces, satirizes,

[12] "James Whitcomb Riley. A Sketch of His Life and an Appraisal of His Work," in *The Century Magazine*, October, 1927, p. 714. Quoted with the permission of Mrs. Masters.

[13] Quoted from *Afterwhiles* (copyright 1887 by The Bobbs-Merrill Company, Inc.) by special permission of the publisher.

or argues; he entertains and moves us. His attitude is
that of a sympathetic admirer, and his humor suggests
that of Dickens in its kinship with the oddities and
pathetic aspects of life. Neither heroic themes nor power
ever tempted his hand; and he has been distinguished by
the invention, sweetness, and melody, found in such works
as "Griggsby's Station," rather than by his fanciful pieces,
as seen in *Flying Islands of the Night,* or by formal verse.

The Riley dialect has always been one of the distin-
guishing features of his work; also it is one of the most
controversial. It has been set down as a conscious exer-
cise in humor of the Artemus Ward variety and as "the
record of a town man's mimicry of country crudeness,"[14]
and it has been attacked by many critics as untrue to
Indiana and to Midwestern speech. However, as Hamlin
Garland points out,[15] Riley writes his dialect verse in
two ways: one, as an uneducated person would write;
and the other, as this same man, or perhaps his neighbor,
would probably speak. He never tries to change nature.
The verse of his first publication, *"The Old Swimmin'-
Hole" and 'Leven More Poems,* may be cited as an example of the first type of dialect, while "The Old Man
and Jim" may be given as an example of the latter.
Meredith Nicholson points out[16] that whenever Riley
uses dialect, he has in mind a specific individual whose
utterances he is reporting and that he never tries to give
the kind of speech which is merely typical. The poet,
therefore, is more interested in peculiar characters with
outstanding eccentricities than in the average person, and

[14] Fred L. Pattee, *A History of American Literature Since 1870* (New
York, 1915), 326.

[15] *Commemorative Tribute to James Whitcomb Riley,* read in the 1920
Lecture Series of the American Academy of Arts and Letters (New York,
1922), 6.

[16] *The Hoosiers,* 162.

the dialect which he utilizes may be richer than the ordinary rural speech. For example, "ministratin' " (ministering), "competenter" (more competent), "familiously" (familiarly), "resignated" (resigned), and "durin' the army" (during the Civil War) all may not be recognized as the Hoosier or Midwestern idiom, yet quite conceivably may have been spoken by individuals whom Riley overheard; or it is possible that Riley coined some of these words and phrases in order to develop certain characters. In spite of this possible breach of authenticity he can be followed rather closely as a guide in the speech of southeastern Indiana, if not of all Indiana and the Midwest. His verse carries the lilt of the real speech of living people, even though now and then there is an inconsistency, as in the interchangeable use of "again" and "agin," often as the rhyme demands. The Raggedy Man, Doc Sifers, and Squire Hawkins emerge as individuals characterized, at least partly, by their speech. Riley's sensitive ear also recorded correctly the speech of children, Negroes, the Germans, and the Irish. In general, then, he set down "the language really spoken by men" in situations and incidents taken from common life—which is exactly what Wordsworth pronounced, in his famous preface to the *Lyrical Ballads,* to be the province of poetry; and one reason for the popularity of his verse lies in the closeness of the reader, even today, to the dialect.

Riley defended his use of dialect as the real speech of many unlettered people accurately reported and as worthy of presentation as the more standard and grammatical speech, because a true writing of dialect is simply nature displayed by art—which is the function of literature. To reject this kind of writing, he says, is to reject Dickens, Joel Chandler Harris, Mark Twain, Lowell, and

many others. Since dialect arose from the conditions accompanying the building of the nation in the wilderness,
it is thoroughly respectable.[17] Furthermore, we might
point out in defense of the poet's use of dialect that the
very people whose speech he reports enjoy reading and
hearing his poetry as much as city residents, and they are
always affected by what seems to them his accuracy of
reporting and his kindliness.

One can also view Riley's dialect as a part of the flood
of dialect literature that followed the success of Harris'
first Uncle Remus book, in 1880, when America became
interested in a new Pike County type of character, the
southeastern "cracker," and when dialect became wonder-
fully popular, as, for example in Richard Malcolm Johnston's *Dukesborough Tales* (1883) and in the work of
Charles Egbert Craddock (Mary N. Murfree) in "The
'Harnt' That Walks Chilhowee," published in the *Atlantic
Monthly* (1883), and *In the Tennessee Mountains* (1884),
and also in Thomas Nelson Page and his story "Marse
Chan" (1884). Yet, whether in spite of—or because of—
this influence, Riley's dialect appeared in book form in
his first publication, in 1883, and it generally succeeded.
The Negro poet, Paul Laurence Dunbar, was later to
learn lessons in the use of dialect from Riley.

Certainly it is not difficult to point out defects of Riley
and his verse. Many are self-evident. It is both fortunate
and tragic that he never grew old and never quite grew
up, that he always looked, not forward, but backward
with nostalgia to a fancied time when romantic youths
and coy maids and hired raggedy men and smiling Aunt
Marys and old sweethearts moved in an idyllic rural or
small-town setting. The tragedy underlying the life of
Orphant Annie or the tottering age of Aunt Mary or the

[17] See Riley, *Dialect in Literature.*

problems of the farmers who raised the pumpkins and turkey cocks left him unscathed. His man with the hoe owned a lush farm. His opinions and sentiments seemed never to change, and the current world of affairs passed him by. He was completely indifferent to politics; he never voted and interested himself in election returns only when a friend happened to be running for office. He did not raise his eyes from his books and papers long enough to notice domestic problems, reforms, or religious questions; and even the drama of the Spanish-American War and World War I moved him not. Instead, he lived in a sort of sentimental dream, wedded to simple and homely joys and ways, a relic of an age that had hardly existed at all, and part of an era which he scarcely understood. He was obsessed by children and childhood, and it has been said that his poems sound as though they had been penned by the young or the old against those middle-aged. The blinders that he placed on his eyes limited his genius so severely that he goes no deeper into the issues of life than the depiction of innocent joys and sorrows and the vivid portrayal of simple characters. He had no power to discern the soul. Riley's philosophy, then, if he can really be said to possess one, is that of a prudent farmer and is composed of simple sentiments and truisms. Not even his emotion is complex, to say nothing of his thought.

Some critics[18] go so far as to say that Riley was artificial and insincere, that he was always primarily a showman

[18] For example, Pattee, *A History of American Literature*, 328; Wallace Stegner, "Western Record and Romance," in Robert E. Spiller, *et al.* (eds.), *Literary History of the United States* (3 vols. New York, 1948), 2:871; Malcolm Cowley and Henry S. Canby, "Creating an Audience," in Spiller, *et al.* (eds.), *op. cit.*, 2:1121-22. On the other hand, Masters, "James Whitcomb Riley," in *The Century Magazine*, October, 1927, pp. 704-15, gives a rather well-rounded evaluation of Riley.

and an entertainer, writing with his eye on the public taste, having practically nothing to say. Often his writing has been cited as showing how low public taste can sink, when such writing is preferred to that of serious poets and dramatists.

On the other hand, the defenders of Riley contend that a writer who has always been so popular with so many millions of people in such varied walks of life must contribute something that cannot be entirely tossed aside or ignored. And popular he certainly was, in a manner shared by few other literary figures of this or any other age.

Probably no poet was ever honored so much in his own state and during his own lifetime as James Whitcomb Riley; and for years before his death it was almost a sacrilege in Indiana to speak of things Hoosier without at least mentioning the Hoosier Poet, as he came to be called, to say nothing of quoting snatches of his verse. To the popular mind he represented Indiana; indeed, he *was* Indiana! No other literary figure has ever achieved such stature with the entire population of the state. Everyone loved him—the Indianapolis school child who gladly dropped his work and listened with awe in an atmosphere of hushed reverence when the poet dropped by the school to recite some of his poems, the middle-aged man who liked to be called back wistfully to the sunlit streams of his boyhood, the old man who was ready to

> . . . strip to the soul,
> And dive off in my grave
> Like the old swimmin'-hole.[19]

Even people who normally would have had no connec-

[19] Quoted from "The Old Swimmin' Hole," in *Joyful Poems for Children* (copyright 1946-1960 by The Bobbs-Merrill Company, Inc.) by special permission of the publisher.

tion with imaginative literature, like the socialist labor-organizer Eugene V. Debs of Terre Haute, loved and entertained him. Debs called him the "God-gifted Hoosier Poet."[20]

Riley's oddities and shortcomings could be overlooked; the fact that he never married and that his love for children was perhaps abstract rather than individualized, his known addiction to the bottle, the impracticality which caused him usually to take the wrong train or get off at the wrong station—all these things were drowned in the flood of love which he engendered.

The honor which he liked best, however, was that accorded on his birthday, October 7, 1911, which the schools of Indiana and New York City celebrated by special exercises, when Riley rode through the Indianapolis streets, hailed by the school children like a conquering hero. The next year this celebration was observed all over the nation, and in 1915 the Secretary of the Interior suggested that one of his poems should be read in every American school. Many dinners were given for him.

During his final illness President Woodrow Wilson sent anxious inquiries to Indianapolis. When the poet died on July 22, 1916, at the age of sixty-six, some thirty-five thousand people passed his body as it lay in state under the dome of the Indiana capitol; his obituary filled entire pages in the nation's newspapers. After an angry contest with Greenfield, Indianapolis won the honor of burial, and Riley was interred in Crown Hill Cemetery. Indiana had lost its poet laureate. And the nation had lost its most popular poet.

But the memory lingers on. For many years after his death his books enjoyed a surprising, though decreasing,

[20] See Debs's article, "Riley, Nye & Field. Personal Notes and Recollections," in *National Magazine*, October, 1915. The Indiana State Library has a separate of this article.

sale. Riley Day is still observed in Indiana schools, and the Greenfield and Lockerbie Street homes are still visited by thousands. A statue of the poet stands in the Greenfield Courthouse Square, erected through the voluntary offerings of pennies from the nation's schoolchildren. Hotels, ballrooms, a streamlined train, canned foods, an Indianapolis children's hospital, and the like, all bear his name.

And his popularity, though centered in Indiana, was yet nationwide, being surpassed only by Longfellow's. Many other American poets have been admired much more than Riley, but probably no other has been as universally loved as "Sunny Jim," not even Bryant, Lowell, Emerson, or even the popular Longfellow, who encouraged the Indiana poet as a young man. Literary men, like Hamlin Garland, Edgar Lee Masters, Bliss Carman, and Edwin Markham,[21] have penned tributes; William Lyon Phelps edited the poet's letters; Mark Twain, William Dean Howells, Joel Chandler Harris, and Charles A. Dana all acclaimed him;[22] and Riley's verse has been analyzed in many studies of American literature.[23] Several universities gave him honorary de-

[21] See Garland's *Commemorative Tribute to Riley;* Masters, "James Whitcomb Riley," in *The Century Magazine,* October, 1927, pp. 704-15; Bliss Carman, *James Whitcomb Riley. An Essay* ... (Metuchen, N. J., 1925-26); Edwin P. Markham, *Concerning James Whitcomb Riley* (Washington, D.C., 1949).

[22] See, for example, in addition to the references already listed, Henry A. Beers, *The Connecticut Wits, and Other Essays* (New Haven, Conn., 1920); Alfred Kreymborg, *Our Singing Strength. An Outline of American Poetry (1620-1930)* (New York, 1929); Horace Gregory and Marya Zaturenska, *A History of American Poetry, 1900-1940* (New York, 1946); Jeannette C. Nolan, Horace Gregory, and James T. Farrell, *Poet of the People. An Evaluation of James Whitcomb Riley* (Bloomington, Ind., 1951). Nearly all histories of American literature at least mention Riley even if they do not devote criticism to him; he is sometimes rated low.

[23] See Masters, "James Whitcomb Riley," in *The Century Magazine,* October, 1927, p. 712.

grees, such as Yale, which awarded him a Master of Arts degree in 1902. Many of his poems have been set to music. Yet, Riley bore all these dignities with humility, wondering how so much could be made of the former sign painter. He never was tempted to leave his native state.

Riley helped put Indiana on the literary map of America as Whittier did New England, Bret Harte did California—and even as Burns made Scotland register in English literature. As Edgar Lee Masters says, "He put Indiana as a place and a people in the memory of America, more thoroughly and more permanently than has been done by any other poet before or since his day for any other locality or people."[24] Probably James Whitcomb Riley will always remain the leading figure of Indiana literature.[25]

To turn from Riley to the lesser lights that followed him in the field of poetry is to experience an anticlimax, for a procession of poets who are pale by comparison now bids for our attention, and no one of the stature of Riley is encountered until we come to William Vaughn Moody. Between the first publication of Riley in 1883 and the first publication of Moody in 1900 only two poets, Evaleen Stein and Max Ehrmann, stand out from a group who are at best no more than mediocre.

PHILIP BEVAN

The first of these minor figures is Philip Bevan (1811-1890). Bevan was born February 27, 1811, in Newport,

[24] *Ibid.,* 705.

[25] Biographies of Riley are readily available. See Banta, *Indiana Authors and Their Books,* 270-71; article by Will D. Howe in *Dictionary of American Biography, Authors Edition,* 15:611-13; Marcus Dickey, *The Youth of James Whitcomb Riley* (Indianapolis, 1919), and *The Maturity of James Whitcomb Riley* (Indianapolis, 1922). The latest study is Richard Crowder, *Those Innocent Years. The Legacy and Inheritance of a Hero of the Victorian Age, James Whitcomb Riley* (Indianapolis, 1957), which was published after my own writing was completed.

England; and after a period of apprenticeship at carpentry and architecture, both of which he disliked, he came in 1834 to the United States, landing at Philadelphia and traveling down the Ohio and Mississippi to Natchez and New Orleans. In 1836 he returned to England, where he married Elizabeth Ablard, the daughter of the man to whom he had formerly been apprenticed. In 1843, accompanied by his wife and son, he came again to this country and settled in Jackson County, Iowa, where he farmed and served as minister of a new church. After the death of his wife he determined upon the ministry as a career, was graduated from the Lane Theological Seminary in Cincinnati in 1849, and spent the rest of his life as a pastor of Presbyterian churches in the New Albany District of Indiana.[26]

At his death on April 3, 1890, he left some twenty manuscripts, some of which may have been published. Of his four known publications, two were religious in nature and will not be discussed; the other two were patriotic. The author has not seen a copy of the first volume, *America. A Poem* (Cincinnati, 1848). The remaining volume, *Songs of the War for the Union* (Cincinnati, 1887), was inspired, as the title indicates, by his loyal devotion to the Northern cause in the Civil War, in which he lost a son. The poems here collected were written during the war and first appeared in newspapers. All but "Delphon; the Mytic Isle," are on patriotic subjects and are composed of wooden and stilted verse, of which the best observation that can be made is that it arises from sincerity and conviction. "Delphon" is intended to be a counterpart or antithesis of "The Island of the In-

[26] Biography of Bevan taken from Banta, *Indiana Authors and Their Books,* 28. Banta spells his name "Bevin," but it appears as Bevan on the title page of his book.

nocent," a poem previously published; and the purpose is to extol the virtue of a life of innocence in contrast to that of vice and luxury, and also to exalt faithfulness in marriage. Bevan's verse has no permanent value and illustrates only the influence of the Civil War.

SILAS B. McMANUS

Neither will the verse of Silas Bettes McManus (1845-1917) live long, although it has the distinction of a little humor and much sentiment. Dr. McManus was born on September 17, 1845, in Rootstown, Ohio, came to Indiana as a youth, was graduated from the Medical College of Fort Wayne, and took a year of postgraduate studies at the University of Michigan. He and Mary Hillegass of Huntertown, Indiana, were married in 1880. During most of his life he contributed to magazines, and he had connections with the Fort Wayne *Journal Gazette* from 1876 to 1882. He served one term as a state senator, commencing in 1892. He died on April 15, 1917, at his home in the vicinity of Howe, Indiana.[27]

The two poetry publications of McManus—the pamphlet, *"Fot Would You Take For Me"; and Nine or Ten Other Rhymes* (Lima, Indiana, 1894), and the book, *Rural Rhymes* (Cincinnati, 1898)—are full of sentiment and dialect of the same general type as Riley's, but are feeble in comparison. Their subjects are somewhat similar—the charms of home and farm life, the flowers, the birds, the woods, the family, the death of his little son. Perhaps he was attempting to imitate Riley.

Albion Fellows Bacon

Albion Fellows (Mrs. Hilary E.) Bacon (1865-1933), who comes next in our study, is known much more as a

[27] *Ibid.,* 206.

social reformer than as a poet. She was born in Evansville, Indiana, on April 8, 1865. She and her sister, Annie Fellows Johnston, the author of the famous Little Colonel series of juveniles, were the daughters of Albion and Mary (Erskine) Fellows. Their father, a Methodist minister, died when the girls were young, and they grew up in McCutchanville, near Evansville. Five years after her graduation from the Evansville High School in 1883 Albion married Hilary E. Bacon; the couple resided in Evansville, where they reared four children. But Mrs. Bacon did not let her homemaking duties interfere with her interest in writing and agitating for social reform, particularly in the field of housing; and during the forty-five years after her marriage she organized, or helped organize, numerous social organizations and movements, such as the Flower Mission, the Anti-Tuberculosis League, the Working Girls' Association, and the Indiana Housing Association. She was a director of the National Housing Association and a member of the Public Health Nursing Association; she influenced the Indiana State Legislature into passing the state tenement law of 1913 and the state housing law of 1917. Becoming known for her writing and lecturing on tenement reform, in 1931 she was made a member of President Hoover's conference on Home Building and Home Ownership. Her death came on December 10, 1933, in Evansville.[28]

In addition to many publications, mostly in the field of housing, and a book of short stories for juveniles, *The Charm String* (Boston, 1929), Mrs. Bacon, jointly with her sister, Annie Fellows Johnston, issued a collection of poetry, *Songs Ysame* (Boston, 1897). Mrs. Bacon's half of the volume contains graceful lyrics, usually short and

[28] Banta, *Indiana Authors and Their Books*, 12, 170; Parker and Heiney (eds.), *Poets and Poetry of Indiana*, 438.

each possessing a single thought, rather well expressed, and often after the style of Emily Dickinson. Many of the poems are of only eight lines. Her subjects are usually life, death, love and, as one might expect from a person of her interests, sympathy with the underdog. A poetic imagination, a close observation, and a questioning of life may be encountered in her verse.

Sister Mary Genevieve Todd

In contrast to Mrs. Bacon, the life of Sister Mary Genevieve Todd (Lottie Mary Todd, 1863-1896) was outwardly uneventful. She was born on December 19, 1863, in Vevay, Indiana, became a member of the Catholic Church in 1886, and entered the community of the Sisters of Providence at St. Mary-of-the-Woods, Indiana, in 1890, where she served as a very pious teacher in the novitiate. She died July 29, 1896.[29] Her one book was issued under two titles, though in the same year, and ran through five editions. The original title was *Poems, with Pious Thoughts and Practices in Honor of Our Divine Master* (New York, 1897). This is a book of religious verse, conventional in poetic form, espousing the Catholic faith and creed. It reflects a peace arising from acceptance of the doctrines of the Catholic Church and life within it and also a yearning for the peace of heaven. Although the poetry is hardly outstanding, the book does contain some rather beautiful pieces; in addition, a few short essays on religious subjects are included.

[29] Biography of Sister Mary Genevieve Todd taken from the unsigned biographical sketch published in the fifth edition of her *Poems* and also from Barry, A Biographical and Bibliographical Dictionary of Indiana Authors (unpublished M. A. thesis, University of Notre Dame, 1943), 56, 628. A copy of this manuscript is in the Indiana Division of the Indiana State Library.

Evaleen Stein

To the name of Evaleen Stein (1863-1923) is attached an entirely different kind of production, for the work for which she is remembered consists of nature poetry and many children's books, although she was also an artist. The poet was born October 12, 1863, in Lafayette, Indiana, and, except for a few journeys out of the state, spent her life in that city. Her father, John Andrew Stein, was born in Pennsylvania and came in 1851 at the age of nineteen to Lafayette, where he soon became successful as a lawyer and politician. As a member of the Indiana Senate in 1869, he introduced the bill for the establishment of the Indiana Agricultural College (later Purdue University) and served as the secretary of its board. The poet's mother, Virginia Tomlinson, a woman of culture, was born at Logansport, Indiana. Both parents wrote stories, essays, and verse for the local papers. Evaleen's brother, Orth Stein, exercised his literary inheritance in journalism, being one of the first well-known columnists.

Miss Stein attended the local schools, and developing an interest in art, was sent to the Art Institute of Chicago, where she learned decorative design so well that some of her illuminated manuscripts were exhibited at the Society of Arts and Crafts in Chicago and elsewhere in the Midwest. Her interests turned more permanently to literature, however; and when she was twenty-three she began sending poetry to *St. Nicholas* and to the Indianapolis *Journal.* Her first collection of poetry came years later, when *One Way to the Woods* (Boston, 1897) appeared. It was followed five years later by *Among the Trees Again* (Indianapolis, 1902); her third and last volume of verse was for children, entitled *Child Songs of Cheer* (Boston, 1918). In addition, she wrote a lengthy narrative poem commemorating the centennial of the Battle of Tippe-

canoe (1911), another ode celebrating the centennial of
statehood, and two books of English versions of foreign
poetry: *Little Poems from Japanese Anthologies* (1922)
and *Poems of Giovannni Pascoli* (New Haven, Connecticut, 1923).

One Way to the Woods and *Among the Trees Again*
contain essentially the same sort of verse, the poet utilizing the traditional forms of rhyme and meter. Although
some of the poetry is evidently written to her brother or
to an unidentified feminine friend, and though there are a
few travel poems and some pieces in which she expresses
awe in contemplation of the universe, still the greatest impact of her work lies in the field of nature poetry, wherein
one marks the advent of a fresh, new voice in Indiana letters. Her verse is sprightly and happy in praise of the glories of nature, and she often includes minute detail in the
names and descriptions of flowers and bushes and trees.
She loves all the outdoors all the year round, but particularly in the warmer months; there is practically nothing seen here of the malevolent aspects of nature, and
except for an isolated poem or two, nature is beautiful
and inspires happy and beautiful thoughts. Miss Stein
has, thus, a sort of animal appreciation of nature; still,
she sometimes approaches a Wordsworthian concept in
that to her nature and God seem closely related.

The best of her verse has a lilt and cadence, as in "By
the Kankakee," or a rushing sweep, as in "A Song of
Thought." Her metric skill and her diction often rise to
unexpected heights; and through her earnestness in her
happy depiction of her subject matter one sees an escape
from the traditional manner of dealing with nature of
the older writers of the Ohio Valley, who had so often
used it simply as a background against which to establish
a moral. Her *Child Songs of Cheer* contains good chil-

dren's poetry and also includes many nature poems. To be sure, Miss Stein has little to say, and her contribution to poetry is slight; nevertheless, she is the first true nature poet in Indiana literature.

James Whitcomb Riley admired Miss Stein's poetry and both encouraged her and gave her advice. On May 22, 1907, he and Charles Major, Meredith Nicholson, and George Ade gave a benefit reading on the Purdue University campus, the proceeds of which made it possible for her and her mother to live in France for several months, where she happily visited the scenes which she had begun to use in her prose tales and which she would utilize still more in the future. Around 1900 she developed a third interest in her life, that of writing stories for children, and the remainder of her work lies in this field.

Her first children's book was *Troubador Tales* (Indianapolis, [1903]), a collection of short stories; and from that date for the remainder of her life she wrote a new children's book approximately every two years. These books were really long short stories, the subject matter arising from events of earlier ages in romantic places in Europe, particularly France. Her experience in illuminating manuscripts appears in *Gabriel and the Hour Book* (Boston, 1906); and this interest in medieval and courtly France, begun by her knowledge of the art of illuminating, is evident in *A Little Shepherd of Provence* (Boston, 1910), *The Little Count of Normandy* (Boston, 1911), and *Pepin: A Tale of Twelfth Night,* published posthumously in Boston in 1924. Many of her tales are simply old legends recounted with charm and simplicity. *Our Little Norman Cousin of Long Ago* (Boston, 1915) was the first of four books written for the Long Ago series, designed to instruct children in the customs of older ages and regions; her others were *Our Little Frankish Cousin of Long Ago* (Boston, 1917), *Our Little Celtic Cousin of Long Ago* (Boston, 1918), and *Our Little Crusader Cousin of Long Ago* (Boston, 1921). These books are entertaining, but Miss Stein does not rise to her usual ease in telling these stories. She also published *The Christmas Porringer* (Boston, 1914), *Rosechen and the Wicked Magpie* (Boston, 1917), *When Fairies Were Friendly* (Boston, 1922), *Children's Stories* (Boston, 1926), and *The Circus Dwarf Stories* (Boston, 1927). In all this production for children she wrote more *about* children than *for* them; thus, the books offer good adult reading. She loved intensely this unreal, romantic world of history and of her imagination; she practically lived in it. And in so consecrating her talents she formed part of that romantic movement in American and Indiana literature which produced such novels as *Ben-Hur, When Knighthood Was in Flower,* and *Graustark.* Her stories are not great literature, but they had a large following in their day.

When Evaleen Stein died in Lafayette on December 11, 1923, she had a minor reputation both as a poet and as a writer of these romantic tales and in her quiet and gentle manner had endeared herself to many people. She can hardly be numbered in the company of the greatest of the Hoosier literati; nevertheless, no recounting of the best-known writers is complete without her.[30]

Max Ehrmann

In contrast to Miss Stein, Max(imilian) Ehrmann (1872-1945) is one of those contradictory combinations found among writers who are both widely recognized and who have yet remained relatively unknown; for even though

[30] Biography of Evaleen Stein taken mostly from the article by Verne L. Samson in the *Dictionary of American Biography, Authors Edition,* 17:561, and the article by William Murray Hepburn in Banta, *Indiana Authors and Their Books,* 301-3.

he enjoyed an international reputation of sorts, still most Hoosiers have never become familiar with his works, and in the popular mind his name was never closely associated with Indiana literature. Much of his work was published in the form of pamphlets. As a poet, novelist, and playwright, however, during his most productive years he was the unofficial laureate of the Wabash Valley—or, at least, of the city of Terre Haute.

Ehrmann was born in Terre Haute on September 26, 1872, attended the city schools, and received the Ph. B. degree from DePauw University in 1894. He did graduate work at Harvard University in the field of philosophy, and upon returning to Terre Haute, began to write. For some years he also practiced law and served one term as deputy prosecuting attorney, but after 1912 he devoted his talents exclusively to writing. In 1910 he was invited to become a member of the Authors' Club of London, and in 1938 he received the degree of Doctor of Literature from his alma mater, DePauw University. He was a bachelor nearly all of his life; after having been married only a few months to Bertha Pratt King, he died in Terre Haute on September 9, 1945.[31]

His first two publications appeared while he was a student at Harvard. They were *A Farrago* (Cambridge, Massachusetts, 1898), a collection of spirited short stories and sketches of student life at Harvard, previously published in Boston newspapers and composed in a natural diction and in an attractive style, and *The Mystery of Madeline Le Blanc* (Cambridge, Massachusetts, [1900]), a rather well-written story of France and the revolution of 1830.

[31] "Max Ehrmann, Author, Dies," in Indianapolis *Star*, September 10, 1945, Sec. 1, pp. 1 and 3; and "Max Ehrmann, Poet, Prophet, Philosopher," in *The Wabash Valley Remembers, 1787-1938*... (Terre Haute Northwest Celebration Committee, [1938]). See also Bertha K. Ehrmann, *Max Ehrmann, a Poet's Life* (Boston, 1951).

A Fearsome Riddle (Indianapolis, 1901) is a breath-taking mystery of the peculiar relationship of Professor Whitmore, of a school that is evidently Rose Polytechnic Institute of Terre Haute, and his Negro servant and the strange death of Whitmore in the Terre Haute House, perhaps in consequence of his experimenting with time.

Ehrmann turned next to poetry in *Breaking Home Ties* (New York, 1904), a poem in blank verse based on the picture of Hovenden which shows the son of a family saying farewell to the family group. Not only is the scene itself described, but the crux of the poem lies in the farewell speeches of the father and mother, in which the poet takes opportunity to interweave his own views on many subjects. *A Prayer and Other Selections* (New York, [1906]) features the famous "Prayer," first published in 1903, which was written by Ehrmann when he was ill and lonely and which received much publicity when a framed copy was stolen from the Indiana Building at the St. Louis World's Fair. Its creed is work and love, and it has been a source of comfort and inspiration to thousands of readers—as evidenced by the sale in some ten years after its publication of over a million copies and its translation into thirty-three languages.

The remainder of Ehrmann's poetry was issued mostly in three volumes: *Max Ehrmann's Poems* (Terre Haute, Indiana, 1906), *The Poems of Max Ehrmann* (New York, 1910), and *The Poems of Max Ehrmann,* edited by Bertha K. Ehrmann (Boston, 1948). The earlier poems are Whitmanesque, and much of the production is in a style of prose-poetry or polyphonic prose. There are narratives and sketches, such as "A Few Hours Ago"; yet much of the material is in conventional verse forms, and he uses the sonnet effectively. At times his poetry is exquisite in its sweetness, careful diction, and melody; but here and there crudities, imperfect images, and incomplete expression mar the over-all effect, as in the case of "His Wife." Throughout all his verse—and, indeed, all his works— there flows a strong idealism, a love of humanity, an appreciation of the worth of toil, the need for quiet and reflection in the midst of a busy life, condemnation of materialism, sympathy for the unfortunate, and a general affirmation of the spiritual values of life. The poet has power, sincerity, originality, a keen understanding of human nature, and courage in his convictions.

This idealism is expressed also in his dramas. *The Light of the Sun* (New York, 1910), a beautiful, intense, and tragic work, was followed by *The Wife of Marobius* (New York, 1911), a play overpraised in some contemporary newspaper reviews, but still a warm and finely chiseled presentation, laid in pre-Christian Rome, of the difference between love of beauty of the body and love of beauty of the soul. *Jesus: A Passion Play* (New York, 1915) attracted some little attention because of its beauty of style, its sense of nobility and heartbreak, and the presentation of the Biblical characters as simple, ardent Orientals; but probably his best play is *David and Bathsheba* (published in *The Drama*, No. 28, November, 1917), another beautiful Biblical work, showing understanding of the historical period and spiritual power. *Farces: the Bank Robbery; the Plumber* (Terre Haute, Indiana, [1927]) are very light but delightful pieces; and a final play, *Eternal Male and Female,* was published only in the posthumous *The Wife of Marobius and Other Plays* (Boston, 1949) and dramatizes the contest between the sexes in the love life.

Several pamphlets show another side of Ehrmann: *The Gay Life; Scarlet Sketches; A Goose with a Rose in Her Mouth, and Other Stories; His Beautiful Wife, and Other Stories* (all issued in 1925 in Terre Haute); and *A Virgin's*

Dream and Other Verses (Terre Haute, Indiana, [1928]). These are all preachments, in the form of short story, sketch, or verse, against the evils attending sexual immorality—condemning men for forcing ignorant, innocent girls into prostitution through their lust or, as employers, through paying low wages, while the men themselves remain outwardly blameless, and condemning women who take up willingly the life of sin. *The Gay Life* also includes condemnation of the type of marriage in which women are little more than prostitutes. In all these pamphlets Ehrmann's scorching social criticism sears the reader with its force; and the poet's plea for a spiritual and intellectual, as well as physical, attraction between the sexes rings out. Other booklets are *Be Quiet, I'm Talking* (Terre Haute, Indiana, 1926), which contains conversations on such subjects as literature, religion, science, and sex, and *Love from Many Angles* (Girard, Kansas, 1926), which is in the form of little sentence and paragraph essays on love.

Ehrmann's two last publications present his final words on life and living. *Desiderata* (Terre Haute, Indiana, 1927), a very short prose-poem, reveals the poet's soul in a state of serenity and confidence and reflects his tolerance, friendliness, sincerity, and love; it is a devotional creed for living. On the other hand, *Worldly Wisdom* (Girard, Kansas, [1934]), his last publication of verse, is based on the apocryphal book of Ecclesiasticus, the Wisdom of Jesus, Son of Sirach and gives practical advice on daily life. Ehrmann's *Journal* was edited and published by his wife in 1952.[32]

In summation we may observe that Max Ehrmann did his best work in his poetry. His novels are interesting but

[32] Published by Bruce Humphries, Inc., 1952. Ehrmann's papers are deposited in the DePauw University Archives.

mediocre; his plays, though in some ways striking, made
little lasting impression; and his Scarlet Women Series,
as he subtitled his booklets on social criticism, is full of
his keen sense of justice, and sympathy with the less fortunate, but is undistinguished. Here, then, was a great-
souled man, but one whose writings, though interesting
and sometimes valuable, missed greatness.

James Buchanan Elmore

If there is any difficulty in evaluating Ehrmann, there
is none whatsoever in pigeonholing James Buchanan
Elmore (1857-1942), "The Bard of Alamo," whose verse is
so utterly wretched and miserable that it is almost good;
and, strangely, it has received much attention. In spite of—
or perhaps because of—this quality no account of the literature of Indiana would be complete without a look into
his work.

In the introduction to his *Indiana Authors and Their
Books, 1816-1916* Banta discusses Indiana poets whose
verse was of a quality high enough to be paid for and also
poets whose verse was produced late in life, often after
their retirement, and who published their work privately.
Then, Banta continues:

> Between the paid and the self-published poets there is an-
> other and an interesting class. This third variety of Indiana
> poet paid for printing, it is true, but he bargained the local
> printer down to the ultimate dime. When an edition of the
> book came out he peddled it from door to door and from
> street corner to street corner and sold it with every art known
> to salesmanship. Not infrequently, if the work descended to
> a really remarkable literary depth, these people made re-
> spectable profits.

Such, to a superlative degree, was James Buchanan Elmore,
"The Bard of Alamo," unofficial Poet Laureate of Indiana,
who combined farming, poesy inspired by a genius of per-

fectly hopeless and unbelievable ineptitude, and a keen sense of personal publicity values. Elmore, author of such classics as "The Monon Wreck," died in his eighties possessed of five hundred acres of Montgomery County land, the fruit of his pen and his plow about equally.[33]

Elmore was born on January 25, 1857, on a farm near Alamo, Indiana, and was graduated from the Alamo Acadamy. He married in 1880 and taught school for some twenty years, farming in the summers. His poems appeared originally in the poet's column of the Crawfordsville *Journal,* whose city editor, Jesse Green, frivolously bestowed upon him the title of "The Bard of Alamo," which stuck with Elmore all his life and by which he is still known. From the *Journal* the poems were soon reprinted in the Indianapolis *News;* and eventually they were taken up by the New York *Sun* and by newspapers in Chicago, Cleveland, and elsewhere. Before long Elmore found himself possessing a nationwide fame of a sort.

He wrote primarily of rural scenes and activities familiar to the Hoosier and Midwestern farmer, as the titles of many of his poems indicate: "Sugar Making," "The Frog," "The Old Sawmill," "Katie Gathers Greens," "The Good Old Sheep-Sorrel Pie," the humorous "Shoe Cobbler," and the oft-recited "The Monon Wreck" with its well-known line, "Cut, oh, cut my leg away!" Although a few stories are included in his books, his production was mainly poetry. The volumes, many of them published in several editions—the original editions for many years now have been much sought after by collectors all over the world—are as follows: *Love Among the Mistletoe and Poems* (Alamo, Indiana, 1899); *Poems* (Alamo, Indiana, 1901); *A Lover in Cuba and Poems* (Alamo, Indiana, 1901); Supplement, *A Lover in Cuba and Poems* (Nash-

[33] Page xvi.

ville, Tennessee, 1902); *Twenty-five Years in Jackville, A Romance in the Days of "The Golden Circle" and Selected Poems* (Alamo, Indiana, 1904); and *Autumn Roses* (Alamo, Indiana, 1907). His son published posthumously *Nature Poems and Pure Literature* (n.p., 1954).

Elmore wrote also on other subjects, such as politics, city slickers, and crime, and soon after the turn of the century he toured the nation, reading his verse. At his death on the same farm where he was born, on March 12, 1942, his estate was found to be worth $50,000, much of which evidently came from the sale of his books.[34]

William Dudley Foulke

William Dudley Foulke (pseudonym—Robert Barclay Dillingham, 1848-1935), fortunately, penned materials of a happier sort than Elmore, the Bard. Foulke was essentially a man of affairs and was known more as a worker for Civil Service reform and woman suffrage, as a writer on social, historical, and biographical subjects, and as a scholar, editor, translator, and orator than as an author of novels and poetry. Nevertheless, his imaginative work entitles him to our consideration.

Son of a minister of the Society of Friends who, at one time, also served as principal of Friends Seminary in New York City, Foulke was born November 20, 1848, in that city, was graduated from the Friends Seminary in 1863, received the A.B. degree from Columbia University in 1869, was graduated from the Columbia Law School in

[34] Life of Elmore obtained from Banta, *Indiana Authors and Their Books*, 102-3; from De Forest O'Dell, "Unheralded Hoosier Poet," in *American Mercury*, 51 (1940), 422; and from Professor Paul Fatout of Purdue University, "The Sweet Poet of Ripley Township," a paper read at the annual meeting of the Indiana College English Association in May, 1941, quoted in Barry, A Biographical and Bibliographical Dictionary of Indiana Authors, 74-77.

1871, and began the practice of law in New York City that year. The following year he received the A.M. degree from Columbia University and married Mary Taylor Reeves of Richmond, Indiana. He continued to practice law in New York until 1876, at which time he and his wife moved to Richmond, Indiana, where he entered a law partnership and then became part owner and an editor of the Richmond *Palladium* for a few months. From 1909 to 1912 he continued his interest in journalism by becoming one of the owners and the editor of the Richmond *Item*. He was a member of the Indiana State Senate from 1883 to 1885 and in the latter year attracted attention, when he was president of the Indiana Civil Service Reform Association, by serving on a committee which exposed abuses in the State Hospital for the Insane. Following his chairmanship of a committee of the National Civil Service Reform League, President Theodore Roosevelt appointed him in 1901 to the United States Civil Service Commission. He was a friend of Albert J. Beveridge and worked with him in the Progressive Movement; he was for some time president of the American Woman's Suffrage Association. In 1890 Foulke ceased practicing law and devoted his time thenceforth to reform movements, journalism, traveling, and literature. He was long active in community affairs, and he gave the dedicatory address at the unveiling of the statue of James Whitcomb Riley in Greenfield in 1918. His death occurred in Richmond on May 30, 1935.[35]

Foulke's novels are only mediocre. His first, *Maya. A Story of Yucatan* (New York, 1900), is somewhat reminiscent of Lew Wallace's *The Fair God,* but falls far short

[35] Biography of Foulke taken from newspaper articles collected in the Indiana Biography Series, 4:185-86 and 14:80-81, in the Indiana Division of the State Library, and from Banta, *Indiana Authors and Their Books,* 113.

of it. Set against the background of the period of the en-
slavement of the Mayas by the Spanish invaders, this is
the story of Sandoval, one of the survivors of a small band
of Balboa's men who were sent back to Hispaniola
to deliver gold and to obtain provisions but who were
shipwrecked in Yucatan and most of whom succumbed to
fevers or to the hostile Mayas. Sandoval escapes from one
tribe, is taken for a god by another, marries a native
princess, and the couple are saved from death only by
the Spanish conquest of the country. The great defect
in what could be a breath-taking narrative is the general
lack of description and dramatization. This same fault
is disclosed also in *The Quaker Boy* (New York, 1910),
which was reissued the next year under the title of
Dorothy Day. In the guise of the autobiography of Robert
Barclay Dillingham, the story, much of which resembles
the life of Foulke himself, is told of a youth from his
childhood in New York City as the overprotected son of
Quaker parents, his schooling and college days, through
his experience as a soldier in the Union Army, when he
was dangerously wounded, to the day when he and his
fiancée listen to Lincoln give his Gettysburg Address.

Foulke's verse is considerably better than his fiction.
Maya. A Drama (New York, 1911) recounts, in good blank
verse, the story already told in his novel, *Maya. A Story
of Yucatan,* but condenses the action somewhat and evidences a slight mysticism. This is definitely closet drama.
In *Lyrics of War and Peace* (Indianapolis, 1916) one finds
nicely tempered and fanciful verse, mostly sonnets, with
much that reflects domestic happiness and that is spiritually comforting; yet, almost all that he has to say has
been said better by others. This same criticism is true in
some measure of most of his poetry. *To-day and Yesterday.
Sonnets and Other Verses* (New York, 1920) contains some

beautiful love sonnets, high-minded pieces on public affairs, and a section of war poems in which he first pleads
for American entrance into World War I and then sets
forth his sympathy with the cause. This volume includes
his "Centennial Ode, Read on Admission Day at the
State House, Indianapolis, 1916," emphasizing the history
of the state, the strength and courage of the pioneers, the
ideals of liberty, and the need to ward off a possible in-
vader; and although the poem was written in sincerity,
it has not deserved remembrance. *Songs of Eventide,
Heloise, Maya* (Indianapolis, 1928) reprints his poetic
drama previously discussed along with a lengthy poem,
beautifully written in blank verse, retelling the story of
Heloise and Abelard. The rest of the book is verse of
better quality than that previously published, serene
and beautiful, giving a sense of calm resignation, of content with life, and of sorrow for the glories that are passed.
The verse is in conventional forms. One of his best poems
is the following:

Looking Backward

Now cometh evening on; the air is still;
The noonday's glare and glitter could not last;
Yet while the shadows creep o'er field and hill,
Bright memories peer from out a golden past.
Like the first star that trembles in the sky
When darkness falls, so through the clear blue deep,
A vision comes from out the years gone by,
Ere I compose my heart to quiet sleep;
A brown-haired girl whose locks are now of snow—
A song that still is ringing in mine ears—
Dark, tender eyes, that ever softer grow—
A love that wanes not with the waning years.
And now we stand beside an opening gate
To the dim world beyond, and smiling, wait.[36]

[36] *Songs of Eventide,* 11.

His last book of verse, *Earth's Generations Pass* (New York, 1930), reissues much of his earlier work, continues the atmosphere of serenity and idealism of the previous volume and contains some of his translations. We must conclude, then, that in spite of some pleasing verse, Foulke is only a minor figure in literature.

William Vaughn Moody

No such characterization, however, can be made of one of the highest ranking American poets of the twentieth century, William Vaughn Moody (1869-1910), who is the next figure in Indiana poetry, a tragic figure in that he died before his capabilities had been fully realized. He was born on July 8, 1869, in Spencer, Indiana, the sixth in a family of seven children, whose mother, Henrietta Emily Stoy, came of pioneer Indiana stock. His father was Francis Burdette Moody, a retired captain of a river steamer which had made runs between Pittsburgh and New Orleans until Southern soldiers seized it at the outbreak of the Civil War. When Moody was a year old, his family moved to New Albany, Indiana, where he grew up and where he began writing poetry at fifteen. In high school he was editor of two school papers, and after graduating he studied art for a year at a school in Louisville. After the death of his mother in 1884 and that of his father two years later, the family was broken up, and for a year Moody taught a country school near New Albany. He then prepared for admission to Harvard by studying at Riverview Acadamy, New York, supporting himself by teaching. He had only twenty-five dollars in his pocket when he entered Harvard in 1889, but he completed the four-year course in three years, meanwhile earning his way and helping a sister by teaching, tutoring, and typing. Still, he managed to find time to participate in literary activities, writing and serving as an editor of the *Harvard Monthly;* and he associated with such fellow students as Robert Herrick and George Santayana. Having completed his graduation requirements, he spent his senior year in Europe, paying his way by tutoring a wealthy boy, and returned for his graduation in 1893 and the reading of his class day poem. He was in the Harvard Graduate School from 1893 to 1895, earning his expenses the first year by doing editorial work for Bulfinch's *Mythology,* along with his good friend Robert Morse Lovett, and by serving as assistant in the English departments of Harvard and Radcliffe College the second year.

In the fall of 1895 he joined the faculty of the University of Chicago, a relationship which was to prove happy for the University but frustrating for Moody. Here in spite of an association with friends like John Matthews Manly, who later edited the poet's works, the young instructor in English found his duties tedious and confining, interfering with his chosen vocation as a poet. Nevertheless, he was an extremely conscientious teacher, carefully preparing his brilliant lectures on English literature and writing long, detailed criticisms on the themes of his students, who called their reserved, sensitive instructor "the man in the iron mask." He looked forward to vacations, when he had freedom to write; in January, 1898, he computed that "April is only eighty-eight lectures, forty committee meetings, and several thousand themes away!"[37] Sometime later he paraphrased Wordsworth in saying, "My heart leaps up when I behold a calendar on the sly!"[38] He took several leaves of absence, such as 1898-99, when he edited the Cambridge edition

[37] *Some Letters of William Vaughn Moody,* edited with an Introduction by Daniel G. Mason (Boston, 1931), xxi.

[38] *Ibid.*

of Milton, but still was advanced to the rank of assistant professor in 1901. In spite of the offer of President Harper to give him full salary if he would teach only one quarter a year, he did not teach after 1902 and retained only a nominal connection with the University from 1902 until 1907. He had felt since boyhood that his life was to be dedicated to poetry, and he resisted all temptations that would prevent him from pursuing that main interest, preferring a lesser security with liberty to do as he wished. One of the reasons why he was able to burn his academic bridges behind him lay in the publication, with Robert M. Lovett, of *A History of English Literature* (New York, 1902), and *A First View of English and American Literature* (New York, 1905), both of which books were successful and were later revised. The first text remains popular even today.[39]

His first publication of imaginative material was *The Masque of Judgment. A Masque-Drama in Five Acts, and a Prelude* (Boston, 1900), which had been begun three years before in the Italian Tyrol and was a part of his dramatic trilogy on the Promethean theme. He took a camping trip in the Rocky Mountains with Hamlin Garland in the summer of 1901, and that same year his *Poems* was published in Boston. While in Greece in 1902 he read Greek tragedy; then he spent the next few years in New York, Boston, and Chicago. The second of his trilogy of verse dramas, meant to be the first in order, was *The Fire-Bringer* (Boston, 1904). He made altogether four trips to the Far West and three more to Europe.

On a visit to Arizona in 1905, during which he lived with the Hopi Indians for a week, he planned *The Great*

---

[39] The 1956 edition was revised by Fred B. Millett.

Divide. A Play (New York, 1906), originally called *The Sabine Woman,* based on a true incident told to him by Mrs. Harriett Converse Brainerd, whom he later married. It was produced first in Chicago in 1906 and, after revision, was performed that fall in New York. Although in 1908 he had been granted the degree of Doctor of Literature by Yale and had been elected to the American Academy of Arts and Letters, it was this play that brought him popular fame. Though some branded it as amateurish, it was generally hailed as an important addition to American drama.

His second prose drama, *The Faith Healer. A Play in Four Acts* (Boston, 1909), revised to three acts and republished in New York in 1910, was inspired by newspaper accounts of Schlatter, a faith healer, and was performed at Harvard, in St. Louis, and in New York. It was not so successful as *The Great Divide,* but it confirmed Moody's place as a leader in the American drama.

Moody, always strong physically, ruddy in complexion and fond of outdoor sports, enjoyed perfect health till 1906, when a growth was removed from his leg, which had been injured four years earlier while he was climbing Mount Parnassus. Then in the spring of 1908, while living in New York, he suffered a severe case of typhoid fever which permanently impaired his health. He convalesced during the summer with the poet Ridgely Torrence, on an island off the Maine coast, where he was nursed by Mrs. Brainerd, who divorced her husband to marry Moody, becoming his wife on May 7, 1909. The work which he did to perfect *The Faith Healer* came too soon after his attack of typhoid. While visiting in London he became very ill and returning to this country, died of a brain disease in Colorado Springs on October 17, 1910,

at the age of forty-one.[40] He had completed only one act of
"The Death of Eve," intended as the last play of the dramatic trilogy. His *Gloucester Moors, and Other Poems* was
published that same year in Boston; and his *Poems and
Plays,* with an introduction by his former department head
and friend at the University of Chicago, John M. Manly,
was issued in two volumes (Boston, 1912). Later publications were *Some Letters of William Vaughn Moody,* edited
by Daniel G. Mason (Boston, 1913), *Selected Poems of William Vaughn Moody,* edited by Robert M. Lovett (Boston,
1931), and *Letters to Harriet,* edited by Percy MacKaye
(Boston, 1935).

Moody's writings, with the exception of the last three
listed and his scholarly books, merit detailed analysis.
First, however, it must be realized that the greater part
of the works of this taciturn poet, who, according to his
friends, required a pipeful of tobacco to make a remark,
was experimental and, hence, was destroyed. He never
succumbed to the temptation to overpublish; therefore,
his total production was rather small—much less, for example, than that of many other literary figures, including
Riley, Nicholson, and Tarkington. But that small production was one of quality, and he saw to it that nothing immature or ill-advised remained.

The trilogy of verse dramas, though unfinished and
never presented, still supplies the key to his two successfully staged prose plays, because all his dramatic production
revolves about one central problem, the age-old question
of sin, which has been so vexing to mankind since the

[40] Biography of Moody obtained mostly from Stanley J. Kunitz (ed),
Authors Today and Yesterday (New York, 1933), 478-81, and the article
by Walter P. Eaton, in *Dictionary of American Biography, Authors Edition,* 13:108-10. Many accounts and studies of Moody are available. See,
for example, David D. Henry, *William Vaughn Moody. A Study* (Boston,
1934).

days of Adam and Eve and which Milton, Pope, Hawthorne, Whitman, Melville, and countless others have
pondered over. More definitely, this is the sense of sin
and its power of destruction of the freedom of the soul.
For Moody draws a distinction between evil as an absolute and the sense of evil or of sin, which may have little
to do with evil itself and which may arise from heredi-
tary prohibitions or inhibitions; and in all his dramatic
writings he attacks this sense of sin, which has so influenced
the American conscience from the days of the Calvinistic
Puritans. Therefore, the philosophical import of his plays
is greater than their stage merits. Indeed, for good
or ill, the verse trilogy presents such a grand Miltonic
design that it is difficult to grasp its full significance; the
central idea is the inseperableness and the unity of man
and God.

This idea is brought forth in the first of the trilogy,
The Fire-Bringer, which, making use of the Greek myth
of how Prometheus stole fire from heaven for the use of
mankind, gives a Messianic cast to the reaction of humanity to the unsuccessful attempt of Prometheus to destroy man's dependence on God. Excellent blank verse
and diction disguise a certain heavy quality of expression;
nevertheless, the play was acclaimed by critics as giving
Moody first place among American poets. In the complex
second drama, *The Masque of Judgment,* the theme is
re-presented in showing that if God were to destroy man,
he would also annihilate Himself. The angel Raphael believes that in permitting sin and then punishing it God
blundered, and the serpent defeats the Hebrew and Puritan God of Wrath because of His error in punishing man
for following his natural instincts instead of teaching
him more fully how to avoid sin.

The last of the trilogy, "The Death of Eve," was in-

tended once more to affirm the unity of God and His creation and the impossibility of separating them. The aged
Eve, now grown wiser through experience, and seeing that
her sin was not necessarily the fatal act that it appeared to
be and that God's creations exist within God, was to bring
Adam and Cain back to Eden, the scene of the original
sin, for a daring attempt at reconciliation of mankind
with God. The sense of sin would be eradicated by Eve's
love of mankind. How unfortunate it is that this play was
unfinished; for in addition to rendering the other two
plays the more intelligible, it would have been in itself a
unique poem, Miltonic in originality! Literal believers in
the Biblical narrative of creation may be somewhat
shocked by the liberties the poet has taken here. Yet, in
the trilogy Moody is interested in Greek myth and Hebrew story only as a foundation on which to build his
philosophy, which is a poetic solution of the problem of
life. The three plays contain much of his best lyric poetry.

The trilogy is consistent with the prose plays in meaning. In *The Great Divide* the cultures of the Eastern seaboard and the West are contrasted through a clever theatrical method of placing an individualistic New England girl, whose personality and soul have been stunted
by the inhibitions handed down to her by her Puritan ancestors, in the Far West on a trip, where, alone in a cabin
one night, she is accosted by three drunken cowboys who
intend to attack her. In order to save herself, she promises
to marry the best of the three. This man defends her from
the other two; and holding grimly to her promise according to her rigid moral code, she becomes his wife. But
then the couple, Stephen and Ruth, strangely, fall in love
with each other; ennobled by love, Stephen rises to
become a settled, successful mining prospector, whereas

Ruth is tortured by his statement that he came to her through "whiskey, the sun, and the Devil." Believing that they must be cleansed by self-denial, she flees to the East, but Stephen follows and fights a difficult, but eventually successful, battle against not only her ideas but the entire sense of sin. Here is an unusual solution of the problem of sin. The wages of sin are not death but rather life and love and happiness; human instinct is not misleading but fundamentally right. This approach is fatalistic, pagan, and Whitmanesque. As one character says, in Act I,

Happiness is its own justification, and it's the sacreder the more unreasonable it is. It comes or it doesn't, that's all you can say about it. And when it comes, one has the sense to grasp it or one hasn't.

Also, the reader can see in this play Moody's philosophy of love as an ennobling and saving force which rescues Stephen from brutality and Ruth, the unwilling wife, from pride and the false sense of sin.

From the point of view of literary interest we might note in passing that the figure of the heroic Western "bad man," the "diamond in the rough," such as Stephen is, in a sense, was not at all new in Moody's day. Bret Harte, long before, had created this sort of character in a rougher, yet more sentimental, role in John Oakhurst, the gambler, in "Tennessee's Partner" and in "The Luck of Roaring Camp." Variations of this character, seen in action against the background of different situations, are found in Augustin Daly's *Horizon* (1871), Augustus Thomas' *In Mizzoura* (1883), Clyde Fitch's *The Cowboy and the Lady* (1899), and David Belasco's *The Girl of the Golden West* (1905). Of course, the type persists today, particularly on the screen. One might add, also, that Moody refused offers as high as fifty thousand dollars from publishing houses to turn this play into a novel, believing that the two art forms can not be confounded.[41]

His play, *The Faith Healer*, considered by some critics as better than *The Great Divide* and by others as only a potboiler, was not so successful, according to Manly, because Moody refused to build up through music and the excitement of a crowd at the beginning of Act I an emotional atmosphere by which the play could have been made more acceptable to an audience.[42] This story, set in a small Midwestern town, tells of Michaelis, a mystic from the Southwest, who heals the invalid aunt of a young girl, Rhoda, and how news of this astonishing event brings many requesting his aid. But as he heals them, he unexpectedly falls in love with Rhoda, to whom sex has signified only sin, because of her former suffering of a seduction. The sense of guilt of the two results in Michaelis' losing his power to heal, with sad results to his followers, until the two realize the truth of the unity of body and soul. Thus, we have again Moody's revolt against the sense of sin, which, he implies, is not evil itself. But the problem of religion is only incidental here, as the main conflict is between dedication to a calling and human love. This was a personal problem with Moody, for he long debated the extent to which a person dedicated to a noble purpose can share the common life. It is interesting that in three versions of the play that are extant, written at different times, the first has Michaelis renounce love for his work, in the second he does the opposite, and in the

[41] However, a contemporary Indiana writer, Joseph A. Hayes, does not share Moody's concept of art. He wrote *The Desperate Hours* (New York, 1954) first as a novel and then as a stage play (New York, 1955), and it was also produced in the movies.

[42] *The Poems and Plays of William Vaughn Moody*, with an Introduction by John M. Manly (2 vols. Boston, 1912), 1:xliv.

last version he realizes that the two can be combined, on an unselfish level.

Both prose plays, then, represent revolt, revolt of the individual against custom and social law. This type of drama found its best expression at the time in the work of Moody, George Cabot Lodge, and Percy MacKaye; but Moody's was the strongest voice of his time in making the stage again a criticism of life. And his trilogy qualified him to share in the revival of poetic drama.[43]

Some part of what has been said thus far in regard to his plays may be carried over into an analysis of his poetry. Moody was the center of a circle of younger poets—Edwin Arlington Robinson, Ridgely Torrence, and Percy Mac-Kaye in particular. As before remarked, much of his poetry he destroyed if it displeased him, and he has left a rather small body of verse, compared with that published by many other poets. He was a meticulous craftsman and a perfectionist; yet with all his deep poetic instinct and sensitivity to rich melody, rhythm, and sonorous diction and with his preoccupation with truth and philosophy, he took pleasure in the physical world, and his verse is in no way unhealthy or removed from life. It is a harmonious mixture of beauty, sensuousness, vivid imagery, careful logic, and philosophy. That his poems must often be reread several times in order for the reader to obtain their full meaning is evident.

[43] For the basic concept of Moody's plays as all centered in the problem of evil and the sense of sin, I am indebted mostly to Sculley Bradley, "The Emergence of the Modern Drama," in *Literary History of the United States,* edited by Robert E. Spiller, *et al.,* 2:1013-15. In this discussion of the dramas I have utilized also ideas found in Robert M. Lovett's Introduction to the *Selected Poems of William Vaughn Moody* (Boston, 1931) and Manly's Introduction to *The Poems and Plays of Moody.* Henry's *William Vaughn Moody* has also been a help, particularly pages 114-16, 192-94. In addition, Lovett and Manly have been of aid with the poetry.

His poetic production is free from response to the unimportant and the obvious and surface attractiveness; and
probably this is one reason why, in spite of his many ex-
cellences, he is not particularly popular, for his verse is
appreciated primarily by the careful student of poetry,
for whom art is not obvious and trivial. His themes are
the same as those of many poets before him—love, God,
the soul, suffering, the meaning of life, patriotism, protest against injustice—yet he always sees his subject from a
new angle or with fresh significance, transmuting the old
into his own. An inexhaustible storehouse of images is ever
at his command. His diction is highly condensed and
meaningful, as in "Good Friday Night," in which poem
throng such arresting combinations of words and thought
as "heart-stung," "throned in its hundred candles," and
"the doll-face, waxen white, flowered out a living dimness." There is veritable magic in the many simple phrases
which call forth a significance beyond the words themselves; his lyrics abound in this indefinable aspect, like the
songs of Pandora in *The Fire-Bringer*. Believing in a
poetic diction, still he did not turn his back on the values
of colloquial language. His images tend at times to supplant his ideas, becoming allegorical and enigmatic, as
seen in "The Brute," "The Quarry," or "The Moon-
Moth"; his is a gorgeousness and sweetness that is not overdone, but is crystal, and as a scholar he was thoroughly
at home in various kinds of rhythm, meter, and stanza.
The ode, nevertheless, was his favorite, and "An Ode in
Time of Hesitation" reaches a highwater mark in public
poetry. It and "On a Soldier Fallen in the Philippines"
show an intelligent, idealistic patriotism unswayed by the
conception of "manifest destiny" of the Spanish-American
War period. Moody, nevertheless, was still a product of
his time. As Robert M. Lovett points out,

With all his forward-looking qualities, Moody was, after all, distinctly a poet of his age. In looking back over his work, it is interesting to note how the forces of the time wrought themselves out in the form and substance of his verse. There is the eclecticism of the dying Victorian period, and its self-consciousness, its moral striving. There is something of the realism which reflected the influence of science, and the tendency of realism to extend itself into symbolism by the intimations which it carries of the world beyond that which we see and touch. Moody passed from the realm ruled by Tennyson and Browning, Rossetti and Swinburne, to that in which he was akin to Maeterlinck, Francis Thompson, Arthur Symons, and Ernest Dowson. Like the last, he confronted the eternal problem of the dualism of flesh and spirit and their inevitable union, although his solution was not the same.[44]

This poet was many-sided and cannot easily be characterized. What appeals to us most about Moody is his humanity, for he accepted man as he found him, pitied and admired and glorified him. However, the copiousness and austerity of his style reflect his divided character, since he was something of a pagan in his joy in life and nature, but he still cherished a sense of the mystery of life, which made him reverent. Added to this complexity was a temperamental mysticism which allowed him the joy of listening to divine melodies unheard by others and of tasting a divine nectar as he searched for a sight of heaven. He felt the nearness of God and the reality of His being. Yet, he was a modern in his thinking and sought the rights of all men, as evidenced by his famous poem, "Gloucester Moors." Achieving a strong union of poet and preacher, he still did not arrive at a happy solution of life, such as, perhaps, in the optimism of Hovey or in the socialism of

[44] Quoted from Robert M. Lovett, Introduction to *Selected Poems of William Vaughn Moody* (copyright 1931 by the Houghton Mifflin Company), xci-xcii, by permission of the publisher.

Markham; and he thought that creation was moving toward some great, far-off end, unknown to man. What a pity that the sensitive seeker after truth died just as his poetry was becoming sweeter and as he showed promise of becoming as eminent in the drama as Eugene O'Neill!

That he has not continued popular is due in part to his being a transitional figure between the nineteenth-century poets and the new group that suddenly burst into prominence shortly after he died. In 1911, the year after Moody's death, the poets who called themselves the Imagists formed an association in London which included Ezra Pound, Amy Lowell, H.D. and Richard Aldington; and these Imagists undertook a rather disorganized crusade against the conventional forms of poetry in rhyme, rhythm, and meter. That they to some extent succeeded is a matter of record, and the tide of poetry turned away from the verse that Moody had written. When Moody had first appeared in print in 1900, interest in poetry was at a comparatively low ebb, and publishers were reluctant to risk a venture with it; but in 1928 a total of fully fifty volumes was presented for consideration for the Pulitzer Prize. Moody's early death came too close to this poetic revolution, and he was partly obscured by it.

An excellent criticism of William Vaughn Moody's work was offered in *The Dial* of December 16, 1912, by a fastidious critic, William Morton Payne, and with it we close this analysis:

   . . . the main thing to be emphasized concerning Moody is that he was a poet by the grace of God, and such a poet as had not been raised up before him in America—or even in the English-speaking world—since the eclipse of the great line of the older singers. . . . He seems to be the one authentic "maker" that our young century has given to the world, achieving a height that none of his contemporary

fellows-craftsmen in the poetic art, either in England or
America, could attain. . . .

The stupendous task which Moody set himself in the
trilogy is the highest which poetry has ever attempted. It
is the task of Aeschylus and Dante and Milton, the task of
Goethe in his "Faust" and of Shelley in his "Prometheus Un-
bound." It is Milton's attempt to "justify the ways of God
to man" coupled with the attempt of the later poets to justify
the ways of man to God.[45]

To pass from someone of the stature of William Vaughn
Moody to six lesser lights, who conclude the poetry of the
Golden Age, is like turning one's eyes from the brilliance
of a comet to the dimness of stars obscured by the glare
of light. Yet, in spite of the comet, the other stars still
twinkle; and if the astronomer is to plot the course of the
heavens, he must at length focus his telescope on the faint
bodies.

Wilbur D. Nesbit

Wilbur Dick Nesbit (1871-1927) was born on September
16, 1871, in Xenia, Ohio, and attended the schools of
Cedarville, Ohio. Taking up the trade of a printer, he
went to Anderson, Indiana, where he began his long career in journalism by serving as city editor of the Anderson *Times;* he then removed to Muncie, Indiana, and to
Indianapolis, where he worked in advertising and contributed to the Indianapolis *Journal.* He lived next in
the East, writing feature articles for the Baltimore *American,* then moved on to Chicago, where for some time he
conducted the column, "A Line o' Type or Two," in the
Chicago *Tribune,* later transferring to the Chicago *Evening Post.* Before he died, August 20, 1927, he had become

[45] "William Vaughn Moody," in *The Dial,* 53 (July-December, 1912):
484-85.

vice-president of a Chicago advertising agency. In addition to his journalistic endeavors he built a reputation as a toastmaster and after-dinner speaker; he published *After-Dinner Speeches and How to Make Them* (Chicago, 1927). He collaborated with the famous cartoonist, C. A. Briggs; among the writings which he produced for the theater was the libretto of a musical comedy, "Girl of My Dreams."[46]

Nesbit's list of publications is long and includes a book on advertising and many ephemeral and journalistic pieces. He has one novel, and several books of poetry. The novel, *The Gentleman Ragman. Johnny Thompson's Story of the Emigger* (New York, 1906), is slight in import but is a humorous portrayal of life in a small Ohio town as seen through the eyes of a boy of fifteen, who usually misunderstands the full significance of events. In addition to two books of children's verse—*The Jolly Kid Book* (Joliet, Illinois, 1926) and *As Children Do. Poems of Childhood* (Joliet, Illinois, 1929)—Nesbit published the following verse: *The Trail to Boyland and Other Poems* (Indianapolis, 1904), *A Book of Poems* (Evanston, Illinois, 1906), *The Land of Make-Believe and Other Christmas Poems* (New York, 1907), *A Friend or Two* (Chicago, 1910), *Friend O'Mine* (Chicago, 1912), *Your Best Friend* (Chicago, 1912), *The Paths of Long Ago* (Chicago, 1926), and *Sermons in Song. Poems of Homely Philosophy* (Joliet, Illinois, 1929). These are all of the popular sort, the kind of verse that finds its way into newspapers and scrapbooks. Some of it is melancholy in its reminiscence of the past, some of it recalls the lost days of youth and the simple life, as in "The Old Well," "Hickory Nuttin'," and "The Old-Time Fiddler"; some of it is scriptural in inspiration; some is in child's dialect, and some is

---

[46] Banta, *Indiana Authors and Their Books*, 236-37.

sentimental; but there is a spontaneity about it all and now and then a lilt and charm. One of his best-known poems is "Your Flag and My Flag."

Charles R. Williams

Charles Richard Williams (1853-1927) was another journalist, but his verse is better favored than Nesbit's. Born at Prattsburg, New York, he at length attended the University of Rochester, then the College of New Jersey (later Princeton), where in 1875 he received the A.B. degree. Following a year of teaching in the Princeton Preparatory School he studied in Europe for two years, then served as principal of the high school in Auburn, New York, 1878-79, and returned to Princeton for a year as tutor in Latin. After a brief term of editing *Potter's American Monthly* in 1881, he became professor of Greek at Lake Forest College, Lake Forest, Illinois, where he met Emma Almira Smith, marrying her in 1884. It was during this period that he edited *Selections from Lucian,* which went through several editions. In 1883 he was appointed literary editor of the New York *World* and was made assistant general manager of the Associated Press. In 1892 he took up the work for which he was to become so well known in Indiana, that of editor-in-chief of the Indianapolis *News,* whose founder, John H. Holliday, then retired from active management. As editor Williams established a correctness of style and language that set a standard for journalism in the Midwest. His wife died in 1895, and in 1902 he married Bertha Rose Knefler. When he retired from the *News* in 1911, he moved to Princeton, New Jersey, where he lived in the former home of Woodrow Wilson and shared in the life of the University. He died in Princeton on May 6, 1927.[47]

[47] Article by Christopher B. Coleman in the *Dictionary of American Biography, Authors Edition,* 20:252.

Though Williams followed mostly a journalistic career, still his interests were primarily scholarly and literary. In addition to his poetry, he wrote *The Life of Rutherford Birchard Hayes* (2 volumes. Boston, 1914), and edited five volumes of Hayes's letters. His three books of poetry evidence his scholarly as well as his imaginative endeavors; and although they include different types of verse, the general effect is one of end-stopped, singsong lines and a straining after dignified poetic diction. *In Many Moods* (Indianapolis, 1910) contains translations from Latin, Greek, French, and German poets and some rather well-worded sonnets. *Hours in Arcady* (Indianapolis, 1926) reprints some of these translations and poems and adds others. *The Return of the Prodigal. A Monodrama,* first published in 1912, was reissued along with other verse in *The Return of the Prodigal and Other Religious Poems* (Indianapolis, 1927). The title poem is a blank verse narrative, giving an imagined speech of the prodigal son of the New Testament narrative to his friends after he has returned home, recounting his wanderings and dissolute life and praising his father for taking him back. It is a pleasing, fanciful rendering of the story. A rhymed narrative of the birth of Jesus, "Christ Was Born in Bethlehem," and other religious pieces express a humble spirit and an abiding faith.

Louise Vickroy Boyd

The verse of Louise Esther Vickroy (Mrs. Samuel S.) Boyd (1827-1909) was published in periodicals during her lifetime and was collected in a single volume two years after her death, edited by another minor Indiana poet, Esther Griffin White. Mrs. Boyd was included in Coggeshall's *Poets and Poetry of the West,* and she contributed to such magazines as *Appleton's Journal, Graham's Magazine,* and *The Knickerbocker Magazine.* She was born on January 22, 1827, in Urbana, Ohio, and lived for a time in Johnstown, Ohio, and in Pennsylvania. Soon after the Civil War she was married to Dr. Samuel S. Boyd, who had served as a surgeon in the army, the couple then moving to Dublin, Indiana, where they remained for some twenty-five years. Here she was active in civic affairs and in the woman suffrage movement and continued to contribute verse to the periodicals already listed as well as to such magazines as *Century, Scribner's, Harper's Young People, The Woman's Journal,* and *Country Life in America.* She was one of the founders of The Western Association of Writers. She died July 25, 1909, in Ada, Ohio.[48]

Poems by Louise Vickroy Boyd (Richmond, Indiana, 1911) has some roughness, but the verse is usually light and lyrical. The volume contains much nature poetry, like "The Voice of the Wind"; some good pieces on history, like "Crossing the Delaware"; several fanciful, romantic stories, as "An Arab's Story," which is a narrative of the three wise men; a few Biblical verses; and some realistic descriptions and incidents. In addition to her verse she wrote also some expository material; and she has the distinction of publishing the first Indiana juvenile, entitled *Twilight Stories for Little People* (Philadelphia, 1869). This book was the beginning of a long and distinguished list of Hoosier contributions in the field of literature for children.[49]

[48] Parker and Heiney (eds.), *Poets and Poetry of Indiana,* 461, and Indiana Biography Series, 2:250-51.

[49] Banta maintains that Indiana has had practically a monopoly on the juvenile series novels since the publication by Mrs. J. R. Hibbard (known as Faith Wynne) , of Richmond, of *Flossy Lee* (1870) and *Flossy Lee at the Mountains* (1871). Then followed many other series, such as those of Elsie Dinsmore, The Little Colonel, The Bobbs Hill Boys, the Twins series, the Brownie Books, and Raggedy Ann. *Indiana Authors and Their Books,* xiii-xiv. More recently Hoosiers have contributed many volumes to the Childhood of Famous Americans series.

Esther Griffin White

Esther Griffin White (1869-1954) was not so important as Mrs. Boyd; her imaginative works are small in quantity and were not published by recognized presses, but she could produce beautiful sonnets. She was a newspaper woman of Richmond, Indiana, who attended the Richmond schools and then studied at Earlham College, 1887-92, and served on the staffs of various Richmond papers. She was known as an art collector and critic; and her political activity included the distinction of being the first woman to have her name on the official Indiana ballot, the first woman delegate to the Republican State Convention, the first woman candidate for mayor in Indiana, and the first woman to run for Congress.[50] *In the Orchestra* (Richmond, Indiana, 1915) and *Passion's Jewels and Other Sonnets of the Senses* (Centerville, Indiana, 1939) are small volumes containing some graceful, deftly written Italian sonnets with only a few artificialities and imperfections to mar their beauty. The first book includes a sonnet describing the sound of nearly every instrument of the orchestra; the latter book, published when the author was seventy, shows deep appreciation of love and the senses.[51]

William Herschell

A once popular, but almost subliterary, poet was the newspaper writer, William Herschell (1873-1939), whose song, "Long Boy," known familiarly from the beginning of the refrain as "Good-bye, Ma! Good-bye, Pa!" was one of the most popular American songs of World War I. Herschell was born on November 17, 1873, in Spencer,

---

[50] Banta, *op. cit.*, 337, and obituary notice in the Indianapolis *Star,* September 1, 1954, p. 17.

[51] Banta lists one other book, *In the Garden* (Richmond, Ind., 1936), which may consist of poetry, but no copy has been found.

Indiana, lived as a boy in Huntingburg, Indiana, where he began his journalistic work as a reporter for the local *Independent,* was connected three years with the Princeton *News,* then spent the rest of his life in Indianapolis, where he was employed for thirty-seven years by the Indianapolis *News,* primarily as a feature writer but later adding verse to his contributions. In 1908 he married Josephine Pugh. Wabash College, recognizing his war verse, awarded him an honorary A.M. degree in 1917. He died on December 2, 1939, in Indianapolis.[52]

Herschell's publications of poetry, collected mostly from the columns of the *News,* are as follows: *Songs of the Streets and Byways* (Indianapolis, 1915), *The Kid Has Gone to the Colors and Other Verse* (Indianapolis, 1917), *The Smile Bringer and Other Bits of Cheer* (Indianapolis, 1919), *Howdy All and Other Care-Free Rhymes* (Indianapolis, 1922), *Meet the Folks* (Indianapolis, 1924), and *Hitch and Come In* (Indianapolis, 1928). A posthumous publication by his widow was *Song of the Morning and Other Poems* (Indianapolis, 1940). The titles of these volumes are in themselves almost a sufficient indication of the type of verse, and little more needs be said. It is evident that Herschell received the mantle of Hoosier folksy poetry from Riley; yet the mantle fitted awkwardly. In spite of such popular poems as "Ain't God Good to Indiana?" and his war songs like "Long Boy," he was unable to capture the same happy combination of pathos, sentimentalism, humor, and homespun philosophy as Riley; even his sympathy with childhood and his excursions into dialect, though entertaining, do not approach the touch of the master, and his emphasis on city life did not complement Riley's emphasis on rural life.

[52] Banta, *Indiana Authors and Their Books,* 146.

Charles Leo O'Donnell

The last poet of the Golden Age is the Reverend Charles Leo O'Donnell, C.S.C. (1884-1934), former president of Notre Dame University. Father O'Donnell was born in the same town as Riley—Greenfield, Indiana—on November 15, 1884. He was graduated from Notre Dame in 1906, then followed advanced studies at Harvard, Holy Cross College, and the Catholic University of America, at which latter institution he was granted the Ph.D. degree in 1910, the same year that he was ordained a priest and was appointed professor of English literature at Notre Dame. He helped edit the book of *Notre Dame Verse* (Notre Dame, Indiana, 1917). During the First World War he served as chaplain with the Rainbow Division and was made Chevalier of the Crown of Italy by King Victor Emmanuel III. Father O'Donnell was the first president of the Catholic Poetry Society of America. He successfully guided the affairs of Notre Dame as president from 1928 until his death, June 5, 1934.[53]

Father O'Donnell published two studies of the English Catholic poet, Francis Thompson, and wrote the "Ode: for Indiana Day, Panama-Pacific International Exposition." His poetry was published primarily, however, in four volumes: *The Dead Musician and Other Poems* (New York, 1916), *Cloister and Other Poems* (New York, 1922), *A Rime of the Rood and Other Poems* (New York, 1928), and *Collected Poems,* compiled and edited by Father Charles M. Carey (Notre Dame, Indiana, 1942), published for the centennial of the university. His verse in all four of these books can be characterized as dominantly religious in tone, as one would expect, and also is inspired partly by nature, by his life at Notre Dame, and by love of Ireland. Although there is some uneven-

[53] Banta, *op. cit.,* 241, and Indiana Biography Series, 13:18.

ness, he often possesses a light, poetic touch, as in his sonnets; and pieces like the mystical "Ballad of Saint Christopher" are well worth the reader's time. He often puts the Catholic creed into pleasant lyrics and now and then into narrative poetry. Father O'Donnell, however, was evidently not much noticed outside his own circles.

Having now come to the close of the poetry of the Golden Age of Indiana Literature, perhaps we may venture a few generalizations. Obviously there are various kinds and qualities of poetry here represented. As far as types of verse go, we see that there is only one writer of humorous poetry, Silas B. McManus; two authors of primarily religious poetry, Sister Mary Genevieve Todd and Father Charles L. O'Donnell; and five poets with a degree of sentimentality: Benjamin S. Parker, Dulcina M. Jordan, Silas B. McManus, Wilbur D. Nesbit, and William Herschell—all of whom to some extent look back fondly to the golden days of yore. Of course, the master of sentimentalism is Riley. Also, we may observe that the influence of the frontier can no longer be seen so distinctly in the poetry of the Golden Age; yet some persons, such as Parker, still hark back frequently to the log-cabin days. The verse forms are now more varied than in the period of early Indiana literature, and the subjects used for poetry tend to be those utilized universally by poets. The famous poems of this period were written by Riley and Moody.

If we wish to rank these figures, we will understand that there is no doubt that the worst poet of all is the impossible, yet popular, James B. Elmore, and not many steps up the stairway from Elmore stands William Herschell, with his songs and folksy verse. Wilbur D. Nesbit, also, might be conceived of as occupying the same step with Herschell, with Dulcina M. Jordan, Philip Bevan, and Silas McManus arranging themselves a little above these two. About half way up the stairs—along about the landing—we see the mediocre poets: Benjamin S. Parker, Lee O. Harris, Albion Fellows Bacon, Sister Mary Genevieve Todd, William Dudley Foulke, Charles R. Williams, Louise Vickroy Boyd, Esther Griffin White, and Father Charles L. O'Donnell. A step or two above this group we find the first Indiana nature poet, Evaleen Stein, and, perhaps, on the next step up the idealist and social reformer, Max Ehrmann. Three or four steps from the top stands the dapper James Whitcomb Riley, with his pince-nez, white vest, and enormous gold watch chain; and on the very top step we see the quiet, shy William Vaughn Moody, with his eyes cast up toward the stars.

Moody's place as the best poet of the Golden Age can not be challenged—or, as a matter of fact, the greatest poet of all of Indiana literature—for in the period of early literature no one, not even Alice and Phoebe Cary or Sarah T. Bolton, can threaten his position; and in the period since the Golden Age only Marguerite Young and Margaret E. Bruner can even be mentioned in the same breath, but these two are far inferior to Moody. Moody, then, is the greatest Indiana poet.

Yet, we must recognize the fact that in the popular mind, not only in Indiana but all over the nation, millions of people who may never have heard of William Vaughn Moody will contend that the greatest Indiana poet is The Hoosier Poet, James Whitcomb Riley. For them, he *is* poetry.

5

THE NOVEL. PART I

As before indicated, the most outstanding contributions to American literature which were made during the Golden Age of Indiana literature fall in the field of the novel. The poets, though numbering nineteen, include only two names that are well known in American literature, James Whitcomb Riley and William Vaughn Moody. In the novel, on the other hand, there are thirty-four writers, eleven of whom—approximately one third—possess some degree of significance in American letters, to say nothing of Indiana literature itself.

The persons studied in this and the following chapter wrote mostly novels, though some of them published additional types of literature, such as poetry. In every case, however, we will discuss the complete literary work of each writer. The following novelists will be found included in other chapters because their primary contributions lie in other literary genres: George Ade belongs to the chapter on humor; and Lee O. Harris, Max Ehrmann, William D. Foulke, and Wilbur D. Nesbit have been discussed in the chapter on poetry.

Edward Eggleston

The first novelist is Edward Eggleston (1837-1902), the man who began the Golden Age of Indiana literature with his publication of *The Hoosier School-Master* in 1871 and who figures so strongly in the early development of realism in the United States. He is a significant figure in American literature and was the brother of another popular novelist, George Cary Eggleston.

The Eggleston brothers' father, Joseph Cary Eggleston, a graduate of the College of William and Mary, a lawyer, and member of both branches of the Indiana legislature, was of an important old family in Virginia; and the mother, Mary Jane Craig, was the daughter of an Indian fighter and frontiersman, Captain George Craig, who came of distinguished Kentucky lineage, with ancestral roots in Virginia.

Edward Eggleston was born in Vevay, Indiana, on December 10, 1837, and before his father's death from tuberculosis in 1846 spent much time on the Craig farm, outside Vevay, and attended a country school. He also made a long visit to an uncle in Decatur County, where he became more familiar with backwoods dialect and manners. After his father's death his mother became the wife of Williamson Terrell, a Methodist preacher; and Eggleston went in March, 1851, to their new home in New Albany. The family lived there a half year, stayed two years in Madison, and in 1853 returned to Vevay, where Eggleston was so fortunate as to have as his high-school teacher the inspirational Mrs. Julia Dumont, herself a writer of short stories and well known in the Ohio Valley.[1] Mrs. Dumont encouraged Eggleston, saying that he would become an author. He was later to write a tribute to her for her influence and good teaching.[2]

Beginning in June, 1854, he spent over a year in Virginia, visiting relatives and studying at the Amelia Academy. An uncle offered to send him to the University of Virginia, but his increasing hatred of slavery prompted

---

[1] See above, 180-86.
[2] See above, 182-83.

him to refuse this opportunity; also, his poor health, which had beset him since early childhood, soon forced him to put all thought of college out of his mind. Thus deprived from continuing his formal schooling, he set to work to educate himself, reading omnivorously and learning languages.

Returning to Indiana, he worked as a Bible agent until his health was completely broken; then to avoid possible death from consumption, he traveled first west, and next to Minnesota, where in the summer of 1856 he regained his health through outdoor labor. After this experience he tried unsuccessfully to reach Kansas to help the antislavery forces and afterwards returned to Vevay. From November, 1856, to April, 1857, he rode a Methodist circuit, much as he was later to describe in his novel, *The Circuit Rider,* translating the Greek classics in the saddle on the ride between appointments. His health again failed, and there followed another trip the following spring to Minnesota, where he remained nine years. In March, 1858, he married his first wife, Lizzie Snider, at St. Peter, Minnesota. He served as a Bible agent, the pastor of several small churches, and worked at numerous other occupations, his health causing frequent interruptions.

In 1866 he left the ministry for journalism and moved to Evanston, Illinois, where he was associate editor of a Sunday-school magazine, *Little Corporal;* and in 1867 he assumed the editorship of the *Sunday School Teacher,* which soon was retitled the *National Sunday School Teacher.* At this time he became a steady contributor to juvenile periodicals and published expository materials on Sunday-school work, also *Mr. Blake's Walking Stick: A Christmas Story for Boys and Girls* (Chicago, 1870), which was the first of his small books of fantastic fairy tales and moral, sentimental stories, and *The Book of Queer Stories and Stories Told on a Cellar Door* (Chicago, 1870), which aimed at teaching moral and religious truth. In 1870 he moved East, and there followed his connection with the *Independent, Scribner's Monthly,* and *Hearth and Home.*

His editorship of the dying *Hearth and Home* was for only a year, but it pumped new life into that magazine and also launched Eggleston on his career as a novelist who was to have an important influence in popularizing realism in American literature. His first novel, *The Hoosier School-Master,* was published in *Hearth and Home,* September 30 to December 30, 1871, and, then, having resuscitated the magazine, was issued in New York in book form that same year, in an edition of two thousand copies. This was the first of many editions; in a few months fifty thousand copies were sold.

Special attention must be given to this novel, for not only is it significant in American literature, but, in spite of its being Edward Eggleston's first novel, it is his most famous one, and it provides a key to understanding his less-known works. The story is based upon the experiences of his brother George in teaching for a year when only sixteen years old at a rural school at Ryker's Ridge, near Madison, Indiana; it includes the figures of the slim young master, Ralph Hartsock; his husky, uncivilized pupil, Bud Means; the villainous Dr. Small; the bound girl, Hannah; the appealing little boy, Shocky; and many other unforgettable characters of backwoods Indiana of about 1850. The author's purpose, as stated in the preface to the first edition, is to depict life in the Western back-country areas, partly in protest against the featuring of New England in American literature to the exclusion of Western life. As he states in his preface,

It used to be a matter of no little jealousy with us, I remember, that the manners, customs, thoughts, and feelings of
New England country people filled so large a place in books,
while our life, not less interesting, not less romantic, and
certainly not less filled with humorous and grotesque material, had no place in literature. It was as though we were
shut out of good society. And, with the single exception of
Alice Cary, perhaps, our Western writers did not dare speak
of the West otherwise than as the unreal world to which
Cooper's lively imagination had given birth.

He achieved eminent success in focusing attention upon
the West—and Indiana—for in spite of sentimentalism,
melodrama in plot, the use of caricatures in character portrayal, and errors occasioned by his haste in writing, the
story was soon being read by increasing thousands of
Americans; and several generations since have shaken their
heads in amazement at the crudities of the characters and
have chuckled at the queer humor. Eggleston had stumbled upon a mother lode of literary gold. Notwithstand-
ing the difficulty occasioned by the dialect, the book was
translated into Dutch, German, Danish, and French, in
which last tongue, translated by Madame Blanc, the title
became *Le Maître d'Ecôle de Flat Rock.* So, the uncouth
Bud Means was soon traveling abroad, amazing Europeans.

It is a realistic and vivid presentation of the dialect, law-
lessness, and backwoods conditions of the West. Eggleston
had been influenced somewhat by the reading of H. A.
Taine's *Art in the Netherlands,* in which the doctrine is
put forth that people may be explained by the formula of
race, milieu, and the moment—that the artist should
depict what he observes. And that is exactly what Eggleston did. He described the back-country area of southeastern Indiana that he had known, with its crudities and
dialect, and, as he said, the "antique Hoosier." He did
not imply that this Hoosier was typical of the state, for

the benighted type was a backwash of immigration into Indiana, a sort of gaunt, backward poor-white, who had squatted on his land and had never enjoyed much progress or education, using outrageous grammar, vulgarisms, and a dialect never heard by large numbers of Indianans. Since most residents of the state, at the time of publication of the book and later, never were aware of the existence of this relatively small segment of population, it is no wonder that the story raised some objections from persons who feared that the world would take the characters and conditions as typical of Indiana, somewhat as Europeans have tended to understand James Fenimore Cooper's characters as average Americans. Yet, modern Hoosiers find the narrative fascinating and interpret the presentation historically, viewing it as the fictional record of the historic fact that such people once lived in the state, and either moved on or lost their identity through an improved educational system.

Edward Eggleston, of course, was not the first to utilize Hoosier character and setting in fiction. But he was the first to depict Hoosier life and Hoosier character, rough as it stands in the book, in a picturesque and favorable aspect. To accomplish this end he had both to present realistically and to romanticize somewhat his actors and setting. We visualize easily the log schoolhouse with its puncheon floor and rough benches, the uncouth boys and shy or giggly girls, the grotesque adults, the barrenness of the rural life, and its humor, too, the superstitious religion, the drinking and roistering—the structure of the simple backwoods life. All this had never before been seriously and successfully utilized by any novelist. And, the Reverend Mr. Eggleston was kept closely in hand by the self-educated novelist, Eggleston, and avoided over-moralizing.

Such unexpected success with his first novel impelled the editor of *Hearth and Home* to attempt to dig more gold in his Hoosier mine; the result was *The End of the World,* serialized in the magazine, April 20 to September 7, 1872, and then published in New York that same year. Here he utilized the Ohio River country and the Millerite excitement of 1842-43, that he had witnessed, to bolster a thin plot. The book shows that Eggleston antedated Mark Twain in the use of a river steamboat in a Western romance,[3] and in spite of some faults its success prompted the publishers of the magazine to release the author from his editorial functions so that he might write *The Mystery of Metropolisville* (serialized December 7, 1872, to April 26, 1873, and issued as a book in New York in 1873). In being dissatisfied with this novel Eggleston exhibited good self-criticism. It was drawn from his experiences in Minnesota and set a melodramatic story with a weak imitation of Dickens' methods of character portrayal against the fraud of boom-town days in Minnesota, when railroads first developed there. Again, he had written too rapidly, and he now resolved to write no other novels till he could do better.[4]

[3] Mark Twain's *Tom Sawyer* was published in 1876, *Life on the Mississippi* in 1883, and *Huckleberry Finn* in 1884.

[4] On p. xxi of the Editor's Introduction to the 1928 edition of *The Hoosier School-Master,* published by The Macmillian Company, Emory Holloway makes this observation concerning *The Mystery of Metropolisville*: "It is interesting to note, what seems not to have been observed before, that it was while Eggleston's story was running in 'Hearth and Home' ... that an after-dinner discussion concerning what fiction should be led Mark Twain and Charles Dudley Warner to plan and to write in collaboration 'The Gilded Age' (finished in April, 1873), which makes such large use of similar material. Mark Twain had firsthand sources of information, it is true, and is said to have long considered making fictional use of them; but to Eggleston's story belongs the credit of prior publication, if not that of having provoked the more readable, if equally melodramatic, story of Twain and Warner." Quoted with the permission of the publisher.

Fortunately, however, he yielded to the request from *The Christian Union* to write for it *The Circuit Rider: A Tale of the Heroic Age* (serialized November 12, 1873, to March 18, 1874, and published as a book the latter year in New York). This was a much better novel, and many critics pronounced it as better constructed and more realistic than *The Hoosier School-Master*. Returning to the setting of the Hoosier backwoods, although he laid the action in southern Ohio, he produced a sympathetic, realistic portrait of the crude but self-sacrificing itinerant Methodist preacher, whom he himself had been seventeen years before, a type now grown heroic and romantic in retrospect. He dramatized frontier life, creating strong portraits of circuit riders in the rough hero, Morton Goodwin, and also in the youth, Kike, whose dynamic preaching gave his scoffing hearers a case of the "jerks." In spite of some raggedness of style, he gave American Methodism its single classic story. Modern Hoosiers would do well to revive this book.

In 1874 Eggleston took his last ministerial charge, as pastor of the Lee Congregational Church in Brooklyn, New York, but only with the understanding that no creed would be featured, because his religious thinking had grown so liberal that he would no longer be bound by sects and creeds. The only qualification for membership was the wish to serve others; the church was called "The Church of Christian Endeavor," something like Bud Means's church of the Best Licks. After four years of successful ministry, however, his poor health forced his resignation, and the remaining twenty-two years of his life were devoted to studying and writing. He first went to Europe in an attempt to better his health, and while there he collected much historical material to be used in his projected *magnum opus*, a history of the culture of the

American people, which was to be more than a rehashing of politics and wars. While continuing these studies at his home on Lake George, he gave historical lectures at Columbia College and elsewhere and wrote many historical articles and books, some of them designed for young people. He lived to publish only two volumes of the ambitious project which he entitled *The Beginners of a Nation* (New York, 1896) and *The Transit of Civilization from England to America in the Seventeenth Century* (New York, 1901).

Yet, in these years he did some of his best writing. *Roxy (Scribner's Monthly,* November, 1877, to October, 1878, and published in book form in New York in 1878) deals with the problem of adultery in marriage with a frankness unusual for the times; here a wife, Roxy Adams, forgives her erring husband and offers to accept his unborn child, begotten upon another. The realistic story is placed against the setting of former Vevay life—the pretty river village, the Swiss residents, the Methodist revivals. The Indianapolis of 1840 is also described. It is a sort of Hoosier *Scarlet Letter.*

The Hoosier School-Boy (St. Nicholas, December, 1881 —April, 1882; published in book form in New York in 1883) was meant to be a companion piece to *The Hoosier School-Master,* but is far inferior; it preaches sentimentally against the harshness found in rural schools, but not having been himself a typical schoolboy, it was difficult for Eggleston to assume this point of view.

A much better book is *The Graysons. A Story of Illinois (Century,* November, 1887—August, 1888, issued as a book in New York in the latter year), which, along with *Roxy,* is his best fiction and ends his series of Western stories. Like *The Circuit Rider, The Graysons* is not set in Indiana proper, but in the vast Hoosierdom which included parts of Ohio and Illinois, and is an authentic study of the pioneer days, written from a thorough knowledge of the people, carefully using their dialect. The climax comes in the murder trial of the hero, Tom Grayson, a diamond-in-the-rough type, like Morton Goodwin in *The Circuit Rider,* with Tom's attorney, the young Abe Lincoln, proving a witness a liar through showing, by means of a calendar, that the witness could not have seen the accused commit a murder because there was no moon that night. The story is artistically told, and Lincoln is delicately handled and later slips quietly out of the story with no foreshadowing of his great future.

Eggleston's wife, Lizzie Snider, died in 1889; and in 1891 he married Frances Goode, of Madison, Indiana. In the latter year appeared *The Faith Doctor* (published in *Century,* February to October, and issued as a book that same year in New York), designed, as the author said, to attack "the prevailing interest in mind-cure, faith-cure, Christian science, and other sorts of aerial therapeutics." Eggleston said the primary purpose of the novel was artistic rather than polemic, but his biographers do not fully agree with his statement. His last imaginative publication was *Duffels* (New York, 1893), a collection of short stories, a literary form in which he never particularly distinguished himself. Eggleston had become more a historian than a novelist in his later years, and in his inaugural address as president of the American Historical Association in 1900 pleaded for history to be written more from the angle of the culture of a people than from their politics—a very modern point of view. He died of apoplexy at his Lake George home on September 2, 1902.[5]

[5] Material on Edward Eggleston was obtained mostly from the article by Ralph L. Rusk in the *Dictionary of American Biography, Authors Edition,* 6:52-54, and from Holloway's Introduction to the 1928 edition of *The Hoosier School-Master.*

This historical bent which he followed for so long was a source both of strength and of weakness to him as a novelist, for most of his novels are little more than fictionized history sometimes weighed down with long disquisitions on customs and manners; still, as such they are valuable and present a vitalized history which is much more palatable to the average reader than the usual history text. In some respects his method resembles that of many early American humorists in their dramatization of the crudities of Western life to arouse the laughter of cultured readers; yet even when he exposed the ignorance, hypocrisy, selfishness, and vice in this life, he was sympathetic with Western civilization, and we find many examples of the diamond-in-the-rough and of the devoted Samaritan among his characters. He was a realist in setting forth life as he saw—or had seen—it; and to balance the barrenness and sordidness of his pictures we find many descriptions of the beauty of the hills and rivers and of the homelike atmosphere of some of the dwellings. He possessed a rich humor, which, though often resulting in mere caricature, added the correct dash of imagination to render his tales the more interesting; his sanity of outlook on life is a corrective to the glamour which has always tended to invest such figures as the highwayman, the Mississippi gambler, and the smooth hypocrite.

Altogether, Edward Eggleston was a remarkable person, who, rising above his environment and successfully combating ill health, stumbled, like Sir Launfal, upon his objective at his own front door. Like Riley, he turned the mud of Indiana into literary gold. And in spite of the excellence of some of his other work and in spite of his later realization of the weaknesses of the book, probably he will always be known as the author of *The Hoosier School-Master*.

One final word about his position in literature. He and James Whitcomb Riley and Booth Tarkington are the greatest interpreters of the Hoosier scene. Although the outlook of Eggleston is essentially that of a realist, the attitude of Riley is that of a sentimentalist, and the approach of Tarkington is that of both a realist and a romanticist, yet they all meet in the use of Hoosier dialect and in a deep love for their native state and its common people.

Also, Edward Eggleston came close to the beginning of realism in American literature as a whole. Although local literature had been written before Eggleston, Bret Harte was the only name of much significance; and his *The Luck of Roaring Camp and Other Sketches* was published only in 1870, just one year before *The Hoosier School-Master*. While Harte had opened up the West as a new and powerful field for literature, it was Eggleston who helped turn this new current of local color in the direction of realism. One of his great contributions, of course, was in the field of dialect. No one in Indiana literature before him had made any serious attempt to use dialect; and very few in American literature as a whole had employed it, the great exception, of course, being James Russell Lowell. Other local colorists and realists were soon to follow. Mark Twain began his typical local-color work with *Roughing It* in 1872; Sarah Orne Jewett, a New England local colorist, published *Deephaven* in 1877; George Washington Cable issued his *Old Creole Days* in 1879; Joel Chandler Harris began his work in 1884 with *Mingo and Other Sketches in Black and White;* and Thomas Nelson Page released his *In Ole Virginia* in 1887. Edward Eggleston, then, was a real literary pioneer.[6]

[6] For more information on Edward Eggleston, see the excellent bibliography in Spiller, *et al.* (eds.), *Literary History of the United States,* 3:485-86. In addition to the sources already listed, see William Peirce Randel, *Edward Eggleston, Author of 'The Hoosier School-Master'* (New

GEORGE CARY EGGLESTON

It is understandable, yet in a sense unfortunate, that Edward has always overshadowed the work of his younger brother, George Cary Eggleston (1839-1911); the latter was an important literary figure in his own day but has been largely forgotten since his death. One looks in vain through most modern histories of American literature to discover any reference at all to George Eggleston. However, his many published works were very favorably received, in general, and for many years he circulated freely as a striking personality among the literary circles of New York as a journalist and as a writer, enjoying the popularity of his books—and, what was surprising for the post-Civil War period, a personal popularity, since he talked freely of his service as a Confederate soldier. As a matter of fact, he made the most of his background of long residence in the South and of his war experiences, volume after volume springing up almost overnight from this rich germination bed. And his Yankee readers, forgetting their prejudice, gloried with him in the gracious chivalric atmosphere of old Virginia. He was one of those who inaugurated and popularized the so-called "magnolia tradition" of the ante-bellum South. Still, because he was strongly influenced by his youth in Indiana and wrote novels with a Hoosier background, he is an Indiana writer.

We shall not repeat here the facts concerning the background of the Eggleston brothers.[7] George Cary Eggleston was born at Vevay, Indiana, on November 26, 1839, the second of three brothers. When he was only seven

York, 1946) and George Cary Eggleston, *The First of the Hoosiers, Reminiscences of Edward Eggleston* (Philadelphia, 1903). Banta, *Indiana Authors and Their Books*, 98, gives a convenient list of Eggleston's publications.

[7] For the family background of George Eggleston, see the account of Edward, above, 262.

years of age, his father died, leaving the rearing of the
three boys and one girl to the mother. The father had
requested that his law library be exchanged for a library
of standard literature so that the children might have
good reading, and the mother guided them in this reading. George attended primitive schools, such as his brother
Edward was to make famous in *The Hoosier School-Master,* and he was privileged to share with Edward the inspiring direction of Mrs. Julia Dumont, his high-school
teacher in Vevay. Like Edward, he later penned strong
praise of her teaching. Edward, having now educated himself sufficiently, prepared his brother for college; and
George entered Indiana Asbury (now DePauw) University at fifteen, where he spent over a year until lack of
money compelled him to interrupt his education by teaching school for a year at Ryker's Ridge, near Madison,
Indiana. As stated earlier, Edward drew material for *The
Hoosier School-Master* from the amusing and frustrating
experiences that George had that year.

The next year (1856) George Eggleston inherited the
family plantation in Amelia County, Virginia, and was
astonished by "the glamour of that easy-going, restful and
exquisitely self-poised Virginian life," as he later described
it. Not sharing the intensity of Edward's hatred of slavery
(though he himself thought it wrong, in spite of the mild
treatment of the slaves which he found in Virginia), he
remained nine years in the Old Dominion. He attended
Richmond College, 1857-58, and studied law in Richmond, making friends with John Esten Cooke and others
of the Richmond literary circle, and was beginning to
practice law in 1861, when the Civil War broke out. He
voted against secession; but when Virginia cast her lot
with the South, he enlisted in the Confederate Army,
serving with distinction throughout the war, first in the

Army of northern Virginia, under Colonel J. E. B. Stuart, who was later to gallop fearlessly and gallantly through several of George Eggleston's novels and historical accounts of the war, later under General Fitzhugh Lee, then in the field artillery. He took part in many skirmishes and in the campaigns of the Wilderness, Cold Harbor, the bloody siege of Petersburg, and in the battles around Appomattox. During most of the war he was a sergeant major and, miraculously, escaped both injury and sickness.[8]

Undaunted by the hot feeling against the South at the close of the war, in 1865 he visited Vevay, then was employed for several years by a banking and steamboating company in Cairo, Illinois, where in 1868 he married Marion Craggs. After practicing law for a time in Mississippi, in 1870 he went, with his wife and one child, to New York, where his brother Edward had recently become a member of the staff of *The Independent.* Here George began a journalistic career which lasted until his voluntary retirement in 1900 to devote his entire time to writing. After working a year as a reporter and editorial writer on the Brooklyn *Daily Union,* he next did free-lance writing; then when Edward became editor of *Hearth and Home,* George assumed the position of managing editor and succeeded Edward as editor a few years later. Together, the brothers built up the magazine, procuring good writers, like Frank R. Stockton. When the magazine was sold in 1874, George returned to free-lance work, writing for many periodicals, such as the *Atlantic Monthly, Appleton's Journal,* and *Galaxy.* After serving

[8] George Eggleston recorded his experiences in a fascinating account, *A Rebel's Recollections* (New York, 1874), which the present author highly recommends. The book is valuable to the historian for a dashing but realistic portayal of J.E.B. Stuart. It was reissued by the Indiana University Press in 1959 as part of the Civil War Centennial Series.

as editor of *The Magazine of American Homes,* he became literary editor of the *Evening Post,* acting as assistant to William Cullen Bryant. From 1881 to 1885 he was literary adviser to Harper and Brothers, from 1884 to 1889 editor of the New York *Commercial Advertiser,* and from 1889 to 1900 was editorial writer for the New York *World,* under Joseph Pulitzer. Since 1872 he had been publishing books, and finally in 1900 he turned away from the lure of the journalistic life, which he termed "the call of the wild." An amazing productivity followed, during which he published twenty-eight miscellaneous volumes to add to the fifteen issued before 1900. He died on April 14, 1911.[9]

Such a tremendous production must be treated and analyzed by types. George Eggleston's books may be classified as follows: (1) history and biography; (2) books for young people; (3) novels about Virginia and the South; and (4) miscellaneous.

His chief contribution to the field of history is the *History of the Confederate War* . . . (2 volumes. Boston, 1910), which is a readable and unbiased treatment of the subject; his historical works continued to appear until the posthumous *Our Colonial Story* (revised and edited by Clarence H. McClure, Chicago, 1921). Essentially, however, Eggleston is not a historian, for he usually wrote too rapidly and too much with his eye on popular appeal to take the necessary pains and time that writing good history requires. He did better with biographical and autobiographical materials. When William Dean Howells,

[9] Material on George C. Eggleston was taken for the most part from the article by Atcheson L. Hench in the *Dictionary of American Biography, Author's Edition,* 6:54-55, and from an article by John C. Metcalf in the *Library of Southern Literature,* edited by Edwin A. Alderman and Joel C. Harris (16 vols. Atlanta, Ga., 1907), 4:1525-31. Many encyclopedias contain biographical information.

the editor of the *Atlantic Monthly,* asked him to write his reminiscences of Confederate army life for the *Atlantic,* he at length responded; and, in spite of misgivings about how such a subject would be received by Northern readers so soon after the war, he wrote a series of papers entitled "A Rebel's Recollections," which, because of the broad, democratic, and nationalistic spirit in which the matter was handled, quickly hushed protests and was greatly praised. Vindictiveness against the North and the rebel yell were both happily absent from these calm memoirs, which abounded in humanized portraits of great personalities, like that of J. E. B. ("Jeb") Stuart, dramatic presentations of the daring spirit of the Confederate cavaliers, and insight into human nature. The "Recollections" were published in book form in New York in 1874. For years it was highly popular and helped, in a small way, to pour oil on the troubled waters of the Reconstruction period.[10]

Southern Soldier Stories (New York, 1898) can also be included in this category because it is partly reminiscence. We shall have more to say of this book later. *The First of the Hoosiers* is explained by its subtitle, *Reminiscences of Edward Eggleston, and of that Western Life Which He, First of All Men, Celebrated in Literature and Made Famous* (Boston, 1903); however, the book also affords psychological insight into the life of the author himself and is valuable for the light it throws on pioneer Indiana. The last significant book of this category, *Recollections of a Varied Life* (New York, 1910), published when he was seventy-one, is both an autobiography and a *Biographia Literaria,* showing an alert mind, a keen wit, and a great humanity. It abounds in references to litera-

---

[10] See George Eggleston's account of the writing of these articles in *Recollections of a Varied Life* (New York, 1910), 148-50.

ture and to contemporary literary figures, and it explains the genesis of many of his books. Anyone making a serious study of George Eggleston should read it.

The second division of his works, books for young people, is large, numbering eighteen very popular volumes. Only a few need be cited as examples. Beginning with expository works, *How to Educate Yourself* (New York, 1872) and *How to Make a Living* (New York, 1875), he soon turned to fiction, as in the Big Brother series, a trilogy about the Creek War in Alabama and Mississippi: *The Big Brother* (New York, 1875), *Captain Sam* (New York, 1876), and *The Signal Boys* (New York, 1878). *The Bale Marked Circle X. A Blockade Running Adventure* (Boston, 1902) is a thrilling story of three young Confederate soldiers. Three books in particular show the influence of his Indiana boyhood: *The Last of the Flatboats* (Boston, 1900), which tells the spirited adventure of five Hoosier boys ("Ed" is Edward Eggleston) who, starting from Vevay, Indiana, take the last of the flatboats down the Ohio and Mississippi to New Orleans; *Jack Shelby. A Story of the Indiana Backwoods* (Boston, 1906); and *Long Knives. The Story of How They Won the West* (Boston, 1907), which is a tale of the George Rogers Clark expedition. All these juveniles arose from an instinctive knowledge of youth and strong sympathy for boys.

Yet, it is in the third division of the writer's works, novels about Virginia and the South, that we find the typical—indeed, the real—George Eggleston. Here he threw his whole heart and being into these thirteen books, harking back time and time again to his nostalgic, treasured memories of Virginia as he knew it before and during the war, and the golden glow of the aristocratic old order with its chivalric code! The setting in most of the novels is in or around Amelia County, Virginia, where

Eggleston's own plantation was located, or in some place seen by him during the war; thus it is an idealized old plantation countryside. Against this glamorized background of stately white mansions set amid groves of tall trees with the quarters of contented Negroes in the rear and surrounded by cotton fields and woods, the stalwart, courteous gentlemen and the beautiful belles with flowing golden tresses take their gay morning rides or deal with the obstacles to their true love—or else the men, now attired in spotless gray, form quickly under the Stars and Bars and, led by the dashing figure of "Jeb" Stuart, rush fearlessly against the rising tide of blue, supported in spirit and also in action by the ardent ladies. These stories, then, are almost all idyllic. The reader wishes that he could have shared this perfect life.

George Eggleston was precipitated into writing novels by a strange situation. While he was on the staff of *Hearth and Home,* a writer who had promised the paper a serial story failed to produce it; and looking frantically about for another story but finding none, Eggleston said absently in a staff meeting that if no other writer could be found, he himself would write the story—whereupon he was drafted for the project, and the meeting was quickly adjourned before he could protest. The novel that slowly grew (*A Man of Honor,* New York, 1873) was not distinguished, but it marked the discovery of the rich silver of Virginia lore, which he continued to mine until the year of his death. Like nearly all his novels, this story is partly autobiographical, about a Midwesterner, who, upon visiting relatives in Virginia, is astonished and delighted by the life there and wins a Virginia girl as his wife.[11] *Southern Soldier Stories* (New York, 1898) followed after a long interval, but is surprisingly good. This

[11] See the *Recollections,* 151-55.

is a well-written book of stories and sketches inspired by his army service. The characters are well drawn and very lifelike; they behave as soldiers do, no matter what the age or war, they fight bravely and fiercely, they dislike some of their officers, they can not understand many of the things they have to do, some desert, are caught, and are shot. As the war drags on some realize they are being defeated but still fight on. The characters and incidents are both real and imaginary and often are a blend of the two. This book has long been neglected, but it gives some interesting sidelights on the war and is fascinating to read. Some day it may be revived. *A Carolina Cavalier* (Boston, 1901) is a fast-moving love story set against the background of the invasion of South Carolina by the British in 1780.

Then followed the popular trilogy of *Dorothy South. A Love Story of Virginia Just Before the War* (Boston, 1902), *The Master of Warlock. A Virginia War Story* (Boston, 1903), and *Evelyn Byrd* (Boston, 1904). The preface to the last of these sets forth Eggleston's design:

This book is the third and last of a trilogy of romances. In that trilogy I have endeavoured to show forth the character of the Virginians—men and women.

In "Dorothy South" I tried to show what the Virginians were while the old life lasted—"before the war."

In "The Master of Warlock" I endeavoured faithfully to depict the same people as they were during the first half of the Civil War, when their valour seemed to promise everything of results that they desired. In "Evelyn Byrd" I have sought to show the heroism of endurance that marked the conduct of those people during the last half of the war, when disaster stared them in the face and they unfalteringly confronted it.

In these books we have high romance with enough truth to carry it well, and no one can pronounce the pic-

ture of Virginia life exactly false; but obviously its charm
and the perfection of the characters are overdrawn. Certain of his themes are worthy of comment: the gallant
figure of Stuart, who gallops through the stories, auda-
ciously and shrewdly leading his cavalry and rescuing Virginia ladies; the observation that originally Virginia was
pro-Union, but seceded when Lincoln called on her for a
quota of troops to subdue the rebellion; the realization
of the author that slavery was an evil which should be
suppressed and that the way of life of the South, despite
its charm, was in reality backward; the presentation of
the Southern point of view but without prejudice or bitterness; analysis and praise of the strategy of Lee and
Grant, but condemnation of the overcaution of General
McClellan and of the Confederate government; and a
foreshadowing of a new, modern era for the South. In
spite of obviously hasty writing, the books were very well
received.[12]

The remainder of George Eggleston's novels about Virginia and the South hardly need differentiation, since they
are all cast in this same mold. They are *A Captain in the
Ranks* (New York, 1904), which was to supplement the
above trilogy; *A Daughter of the South. A War's End
Romance* (Boston, 1905); *Love Is the Sum of It All. A
Plantation Romance* (Boston, 1907); *Two Gentlemen of
Virginia. A Novel of the Old Regime in the Old Dominion* (Boston, 1908); *The Warrens of Virginia* (New York,
1908), a novel based on the play by William C. DeMille;
Irene of the Mountains. A Romance of Old Virginia
(Boston, 1909), and *Westover of Wanalah. A Story of Love
and Life in Old Virginia* (New York, 1910). Most of the
heroines in all these romances, particularly in *Dorothy*

---

[12] See the author's comments on these books in *Recollections, passim.*

South, are in reality Eggleston's wife, who appears in many attractive aspects.

The fourth division of George Eggleston's books, the miscellaneous works, includes only his editorship of *American War Ballads and Lyrics* (2 volumes. New York, 1889) and two novels—very strange novels indeed for this romantic writer to produce inasmuch as they contain strong elements of realism: *Juggernaut* (with Dolores Marbourg, pseudonym of Mrs. Mary Schell Bacon [1870-1934]) (New York, 1891) and *Blind Alleys* (Boston, 1906). *Juggernaut* is a powerful book that gains strength as it progresses from a mild beginning to a soul-searing ending, utilizing the theme that he who gains the whole world but loses his own soul has profited nothing. This is the story of Edgar Braine, who upon graduation from Hanover College in Indiana goes to a little river town, which seems to be Vevay, and there becomes the civic-minded editor of the town newspaper, but succumbs to temptation and devotes his life to personal advancement and craving for power, without reference to ethics. His virtuous wife Helen is made to lead a "doll's house" type of life, ignorant of her husband's increasingly unscrupulous ways, until, after he becomes a United States senator, he forces her to grant personal favors to a political rival, over whom Edgar desires control. Finally she deserts him. Edgar is shocked into repentance and morality, whereas the disillusioned Helen now gladly embraces evil and lowers herself to the point where eventually she dies in shame. Except for the vagueness of the latter part of the book, this novel is very realistic. It might be noted in passing that in its exposure of corruption in political life, particularly in Washington, the book is somewhat like *The Gilded Age* (1873) of Mark Twain and Charles Dudley Warner.

So also is *Blind Alleys* realistic. In spite of an ambiguous theme, which seems to be that "nearly all our efforts to better our fellow men, whether positively or negatively, lead us into blind alleys,"[13] and despite confusion about the necessity for social reform, this is a very well-plotted novel, much unlike anything else Eggleston wrote. Indeed, it hardly seems to be the same author at all, for the happy glow of Virginia romance is totally absent; and through the interweaving of the threads of the plot there appears some preaching about the evils of slums and tenements, the wretched condition of the poor and how they can really be aided, the hypocrisy of church corporations in secretly owning saloons, the withdrawal of ministers from unpleasant reality, the mistake in blaming all social evil on liquor, the shallowness of narrow-minded Christianity, and work as the correct way to happiness. Perhaps in this novel Eggleston gave expression to many opinions that he had allowed his romantic novels to submerge. But since much of this philosophizing confuses the reader, he will probably remember the book for its story, which is that of the eventual revelation to a young doctor who has been brought up by a tutor working for a secret, mysterious benefactor, of the identity of this benefactor, a woman philanthropist who had once been his father's fiancée, and of the strange circumstances of the doctor's early life. An autobiographical note is sounded in the person of an alert young newspaperman as a leading character. This book, however, though very interesting, falls short of greatness because of its ambiguity.

Essentially a Southerner, and only incidentally a Hoosier, George Cary Eggleston, then, is a popular writer of history, juveniles, and romances and is a minor American literary figure—but an interesting one. In spite of the

[13] Page 339.

realism of *Blind Alleys* and *Juggernaut,* both of which come closer to greatness than anything else he did because they have much more substance than his other novels, he is a confirmed romantic seeking a never-never land in the misty bygone days of the old South. Undoubtedly there is much truth in his picture of life there—indeed, he always swore that he was in no way exaggerating it—yet his presentation is too perfect to be believed.

His fiction is almost all autobiographical in some sense. The novels are mostly love stories with a minimum of obstacles to supply interest, but the reader never despairs that The Land Where Dreams Come True is just around the corner—neither do the lovers themselves seem much to doubt the outcome. His usual formula for developing character is to string illustrative anecdotes on a thread of biography. This method results in some striking portraits, but there is an almost complete absence of real villains in his tales. He excels in presentation of the Negro. His heroes, though usually Southerners, are broad-minded American citizens, alert, thoughtful, and courageous, desiring to achieve an adjustment of old traditions to the new day; and Eggleston is sympathetic with the North as well as with the South. In other words, he is a liberal. His style is highly colored, vivid, and journalistic. Like his brother Edward, he wrote too rapidly; he who turns out several books a year can not take time to encompass deep philosophy or excel in "fine writing." Still, his imaginative work makes him a popularizer of the "magnolia tradition" of the ante-bellum South and as such has offered a valuable contribution to American life and literature.

He is not so important as Edward—he penned nothing of the force of *The Hoosier School-Master, The Circuit Rider,* or *The Graysons*—but he has more imagination and greater sympathy; and he has done for the South, though less strikingly, what Edward did for the West. He has suffered an undue eclipse in American literary history. George Cary Eggleston deserves to be revived.

The next novelist, Lewis (Lew) Wallace (1827-1905), has no need of a revival; for his famous book, *Ben-Hur*, like an old soldier, never dies. Indeed, it has hardly ever faded away and well past the middle of the twentieth century is still selling, with thousands and thousands of copies to its credit since publication in 1880. Through it especially Wallace earned during his lifetime the admiration of his fellow Americans and of a high percentage of the literate people of the world, whether they read the book or not; for it was known, at least vaguely, to almost everyone. As a matter of fact, along with *Uncle Tom's Cabin* and *In His Steps*, it is one of the three longest-lived and most popular American novels. Here, then, we have the curious combination of a celebrated writer, yet one who never impressed the critics very favorably.

His was an interesting, impetuous, romantic life. He was a writer only by avocation, since his vocations were those of a lawyer, soldier, governor, and diplomat—and he managed also to do something with playing the violin and with painting in his spare time.

Lew Wallace was born on April 10, 1827, at Brookville, Indiana, which was then only twenty years old and an important town in the state. His father was "Colonel" David Wallace, a fourth-generation Scotch-Irishman, who attended and later taught mathematics at West Point, then studied law in the office of Judge Miles C. Eggleston, first cousin, once removed, of Edward Eggleston, and after admission to the bar and some law practice married seventeen-year-old Esther French Test, daughter of a Brookville judge. David Wallace served in three sessions of the legislature, became lieutenant governor (at a salary of two dollars a day), moved his family to Covington, Indiana, where he organized a company of militia (which never was needed) for the Black Hawk War, and when he was elected governor on the Whig ticket in 1837, moved the family to Indianapolis. The son, then, came by his military and political interests naturally.

Lew early manifested a strong dislike for formal education. He was so often truant from the various schools to which he was sent, including the preparatory department of Wabash College, that in spite of parental floggings he had little formal education and learned what he knew from adventure in the woods and from voracious reading in his father's library and also in the Indiana State Library, where he became attached to Cooper, Irving, and Plutarch. His mother died of consumption during his childhood. His father's second wife, the nineteen-year-old beautiful Zerelda Gray Sanders, helped direct his reading. In Indianapolis he took the part of Numony in the Indianapolis Thespian Corps' presentation of Robert Dale Owen's drama, *Pocahontas*. Henceforth Lew tended to think and act dramatically. Inspired, perhaps, by noble thoughts thus engendered, he and another boy ran away from home in an attempt to join the Texans in their struggle with Mexico, but they were intercepted and returned home. He wrote some juvenile poetry, never published, which told heroic and military tales, for Lew's romantic attitude was taking strong form; he became so enamored of Prescott's *Conquest of Mexico* that he prepared to write on the subject. Thus early did his novel *The Fair God* have its genesis.

After earning money by copy work in the county clerk's office and by reporting for the Indianapolis *Daily Journal* the deliberations of the Indiana House of Representatives, he studied law in his father's law office, but failed the bar examination in his haste to organize a company for the Mexican War. He was elected second lieutenant of the company; and under a fanfare which included the presentation to the unit of a beautiful flag from the women of Indianapolis and a solemn charge from the Indiana poet, Sarah T. Bolton, to bear it honorably, the company marched off to war. Lew's heart's desire—an opportunity for distinction in war—was doomed to disappointment because the men saw no real action and returned without the cheering and flag waving he had anticipated.

He campaigned shortly thereafter against Gen. Zachary Taylor, for whom he had contracted a dislike in the war, and became a Democrat temporarily. In 1849 he redeemed himself academically by passing his bar examination, then moved to Covington, where in 1850 and 1852 he was elected prosecuting attorney. In the latter year he married Susan Elston, third daughter of Major Isaac Elston, of Crawfordsville.[14] Moving to Crawfordsville in 1853, he was elected to the state senate in 1856; in that year he organized a military company, whose official title was the Montgomery [County] Guards, but known popularly as the Zouaves because the romantic Captain Wallace dressed them in the baggy gray pants, blue-and-red jackets, and red-visored French caps of Algerian troops. Their well-disciplined parades set many a heart aflutter, and Wallace soon found himself known throughout the state.

Now the young soldier felt the hand of fate resting upon him, for with the outbreak of the Civil War Governor Oliver P. Morton appointed him adjutant general of the

[14] Mrs. Wallace was a cultivated person who wrote poetry and a few religious and travel books. She was critic and editor of her husband's works. A brief biography can be found in Banta, *Indiana Authors and Their Books*, 331. For a bibliography of her writings, see Russo and Sullivan, *Bibliographical Studies of Seven Authors of Crawfordsville*, 419-46.

State of Indiana and promised him the command of one of the regiments to be raised. In a week's time he had assembled 130 companies, seventy more than the quota for Indiana, and he soon was made colonel, commanding the eleventh regiment. (Almost all of Wallace's Zouaves enlisted in the army, and most of them became officers.) After training at Camp Morton, the bearded, handsome, fierce-eyed colonel paraded his regiment in Indianapolis in Zouave uniform and had the men kneel on the State House lawn and swear a tremendous oath to wash away by their acts the stain of the defeat of Indiana troops in the battle of Buena Vista in the Mexican War. Wallace shortly received the rank of brigadier general, and after the battle of Fort Donelson he was promoted to major general. But in spite of his high rank, he was kept on the sidelines during most of the war. His most important contributions were his defense of Cincinnati in 1862 and the delaying action which he fought in the battle of the Monocacy in 1864 which helped to save Washington, D. C., from capture. Wallace was a member of the court martial which tried those accused of the murder of Lincoln, and he was president of the court that tried and sentenced Henry Wirz, the commandant of the ill-famed Andersonville prison.

During the last months of the war General Wallace engaged in diplomatic and military activities in the Southwest, aimed at bringing Texas and certain other adjacent rebel territories back into the Union, and aided the followers of Juarez, who were attempting to drive the French out of Mexico.[15] He forwarded munitions to the Mexican liberals, attempted to raise money and troops, and re-

[15] Much that Wallace did in the Southwest and in behalf of Mexico was secret and almost of the cloak-and-dagger type. See Chapter VIII, "Mexican Mission," in Irving McKee, *"Ben-Hur" Wallace. The Life of General Lew Wallace* (Berkeley, Calif., 1947).

ceived a commission as major general in the Mexican Army.

After some time in Mexico he returned to private law practice in Crawfordsville. Defeated for election to Congress as a Republican, he was appointed by President Hayes in 1878 governor of New Mexico Territory and served till 1881, when he was appointed by President Garfield minister to Turkey and served until 1885, enjoying the confidence of the notorious sultan, Abdul-Hamid II. In 1890 he refused the appointment offered by President Harrison of a diplomatic mission to Brazil. After his retirement from diplomatic service he lived in Crawfordsville, usually wintering in Indianapolis. This dashing, colorful, versatile figure died at his home in Crawfordsville on February 15, 1905. Five years following his death his statue was erected in the Hall of Fame in Washington, D. C.[16]

Wallace's works are the product of his fanciful, dramatic life and of his daydreams. We can expect only romantic materials, and this is exactly what we find. His works are few and can be divided into major and minor writings, the major items consisting of his three famous novels. The minor works, except for some expository items, such as two biographies of Benjamin Harrison and his unfinished autobiography,[17] include only two long poems, *Commodus. An Historical Play* (Crawfordsville, Indiana, 1876) and *The Wooing of Malkatoon* (issued with *Commodus*, New York, 1898).

[16] The biography of Wallace was taken mostly from the interesting comprehensive biography by McKee, the article by Anna L. Lingelbach in *Dictionary of American Biography, Authors Edition*, 19:375-76, and the article by John D. Forbes in Banta, *Indiana Authors and Their Books*.

[17] Wallace's autobiography ended with the Civil War; it was completed, rather sketchily, by his wife with the aid of Mary Hannah Krout and published in two volumes in 1906.

Commodus is a five-act drama in good blank verse which tells the story of how Maternus, formerly a Roman slave, having gathered together others like him (evidently in modern Transylvania) and having lived as a sort of robber baron with his own army, at length finds himself set upon by Roman armies on all sides, by command of the emperor Commodus. Maternus tries to slip his men through the Romans in order to reassemble them near Rome, kill Commodus, and proclaim himself emperor; but he is betrayed by one of his officers and is seized and executed. The plot, though Shakespearean in type, is essentially immoral, whereas the magnificence, the cast, originally of forty-four players, and the tremendous scenes were all beyond the possibilities of the contemporary theater. In spite of Wallace's frequent revisions, he could not get the play produced, and it remained closet drama. *The Wooing of Malkatoon* is a romantic poem composed in surprisingly good blank verse, the story based on the thirteenth-century Turkish legend of Prince Othman, who, after surmounting many obstacles placed in his path by Edebali, the father of Malkatoon, has a vision of the conquest of Constantinople and wins his beloved. The Oriental imagery here is beautiful, but the narrative is close to a bedtime story. The verse is better than the tale. Both *Commodus* and *Malkatoon* have remained little known and can not be compared with the novels.

These novels, forming the major work of Wallace, are *The Fair God; or, The Last of the 'Tzins. A Tale of the Conquest of Mexico* (Boston, 1873); *Ben-Hur. A Tale of the Christ* (New York, 1880); and *The Prince of India Or Why Constantinople Fell* (New York, 1893).

The Fair God, begun when the author was a mere boy and continued and revised at various times, tells a highly colored story of ambition and love entwined in the history as recorded by Prescott, which had so intrigued Wallace. Although having an air of veracity through rather heavily authenticated facts and descriptions taken from Prescott and other historians, the novel is still an exotic parade of nearly unpronounceable names, splendid costumes, picturesque scenes, and physical and heroic actions—all of which set off the contrast between the crumbling pagan but noble culture of the Aztecs and the cruel and vicious so-called Christian civilization of the Spanish invaders. Eddies of savagery, nobility, heroism, love, religion, and superstition whirl about the characters and incidents; and the glory which once was Mexico glitters like dazzling sunlight upon the struggle. The battles which throng the book, in contrast to some of the indecisive and frustrating battles of the Civil War in which Wallace had participated, are heroic and dramatic. Indeed, much of Wallace's own life is here disguised and idealized, as in his transformation of a demonstration of hypnotism involving a tailor and his apprentice, which he had witnessed in Covington during his residence there, into the chapter in which the coming of Cortes is prophesied. Also, his description of the organization of Guatamozin for the defense of Tenochtitlan, the capital of the Aztecs, is reminiscent of Wallace's defense of Cincinnati in 1862. All of this made an action-packed tale told against a luscious and sensuous setting.

But critics, though in general favorable—some quite lavish in their praise—were quick to pick faults, to show, for example, that the characters, including the hero, Hualpa, and even the imposing figure of Montezuma, going tragically but nobly down to destruction, are mostly conventional and unindividualized and that the women are carbon copies of Cooper's respectable and helpless innocents. Wallace's models—Scott, Cooper, and G. P. R.

James—shine through the work. Yet, the verdict of the public at large, both in this country and abroad, was very favorable; and edition after edition streamed from the presses. By 1941, 217,000 copies had been sold, and the book was still moving.[18]

Ben-Hur enjoyed a much greater reception—at least from the public. Wallace selected the subject of the origin of Christianity because it is the climax of the Bible, the most popular of all books, and because of his interest in the story of the Magi, into which medieval tale he introduced an allegory, making Gaspar a Greek symbolizing faith, Melchior a Hindu standing for love, and Balthasar an Egyptian doing good works. He then added a Jew for hero, a Roman as villain, mixing the potion with the proper ingredients of miracles, local color, heroic and villainous actions, pageantry, history, Biblical narrative, vengeance, religious adoration, physical and military action, and excitement—and the result was nearly hemlock for some of the critics, but nectar for others and also for the populace of America, for whom the novel and the theater now became for the first time respectable and popular art forms. It was *The Fair God* further developed, along the lines of *Ivanhoe*. Instead of Prescott as the foundation, Wallace had discovered Gibbon and Flavius Josephus, and through painstaking research he obtained

---

[18] For some of the analysis of *The Fair God*, the author is indebted to McKee, *"Ben-Hur"* Wallace, particularly pages 123-27. As McKee remarks, at first the novel was a cause of embarrassment to Wallace in his law practice, for in order to turn a case against him the opposing attorney had only to mention in court that Wallace had written a novel, whereupon the jury of merchants and farmers would join in a loud guffaw. Apparently interest in literature had not captured all Hoosiers by 1873! Wallace's situation may be compared to that of Judge John S. Reid, whose exotic narrative poem, *Gulzar; or, the Rose-Bower*, was frequently quoted to his embarrassment in his own court with the result that he finally disavowed authorship. See above, 90n.

much information for the setting. After having written
sixteen chapters, he fell in company with Colonel Robert
G. Ingersoll on a train going from Crawfordsville to Indianapolis, where both were to speak at the Third National
Soldiers' Reunion. Having listened to Ingersoll's agnostic
arguments, Wallace, though never in his life a member
of any church, determined to turn his novel into a refuta-
tion of Ingersoll. Later, in magazine articles, the novelist
was to say that the composition of the book converted
him to belief in God and in the divinity of Christ. He
finished the last quarter of the book mostly in the executive mansion at Santa Fé while governor of New Mexico
Territory; after his seven years' work on it, Harper's published the novel in 1880.

There are problems and paradoxes here. In the story
the paths of Jesus and the hero, Ben-Hur, cross, and in this
strange situation may be found the key to the appeal of
the tale, for the romantic Ben-Hur is a warrior and a
worldly figure, yet a dreamer; and these mutually repel-
lent components are both presented to the puzzled reader
to be reconciled and admired. Yet, perhaps the reason for
Wallace's success in getting them admired is the fact that
Americans, and people everywhere, do admire both the
religious and the wordly and that there is a contradiction
in their own natures. Critics have also pointed out the
overuse of coincidence, the fact that the women are of
the same innocent and passive types as in *The Fair God,*
that the spirit of the novel is Victorian, that it is melodramatic, that it is an artistic failure, and that Wallace in
his attempt to prove Christianity demonstrates only his
misunderstanding of it. Probably one of the reasons for
the attitude of many critics in either ignoring or attacking
it was Wallace's position as a literary amateur, one who
had not even migrated to worship at the centers of litera-

ture in Boston or New York, as had the Eggleston brothers. Also, he had tried to re-glamorize the Holy Land, which Mark Twain had debunked in *Innocents Abroad* (1869).

But the public brushed these objections aside and after some hesitation read, approved, and bought the book in increasing quantities till the sale became a landslide and almost every literate American had read or heard of it or one of its many adaptations, some of which Wallace himself made. About 2,800 copies were sold during the first seven months after publication; then after a decline to a trickle in 1881, 750 copies a month were sold in 1883, 4,500 a month in 1886-87, until at the end of 1889, 400,000 copies had been sold. By 1944 Harper's estimate of the total number of sales was 2,500,000 copies in all of the numerous editions, including fourteen luxurious editions with illustrations, one of which was advertised as "the most elaborately illustrated book in the country" and was bound in gold and silk and priced at $30.00 a set. In 1913 Sears, Roebuck and Company ordered an edition of one million copies to sell at thirty-nine cents. Translation was made into nearly every European tongue and some Asiatic languages, and unauthorized and plagiarized excerpts appeared here and abroad.

After resisting many offers to turn *Ben-Hur* into a play, including one from a company that planned to lease a thirty-acre tract on Staten Island, on which to present the famous chariot race, Wallace at length allowed Abraham Erlanger, a theatrical manager, to construct and produce a play, with the stipulation that it would use mostly the book's phraseology and that Christ was not to be presented. Erlanger instead represented the figure of the Savior by a shaft of light of 25,000 candle power. The play, with specially composed music, a cast of four hundred, and such tremendous sets as never before seen on

the stage, complete with treadmills and live horses for
the chariot race, was produced in six acts and thirteen
scenes and opened in New York on November 29, 1899.
It continued for twenty-one years all over the country on
enlarged stages, being performed by various companies
and casts, including famous actors, like William Farnum,
a total of 6,000 times, 20,000,000 people paying $10,000,-
000 in admissions, with standing room jammed full. Special trains were run to cities such as Louisville. *Ben-Hur's*
record as a stage production is unequaled in the history
of the American theater. And as the novel helped break
down the barrier to the reading of novels (General Grant,
for one, who had not read a novel in ten years, stayed up
all night to read it), so the staging of the book brought
millions of new faces to the theater. Religious leaders,
though divided on the subject of *Ben-Hur,* mostly supported it vigorously, as did Billy Sunday and William
Jennings Bryan. To millions of readers, theater-goers,
and movie-goers, when the book was rendered into a
Hollywood extravaganza by Metro-Goldwyn-Mayer in
1925, and again in 1959, *Ben-Hur* became a definitely
religious experience, causing tears to flow freely. Whether
the novel was good or bad as art, at least it must be said
that Wallace played a lion's share in popularizing fiction
and the theater with the American public. And the novel
earned for him more than writing had earned for any
other author of his generation; by 1936 *Ben-Hur* had
made more money for its various owners than any other
American novel. As Wallace said in 1899 when first viewing the stage sets for the play, "My God! Did I set all
this in motion?" He had.

The novel gave birth to a host of imitations, none of
which ever seriously approached the original in popularity: G. J. Whyte-Melville's *The Gladiators. A Tale of*

Rome and Judæa (1890); Marie Corelli's *Barabbas. A Dream of the World's Tragedy* (1894); Florence M. Kingsley's *Titus. A Comrade of the Cross* (1895); Robert Bird's *Paul of Tarsus* (1900); J. Breckenridge Ellis' *Adnah. A Tale of the Time of Christ* (1902); *Saul of Tarsus. A Tale of the Early Christians* (1906) by Elizabeth Miller (Hack); and Roe R. Hobbs's *The Court of Pilate. A Story of Jerusalem in the Days of Christ* (1906). The type still marches on today.[19]

After the meteoric success of *Ben-Hur*, Lew Wallace's last novel, *The Prince of India*, could be nothing but an anticlimax. The book had its origin in President Garfield's appointment in 1881 of General Wallace as minister to Turkey and Garfield's suggestion that he write a novel about Constantinople. The fall of that city in 1453 excited Wallace's imagination, and he planned to weave around this event a novel that was to be his *magnum opus*. It was aimed to be a revelation of the heroism of the Turks and was to weave into the events of the fall of the city the legend of the Wandering Jew. The book was

[19] For the information concerning *Ben-Hur* and some of the analysis of it, the author is indebted to McKee, *"Ben-Hur" Wallace*.

The newest *Ben-Hur* motion picture, released in 1959 with great "ballyhoo" by Metro-Goldwyn-Mayer, is said to have cost more than $14,000,000 to produce. It was voted the best film of that year by the New York film critics. This movie stimulated the Ben-Hur festival held in Crawfordsville on November 13-14, 1959, which featured speeches about Wallace, exhibits, and a parade ending at the Wallace study. The original manuscript of *Ben-Hur*, insured for $100,000 and protected by armed guard, was brought from Indiana University for the event. The movie has also resulted in a new flood of editions of the novel, with millions of copies now in print.

The original manuscript of *Ben-Hur* is now (1961) in the Lilly Library at Indiana University. At the time of the dedication of the library in the spring of 1961, twenty-seven pages of the manuscript which had been "lost" for many years and then discovered at Harper's in 1959, were given to the library and placed with the rest of the manruscript.

written for President Garfield and the Turkish sultan, Abdul-Hamid, now Wallace's friend. The admirers of *Ben-Hur* waited impatiently for the completion of the new novel, but the actual writing began only in 1887, and the book was not published until 1893.

The Prince in the novel, who was able to assume any religion — pagan, Mohammedan, Christian — was really Wallace himself, who had often puzzled people because he seemed to be anything but Hoosier Methodist. In this guise Wallace, as the Prince, proposed a federation of religions, which was, at least, an original touch. And it fell as much on deaf ears in 1893 as it does in the twentieth century. The novel was composed on as broad a canvas as *Ben-Hur,* but it was more elaborate, it abounded in the heroic, the physical, the marvelous, the strange, the noble, the picturesque, the exciting, and happily, the original. As Wallace is the Prince, so are his Zouaves the knights and courtiers, and the eve of the great battle is the eve of Wallace's battles in the Civil War; the places described are those he had visited in the Near East. But Wallace could not understand that nineteenth-century American efficient management and standardization could not be applied to fifteenth-century religious phenomena; hence, the Prince's attempt to unite all Christian and non-Christian religions under the banner of monotheism did not appear so implausible to him as to most readers. Yet, the tale is well told and gathers interest as it speeds along.

Most of the critics chose to ignore the book, as they had *Ben-Hur.* Of the ten or so that spoke none was more than lukewarm; and most picked flaws: in the universal religion, in the style, or in the melodrama. The real insult, however, came when Ernest A. Baker in his *Guide to Historical Fiction* judged *The Prince* to be "juvenile."

At first, the reading public, expecting another *Ben-Hur* and spurred by much advance sales promotion, rushed to buy the book, and 100,000 copies were purchased within six months; but evidently not finding what it wished, the public, like the reviewers, grew lukewarm, and only 100,-000 more copies were sold in the next fifty years.[20] The real defects in *The Prince of India* lay in the fact that the fall of Constantinople in 1453 and ecclesiastical history were not of much interest to contemporary Americans, and the story was too unreal and lacked the Christian appeal and the roaring climax of the chariot race in *Ben-Hur*. Furthermore, its universalism had for many the taint of a movement opposing all religion only recently encountered in the Midwest. An attempt to dramatize the book with lavish settings, machinery, and famous actors, as in the case of *Ben-Hur,* ran only eight weeks in Chicago and, in spite of some changes, only nine weeks in New York. What a pity it was that *The Prince of India* did not precede, instead of follow, *Ben-Hur!*[21]

Can we say, then, in conclusion to the study of Lew Wallace, that throughout his life he was an amateur—a very gifted amateur to be sure—but still a jack-of-all-trades, yet in none a master craftsman?[22] In none of his many careers was he a professional. The law, which he pursued intermittently, he did not especially like; he reveled in soldiering, but he was no Grant; the role of governor and diplomat were for him just a passing fancy, a

[20] Wallace, however, realized enough from the advance sales to build the first modern apartment house in Indianapolis, at Meridian and Vermont streets, which he named The Blacherne, after the palace of the emperor of Constantinople in the book. The apartment house is still in use.

[21] Again, for much of the material on *The Prince of India* I am indebted to McKee.

[22] Forbes, in Banta, *Indiana Authors and Their Books,* is the source of this general idea.

plum for his pride; writing was only an avocation. Still, it is as the author of his novels, particularly *Ben-Hur,* that he will be remembered, in spite of the snubbing of the critics. In general, the criticisms leveled at his novels were justifiable in pointing out the melodrama and the lack of characterization and originality. They are each far from being the great American novel, though the publishers of *Ben-Hur* once thus advertised it. Yet anyone who can so capture the average American's imagination as Wallace did in his greatest book and who can draw millions of people to the world of fiction and to the theater deserves better treatment than he has received from literary critics. He paved the way for a much greater public attention to fiction and to drama which many writers to come would enjoy, and many a novelist today has reason to thank Wallace for the indirect benefit he receives through interest in novel reading which the author of *Ben-Hur* stimulated.

But why did not Wallace, with his own brilliant and colorful life, full of adventure and fascinating incident, write about some of these subjects? Why did no novel like *Miss Ravenel's Conversion from Secession to Loyalty* or *The Red Badge of Courage* flow from his pen? The answer lies in his nature. Lew Wallace was a man born too late. Like Miniver Cheevy, he "loved the days of old when swords were bright and steeds were prancing"—but he was an enormously successful Miniver. He was of the order of Scott and Dumas; that is, he was about as far from the tenets of realism as one could be, and his romantic attitude toward life stimulated his rejection of the present and his escape to the storied past, in the long ago and the far away. Only large subjects and great movements interested him; he was, as Meredith Nicholson points out, "an Oriental with medieval tastes, another Sir

Richard Burton."[23] He was a link between the old days of the dauntless knights and the present world of fact; he was of the atmosphere of Thermopylae continued to Shiloh. He could be only a romanticist. The debt Indiana literature owes to him is enormous.[24]

MARY HARTWELL CATHERWOOD

The next Indiana novelist, Mary Hartwell (Mrs. James Steele) Catherwood (1847-1902), was likewise a romanticist, but only in the latter part of her career; for she was a realist for many years before she wrote her romances. She met with less fame than the Eggleston brothers or Wallace. Still, she was a writer of importance in her time, and her life touched the lives and careers of many literary figures, particularly the local colorists and realists—and also a Brahmin or two, like William Dean Howells. Some of her stories are significant in that they precede novels which have often been thought to hold the distinction of being the first in their field; and her romances, though in some ways rather thin, were popular. She holds yet other importance for us. As the foremost scholar to investigate her work, Robert Price, has said,

Mrs. Catherwood was the first American woman novelist of any significance born west of the Appalachians. That fact when viewed by itself is of little worth in the main story of American fiction except as an interesting chronological "first." It assumes considerable significance, on the other hand, when one considers that Mrs. Catherwood was also the first woman of any prominence in American literature to acquire a college education, that she was graduated not from a school in the

[23] "Lew Wallace as an Author," in *In Memoriam. Major-Gen. Lew Wallace* (Military Order of the Loyal Legion, n. p. 1905), 17.
[24] Any student of Lew Wallace should begin with McKee's book. See also Russo and Sullivan, *Bibliographical Studies of Seven Authors of Crawfordsville*. Wallace's letters are to be found in the Indiana State Library.

East but from a new college sprung up in Ohio, that she won this education by her own efforts against extremely difficult odds, and that she was probably the first woman writer from the new West to support herself independently, even for a short time, by free-lance authorship. Mary Hartwell Catherwood was not merely one more gifted woman among the large number of such American writers who appeared in the generation after Emerson. She was the pioneer woman writer in the first generation of Middle Western authorship. Her career epitomizes the struggle faced by any woman of her region and generation who chose writing for a vocation. Her work stands as a significant product of the forces necessarily at work in that particular milieu.[25]

We must differ with the above statement in two respects: Alice and Phoebe Cary, rather than Mrs. Catherwood, were evidently the first women writers from the West to support themselves by their pens (they did so nearly their entire adult lives); and Mrs. Catherwood, instead of being "the pioneer woman writer in the first generation of Middle Western authorship," followed not only the Cary sisters but also Julia Dumont and Sarah T. Bolton. Nevertheless, Price has indicated the significance of Mrs. Catherwood, and it is evident that no serious student of American literature—to say nothing of Indiana literature—from the Civil War to the turn of the century can afford to overlook her work.

Mary Hartwell Catherwood was born in the small settlement of Luray in Licking County, Ohio, the daughter of Dr. Marcus Hartwell, who had attended Marietta College and had studied medicine in Columbus, and Phoebe Thompson Hartwell. For several years Mary watched the current of western migration flow past her very door;

[25] Robert Price, "A Critical Biography of Mrs. Mary Hartwell Catherwood: A Study of Middle Western Regional Authorship, 1847-1902," reprinted from *Abstracts of Doctoral Dissertations*, No. 43, The Ohio State University Press, 1944, p. 125. Quoted by permission of the University.

then when she was ten, the family joined it, settling at length in Milford, Illinois, where the parents soon died, leaving Mary, a younger brother, and a younger sister to be reared by their maternal grandparents at Hebron, Ohio. The early trip on the National Road to Illinois was later to be featured in an autobiographical sketch for children, *Old Caravan Days* (Boston, 1884). A novel, *Craque-O'-Doom* (Philadelphia, 1881), written in Indianapolis, tells of her unhappy girlhood in Hebron, called Barnet in the book, a town on the National Road at the Ohio Canal. The respectable but decadent life of the town is pictured in very bitter terms, making this novel a prototype of Sherwood Anderson's *Winesburg, Ohio* (1919) and several other such books and anticipating Edgar Watson Howe's *The Story of a Country Town* (1883) by two years. At fourteen she began to teach country schools to relieve her poverty, and two years later she commenced to publish her stories and poetry in *The North American,* of Newark, Ohio. By teaching she worked her way through the Granville Female Seminary, entering in 1865 and finishing the four-year course in three years, graduating in 1868. From 1868 until 1874 she continued her teaching, taking schools in Granville, Ohio, and Danville, Illinois, varying her routine by writing poems, articles, and stories. One of these stories, published in 1871 in *Wood's Household Magazine,* won a prize of $100. None of this early material, however, was more than mediocre, and it was perfunctorily romantic.

Encouraged by the reception of her work, in 1874 she took the bold step of giving up teaching for the hazardous career of a free-lance writer, which she successfully pursued, in Newburgh, New York, and then in Cincinnati, until 1877, when the economic depression coming in the middle seventies forced her into a brief dependence on relatives and friends in Illinois. Potboilers during this brave venture included her undistinguished first novel, *A Woman in Armor* (New York, 1875), which appeared initially in *Hearth and Home.*

In December, 1877, she married James Steele Catherwood, of Hoopeston, Illinois; and the couple lived over the railway station in the little town of Oakford (formerly Fairfield), in Howard County, Indiana. Here Mrs. Catherwood, no longer having to support herself, began to report on Western life as she saw and felt about it, not caring any longer whether the material sold. Her dislike of the ugliness and narrowness of mind found in rural life and in small towns now came to the fore and was translated into stories that are startling in their critical realism even today.

One such story, "The Monument of the First Mrs. Smith," published in the Kokomo (Indiana) *Weekly Dispatch,* of November 7, 1878, tells an unlovely story of how Susan Smith, a farmer's wife, grown gaunt and ugly through overwork and privation in developing the farm, dies and is superseded by a new, demanding wife who has much more expensive tastes; yet Smith is now able to afford these excesses because of the industry of Susan, whose gravestone he has not yet got around to erecting.

Another story, "A Little God," serialized in the same newspaper from December 19, 1878, to January 16, 1879, provided a similarly realistic picture of the boom-town development of Hoopeston, Illinois, which she disguised slightly as Whoopertown or Whooper City, showing the squalor, the vicious bickering of factions about planning the town, and the greedy rush for salable lands to turn into town lots. Eighteen years later Mrs. Catherwood was to rework this story into a novelette, *The Spirit of an Illinois Town* (Boston, 1897), which received at least one favorable review and which Professor Fred Lewis Pattee termed "a realistic story of a typical boom town," "the very soul of the new West."[26] But despite this praise, the book is no longer read.

Even Oakford itself appeared in her stories, hardly disguised under its earlier name of Fairfield, as in "Mallston's Youngest," a local-color story published in *Lippincott's Magazine* in August, 1880. "The Career of a Prairie Farmer," the simple story of how some young Ohioans finally conquered prairie farms in Illinois, was issued in the same magazine in June of that year and was reprinted, along with similar stories, in *The Queen of the Swamp and Other Plain Americans* (Boston, 1899). These stories can stand as samples of her early local color and realistic efforts.[27]

While she was perfecting her style in this early fiction and was gaining a sort of recognition, she met in Kokomo in February, 1879, James Whitcomb Riley, whose work was yet unrecognized and who, therefore, was greatly discouraged. Mrs. Catherwood, likewise, was not completely happy, since she had given up literature for marriage in an unloved country town. Their ripening friendship resulted in mutual literary inspiration, and they collaborated on several projects, among which was "The Whittleford Letters," a romantic story of the lives of two writers that, strangely, resembled theirs; but the story was abandoned when the writers realized that the romance was becoming too true.

The Catherwoods moved to Indianapolis late in 1879, where Riley had just gone to work on the *Journal* and

[26] *A History of American Literature Since 1870* (New York, 1915), 262.
[27] For much of the material concerning these early stories of Mrs. Catherwood I am indebted to Robert Price's article, "Mrs. Catherwood's Early Experiments with Critical Realism," in *American Literature*, 17 (1945):140-51.

where Mr. Catherwood operated a confectionery. His wife was quickly swept into the literary life of the city, and for some two years she contributed to George C. Harding's *Saturday Review* and served as drama critic for the magazine. She is described as being then an attractive, graceful person with hazel eyes and auburn hair. The association with like-minded people must have greatly inspired her, because while she lived in Indianapolis her literary production was large. In addition to *Craque-O'-Doom* (the title coming from one of Riley's poems), she published many of her best local stories, like "Mallston's Youngest," and two juveniles, *The Dogberry Bunch* (Boston, 1879) and *Rocky Fork* (Boston, 1882). These juveniles were eventually followed by others—*The Secrets at Roseladies* (Boston, 1888), *Bony and Ban* (Boston, 1898), and *Heroes of the Middle West* (Boston, 1898). During this period she also wrote stories like "Serena," published in the June, 1882, *Atlantic Monthly*, which in recording a death and funeral on an Ohio farm was deficient in plot but was crammed full of perfect reporting of customs, incidents, and manners of the Midwest. Then, perhaps as a result of her association with Riley, she began to see country and village life in a less caustic and more sentimental light. It was a natural, but slow, shift to the point of view of *The Romance of Dollard* (New York, 1889).

In the meantime she and her family moved to Hoopeston, Illinois, where they lived from 1882 to 1899 and where Mr. Catherwood was postmaster and was associated with a real-estate firm. Here, in spite of living again in a small town with all its defects, she awoke to her best subject in writing, that of the early history of the French in North America as recorded and popularized by the accurate and vivid histories of Francis Parkman. She was captivated by the spirit of romance which she saw abounding everywhere in these French materials. Now occurred the metamorphosis of Mrs. Catherwood the realist into Mrs. Catherwood the confirmed romanticist, who became so imbued with romance that in 1893 at the Chicago World's Fair she defended that point of view effectively in a public debate with the young Hamlin Garland, who was an exponent of realism. Nearly everything she wrote from 1889 till the publication of her last book, *Lazarre* (Indianapolis, 1901), was romantic, and most of it dealt with French subjects.

The Romance of Dollard is representative of Mrs. Catherwood's romantic novels. It grew out of a friendship with an Indiana poet, Benjamin S. Parker. While living in Indianapolis Mrs. Catherwood had met Parker, who at that time was American consul at Sherbrook, Canada. Taking an interest in her literary aspirations, Parker invited her to pay his family a visit; this she did soon, and while there she witnessed the celebration of St. John's Day. In the procession there was a float which represented the historical figure Dollard and his sixteen men, all of whom willingly sacrificed their lives in 1660 in order to check the advance of the hostile Iroquois on Montreal, then a small French outpost. Mrs. Catherwood conceived the idea of her story from this sight. She spent some time in Canada collecting material for it, then wrote the story of the incident much as it had actually occurred. Instead of following the usual manner of the writers of historical romances in creating nonhistorical characters to add to the cast of historical figures, she altered the historical characters themselves. For example, she gave the hero, Adam Dollard, Sieur des Ormeaux, a sweetheart, Claire Laval, who had been unattainable in France but who, fleeing her guardian's plans for distasteful marriage matches for her, comes to Canada, where she and Dollard are married. Claire accompanies her husband to the lonely little fort, where she is killed along with the rest of the band. Many historical persons flock through the story, such as several Sisters of the old Hôtel-Dieu (the hospital) at Montreal and the Huron chief Annahotaha, who with a few Hurons participates in the expedition and dies with Dollard; many places, such as old Quebec and Dollard's seigniory on the island of St. Bernard in the broad St. Lawrence, are well depicted. Indeed the whole atmosphere and spirit of old French Canada are well set forth.

Mrs. Catherwood's old friend, James Whitcomb Riley, helped introduce the writer and the manuscript to the editor of *Century Magazine,* in which it was first serialized in 1888. Her model, Francis Parkman, himself wrote a preface which was published with the book, in which he praised the romance for its historical accuracy, adding that

the author is a pioneer in what may be called a new departure in American fiction. Fenimore Cooper, in his fresh and manly way, sometimes touches Canadian subjects and introduces us to French soldiers and bush-rangers; but he knew Canada only from the outside, having no means of making its acquaintance from within, and it is only from within that its quality as material for romance can be appreciated. . . .
The realism of our time has its place and function; but an eternal analysis of the familiar and commonplace is cloying after a while, and one turns with relief and refreshment to such fare as that set before us in Mrs. Catherwood's animated story.

In the main Parkman was correct in that Mrs. Catherwood was a pioneer in the subject field, but one is somewhat astonished to see Parkman condoning such liberties as she often takes with her historical figures with no authenticating evidence, in spite of her many footnotes confirming much of the rest of the action. One wonders also why she does not use more foreshadowing and why some of the action is described in vague terms. Still, in spite of these faults and an overly simple plot, this is a well-written, fascinating story, full of the exciting vigor of the North, a happy selection of romantic elements, and a power a little like that of Thomas Hardy to personalize the setting. *Dollard* sold widely, and with it Mrs. Catherwood achieved considerable recognition.

Many similar romances of New France followed, most of them first being serialized in the *Atlantic, Century,* or *Harper's: The Story of Tonty* (Chicago, 1890); *The Lady of Fort St. John* (Boston, 1891), which Pattee calls the best of her romances, probably because of the character Rossignol;[28] and *Old Kaskaskia* (Boston, 1893). *The Chase of Saint-Castin and Other Stories of the French in the New World* (Boston, 1894) is a collection of her second type of regional short story, this group centering in the French life along the border of the United States and including the powerful tale, "The Windigo." This collection of stories and *Mackinac and Lake Stories* (New York, 1899) are her best. *The White Islander* (New York, 1893) evidences transition from French subjects and descends to melodrama in the scene in which the Indians start to burn the hero at the stake and his sweetheart Marie, unable to save him, springs into the flame to die by his side. The priest, powerless to help, marries them as the flames crackle; then a rescuing party dash in just in the nick of time to save the couple. *The Days of Jeanne d'Arc* (New York, 1897), written after much research and reading on the peasants in France, she said originated in an impulse from God; and *Spanish Peggy. A Story of*

[28] *A History of American Literature,* 260.

Young Illinois (Chicago, 1899) contains the figure of the young Lincoln. In 1899 she separated from her husband and lived thenceforth mostly in Chicago. Her *Lazarre* (Indianapolis, 1901), a historical romance growing out of the career of Eleazar Williams, claimed to be the "lost dauphin" of France, was her greatest success; and it was soon produced as a play, starring Otis Skinner. Mrs. Catherwood died in Chicago on December 26, 1902, leaving some unpublished work.[29]

Mary Hartwell Catherwood can not be quickly summarized and dismissed. Her most popular work was done in the field of historical romance, and in that she tapped with sure touch time and again the riches of the early French romantic lore. She was never adept in skilful plotting. She often sentimentalizes her characters; she over-documents her historical materials, yet she takes much liberty with her historical characters, and she falls occasionally into melodrama. Still, her books show careful research, a strong feeling for the wilderness, and an ability to vitalize the past. As Pattee states it:

Amid this wild landscape a wild social order—savage Indians, explorers, *voyageurs,* flaming Jesuits, *habitants, grands seigneurs,* soldiers of fortune—Frontenac, Tonty, Dollard, La Salle, Bigot, Montcalm, and perhaps the lost dauphin, son of Louis XVI and Marie Antoinette—and in the heart of it all and the moving force of it all, beautiful women, exiles from France, exquisite maidens educated in convents, charmingly innocent, little Indian girls, Indian queens, robust daughters of *habitants.* Swords flash in duel and battle, love rules utterly even such stormy souls as La Salle's, plots with

[29] Biographical material concerning Mrs. Catherwood was obtained from the two articles by Price already cited, the sketch in Banta, *Indiana Authors and Their Books,* 54-56, and the article by Dorothy A. Dondore in the *Dictionary of American Biography, Authors Edition,* 3:573-74. Memories of Mrs. Catherwood lingered long in Indianapolis, as she was greatly beloved there.

roots that extend even across the ocean into France are worked out in secret fastness—with such material and such background romantic combinations are endless.[30]

Probably Mrs. Catherwood's romances have not stood well the test of time because of their flimsy quality, but this romantic work came at the beginning of the sudden flowering of romances around the turn of the century and as such is significant of the dawn of that movement. Such tales as *Alice of Old Vincennes* and *Monsieur Beaucaire* logically followed.

Perhaps still more significant, however, are her realistic works, which have been so overshadowed by the romances. Had she better developed this vein, she might have become, as Pattee says, the Miss Wilkins or Miss Jewett of her area. In her stories of critical realism she antedated the novels that have usually been given the credit as chronological firsts, and she might have become a much greater writer had she retained this attitude toward literature. Perhaps it was not only the force of Riley's example that lured her away from realism; she may have found her constant confinement in the villages which she considered ugly and spiritually limiting so unpleasant that she escaped into romance. At any rate, she deserves the reevaluation that has been slowly developing.[31]

MAURICE THOMPSON

The next novelist, (James) Maurice Thompson (1844-1901), has fared better by the hand of time, for his name is well remembered today, and his *Alice of Old Vincennes*

[30] Quoted in Fred Lewis Pattee, *A History of American Literature Since 1870* (Copyright, 1915, The Century Company), 260. By permission of Appleton-Century-Crofts, Inc.

[31] Suggestions for the analysis of Mrs. Catherwood's works have been found in the four sources cited in Note 29 above and in Dorothy A. Dondore, *The Prairie and the Making of Middle America* . . . (Cedar Rapids, Iowa, 1926), 258-62.

still thrills the young in heart. As a romanticist who published novels in the last twenty years of the nineteenth century he is less significant in the history of American literature as a whole than Mrs. Catherwood in her early tales of realism, since Thompson mostly followed the current trend of blossoming romanticism. Yet this versatile writer excelled in many fields of endeavor, being a civil engineer; a politician; an outdoor man who called frequent attention to nature and who helped popularize archery as a sport; a scientist making valuable contributions to the fields of botany, zoology, and geology; a literary critic who fought relentlessly against the rising tide of realism in literature; a Confederate soldier, who later was a law partner of his former arch enemy, General Lew Wallace; and also a poet and a novelist. In a sense Thompson was a cross between his friend, Lew Wallace, and his fellow rebel soldier and romanticist, George C. Eggleston. He is one of the best-known figures of Indiana literature.

Maurice Thompson (he early dropped his first name, James) came of a thoroughly American background, his cultured mother having descended from Dutch stock and his father's Scotch-Irish forebears having come through Virginia, North Carolina, and Tennessee into Kentucky. His great-great-grandfather enjoyed the friendship of Daniel Boone. Maurice was born on September 9, 1844, to the Reverend Matthew Grigg and Diantha (Jaeggar) Thompson, in Fairfield, Indiana, where his father was pastor of the Primitive Baptist Church. After a time the Reverend Mr. Thompson was transferred to a pastorate in Missouri, and then to Georgia, where another son was born, Will Henry Thompson, who was to write two famous poems about the Civil War.[32] By 1854 the father had inherited a plantation with slaves in the Coosawattee

[32] For Will Henry Thompson, see above, 197-98.

Valley of northern Georgia and for this or some other reason left the ministry and established his family on the plantation, where, schools being few and poor, he had his sons tutored. Maurice was taught Latin, Greek, Hebrew, French, German, and mathematics. The last subject was important, since he chose to become a civil engineer. But education did not represent for the boys simply something enclosed within the covers of books; in the outdoors they learned science, and also they picked up woodcraft and archery from men who had been taught by the Cherokee Indians. The brothers were later to make full use of this knowledge.

When the war broke out, Maurice, not yet eighteen, enlisted in the Confederate Army, and Will soon followed suit. Probably it was in part his knowledge of woodcraft that made Maurice an able scout for the Confederacy. Though during the conflict he became convinced that the North was right, he still gave faithful service to the South. He returned from the conflict to recover from a bullet wound in the chest and found his family destitute, their home having been in the line of Sherman's march to the sea. He worked in the fields, sold squirrels at ten cents to buy books, and soon went to Calhoun, Georgia, where he continued his studies in engineering, read law, and was admitted to the bar. Here in Calhoun he evidently did his first serious writing, contributing poetry to *Scott's Monthly Magazine* and to other struggling Southern literary journals which were barely treading water in the tempest of Reconstruction. In 1867 he commenced a scientific survey—botanical, zoological, and ornithological—of Lake Okeechobee, Florida, of the Okeefinokee Swamp, and of other such regions in the South.

Although these scientific pursuits were interesting and perhaps rehabilitating to a war veteran, there seemed to be little future in them—or in any other line of work in these dark days in the South, for that matter—so Maurice and his brother Will considered the matter carefully and decided upon a bold course. Since the South was overrun by carpetbaggers, who seemed to be milking the area of what little the war had left untouched, why could not the North use two good former rebel soldiers? Packing knapsacks, they set out in 1868 to walk north.

Several weeks later they wandered into Crawfordsville, Indiana, probably unaware—or not caring—that General Lew Wallace and three other retired Union generals lived in this hotly pro-Union town. The brothers were slight of build but erect and muscular and had dark hair, olive skin, and gray eyes. Luck was with them, for they were received by the townspeople much more hospitably than they expected; and quickly a Crawfordsville resident, John Lee, who was in charge of constructing a railroad near by, gave the brothers jobs as engineers. Once when Maurice called at the house of Lee on business, his daughter Alice answered the doorbell; and, to make a long story short, within a year the two were married and settled in Crawfordsville. Some years later Will Thompson married Alice's sister Ida.

In 1871, after he had established himself financially, Maurice dropped engineering to open a law office with his brother in this same town, their chosen home; this pursuit permitted him to devote some time to his first love, literature. He practiced law until 1884, being a partner for a time with Lew Wallace, for the two former enemies in war quickly forgave each other and became fast friends, particularly enjoying together outdoor sports, such as fishing, to say nothing of their interest in literature. An honor bestowed upon few former rebel soldiers came to Maurice in 1879, when he was elected to the

Indiana legislature. In 1884 he gave up law for literature; and, except for serving two terms as Indiana state geologist and head of the department of natural history, from 1885 to 1889, he followed writing and lecturing as a career until his death.

He was a shy, retiring person who shunned publicity but was friendly and a gracious host at his beautiful home near Lew Wallace's in Crawfordsville, called Sherwood Place after the forest frequented by the great legendary archer, Robin Hood. Here he and his charming wife entertained, among others, William Dean Howells, who came to Crawfordsville to secure local color and information on divorce courts while writing *A Modern Instance*. These two friends disagreed on the subject of realism, for Thompson always was a romanticist, but they enjoyed each other immensely. The Thompson family always wintered in Maurice's beloved South, at their winter home in Bay St. Louis, Mississippi, where Thompson delighted in the semitropical waters and woods. In 1900 Wabash College, in Crawfordsville, awarded Thompson the degree of Doctor of Letters. When he died of pneumonia at Sherwood Place on February 15, 1901, the local G. A. R. post attended the funeral of this former rebel in tribute to him, and the local schools observed Maurice Thompson Day with fitting exercises and readings from his works. Here was a rebel who had captured the hearts of his enemies.[33]

[33] Biographical information on Maurice Thompson was obtained from many sources, but particularly the following: Banta, *Indiana Authors and Their Books*, 317-19; the article by Frank H. Ristine in *Dictionary of American Biography, Authors Edition*, 18:460-61; the article by William H. Hayne in the *Library of Southern Literature*, 12:5255-58; Charles F. Smith, *Reminiscences and Sketches* (Nashville, Tenn., 1908), 113-35; obituaries in the Indianapolis *News* and *Sentinel* of February 16, 1901; and Russo and Sullivan, *Bibliographical Studies of Seven Authors of Crawfordsville*, 175-77.

Thompson published many scientific studies, as in the field of geology, which can not be considered in this present analysis. He began his imaginative works, however, with *Hoosier Mosaics* (New York, 1875), a collection of gracefully written dialect sketches and stories, rather realistic in a faithful depiction of Indiana people, small towns like Colfax, and rural scenes like the Kokomo Fair Grounds. But it had also an aura of romance in its simplicity, beauty, and even, at times, mystery, as in "Was She a Boy?" the story of a youthful and strange figure who may have been a disguised criminal. The book made Thompson famous in Indiana.

Now followed two books drawn from youthful experience on the subject of archery, which came after magazine articles on the subject: *The Witchery of Archery: A Complete Manual of Archery. With Many Chapters of Adventures by Field and Flood* ... (New York, 1878) and *How to Train in Archery. Being a Complete Study of the York Round*, written with his brother Will (New York, 1879). Because of the subject and the breezy treatment of it these two books were surprisingly successful, and they and the articles on this same theme created a nationwide interest in the sport, which has continued till the present.[34] All his life Maurice Thompson retained his interest in archery, often winning competitions. He also published three collections of nature sketches: *By-Ways and Bird Notes* (New York, 1885); *Sylvan Secrets, in Bird-Songs and Books* (New York, 1887); and *My Winter Garden. A Nature Lover under Southern Skies* (New York, 1900). Juveniles from his pen also reflected his outdoor interests and include *Claude's Big Trout* (Boston, 1884); *The Boys' Book of Sports and Outdoor Life* (edited

[34] Many modern manuals of archery give the Thompson brothers credit for reawakening national interest in the sport.

by Thompson and partly written by him, New York, 1886); *The Ocala Boy. A Story of Florida Town and Forest* (Boston, 1895); and *Stories of Indiana* (New York, 1898), which latter book is Indiana history told in the form of stories. Various expository works on history and literature also appeared; *The Ethics of Literary Art. The Carew Lectures for 1893, Hartford Theological Seminary* (Hartford, Connecticut, 1893) dealt with morality in literature and attacked realism.

But it is as a poet and a writer of romances that Thompson will be best remembered. His verse is published in two collections only, *Songs of Fair Weather* (Boston, 1883) and *Poems* (Boston, 1892). Though some critics predicted about the time of his death and shortly afterward that Thompson would be remembered for his poetry, such has not been the judgment of history, for his *Alice of Old Vincennes* overshadows all of his other works. Nevertheless, there is much to be said for his verse. It is primarily nature poetry of unequal merit, full of scenes of Indiana, Georgia, and Florida; but there are not the usual landscapes of poetry described in a merely pretty manner. Against a background traced with delicacy he conjures up surprisingly and briefly some spirit of the forest, and there is often in his diction a novelty and freshness that pleases the reader, as in "Before Dawn." He usually handles his subjects so well that they leave one with a feeling of awe and wonder as though something of rare beauty had appeared fleetingly. A feeling for and thorough knowledge of the out-of-doors pervades the poems—for example, in "A Flight Shot," "The Death of the White Heron," and "In the Haunts of Bass and Bream," which describes the catching of a bass. The poems on archery are realistic and musical, and his odes, such as "In Captivity," evidence a broadening of his horizons. His verse is thoroughly American—he prefers the mockingbird to the nightingale—and he deals fervently with patriotic subjects, as seen in his stirring poem on Reconstruction entitled "To the South." "Lincoln's Grave" was the Harvard Phi Beta Kappa poem of 1893. Yet, in spite of these merits, his verse often lacks finish and spontaneity, and he is not a first-rate poet. Thompson's nature poetry came a few years before the publication of Evaleen Stein's nature verse in *One Way to the Woods* (1897) and *Among the Trees Again* (1902); and these two are Indiana's main nature poets.[35]

Except for *Alice,* Thompson's romantic novels are of much the same type and can be treated together. *A Tallahassee Girl* (Boston, 1882); *His Second Campaign* (Boston, 1883); *At Love's Extremes* (New York, 1885—reissued in 1901 as *Milly: At Love's Extremes. A Romance of the Southland); A Fortnight of Folly* (New York, 1888), *The King of Honey Island* (New York, 1893); and *Sweetheart Manette* (Philadelphia, 1901) are all cut from the same tapestry of romance and are sentimental, colorful stories of the post-bellum South. In *His Second Campaign* characters from the West and South are contrasted, and the author anticipates his use of the romantic historical novel later seen in *The King of Honey Island* and in *Alice.* Thompson returned to the short story in *Stories of the Cherokee Hills* (Boston, 1898), reminiscent of his Southern boyhood in a slave state. Both *A Banker of Bankersville* (New York, 1886), a study of village life, and *Rosalynde's Lovers* (Indianapolis, 1901), a romantic novel, have their settings in Indiana. Although two or three of these books enjoyed a good sale, most of them were not much noticed, and none of them was of consequence.

[35] Nicholson's *The Hoosiers*, 205-8, has been of help in analyzing Thompson's verse.

It was only at the last of his career that Maurice Thompson was able to write a very successful novel, a best seller that sealed his reputation as one of the foremost literary figures of the Midwest. It was, of course, *Alice of Old Vincennes* (Indianapolis, 1900). Why he had not been able to hit before upon this sure formula of a mixture of fiction and the history of a significant event in American—and Indiana—history is not clear. The story is based on the early history of the little French settlement of Vincennes on the lower Wabash, its vicissitudes under British rule, and the victorious expedition of George Rogers Clark which won the town for the Americans. Thompson had little to change in his historic characters—he had only to fill out the characters, add a few extra figures, and supply incidents. Actually he capitalized on the recent publication of William H. English's *Conquest of the Country Northwest of the River Ohio 1778-1783 and Life of Gen. George Rogers Clark* (Indianapolis, 1897), but over all the authenticated facts he wove expertly the fabric of romance. Though the story has the air of historical accuracy,[36] the characters come alive in a way that Thompson had never before achieved. Best drawn are the beautiful, athletic, brave, and spirited Alice; the conscientious old Father Beret, of mysterious antecedents; the wizened, physically repulsive, but courageous and likable scout, Oncle Jazon; and Long Hair, the hideous, cruel savage, and other Indians as well—but Lieutenant Beverly is only the conventional hero, and the love element, likewise, is conventional. Strangely for the nature lover which

[36] The letter of Gaspard Roussillon (Francois Bosseron) written in 1788, to which the author refers in his dedication as the historical basis for his heroine Alice, has not been found and may be a bit of fiction. There have been several analyses of the history in Thompson's novel. One of these is "Judge Charles B. Lasselle's Notes on Alice of Old Vincennes," in *Indiana Magazine of History,* 4 (1908):81-85.

Thompson was, there is small feeling for nature in the book; Mrs. Catherwood would probably have featured it almost as a character itself. Also, the mystery concerning Father Beret's past is never resolved. The interest of the book lies mostly in externals; nevertheless, its strong, vivid movement and suspense carries the reader breathlessly through to the end.[37]

Alice was a best seller in 1900, and its record was improving, perhaps giving Thompson hope that its sales would equal the revival of the best seller of his friend down the street, Lew Wallace, whose success with *Ben-Hur* had made its author a trifle arrogant; but, as Banta remarks,[38] *Ben-Hur* continued its huge volume of sales after *Alice* had slowed in four or five years to a few thousand a year. By that time, however, the friendly competition was meaningless to Maurice Thompson, for he had expired quietly in 1901—at the peak of his fame.

James Maurice Thompson, then, lived and died a romanticist. As nonresident editor of *The Independent* during the last twelve years of his life, he spoke always, in a fresh, original style, for morality in literature and against realism.[39] He contributed 253 articles and poems to *The Independent* from 1883 to his death; his reputation as a Midwestern literary figure was of the highest.[40] He was a strong believer in the literary future of the West, considering it a nearly unworked field. In his works on archery and nature he stands nearly alone; in

[37] Another good novel on the capture of Vincennes by Clark is Caroline Krout's *On the We-a Trail* (see below, 387, 389). It is not of the quality of Thompson's, however.

[38] Page 319.

[39] See the unsigned editorial in *The Independent,* February 21, 1901, pp. 452-53.

[40] The article in the *Dictionary of American Biography* says Thompson's reputation was "the most commanding of his generation in the Middle West." I doubt that this extreme position is correct, however.

his poetry he is hardly more than mediocre; but in his novels, as a follower of Scott and also Southern imitators of Scott such as William Gilmore Simms, John P. Kennedy, and John Esten Cooke, he was a Southern romanticist transplanted to the fertile banks of the Wabash, who helped in the rebirth of romance at the end and turn of the century. His *Alice of Old Vincennes* served along with the novels of New France of Mary Hartwell Catherwood as a model for the great majority of the later historical novels. Thompson, thus, is significant both in Indiana letters and in American literature.

Maurice F. Egan and Dwight Le Roy Armstrong

Nothing of the sort, however, can be said about the next two novelists, Maurice F. Egan and Dwight Le Roy Armstrong, for they are definitely minor.

Maurice Francis Egan (1852-1924), diplomat, college professor, journalist, and writer of prose and poetry, devoted much of his life to the political and diplomatic world; and even though his books are numerous, his literary work served, at least in part, as an avocation, and most of it is not enduring. He was born in Philadelphia on May 24, 1852, and received from his mother, Margaret MacMullen, of a Scotch-Irish Philadelphia family, a love of literature and a devout Catholic faith; from his handsome father, Maurice Florent Egan, of a good Irish family who had emigrated to Philadelphia in 1825, came geniality, humor, and a sense of democracy—all traits that kept the son ever surrounded by friends. Maurice, Jr., became a connoisseur of good food, good wine, good music, and good society.

He attended St. Philip's Parochial School and LaSalle College, from which he received his A.B. degree in 1873. In both these institutions he followed classical studies but also read widely, and he began his writing by publishing at seventeen an essay in *Appletons' Journal* and soon was writing for the Philadelphia newspapers. From 1875 to 1878 he studied philosophy, taught at Georgetown University, and entered into the social and diplomatic life of Washington, D. C. He then undertook some study of law, obtained a Master's degree at Notre Dame University in 1878, and went to New York that year to pursue a career in journalism. In New York he was sub-editor of *Magee's Weekly* and in 1880 married Katharine Mullin of Philadelphia. After 1881 he was associate editor of *Freeman's Journal* and editor in 1888. During this period he wrote as many as fifteen thousand words a week—articles, verse, and book reviews—for newspapers and other magazines.

Partly for the sake of his children and partly because he desired a less strenuous life, in 1888 he became professor of English Literature at Notre Dame. He was an excellent lecturer and a leading figure in university and town life.[41] In 1896 he transferred to the Catholic University in Washington, where he resumed his participation in the political and social world and where he attained prominence as a liberal Catholic. He became, as Theodore Roosevelt expressed it, "unofficial diplomatic adviser" to Presidents. He helped Roosevelt and McKinley settle the problem of the friars' lands in the Philippines; and in 1907 Roosevelt appointed him minister to Den-

---

[41] Egan's account of his life while teaching at Notre Dame is to be found in his *Recollections of a Happy Life* (New York, 1924), 158-78. See also the account in Arthur J. Hope, *Notre Dame. One Hundred Years* (Notre Dame, Ind., 1943). Egan must have been something of a dilettante at Notre Dame and apparently did not allow his teaching duties to interfere with his extracurricular activities. He must have been delightful in his personal charm, yet rather odd. He claims to have worn the first top hat seen in South Bend, Indiana; and he seems frequently to have invited friends to his home for dinner, then forgotten about extending the invitation and expressed surprise when they appeared.

mark, where until the end of World War I, as a shrewd, patriotic, and charming public servant, he relayed to the administration information on European affairs and finally succeeded in arranging the purchase of the Danish West Indies. He declined the position from both Taft and Wilson of ambassador at Vienna and became in 1916 the senior diplomat in Copenhagen and was recognized as dean of the American diplomatic corps. His account of his successful service, *Ten Years Near the German Frontier* (New York, 1919), was well received at home.

After his return to America he resumed his old habit of writing articles, essays, reviews, verse, and stories—to say nothing of the flow of books. The latter part of his life was brightened by many honors, memberships, and lectureships. He died from kidney trouble in Brooklyn on January 15, 1924.[42]

Egan's literary output was enormous and, in addition to the articles, stories, and verse already mentioned, included school textbooks, translations, expository materials, novels, poetry, some literary criticism, and altogether thirteen juveniles. A few of these works, however—some of them products of his years in Indiana—may serve as examples of his entire contribution because of the peculiar quality that permeates nearly all his writing.

His first book was a novel, *That Girl of Mine* (Philadelphia, 1877). *The Life Around Us* (New York, 1885) is "a series of stories made by a Catholic for Catholics"[43]

[42] Biographical data on Egan was obtained from the article by Allan Westcott in *Dictionary of American Biography, Authors Edition*, 6:49-50, and from *Who Was Who in America*, Vol. 1 (1897-1942). For further biographical details and a complete list of his writings, see the biographical sketch by T. F. Meehan included in Egan's *Recollections of a Happy Life*. See also the commemorative tribute by David Jayne Hill published by the American Academy of Arts and Letters in 1924.

[43] Preface, p. v.

which had been first published in various periodicals, such as *The Catholic World*. These are good stories, with a heavy Catholic flavor touching on such questions as whether a worldly boy should become a priest or a girl should enter a convent. *A Garden of Roses. Stories and Sketches* (Boston, 1887) contains rather slight material, again with a definite Catholic tone. The characters are almost always Catholics, and the Church enters somehow into the action. *How They Worked Their Way and Other Tales* (New York, 1892; revised in 1898) is a book of stories about Catholic American children for Catholic American children. *A Marriage of Reason* (Baltimore, 1898) shows the resistance of some selfish people to acceptance of the Catholic Church and how they came to realize their error; *The Watson Girls. A Washington Story* (Philadelphia, 1900) is an unimportant book for girls. *Songs and Sonnets and Other Poems* (Chicago, 1892) is conventional in form and mediocre in quality; it has as its themes love and the Catholic faith, and the author has little to say. In general, then, Egan's imaginative work is that of a mediocre writer of poetry, novels, and stories, whose products in one way are conventional and in another are so colored by the Catholic creed that his art is much restricted and lacks universality of appeal. While Catholics, perhaps, may welcome this bent, his reading public is much reduced thereby.

Yet we should observe that this criticism does not hold for his two popular books, *Ten Years Near the German Frontier* and *Recollections of a Happy Life* (New York, 1924), which, although no longer much read, are still very readable. The debonaire charm of the author shines throughout the *Recollections*. It is unfortunate that his other works lack this universality. Maurice Francis Egan, therefore, must be counted as having been more important in his political and diplomatic life than in his literary production.

(Dwight) Le Roy Armstrong (1854-1927) made a smaller contribution than Egan and is known almost entirely for one of his few novels. He was born on May 13, 1854, at Plymouth, Indiana, was educated in the schools there, and studied law for a while at Indiana University, but abandoned his law books for a career in journalism. After newspaper reporting in Ladoga, Indiana, in 1896 he became editor of the Lafayette *Morning Journal* and was connected with that paper and with the Lafayette *Democrat* until 1905, when he moved to Salt Lake City and edited the *Herald-Republican*. He also worked with the Chicago newspapers for some years and died in Salt Lake City, March 29, 1927.[44]

Armstrong wrote expository works and novels, such as *An Indiana Man* (Chicago, 1890), an exposé of political corruption in the election of a sheriff; and *Dan Gunn* (Chicago, 1898), a worthless popular novel about how a raw country fellow journeyed to Chicago to find the local belle and a dandy that she had run away with. *The Outlaws. A Story of the Building of the West* (New York, 1902) is, fortunately, much better. It is a rather vigorous tale of the early Wabash country and the rapid growth of its heterogeneous population of common folk and features house raisings, the building of canals, raids of outlaws, and the cholera epidemic of 1832-33—a menace employed as a convenient device to kill off the undesirable characters.

[44] Banta, *Indiana Authors and Their Books*, 9.

Meredith Nicholson

It is a pleasant change to turn to one of the most eminent of Indiana literary figures, Meredith Nicholson (1866-1947), the dean of Hoosier writers, who discovered that the way to attain success is to stay in your own home town.[45] He stayed there, becoming one of the most famous of Midwestern literary men—and, incidentally, one of the most rabid of Hoosiers. His well-known books —such as his study of Indiana, *The Hoosiers;* his essays, such as *The Valley of Democracy;* and his novels, such as *The House of a Thousand Candles* and *A Hoosier Chronicle*—gained him a large popular following and carved a niche for him in the halls of fame. He was an important member of the literary circles both of his native Crawfordsville and of his adopted home, Indianapolis; and as journalist, poet, essayist, novelist, lecturer, and American diplomat, he attracted favorable attention both in the United States and abroad.

Meredith Nicholson's father, Edward Willis Nicholson, whose family history extended back to the colonial era, was born in Kentucky and moved when a young man to Montgomery County, Indiana, where he became a respected farmer and a member of Lew Wallace's company of Montgomery Guards, called familiarly the Zouaves. When the Civil War began, he served with other Zouaves in the eleventh regiment for three months, then transferred to the artillery—serving in the ninth and twenty-second batteries throughout the war. Likewise the fortunes of war affected Meredith's mother, Emily Meredith. She was born in Centerville, Indiana, the daughter of Samuel Caldwell Meredith, an early settler and a pioneer publisher and editor. During the war she

---

[45] See Nicholson's popular essay, "Stay in Your Own Home Town," in *Old Familiar Faces* (Indianapolis, 1929).

served as a nurse. Having met Edward Nicholson at Camp Morton in Indianapolis, soon after the war she married him, and the couple settled in Crawfordsville, where their son Meredith was born on December 9, 1866. Meredith Nicholson, therefore, came naturally by an interest in the Civil War, in pioneer Indiana, and in all that is characteristic of Hoosier life and culture.

When the son was six, the family moved to Indianapolis, where, except for three years in Denver and ten years in diplomatic service, Meredith was to spend the rest of his life, maintaining, nevertheless, close ties with Crawfordsville. In Indianapolis he attended the public schools but left high school during his first year, taking successively jobs as a drug store clerk, a worker in a print shop, a court reporter, and law clerk. At nineteen he began to study law; for a while he was in the office of William Wallace, brother of Lew Wallace, one of the leading attorneys of Indianapolis. The young student had the experience that so many students of law or practicing attorneys encounter, that of finding his real love to be writing instead of law.

The immediate impetus toward literary aspirations is not difficult to find. While working in William Wallace's office he was dazzled by the frequent visits of General Lew Wallace, who, from a youth's point of view, "glittered when he walked." Lew Wallace, of course, took an interest in Nicholson because of his father and encouraged him to write, as did another Crawfordsville literary figure, Mary Hannah Krout. Probably the greatest stimulus, however, came from meeting James Whitcomb Riley in the same law office. Later Riley made a special effort to congratulate Nicholson on the publication of a poem printed beside one of his own in the Cincinnati *Enquirer*, and he invited the fledgling, still only nineteen, to dinner and accepted him as a fellow author. The friendship of

Riley and Nicholson, begun in this manner, lasted throughout their lives, and some years later Nicholson and his family visited Riley regularly on Sunday afternoons.

Nicholson, thus inspired, made contributions to the Indianapolis newspapers and soon had deserted law for journalism. During the year 1884 he was with the Indianapolis *Sentinel,* then joined the editorial staff of the Indianapolis *News,* where he continued until 1897. Regretting his previous action in leaving school against his mother's advice, he attempted during his newspaper days to compensate for his educational deficiency by home study. He more than succeeded, teaching himself Latin, Greek, French, and Italian. His first book, *Short Flights* (Indianapolis, 1891), a collection of mediocre poems, abounding in clichés, was published in 1891 and prompted the award of an honorary A.M. degree by Wabash College in 1897.

In 1896 he married Eugenie Kountze, an attractive, charming, cultured, and wealthy girl of Omaha, Nebraska, whom he had met in Indianapolis, and who was to bear him three children. Nicholson's best man at the wedding in Omaha was a young Indianapolis writer who was having a dismal time getting anything published and was despairing of success. His name was Booth Tarkington.[46]

When Nicholson left the *News,* he spent an unsuccessful year as a stockbroker, then violated his own precept, as he later stated in one of his essays, about staying in one's home town, and moved in 1898 to Denver, Colorado, where for three years he was the unhappy treasurer and auditor of a coal-mining company, a kind of work which

[46] A feeling of competition and jealousy later grew up between Nicholson and Tarkington. Jean B. Sanders, Meredith Nicholson: Hoosier Cavalier (M. A. thesis, De Pauw University, 1952), 89. A copy of this thesis is in the Indiana State Library.

he disliked. Suffering from nostalgia, he wrote his study of Indiana, *The Hoosiers* (New York, 1900), which was well received and which remains one of the best works on Indiana culture and literature. Soon he was called back to Wabash College to receive a Doctor of Literature degree.[47]

In 1901 the Nicholsons decided to return to Indianapolis, and Meredith Nicholson determined to see if he could make a career of writing. His few years out of the state had given him a broader perspective and a deeper appreciation of the home scene and the culture of the Indiana people. Mrs. Nicholson provided the means whereby he could try this experiment, supplying an income and a house with a private study. His first task was to make a second collection of his poems, which had been appearing in various periodicals. It was not immediately accepted for publication, and when it did appear, under the title *Poems* (Indianapolis, 1906), it did nothing to add to his reputation, for the verse was of the same mediocre type as his first collection. He had done nothing to fulfill the great promise as a poet that some had originally predicted for him. About the only significance of the *Poems* lay in its prefatory poem "To James Whitcomb Riley," which so pleased Riley that he bought seventy-five copies and sent them here and there; this, according to Nicholson, evidently constituted most of the book's circulation. It was evident that his field lay elsewhere.

In the meantime he had speedily penned his first novel, *The Main Chance* (Indianapolis, 1903). It was dedicated

[47] Though Nicholson never attended Wabash College, he was always considered "a son of the college community." Letter of Dean (now President) Byron K. Trippet to Mrs. Jean B. Sanders, quoted in her thesis, Meredith Nicholson: Hoosier Cavalier, 21. Nicholson spoke frequently at Wabash College.

to his wife and was about her native city, Omaha, written as an indictment of big business and its extralegal methods, blackmail, and violence. In spite of its realism it is more of a love story with a happy ending than a cry against injustice.[48] It provoked much discussion in Omaha, and the *Bookman* of November, 1903, listed it as a best seller. It is said that Nicholson refused offers from New York dramatists who wished to turn the novel into a play, because he did not think it fitting for drama. This was his first success, and he found that he could write this sort of story easily and that it made money. Also, he found satisfaction in having it accepted by the local Bobbs-Merrill Company, whose officials he knew, since he had submitted it under the pseudonym "Mr. Wheeler."

His experiment in pursuing a literary life having proved an obvious success, Nicholson followed his first novel with a second, *Zelda Dameron* (Indianapolis, 1904), this time changing the locale to Indianapolis and making an attempt to link, in a semirealistic manner, pre-Civil War Indianapolis with the contemporary city. Many of its scenes could be identified.[49] This second story, however, did not sell as well as the first.

The production of novels once begun, Nicholson maintained the pace of publishing nearly every year until 1929. Next appeared his greatest success, *The House of a Thousand Candles* (Indianapolis, 1905), a romantic thriller which sold over 250,000 copies in the United

[48] Compare the tepid realism of *The Main Chance* with the harsher realism to be found in such novels as Alfred Henry Lewis' *The Boss*, an indictment of municipal corruption, published the same year.

[49] Russo and Sullivan, *Bibliographical Studies of Seven Authors of Crawfordsville*, 85, report that " 'Mariona' is Indianapolis; 'Jefferson Street,' Washington Street; 'High Street,' Virginia Avenue; 'Hamilton Club,' Columbia Club; 'Tippecanoe Club,' University Club."

States and was soon translated into other languages. Whereas his reputation became national with the publication of his first two novels, it was now international, and French critics gave him praise. This is a "plot" story and bears a brief recounting. John Glenarm, a young engineer who has dissipated the fortune inherited from his father in wandering over the world, receives in Naples a letter from a former schoolmate, Arthur Pickering, now a proud, tight-lipped lawyer, saying that Glenarm's grandfather is dead and has left his house and estate in Wabana County, Indiana, to his grandson. Glenarm returns to Indiana and discovers that in order to claim the property he must live on it a year "in an orderly and temperate manner." He finds it to be a large, unfinished house situated on a lake (Lake Maxinkuckee), near the village of Annandale (Culver). Bates, an inscrutable but perfect servant, is the only inhabitant.

Glenarm establishes himself in the house, studies his grandfather's books on architecture, and has many exciting adventures, in which he is shot at by an unknown assailant, hears mysterious noises in the house, grapples in dark underground passages with a stranger who is evidently searching for a treasure concealed by the grandfather, and finds in a recess in the wall of a tunnel notes for a large sum of money owed to the grandfather by Pickering. As Pickering and a sheriff attempt to evict Glenarm for violating the will, the grandfather, very much alive, steps out of a concealed door in the fireplace and explains that he had played dead in order to call his grandson home and inveigle him into choosing architecture as a profession. Pickering is confronted with evidence of his rascality, Glenarm marries the beautiful girl who has hovered about the edges of the action, the couple settle down in the house with the grandfather, and the tale ends happily. Of course, the entrance of the grand-father is a *deus ex machina* device, but all this adds up to a story told with zest and good characterization and action.

Nicholson wrote the following note, dated May 23, 1932, in a copy of the book now in the Indiana State Library:

This novel was written at 1500 N. Delaware Street, In-dianapolis, (a new home we had built), between October, 1904 and the following May. At this time there was a deluge of tales in imitation of Anthony Hope's "Prisoner of Zenda." It occurred to me to show if possible that a romantic tale could be written, without an "imaginary kingdom," with the scene in our own Indiana. Lake Maxinkuckee suggested the scene. . . . The success of the story surprised me. It was translated into five languages, was popular in England, and was dramatized with E. M. Holland, a distinguished actor, in the role of Bates. Two motion picture versions have been made. The title is still being paraphrased by advertisers. I have had more fun out of this tale than out of any other I have written. . . .[50]

The play taken from the novel broke all stock records during its first year, and it was repeated for years, being produced even in England, Australia, and South Africa.[51] The book itself is still read. Its sequel, *Rosalind at Red Gate* (Indianapolis, 1907), was not nearly so successful, but was also dramatized.

For a time Nicholson deserted Hoosier settings. In *The Port of Missing Men* (Indianapolis, 1907) he contin-

[50] Russo and Sullivan, *op. cit.*, 89n-90n, report that "according to the Peoria, Illinois, *Star,* December 16, 1906, a railway was advertising 'The Road of a Thousand Wonders,' two widely separated candy manufacturers described their respective enterprises as 'The House of a Thousand Candies,' and a summer resort hotel was called 'The House of a Thousand Delights.'"

[51] The author happened to encounter one of the movies made from the novel running as a television show on June 22, 1955.

ued what he had begun in *The House of a Thousand Candles*—trying to bring romantic adventure to America without aid of costumes or exotic scenes. This time he chose the Virginia hills as a background against which to place an intrigue of the Hapsburgs and a hero who is eventually disclosed as an Austrian nobleman. The novel was not so well received as *The Candles;* yet it too was made into a motion picture. *The Little Brown Jug at Kildare* (Indianapolis, 1908) was suggested by the current election and was a light comedy and romance about two governors and their families. Nicholson's friendship with the governor-elect of Indiana, Thomas Marshall, who later became Vice-President, supplied the inspiration. Then after gathering material on labor conditions in Pittsburgh—and recalling his three years of experience in the coal industry in Denver—the novelist penned *The Lords of High Decision* (New York, 1909), a story of the Pittsburgh coal barons in which he tried to construct a better novel by doing more thorough characterizations; yet his expectation that he would thereby lose with his public was realized.[52] And in *The Siege of the Seven Suitors* (Boston, 1910) he bade farewell to cloak-and-dagger intrigue in a farce comedy; but strangely—or perhaps we should say of course—his readers, now educated in Nicholsoniana, took the story as straight romance, and he complained in a note written on the flyleaf of a gift copy that no one had found it funny.

In *A Hoosier Chronicle* (Boston, 1912) he returned to a Hoosier setting and wrote what many critics consider his best novel; yet it is not a finished product, for the story at times drags, and it includes much authorial intrusion of an expository nature, often singing the praises of Indiana. This is a semi-autobiographical novel,

---

[52] See his "Confession of a Best-Seller," in *The Provincial American and Other Papers* (Boston, 1912), 219 ff.

describing the campus and early times of Wabash College in Crawfordsville (called Madison College) and is a serious work presenting Indiana politics in a realistic manner. It was accorded a good reception and helped increase interest in Indiana among non-Hoosiers. In a sense it was a very different kind of novel to be written by the author of light romances; it does not possess the interest inherent in *The House of a Thousand Candles*.

This seriousness of purpose is continued in *The Provincial American and Other Papers* (Boston, 1912), a compilation of essays that had appeared in periodicals from 1902 to 1912 and which form a strong defense of the American village as a bulwark of democracy. Nicholson made three more collections of his essays, all previously published in periodicals: *The Valley of Democracy* (New York, 1918), *The Man in the Street. Papers on American Topics* (New York, 1921), and *Old Familiar Faces* (Indianapolis, 1929). These are mostly familiar essays, written out of his own experience, differing in style, some including narratives, and containing minor faults in the use of clichés and in a rambling style. But this diffuseness is made effective through an expert sense of timing—the same sense which made Nicholson an effective writer of romances and a striking public speaker. The pieces are enlivened through strong assertion, a racy humor, and occasional sentimentality; his strong belief in democracy, tolerance, and the necessity for good self-government shines strongly through the bulk of his essay production, featuring the Middle West and particularly Indiana. Three main ideas recur: the desirability of decentralization of government, the necessity of separation of partisan politics and municipal government, and the necessity of universal participation of the people in a democracy.[53]

[53] See Sanders, Meredith Nicholson, 139 ff.

From 1913 to 1917 four additional romances increased
Nicholson's popularity, but not his integral worth as a
man of letters, and a fifth novel proved a hybrid of realism and romance. The four romances were *Otherwise
Phyllis* (Boston, 1913), *The Poet* (Boston, 1914), *The
Madness of May* (New York, 1917), and *A Reversible
Santa Claus* (Boston, 1917). In *Otherwise Phyllis* he returned to Crawfordsville for the setting; *The Poet* was a
fictional biography of his old friend, James Whitcomb
Riley, and a tribute to him.[54] The hybrid was *The Proof
of the Pudding* (Boston, 1916) and is realistic in its description of early Indianapolis and a slowly changing
moral order, but it is marred by his usual happy ending.
Turning then from realism, after this rather unsuccessful
book, he produced next the picaresque *Lady Larkspur*
(New York, 1919) and *Blacksheep! Blacksheep!* (New
York, 1920), both of which were much more popular.

Meredith Nicholson's last books were a mixture of
several types. *Honor Bright* (New York, 1923), a three-act
comedy written with Kenyon Nicholson (no relative),
was first produced at the Murat Theater in Indianapolis
on August 22, 1921. *Best Laid Schemes* (New York, 1922)
is a book of short stories which is better than his last
three novels, several of the stories being close to familiar
essays. The story Nicholson liked best, as one might guess,
is about politics, "The Third Man." Then appeared three
pseudo-realistic novels: *Broken Barriers* (New York,
1922), *The Hope of Happiness* (New York, 1923), *And
They Lived Happily Ever After!* (New York, 1925).[55]

---

[54] Nicholson's notes, written on the flyleaves of the copies of several
of his books in the State Library, giving information about the circumstances of composition, setting, characters, and the like, have been
of great aid to the author in this study.

[55] *And They Lived Happily Ever After* grew out of visits made by
Nicholson to the office of the clerk of the Marion County Circuit Court
in Indianapolis.

In these the novelist depicted changing times, but he was still too much of a romanticist to let the realistic actions of his characters follow to their logical conclusions, and he invariably broke into the narrative somewhat as in the role of God, killing off the obnoxious and showering happiness upon the deserving. Even his serious treatment of the problems of love, marriage, and sex in *Broken Barriers* suffers from this failing. His last work, *The Cavalier of Tennessee* (Indianapolis, 1928), is an historical novel about Andrew Jackson; it was based on research on this figure, long glamorous to Nicholson, and the treatment is both sympathetic and, as one might guess, romantic.

Nicholson's success in writing popular works made him a famous figure not only in Indianapolis but everywhere he went, and he thoroughly enjoyed this publicity. Affable and personable, he was an inveterate joiner of organizations and was an entertaining speaker much sought after. In every speech, he managed to work in somewhere his strong conviction that Americans should insist on the best in government. He was elected to honorary membership in Phi Beta Kappa, the National Institute of Arts and Letters, and other societies; and he received honorary degrees from Butler and Indiana universities. His literary activity declined in the twenties and ended with the death of his wife in 1931. Henceforth, his career was diplomatic, rather than literary. He served as American envoy to Paraguay, 1933-34; to Venezuela, 1935-38; and to Nicaragua, 1938-41, after which he returned to private life in Indianapolis. From this time until his death he contributed articles of various sorts to the Indianapolis papers, mostly on the subject of Indiana and its culture. He married Mrs. Dorothy Wolfe Lannon in 1933; they were divorced in

1943. He died, the respected chief among Indiana authors, on December 22, 1947, at the age of eighty-one.[56]

There are many elements apparent in his works. Certainly he loved Indiana—the life of the small town and the life of Indianapolis—and the Indiana setting, authentically portrayed, figures strongly in his writings; he believed thoroughly in the superiority of his native state, saying that his travels elsewhere only made him better appreciate home. He was, as he said, an "incurable hick." Yet, he was aware of what was going on elsewhere and was no mere provincial; he knew the Middle West as did few other writers of his time.

It is unfortunate that he swung between romance and realism, for he was too optimistic to be a thorough realist and always spoiled his attempts at realism by tacking on a happy ending. Undoubtedly he wrote his novels for money,[57] and the continued success of his romances (eight made the best-seller lists between 1903 and 1916) ever lured him from more serious writing. It is in his essays, rather than his novels that one finds his sincere convictions about the worth of democracy. As a matter of fact, he preferred to be known as an essayist rather than a novelist; therefore, one must not dwell too strongly upon the thinness of his romances, for the real Nicholson was not there. Probably he hoped that he would live in the history of literature because of his essays, such as those in *The Valley of Democracy;* but, for good or ill, these are no longer much read, except for his scholarly work, *The Hoosiers,* which remains the seminal study of Indiana cul-

[56] The biography of Nicholson was obtained mostly from Banta, *Indiana Authors and Their Books,* 237-39; from Sanders, *op. cit.;* and from Russo and Sullivan, *op. cit.,* 71-72. These sources have also been of aid in analyzing his works, as has been *Meredith Nicholson, American Man of Letters,* published by Charles Scribner's Sons (New York, n.d.).

[57] His family confirm this fact. See Sanders, Meredith Nicholson, 93-94.

ture and letters. What he is known for today is mostly his *Hoosier Chronicle* and, especially, *The House of a Thousand Candles.* To thousands of Hoosiers, then, the name of Meredith Nicholson spells romance.

OTTO STECHHAN—MARY ELIZABETH LAMB— CHARLES F. EMBREE

In leaving Meredith Nicholson, we do not encounter anyone of like stature until we come to Charles Major. Three minor novelists now follow, none of whom needs detain us long: Otto Stechhan, Mary Elizabeth Lamb, and Charles F. Embree.

Otto Stechhan (1851-1922) was born in Prussia and came to Indianapolis with his family when he was about six years old. He became an upholsterer and a furniture manufacturer, a member of the city council in the 1880's, and later a representative in the state legislature from Marion County, in which latter capacity he introduced the bill which provided for the establishment of training in trades under the public school system. Well known as a sportsman, he built one of the first hunting and fishing lodges at Lake Maxinkuckee. He spent the last two years of his life with his son[58] in California, where he died on January 19, 1922.[59] Stechhan was the author of five books of very mediocre quality. *I Fear Thee Not and Other Poems* (Indianapolis, 1893), translated into German as *Lieben und Leben* (Chicago, 1894), consists mostly of nature poetry cast in a conventional, singsong

[58] Otto Stechhan's son, Hans Otto Stechan, changed the spelling of the family name and became a Hollywood writer for the motion pictures. He was the author of such plays as "Balboa" and "The Great Apostle."

[59] The biographical data on Otto Stechhan was found in Banta, *Indiana Authors and Their Books,* 301, and in the obituary in the Indianapolis *News,* January 20, 1922, p. 23.

form; the only verse of merit is in the title poem, in which he sharply questions God. Of the same type is the verse in *Rudder, Rod and Gun. Poems of Nature* (Indianapolis, 1898), wherein is seen Stechhan's delight in outdoor life; many settings in northern Indiana, such as lakes Maxinkuckee and Wawasee, are featured. Two novels—*Unrequited Love* (New York, 1900), the romance of a city artist and a beautiful country girl, and *Whither Are We Drifting?* (New York, 1901), a fictional discussion of economic and social problems—are summarized and narrated rather than dramatized. His last work, *Love Letters of a German American* (Dresden, Germany, 1904), was written in German and published anonymously in Germany, as the supposed letters of a woman of German ancestry but American birth; a story connects the various letters.[60]

Little information is available concerning Mary Elizabeth Jordan Lamb (1839-1916). The obituary notice in the Crawfordsville *Journal and Review*, June 5, 1916, states that she was born in Montgomery County and spent practically all her life there. Her husband, George W. Lamb, died in 1902. Mrs. Lamb contributed prose and poetry to the Indianapolis *Sentinel*. Her two romantic novels (one laid in the South and the other, with a Southern girl as heroine, in a European scene) appear to have been rather widely circulated. The novel with a Southern setting is *Irene Liscomb. A Story of the Old South* (New York, 1908); and the other, *The Mystery of Walderstein. A Story from the Life of Two Prussian Officers* (Chicago, 1894), a conventional novel full of the usual trappings of romance.

Charles Fleming Embree (1874-1905) died before he had opportunity to develop his powers fully. Born on October 1, 1874, in Princeton, Indiana, of pioneer south-

---

[60] See "Otto Stechhan's Book," in Indianapolis *News*, July 16, 1904.

ern Indiana stock, he attended the Princeton schools and entered Wabash College in 1892, but left before his senior year to pursue professional writing. He soon succeeded, publishing in 1897 *For the Love of Tonita, and Other Tales of the Mesas* (Chicago), which reflected his own change of residence to California and Mexico. In 1898 he married Virginia Broadwell. His next novel was *A Dream of a Throne. The Story of a Mexican Revolt* (Boston, 1900), a dramatic romance of adventure with its setting around Lake Chapala. His last novel, *A Heart of Flame. The Story of a Master Passion* (Indianapolis, 1901), is a stirring love story. During his short lifetime he lived also in France and Spain. In recognition of his writings Wabash College awarded Embree an honorary A.M. degree in 1903, but his career was cut off by his death on July 3, 1905, in Santa Ana, California.[61]

CHARLES MAJOR

In contrast to the above three authors, Charles Major (1856-1913) is one of the significant literary figures of Indiana. Although he lived very much in the present, he preferred the glorious days "when knighthood was in flower." To his name are attached glamour and romance —the flashing of swords, the brilliance of European courts with bright-eyed ladies and strong-hearted knights, the menace of dark intrigue, the pomp of the fiery-tempered English monarch, Henry VIII, clandestine meetings of lovers, the gallantry of old France. And all this high-flown adventure issued from a prosaic law office in Shelbyville, Indiana! A small-town Hoosier lawyer who turned into a novelist and historian of sorts of the English Tudor and

[61] Information on Embree taken from Banta, *Indiana Authors and Their Books,* 103-4, the obituary in the Indianapolis *News,* July 7, 1905, and from notes supplied by Clotilde Embree Funk, of Indianapolis.

European renaissance period, Charles Major became one of the most popular American novelists of his day.

He came of an interesting background. According to Maurice Thompson,[62] the Major family claims to date from the d'Fys, who came to England with William the Conqueror and fought at the Battle of Hastings. The Majors lived in Scotland; but during the tempestuous days of Cromwell three brothers of the family went to the town of Granard, County Longford, near Edgeworthtown, in Ireland, where Stephen Major, father of the novelist, was born and where his early education was directed by the Irish novelist Maria Edgeworth and her brother. Charles Major thus came naturally by an interest in English history. Stephen Major came to the United States in 1829, studied law, became one of the foremost lawyers, a judge of Indiana's Fifth Judicial Circuit, and one of the most prominent men of the state.

To him and his wife, Phoebe (Gaskill) Major, their son Charles was born on July 25, 1856, in Indianapolis.[63] When Charles was thirteen, the family moved to Shelbyville, where the author was destined to spend the rest of his life. Here he attended school, being attracted particularly to English literature and history, and was graduated from the high school with its first graduating class in 1872, giving a brilliant class oration which led many to predict a great future for him. He was graduated from the University of Michigan in 1875 and then returned home to read law in his father's office. In the two years during which he prepared himself for admission to the Shelby

[62] "The Author and the Book," pp. 3 ff., printed in several editions of *When Knighthood Was in Flower* after the text of the novel. See, for example, the Mary Tudor edition.

[63] Major was born in a house occupying the present site of the office of the Indianapolis Public Schools at Meridian and Ohio streets.

County bar he not only traveled and studied law but became even more fascinated with history.

While practicing law, Major did not neglect his civic responsibilities. He was elected city clerk in 1885 and, as a Democrat, was a member of the Indiana legislature for one term in 1887, but declined further service. In 1885 he married a Shelbyville girl, Alice Shaw, who proved the ideal wife for him. He was a trustee of Purdue University from 1902 until his death. Though he devoted his efforts mostly to his profession, he stole as much time as he could for his main interest, the study of English and French history during the Renaissance; he carefully examined all available state papers, memoirs, diaries, letters—everything of the nature of source material, particularly of the Tudor Age in England. Upon occasion he would even send to England for materials not available elsewhere. He believed that a novelist desiring to lend a historic atmosphere to his work must be steeped in his period;[64] hence, when he came to write, he was well prepared by his absorption of a great mass of historical details.

Major conceived his first novel, *When Knighthood Was in Flower,* two years before it saw print. Knowing the period so well, he found the plot and characters leaping into life. The Indiana historian, Jacob P. Dunn, quotes an English critic, James Milne, as saying that Major confided to him that the idea for the book was provided by the reading of the *History of France,* by Francois Pierre Guillaume Guizot, in which it is mentioned that when Mary Tudor, the sister of Henry VIII of England, married Louis XI, King of France, she was in love with the handsome Charles Brandon, a favorite of her brother. Later, in the edition of 1548 of Edward Hall's *The Union*

[64] See Major's article, "What Is Historic Atmosphere?" in *Scribners,* 27 (1900):753-61.

of the Two Noble and Illustre Famelies of Lancastre and Yorke, originally published in London in 1542, Major found another brief reference to these two persons, saying that after Louis died, Mary wrote to her former lover that if he now desired to marry her, he should come to her in Paris without Henry's consent before he had opportunity to prevent the marriage.[65] Out of these two scraps of historical record, Major composed his story against the background of the characters, actions, and setting of the period of Henry VIII, which he knew so well. The book was written in his law office in the evenings and on Sunday afternoons.

When the manuscript was finished, Major submitted it to Harpers, which made one of those mistakes, so well known among publishers and so bitterly regretted afterward, of misjudging the material and rejecting it. A little while later, however, in 1897, Lee Burns, a salesman for the Bowen-Merrill Publishing Company of Indianapolis (now The Bobbs-Merrill Company), dropped into Major's office to attempt to sell him a set of law books. As it turned out, Mr. Major did not believe that he needed any law books that day, but he did just happen to have a manuscript that perhaps Mr. Burns's company might be interested in, and would Mr. Burns take it back to the company and see? Fortunately, both for Charles Major and Bowen-Merrill, Mr. Burns did; and John J. Curtis, the secretary of the firm and director of publications, read and approved the manuscript, all except the title, which Major had written as "Charles Brandon, Duke of Suffolk." Thinking this far too prosaic for a romantic and exciting love story of the early sixteenth century, Curtis at length chanced upon this couplet in the poem, "The Gentle Armour," by the English romantic writer, Leigh Hunt:

[65] Jacob P. Dunn, *Memorial and Genealogical Record of Representative Citizens of Indiana* (Indianapolis, 1912), 206.

There lived a Knight, when Knighthood was in flow'r,
Who charmed alike the tilt-yard and the bow'r.

His suggestion of borrowing part of the first line impressed everyone as a happy solution. *When Knighthood
Was in Flower* was published in September, 1898, with
the subtitle, "The Love Story of Charles Brandon and
Mary Tudor, the King's Sister, and Happening in the
Reign of His August Majesty, King Henry VIII. Rewritten and Rendered into Modern English from Sir Edwin
Caskoden's Memoir by Edwin Caskoden." This being his
maiden voyage upon the perilous sea of literature, Major
had chosen a pseudonym, pretending that the book was
based upon the memoir of Sir Edwin Caskoden, Master of
the Dance for Henry VIII.

The success of the book was both sudden and over-
whelming. Within a few days after publication the Chicago *Times-Herald* gave it a lead review, comparing it
favorably with the work of Anthony Hope. Other reviews,
each one tending to be more enthusiastic than the last,
followed close upon each other, the real author was soon
discovered and elevated to a position of fame, and the
novel went into edition after edition. During a large part
of 1899 it ranked as one of the three most popular novels
and continued to be a best seller for fourteen consecutive
months, over 200,000 copies being purchased in two
years.[66]

And this success was only the beginning, for the great
Julia Marlowe, the beautiful and charming Shakespearean
actress, quickly asked for dramatic rights; and after talking
with her and witnessing her performance in *As You Like
It,* Major conquered his doubts about the success of the

[66] Howard G. Baetzhold, "Charles Major: Hoosier Romancer," in
Indiana Magazine of History, 51 (1955):34; article by Donald A. Roberts
in *Dictionary of American Biography, Authors Edition,* 12:214.

story as a play and allowed Paul Hester to dramatize it. With Miss Marlowe taking the part of Mary Tudor, the play began in St. Louis on November 26, 1900, and opened in New York on January 14, 1901. It came to Indianapolis, at English's Opera House, on December 17, 1900, where it was given a tremendous reception and Major was called to the stage to speak to the audience. The play enjoyed capacity crowds at English's, about 10,000 persons paying $12,000 in admissions—the best seats being priced at only $1.50.[67] In London Julia Marlowe again starred in the play, as did Nellie Stuart in Australia. In addition to the dramatization of *Knighthood,* it was made into a comic opera and into a motion picture, all these versions earning a fortune for Charles Major. Small wonder that other Indiana lawyers did not immediately desert their dusty law books and spittooned courtrooms for dreaming in the world of romance!

The novel tells the story of the stormy road to eventual happiness of Mary Tudor and Charles Brandon and how they overcame the obstacles placed in their path, mostly by King Henry. In having the fictitious Edwin Caskoden act as narrator Major avoids having to use only sixteenth-century idiom. The characters, though in many ways the usual romantic types, possess youth, spirit, and vivacity— qualities always attractive in fiction. All womankind is epitomized in the complex character of Mary Tudor, who is proud, loving, cold, passionate, willful, trusting, fearing, faithful, scheming, spoiled, and virtuous. There is a rush and dramatic force of incident, adventure, and suspense; but the tale remains essentially sentimental and simple in design. Probably Major whitewashed somewhat the character of the real Charles Brandon; yet his knowledge of history permitted him to be accurate in historical detail,

[67] Baetzhold, *op. cit.,* 35.

even though some critics said that his work lacked real historical atmosphere.[68] And although he knew political history, he was largely unfamiliar with social history, with the result that as a true reconstruction of life during the reign of Henry VIII the book is in some ways ridiculous. One can not deny, however, that *When Knigthood Was in Flower* was one of the most popular books in Indiana—and American—literature. It was Major's greatest success, and it is still famous today.[69]

After the publication of his first book, Major tended to do less legal work, though he used his office as a place in which to write. In the romantic vein he published *Dorothy Vernon of Haddon Hall* (New York, 1902), which turned out to be next in popularity of his works, ranking also as a best seller and, as dramatized again by Paul Hester, enjoying a long run on the stage. Utilizing once more the first person, he presents another pair of theatrical, though likable, lovers who conquer the obstacles to love, at the time of the conflict between Queen Elizabeth I and Mary, Queen of Scots. The heroine, the high-spirited Dorothy Vernon, we must admit, pursues the willing Sir John Manners, glamorous son of her father's enemy, to a happy conclusion. Again, accuracy of historical detail to some extent outweighs the failure to re-create the true spirit of the past. Less successful romances now followed: *Yolanda, Maid of Burgundy* (New York, 1905), a story of sixteenth-century France; *A Gentle Knight of Old Brandenburg* (New York, 1909), a tale of the period of the boyhood of

[68] See Roberts' article, for example.

[69] Major, like other famous authors, paid the price of being a celebrity. After *Knighthood* was published, he was hounded in his law office by the curious, who wanted to obtain an autograph, take his picture, or simply stare at him. Several times he looked up from his desk to see someone planted in front of him ready to take a snapshot. See Thompson, "The Author and the Book," 6.

Frederick the Great; *The Little King. A Story of the Childhood of Louis XIV, King of France* (New York, 1910), and *The Touchstone of Fortune. Being the Memoir of Baron Clyde, who lived, thrived, and fell in the Doleful Reign of the So-Called Merry Monarch, Charles II* (New York, 1912).

In the meantime, Major had made three excursions into subjects closer home and nearer to his own time. His second book, chronologically, was *The Bears of Blue River* (New York, 1901), probably the best known and most loved of his books about Indiana, which has a slight edge in popularity over the adventures narrated by his Thomas Andrew William Addison, known as *Uncle Tom Andy Bill* (New York, 1908). Both books tell stories that have the action, suspense, and adventure all boys love. The thirteen-year-old Balser Brent, his brother Jim, and a friend, Tom Fox, in *The Bears of Blue River,* and Tom Addison, in *Uncle Tom Andy Bill,* fight the forest, the elements, and ferocious animals. These books are still popular.[70]

Major's third book, also having an Indiana scene, *A Forest Hearth. A Romance of Indiana in the Thirties* (New York, 1903), was practically a failure. In it he attempts to transplant all the machinery of romance of the European past to the realism and hardship of the Indiana frontier—and the exotic plant makes but a ridiculous showing in the wild Hoosier forest and quickly withers. High-spirited nobles speaking in an elevated style may be credible in the history of far-off Europe, but when backwoods Hoosiers are made to behave and talk like the characters in *Knighthood* or *Dorothy Vernon,* the result is fantastic. Once more we find here an idealized, romantic

[70] I am indebted to Baetzhold, *op. cit.,* 36, for some ideas which I have used in this analysis.

couple, loyal and true to each other, who eventually surmount the road blocks on the highway to love's fulfillment; but the gentle, great-hearted backwoods hero, Diccon Bright, and the heroine—the truth-loving, submissive woodland flower, Rita Bays—are only stock types. So also is the villain, Williams, who attempts to force Rita to marry him by threatening to foreclose on the various business debts that her impractical father owes him. The best-drawn character is the postmaster-teacher, Billy Little, who advises, cajoles, and blusters his way through the action, aiding the lovers. All the characters talk like English nobles or college professors. Perhaps this is one reason why *A Forest Hearth* was better received in England than in the United States.

Major's last book, *Rosalie,* revised and published posthumously (New York, 1925) by his wife and Test Dalton, had been first entitled *The Canadian Story.* Probably it is unfortunate that the novel was issued, for it added nothing to Major's fame, dealing with two unpopular topics—a faithless priest and unethical practices of physicians—and lacks a final polish. Still, it is an interesting change from his usual type of story.

When Major died on February 13, 1913, he had long been a famous Indiana and American writer and had achieved financial success as well.[71] His principal fault lay in the repetition of his favorite plot of providing obstacles to the union of a romantic couple and in his lack of sufficient characterization of his personages, most of whom remain only stock types. Yet we must remember that that which is to us today a hackneyed plot, a melodramatic device, or a stock character was much newer in Major's day. It can not be denied that he had his faults, yet he knew

---

[71] Major used his royalties to purchase some six hundred acres of valuable Shelby County land.

that the public liked spirited romantic tales and gave them what they wanted. *When Knighthood Was in Flower, Dorothy Vernon of Haddon Hall,* and *The Bears of Blue River* are his most famous books; and his romances were widely imitated. He was, in a sense, the Sir Walter Scott of his town and one of the great romancers of Indiana literature.[72]

MILLARD F. COX—FRANK A. MYERS

No such fame attends the next two novelists, Millard F. Cox and Frank A. Myers, but each published a novel that was widely circulated.

Millard F. Cox (1856-1914) was born in the vicinity of Noblesville, Indiana, on February 25, 1856, and attended the schools of Noblesville and Tipton. He learned printing as a boy on the Tipton *Times,* and sometime later he taught a term in a rural school. In 1876 he moved to Indianapolis to study law and was admitted to the bar in 1880. After practicing in Tipton from 1881 to 1884, he resided in Indianapolis, serving a term beginning in 1885 as deputy reporter of the Supreme Court; he was elected judge of the Criminal Court of Indianapolis in 1890 and served four years. In 1892 he married Hattie P. Weed. Discontinuing the practice of law in 1904, he became the chief editorial writer for the Indianapolis *Sentinel;* in 1909 he was made secretary of the State Board of Accounts. Cox died in Indianapolis on March 16, 1914.[73]

[72] Information for the biography and criticism of the works of Charles Major has been obtained mostly from the sources listed above and also from William M. Hepburn, *The Charles Major Manuscripts in the Purdue University Libraries,* reprinted from *The Indiana Quarterly for Bookmen,* July, 1946. The Purdue collection contains the manuscripts of Major's ten principal works, his private library, and all materials about Major available at the time of presentation in 1925.

[73] Biography of Millard F. Cox was obtained from Banta, *Indiana*

Cox's one novel, *The Legionaires. A Story of the Great Raid* (Indianapolis, 1899), published under the pseudonym of Henry Scott Clark, is a well-written romantic novel on the subject of General Morgan's raid into Indiana during the Civil War. It demonstrates a good understanding of the political and social conditions of the Kentucky-Indiana border. The book sold in several editions.[74]

Frank A. Myers (1848-*c*.1928) was born in Tuscarawas County, Ohio, the son of the Reverend Absalom and Nancy Myers. The family moved to Daviess County, Indiana, in 1861. Frank attended Hartsville College, taught school for several years, and then became editor and manager of the Washington *Gazette*. He married Ella Elliott of Knox County, Indiana, in 1882. He is listed in the Evansville city directories from 1895 through 1928. Myers wrote a few expository materials on Indiana history and child training and published at least one book, *Thad Perkins. A Story of Indiana* (New York, 1899). This is a semi-autobiographical novel, set against the background of pioneer life in southern Indiana, particularly around Washington, and depicts a boy's eventual triumph over hardships. The manners and traditions of this area of Indiana, with its dangerous groups, such as the White Caps and the Knights of the Golden Circle, are depicted, and there is much use of dialect.[75]

Authors and Their Books, 76, and obituary in the Indiana Biography Series, 2:111.

[74] A modern novel on the subject of Morgan's Raid is *The Raiders* (New York, 1955), written by William E. Wilson, author and member of the English Department of Indiana University.

[75] *History of Knox and Daviess Counties, Indiana* . . . (Chicago, 1886), 791-92; unsigned article in Indianapolis *News*, May 13, 1899, p. 1.

6

THE NOVEL. PART II

BOOTH TARKINGTON

Now RISES a shimmering star on the literary horizon. It is Newton Booth Tarkington (1869-1946), the "Gentleman from Indiana"[1]—novelist, playwright, short story writer, artist, critic, art collector, and politician. Hardly anyone need be told that Tarkington is one of the leading figures of Indiana literature and that he made his mark in the larger field of American literature as well. Twice winner of the Pulitzer Prize for his novels, *The Magnificent Ambersons* and *Alice Adams;* a member of the American Academy of Arts and Letters, holding William Dean Howells' "chair"; winner of the Gold Medal for fiction in 1933 presented by the National Institute of Arts and Letters; winner of the William Dean Howells medal in 1945 from the American Academy of Arts and Letters; author of such favorites as *The Gentleman from Indiana, Monsieur Beaucaire,* and the Penrod stories, Tarkington depicted not only his beloved Indianapolis in the era before the capital had become a big city, but also provided his readers with keen insight into the middle class of America—and into human nature. In his tremendous production of novels, plays, stories, and essays one can find humor or social history, and sometimes both. His

[1] See the definitive biography of Tarkington by James Woodress, *Booth Tarkington. Gentleman from Indiana* (Philadelphia, 1954). I have been guided in my discussion more by this book than by any other source.

strong contribution to the American theater gives him a place as an important playwright of the early twentieth century; his plays held the stage for many years, still enjoying today an occasional revival. And overshadowing his long list of titles—for he wrote industriously all his life and found his greatest pleasure in writing—is the man, Tarkington, the genial, kind, understanding soul and warm friend of many prominent Americans in different walks of life, who saw his generation clearly and recorded it carefully through satire and humor.

He was born on July 29, 1869, in Indianapolis into the environment that he wrote about so often, the prosperous Midwestern middle class. His father, Judge John Stevenson Tarkington, was graduated from Indiana Asbury (now DePauw) University in 1852, served as private secretary to Governor Joseph A. Wright, and practiced law in Indianapolis. During the Civil War he served one term in the legislature and was captain of a company of the 132d Indiana Infantry. After the war he continued to practice law in Indianapolis and served a term as judge of the Fifth Judicial Circuit. He was a gentle and understanding father to Booth, who gained his own qualities of gentleness and kindliness from his father, and between the two there always existed a strong affection. Judge Tarkington published two books of essays, the first, however, appearing eleven years after his son's first publication.[2] Booth's grandfather, the Reverend Joseph Tarkington, was a conscientious Methodist circuit rider during the pioneer period in Indiana, having been born in Nashville, Tennessee, in 1800 of parents who had come from North Carolina in 1798 and who then migrated north to Indiana along with the surge of population. Joseph Tark-

[2] For a discussion of Judge John Stevenson Tarkington, see below, 493-94.

ington later acted as agent, 1855-57, for the university which his son John was to attend.

Booth's mother, Elizabeth Booth Tarkington, came of a New England ancestry that extended back to Thomas Hooker, the founder of Connecticut. Her father, Beebe Booth, a Yankee shopkeeper, after service in the War of 1812, had brought a load of merchandise by horseback over Daniel Boone's Wilderness Road and established a store in Salem, Indiana, where Elizabeth was born. When her family moved to Terre Haute, her father sent her to the best school available, St. Mary-of-the-Woods. She brought to her marriage an intelligent, cultivated mind, as well as ambition and pride. Her marriage with John Stevenson Tarkington was symbolical of the union in Indiana of the Southern and Eastern streams of immigration into the new state. Her brother, Newton Booth, migrated West and made his fortune in California, where he ultimately became governor and United States senator; remaining a bachelor, he doted on his sister's family. His nephew received not only his name but also financial help, including a legacy that supported him during the lean years after college when he was trying to establish himself as a writer.[3] Booth Tarkington, then, was well born.

After surviving the financial panic of 1873, the family built a brick house in a fashionable residential section at 1100 North Pennsylvania Street, a place which remained home to Booth for forty-six years, a lighthouse

[3] In 1872, when Booth was three years old, his mother took him to visit his uncle, then governor of California; and during a banquet that the governor gave, some of the guests, who were mostly ex-miners of the days of the Gold Rush, filled the child Booth with champagne—with spectacular results. Booth afterward recorded in his memoirs, as reported by Woodress, that "In one particular line of accomplishment I am now probably without a living colleague. I doubt that any other inhabitant of the year 1941 has the right . . . of recording that he got howling drunk in the State of California in 1872." Woodress, *Booth Tarkington*, 25.

illuminating a buffeting sea of change. Here he grew up, and here he wrote his best works; here his mother died, his first marriage collapsed, and his daughter died.[4] In his boyhood he was modest and humble and, in addition, like his characters Willie Baxter and Ramsey Milholland, was ill at ease in the presence of girls. He compensated for his lack of physical vigor by reading widely in his father's good library, particularly history, Shakespeare, and the novels of Dickens, Scott, Hugo, Goldsmith, and Wilkie Collins. Very early the creative impulse manifested itself, and even before he attained school age he was dictating stories about California to his long-suffering older sister, Hauté. At one time he endured the tyranny of a very unsympathetic teacher, with the probable result that he retained throughout his life an interest in children and their inward lives and problems.

One highlight of his early life was the appearance of a young, as yet unknown, journalist on the staff of the Indianapolis *Journal* who was attracted by Booth's sister Hauté. This was James Whitcomb Riley. He became a friend of the family and an idol of the eight-year-old Booth. The poet soon was reciting verses to the boy, acting out stories for him, and even asking his advice about poems. Both liked to draw, and in 1886 Booth gave a suggestion for the cover design of *Boss Girl* which Riley followed,[5] and Riley afterward called Booth his

[4] Booth Tarkington was born in a house at 520 North Meridian Street, then the best residential area of the city. In 1923 the changing character of the area around the home at 1100 North Pennsylvania Street drove him to a comfortable residence at 4270 North Meridian, where, except for spending part of the year in Maine, he lived until his death. The old home at 1100 North Pennsylvania was desecrated, in Tarkington's eyes, by the erection of a hamburger stand on the front lawn, and in 1940 the house was razed to provide space for a parking lot.

[5] Woodress, *Booth Tarkington*, 44-45.

collaborator. This happy friendship between the two lasted for many years.

A period of truancy from Shortridge High School resulted in Booth's being sent to Phillips Exeter Academy for two years, an experience which helped him mature. He spent two years at Purdue University, where he began a lifetime friendship with George Ade and John T. McCutcheon, both of whom had graduated before Tarkington entered but who returned frequently from their newspaper jobs in Chicago to make uproarious the weekends at the Sigma Chi fraternity, to which Booth belonged. He took part in many extracurricular activities at Purdue, including the writing of a newspaper column. In contrast to his careful studying at Purdue, his last two college years at Princeton, 1891 to 1893, were gay. Lacking a background in the classical languages (his uncle Newton had seen no use in them in building the state of California and had convinced his sister that Booth should have nothing to do with such claptrap), he had to register as a special student; he took mostly the courses that interested him, seemed never to study, but, happily possessing a nearly photographic memory, passed his examinations easily. He turned his student days into a prolonged frolic and attained distinction as a writer, editor of student publications, soloist in the glee club, for which he composed songs, and president of the Dramatic Association. During his presidency, the Association changed its name to the Triangle Club and began its tradition of productions with "The Honorable Julius Caesar," which Tarkington wrote. Though he was not graduated, he always remembered the teachers (one of them was Woodrow Wilson, then professor of political economy) and the many friends he made there, and he remained a loyal Princeton alumnus.

Now followed a difficult period for Tarkington, that of attempting to find himself as a writer. Rejecting an opportunity to begin a journalistic career with the New York *Tribune,* he returned to his home in Indianapolis, where for five years he labored to break into the field of free-lance writing and illustrating. It was almost entirely a frustrating, fruitless time, during which his long vigils at the desk, often of sixteen hours' duration and lasting all night, were interrupted by the dispatching of a manuscript or a drawing and the quick return of it accompanied by the inevitable rejection slip. Once he made a long trip to New York to advance personally his case with the publishers and while there had the fortune of meeting William Dean Howells, but also the misfortune of becoming tongue-tied in the great man's presence. He was teaching himself to write. Yet, to his head-shaking Indianapolis neighbors he was a lazy roisterer, spending himself in drink and midnight debauches, who would come to no good. Much of his early, unpublished material is interesting to the student of the successful Tarkington,[6] but all that he had gained from it by 1895, in addition to needed experience, was twenty dollars from the old *Life* magazine for a drawing with accompanying text. This success was followed by thirty-one consecutive rejections. He wisely decided then to concentrate on writing rather than drawing.

He turned out plays and stories, many of them laid in one of his favorite periods—the eighteenth century in America, England, and France. One of these, "Mlle. de Marmantel," a one-act comedy written for the Indianapolis Dramatic Club, was later published as *Beauty and the Jacobin. An Interlude of the French Revolution* (New York, 1912). His drawings, though never exciting

[6] Woodress, *Booth Tarkington,* Chapter III, "Literary Apprenticeship."

much interest from publishers, did stimulate his own imagination; and one of his sketches showing two men in eighteenth-century costume—a large, angry Englishman and a dapper young Frenchman, facing each other over a gaming table—so caught his fancy that he concocted a story to go with it which he eventually entitled *Monsieur Beaucaire*.[7] It was quickly rejected by a publisher, who thus lost a golden opportunity, for when McClure later brought it out in 1900, it became a best seller. It is a delightful, young costume romance laid in Bath, England, during the time of Beau Nash and narrates how the French Duke of Orleans, in disguise as a barber, unmasks the rascality of the English Duke of Winterset and the snobbishness of the beautiful belle of Bath, Lady Mary Carlisle. Tarkington later helped turn the story into a play, in which Richard Mansfield starred. During all this period of apprenticeship had it not been for the legacy from his uncle Newton Booth, he would have been forced to "do something," as his friends and neighbors had long counseled.

But the wheels of fortune were soon to grind out a better fate for the young author. Shortly after he left Princeton in 1893 he had begun work on his first novel, to be called *The Gentleman from Indiana,* but after writing about forty thousand words, he found the story stuck

[7] See the discussion of *Monsieur Beaucaire* in Robert Cortes Holliday, *Booth Tarkington* (Garden City, New York, 1918), 68-77. As Asa Don Dickinson reports in *Booth Tarkington: A Sketch* (Garden City, New York, 1928), p. 10, Riley, as might be imagined, had no appreciation for *Beaucaire;* and although his friendship with Tarkington suffered no interruption, he neither read anything more from his friend's pen nor mentioned Booth's works till he chanced upon *The Flirt,* a powerful transcript of American life which so fascinated him that he spent half the night finishing it. He called on Tarkington the next morning before breakfast to express his appreciation of the book. Henceforth Tarkington's books in addition to Riley's were subjects in their conversation.

fast, and he could do nothing to coax it into action again; hence he turned to other tasks. Then in December, 1897, he was shocked when his closest Princeton friend, John Cleve Green, died in Philadelphia, and he realized that perhaps subconsciously he had been modeling the character of his hero, John Harkless, on Green. Resolving to turn the book into a memorial to his friend, he obtained a fresh perspective and in April, 1898, began the novel anew and soon found it clearly framed in his mind. He wrote furiously but carefully and had it finished by fall. It was published through a peculiar circumstance. Unknown to him, his admiring sister Hauté (now Mrs. Ovid Butler Jameson) had carried with her on a visit to New York the manuscript of *Monsieur Beaucaire,* in which she attempted to interest the publisher, S. S. McClure. McClure was not completely sold on *Beaucaire,* however, but Hauté's mention of her brother's novel about Indiana interested the publisher; the result was that she telegraphed the amazed Booth to rush the manuscript to McClure. He did and an anxious two weeks dragged on; then a letter arrived in Indianapolis, signed by Hamlin Garland. It commenced: "Mr. McClure has given me your manuscript, The Gentleman from Indiana, to read. You are a novelist."[8]

Those last four thrilling words changed life for Tarkington! Now his labors were vindicated, not only in the eyes of the world, but particularly in his own opinion. Henceforth he was an author—and a famous one. An offer from McClure to publish the novel followed hot upon Garland's letter, and invited to New York to cut the manuscript in half so that it might be published also as a serial in *McClure's Magazine,* he found himself whisked into a dream world of opened doors, of friendly,

[8] As quoted in Woodress, *Booth Tarkington,* 74.

smiling editors and publishers, and of famous authors, all of whom greeted him as an equal. When he was first ushered into the sanctum sanctorum of the offices, McClure bounded up from a conversation with Hamlin Garland to meet him, exclaiming, "You are to be the greatest of the new generation, and we'll help you to be."[9] In the delirious whirl of the next few days he met Garland, Ida Tarbell, Frank Stockton, Paul Leicester Ford, F. N. Doubleday, Rudyard Kipling, and Bliss Perry, with some of whom he was to form lasting friendships. And as he luxuriated in his air castles, now come true, he turned down an offer from McClure of an editorial position at seven thousand dollars a year, for he had no editorial ambitions; he simply wanted to write. Some months later he returned to Indiana, a famous young man of thirty, and had the pleasure of experiencing newspaper interviews, reading flattering editorials about himself, and being invited to write a book column for a newspaper.

The Gentleman from Indiana (New York, 1899),[10] except for—and partly because of—some opposition from rural newspapers which said he was attacking Indiana, was enthusiastically received almost everywhere. The novel arose indirectly from Tarkington's necessity during his Exeter and Princeton school days of defending his home state from the friendly slurs of his Eastern schoolmates, and he determined to produce a narrative laudatory of Indiana. So he told the story of John Harkless, the popular and promising graduate of an Eastern college, who buys, sight unseen, the Plattville (Indiana) Herald and finds himself saddled with a broken-down, unpromising country newspaper. But Harkless plunges into the

[9] Quoted in Woodress, Booth Tarkington, 77.
[10] See the discussion of The Gentleman from Indiana in Holliday, Booth Tarkington, 47-67.

community life and politics of the town and Carlow County and by his fearless and virtuous leadership revitalizes the paper. In opposing the vicious and criminal White Caps—mobsters disguised in sheets, predecessors of the Ku Klux Klan—Harkless is nearly killed but returns home from death's door to find himself a state hero and the nominee of his party to Congress.

This is a romantic and sentimental novel, unlike much of Tarkington's later work, and its popularity is derived partly from the virtues and charm both of the hero, Harkless, and the heroine, Helen Sherwood, and from the freshness of the local color, which is expertly presented. The author makes the seemingly uninteresting, prosaic county seat come into real and fascinating life; he molds the indolent, drowsy but capable townspeople into a type —a sort of Brown County caricature, such as Kin Hubbard was later to create—and the type is lovable for all its provincial seediness and the mud and drabness of its habitat. As one might expect from a first novel, the style is somewhat uneven and the story drags in places, but the fame of the book increased steadily; it was a best seller in 1900, has continued in demand, and has never been permitted to go out of print.[11] It was the best study of Indiana in the form of a novel since publication of *The Hoosier School-Master* in 1871.

The ice had now been broken. Tarkington was quick to launch other boats upon the waters. His informal, undogmatic literary criticism, now contributed weekly to the Indianapolis *Press,* turned gradually away from romanticism and toward realism as his creative writing experienced the same change. A curious work, *Cherry*

[11] Woodress reports (*op. cit.,* 83-84) that *The Gentleman from Indiana* "has been reissued and reprinted more than two dozen times, translated into at least six languages, made into a movie, and excerpted for anthologies."

(New York, 1903),[12] demonstrates this. Set in Princeton in the year 1762, it is a burlesque, both of the historical romance and also of the device of the first-person narrative, which had amused Tarkington when he read *Richard Carvel,* which appeared in 1899. McClure, who by this time had serialized *Monsieur Beaucaire* and had it in press for publication, hesitated to publish *Cherry,* thinking the satire not up to Tarkington's standard; and Harper's, seizing the opportunity, brought it out in their magazine, then published it as a book, but only after a delay of thirty-one months. The satire deservedly lagged behind Tarkington's first two published books in appreciation and attracted little attention from a public now expecting entertainment from the author. Perhaps it failed because he attempted to satirize too many things at once—not only the historical romance and the first-person device but also the prudish in human nature.

The Two Vanrevels (New York, 1902)[13] was much more successful and proved a best seller; although a historical romance, the book may still be seen as transitional to later studies of Hoosier life. The novelist utilized his mother's memory of her education at St. Mary-of-the-Woods in Terre Haute (called Rouen) as inspiration for the story; and choosing the period of the Mexican War, he has his heroine, Betty Carewe, fall in love with an attorney, Tom Vanrevel. The Carewe family typifies the old French culture of the town, while the Vanrevels represent the newer Yankee civilization—all of which would add up to a pure novel of manners were it not for the addition of a sensational murder.

During all this time Tarkington played the role of

[12] See the discussion of *Cherry* in Holliday, *Booth Tarkington,* 93-100.

[13] See the detailed discussion of *The Two Vanrevels,* including its device of mistaken identity, in *ibid.,* 77-93.

one of the most eligible gay bachelors in Indianapolis and made many a feminine heart thrill in his perfect-mannered, quiet presence, until on June 18, 1902, he married Louisa Fletcher, a girl ten years younger than he, the daughter of an Indianapolis banker, Stoughton J. Fletcher, of the Fletcher "dynasty" which figured so long in Indianapolis social and financial history. She was interested in the arts and literature, and some time later she was to publish a book of rather mediocre verse, *The Land of Beginning Again* (Boston, 1921). The marriage was to prove an ill-fated union.

At this same time the novelist followed the lead of his father and uncle and made his one and only entrance into politics. He did so out of a feeling, common among many writers early in the century, that good citizens should run for office to help combat political corruption. Perhaps, also, he was looking for ideas for writing. Filing as a Republican candidate for the Indiana House of Representatives, he conducted no campaign, but his name on the ballot was enough to secure his nomination, and he was easily elected. His term in the legislature of 1903 was notable for his conscientious, honest service and his successful stand against a bill sponsored by Governor Winfield T. Durbin to oust—needlessly—the board of the state reformatory at Jeffersonville. Tarkington's leadership of the opposition won him public favor. With great difficulty he made a single speech during the session, nominating Charles W. Fairbanks for re-election to the U. S. Senate—and thereafter steadfastly attempted to avoid again undergoing such an ordeal. Tarkington was no speaker; and he remained shy in public, shunning the spotlight. But the legislative session did provide him with ample literary material, which he stored away for future reference.

The first use of it came with *In the Arena. Stories of Political Life* (New York, 1905).[14] In these six short stories he dramatized realistically the inner workings of a legislature, sparing no aspect of dirty politics, dishonesty, or shameless sellout. At least one of these, "The Aliens," a story of filthy ward politics, is actually naturalistic. Tarkington was indeed changing! The stories, appearing first through magazine publication, were enjoyed by Theodore Roosevelt, who invited the author to luncheon at the White House to discuss them. The President voiced his fear that they would deter men of integrity from launching into politics. When the stories were collected in a book, Roosevelt wrote a strong commendation, lauding the preface in which Tarkington advised honest citizens to enter politics.

In order to aid his convalescence from a near fatal attack of typhoid, Tarkington, with his wife and his parents, spent 1903 to 1904 in Europe. He created something of a sensation in London. Booth returned, in much improved health, to settle for a time in New York and hobnob with literati like the McClures and Mark Twain and to entertain George Ade, who had come to New York for the opening of his hilarious play, *The College Widow*.

Tarkington again turned to his writing, and the first product was a minor work, *The Beautiful Lady* (Garden City, New York, 1905).[15] This tale was suggested by his European trip and utilizes an elaborate plot to show how an impoverished Italian nobleman hires himself out as a human signboard in Paris, advertising a musical review on his shaven head, and saves the beautiful lady of the review, who pities him, from an unfortunate match. Another book published at nearly the same time was *The*

[14] *In the Arena* is discussed in Holliday, *Booth Tarkington*, 103-8.
[15] For a discussion of *The Beautiful Lady*, see *ibid.*, 119-22.

Conquest of Canaan (New York, 1905),[16] an Indiana story full of local color and evidently laid again in Terre Haute, with a lawyer as hero, who, as well as the heroine, pulls himself up in the world by his own boot-straps and triumphs over the black villain. This novel quickly became a best seller, and it was reissued in 1935.

The Tarkingtons soon returned to Europe, where, in a rented villa on the beautiful isle of Capri, Booth tried unsuccessfully for a time to collaborate with Harry Leon Wilson in play writing. In Rome the Tarkington's daughter, Laurel, was born. At another rented villa, this one very close to Paris, he wrote *His Own People* (New York, 1907), a study of a smug, naïve Midwestern young man in Rome on a vacation who is exhilarated by the brilliant society and awed by a French countess but fleeced at poker by her companions and returns home, "a sadder and a wiser man," to "his own people," where he really belongs. Harper's refused the story on moral grounds, but *The Saturday Evening Post* brought it out, and Doubleday published it as a novelette.[17]

A second novel produced in France was *The Guest of Quesnay* (New York, 1908), a curious piece, not at all typical of Tarkington. This is the tale of a dissolute, rich young American, Larrabee Harman, a type that the author had frequently seen in Paris, who, engaged in a scandalous affair with a Spanish harlot and dancer, loses his memory in an automobile accident, in which he is critically injured, and is nursed back to health by his own wife, whom he does not recognize and who protects him from his former mistress and other evil. The Christian symbolism is apparent in Harman's being born again—

[16] For a discussion of *The Conquest of Canaan*, see *ibid.*, 108-18.

[17] Holliday analyzes *His Own People*, in *ibid.*, 123-27.

through the automobile accident—and assuming the role
of a penitent before he can enter the kingdom of God
(his new spiritual vision) and in his wife's pardoning him
for his former sins. The novel went through at least
ten editions.[18] After finishing this book, Tarkington came
home from the life of an author and gay man-about-town
in Paris, for the first time in almost two years.

He brought with him the manuscript of a play on which
he and Harry Leon Wilson had collaborated, *The Guardian* (New York, 1907), produced and published later as
The Man from Home (New York, 1908).[19] It features
the character, Daniel Voorhees Pike, a Kokomo, Indiana,
lawyer, modeled on two Hoosiers who had visited Rome—
Jim Stutesman, a witty lawyer and politician from Peru,
Indiana, and Stoughton Fletcher, of Indianapolis, who
had been unimpressed by Europe. As a combination of
these two, Pike goes to Italy to save his two rich but
foolish wards from falling matrimonial prey to fortune-
hunting titled Europeans. He eventually succeeds in his
purpose and in doing so disparages Europe and brags
continually and ludicrously about Indiana. To the aston-
ishment of the authors and to the disgust of some critics,
Pike's extravagant praise, instead of being laughed at,
was vigorously applauded by American audiences everywhere, and the play proved a great success.[20]

[18] I am particularly indebted to Woodress, *Booth Tarkington*, 136-46,
for the main ideas in the interpretation of *The Guest of Quesnay*.

[19] According to Dorothy R. Russo and Thelma L. Sullivan, *A Bibliography of Booth Tarkington, 1869-1946* (Indianapolis, 1949), 23, "In
September 1927 at George Tyler's request the play was rewritten and
produced under the title, 'Hoosiers Abroad.'" The play has appeared
in various versions.

[20] Woodress, *op. cit.*, 146-47, reports that *The Man from Home* was
the second largest money-maker that Tyler ever produced, netting $600,-
000 during the five years of its run in Chicago, New York, and elsewhere,
and paying Tarkington about $200 a week for this period. After the play

This success may have been a mixed blessing, however; for although Tarkington never regarded himself seriously as a playwright, he was thus induced to continue collaboration with Wilson and to write plays for three years, from 1907 to 1910, with decreasingly effective results. Most of them were produced with varied success, having short runs on Broadway and playing on the road, but evidently were never published. They included "Cameo Kirby," a romantic melodrama about a hard-boiled Mississippi gambler (which was made into a movie at least three times); "Your Humble Servant," written for Otis Skinner, a play about an aging actor and his ward, an actress on the way up; "Getting a Polish," which contrasted the cultures of New York and the Far West; and "Springtime," set in Louisiana at the time of the War of 1812, a sort of Romeo and Juliet story ending happily. "Foreign Exchange," a failure, displayed the difference between the morals of America and Europe as seen in the relationship of an American wife and her French husband. "Cinderella of Tompkins Square," on reconsideration by the authors, was filed in the wastebasket.

An interesting novelette reflecting these playwriting experiences is *Harlequin and Columbine* (New York, 1921), which presents the problem of writing and producing plays.

This was an unsettled period in Tarkington's life, for he was often rushing back and forth from New York to Paris and then about the United States, writing and aiding with the production of his plays; and his domestic situaton was deteriorating rapidly. Under such stress lengthy fiction was out of the question, and all he could get

set a record in Chicago with 375 performances, it moved to New York and ran for over a year before starting on tour. Also, see Holliday, *Booth Tarkington*, 128-32.

together was an expansion to a novelette of his short story, *Beasley's Christmas Party* (New York, 1909). This tale, inspired by his Uncle Newton, was a portrait of David Beasley, a bachelor and politician. Still, on the exterior, Tarkington was a gay and witty companion of many famous people—Howells, Mark Twain, John Barrymore and others—and the life of every party he attended, particularly if the occasion was lubricated by liquid refreshment. But he was hiding a personal tragedy.

This tragedy came to the fore when on November 13, 1911, his wife was granted a divorce, and for a time he suffered in public esteem. Evidently it was a situation of conflicting temperaments and desires in life and marriage, and Louisa had tired of Booth's frequent absences. Laurel was to remain in her mother's custody, but Booth was to have frequent visits with her. This was a catastrophe to Tarkington, yet it did not interrupt his productivity. Instead, he set to work to reorganize his life, and he soared to greater literary heights than before. Settling in his old home on Pennsylvania Street in Indianapolis, he soon was turning out a stream of good books, which included the best he ever wrote.

One of the main reasons for this new success was the entrance into his life of his second wife, Susanah Robinson, of Dayton, Ohio. He had first met her at a dinner party in 1907 and had been immediately attracted to her but had chanced to see her only once after that. Not long after his divorce he began to make trips to Dayton to see her, and on November 6, 1912, they were quietly married. They came to live in Tarkington's family home in Indianapolis, and they enjoyed a very happy married life for thirty-three years. Susanah was exactly the kind of wife for Tarkington, for she was interested in literature and in his work; and she efficiently ran the household and acted as a tactful buffer between Booth and the distractions of ordinary living and the many visitors, telephone calls, and interruptions that interfered with his writing. And, of course, Tarkington had learned by his mistakes in his previous marriage. Also, she and the novelist's physician helped Booth give up liquor (for he had become an alcoholic). When he was warned that drink was interfering with his work, he became a teetotaler.

The first novel published after this happy change in marital status was *The Flirt* (Garden City, New York, 1913). It is by no means his best novel, but it is the first in his new manner of writing; for here he discarded elaborate plot and let the characters take the bit in their teeth.[21] Also, it is Tarkington's first domestic novel, his first novel making use of Indianapolis as a setting, though the city is disguised, and the first of many books dedicated to Susanah. Here is related how Valentine Corliss, of a well-known Midwestern family (a type of family to be developed later in *The Magnificent Ambersons),* returns home after many years abroad and cheats people through selling stock in an imaginary Italian oil field. He is eventually exposed and killed. Rejecting the temptation to write melodrama, the author creates in his heroine, Cora Madison, the flirt—a devastatingly beautiful, yet terribly selfish, girl who is the first of many such Tarkington heroines that cause only misery for others—truly a Becky Sharp character. The Madison family suggests that of *Alice Adams,* and the book is full of realistic actions and characters, among them Cora's younger brother, Hedrick Madison, a predecessor of Penrod Scho-

[21] Tarkington later disparaged everything he had written before 1913, saying that he had relied too heavily on plot. Woodress, *Booth Tarkington,* 168.

field. The story is not completely successful, however, because the confidence man, Corliss, is not very convincing in such surroundings, and there are defects in plot.[22]

In some ways *The Flirt* looked forward to *Penrod* (Garden City, New York, 1914); and with the latter book the novelist attained enduring success, simply because he created real children, instead of miniature adults. All his life he had subconsciously been preparing to write the Penrod stories and other tales of childhood; for not only did he remember vividly his own boyhood and its vicissitudes, with the dancing classes, the trouble with his teacher, the shows presented in the stable, but he had usually before him the examples of his sister's boys, whose family home was across the street and who, with other boys, played in Tarkington's back yard and stable. It was his wife Susanah, however, who awakened his active interest in child subjects. She read and admired *The Hill*, by Horace Vachell, a story of the hazing of small boys at Harrow in England, and she showed it to her husband. To her surprise, however, he said that although the hazing probably was well described, no boys, not even English boys, had ever talked like the characters in the novel. "Why don't you write about boys as they really are?" she asked. The challenge impelled him to his desk, and the result was the first Penrod story, "Penrod and the Pageant."[23] It was followed by many more.

The Penrod stories and similar books—*Penrod and Sam* (Garden City, New York, 1916), *Seventeen* (New York, 1916), *Penrod Jashber* (Garden City, New York, 1929), and *Penrod: His Complete Story* (Garden City, New York, 1931)—succeeded because Tarkington believed that boys should be presented in fiction as they are in life,

---

[22] For a discussion of *The Flirt*, see Woodress, *Booth Tarkington*, 168-71, and Holliday, *op. cit.*, 159-70.

[23] This incident is related in Woodress, *op. cit.*, 174.

certainly not as adults think they are nor as adults would like them to be. The children in all of Tarkington's child books are neither overwhelmingly bad nor spotlessly good, but are the creation of an environmentalist who believed that they relive the experience of the race in their growth and only with difficulty are forced by adults gradually to conform to civilization. Thus, a boy is destructive, combative, artistic, friendly, mischievous, thieving, adventurous, proud, irreverent, amoral—in short, a naïve savage, and, to adults, both horrifying and lovable. The little-gentleman kind of boy the novelist firmly rejects, or he makes him a hypocrite, such as Georgie Bassett, the paragon of conduct, whose saintly living is a source of awe and hatred to the boys of Penrod's gang. Instead, we have boys like Penrod, Rupe Collins, and the Negroes Herman and Verman, who are always in some sort of adventure or scrape, who resist school, girls, and dancing classes, and instead write gory adventure stories, enact theatricals, laugh with and at one another, fight, romp, rescue the cat fallen into the cistern by holding the pants peeled off one of the boys down to it and dropping them into the water when the cat claws its way over the holder to freedom, and so on and on—to the intense delight both of juvenile readers, who are absorbed by the action, and of adults, who find the workings of Penrod's mind a source of amused fascination. The characters make their own story. There is an absence of intense plotting, and Tarkington writes it all cleverly, yet simply, and without much comment, as if in the role of recorder. Through details he makes the commonplace, like the language of the boys and everyday activities, real and important, and he uses much humorous irony.

The novelist rejects the concept of boyhood seen in such books as Thomas Hughes' *Tom Brown's Schooldays*

and Thomas Bailey Aldrich's *The Story of a Bad Boy* as
unreal and as reflecting an adult morality. And yet the
type of Tarkington's realistic boy stories was by no means
new in literature, for it began with Mark Twain's *Tom
Sawyer* (1876) and continued with such books as William
Allen White's *The Court of Boyville* (1899) and Stephen
Crane's *Whilomville Stories* (1900). That the public
enjoyed Tarkington's child stories is reflected by their tremendous sale.[24] In connection with the Penrod stories
mention should be made of *Ramsey Milholland* (Garden City, New York, 1919), the realistic story of boys
who went to war in 1917, which was in part propaganda
for the Allied cause.

But the adult world and its problems was by no means
sidestepped by the Hoosier author. When, after his
wanderings, he settled down, he always considered himself
a resident Indianan, even though he was later to build a
summer home, called Seawood, in Kennebunkport, Maine,
where he and his wife lived each year from May through
December; and even though he really preferred Maine to
Indiana, Indianapolis still held him. His roots were there.
It was home. Yet, during his long absence, things had
changed at home. He had left it a small, homey city
primarily of settled, respectable families living in large
Victorian houses set in broad, shaded yards, and moving
in an unhurried routine. When he again took up residence on Pennsylvania Street, the mode of living had
changed to one of tenseness and hurry, the city was
expanding rapidly, slums had developed, business was

[24] *Penrod* and the other boy stories were a huge success, as evidenced
not only by the sales of the books but also by translation into many
languages and the release of frequent movies made from them. See Russo
and Sullivan, *A Bibliography of Tarkington*, 29-33, *et passim*. For a discussion of *Penrod* and other boys' books see Holliday, *op. cit.*, 168-77,
and Woodress, *op. cit.*, 174-80.

booming and was encroaching even on his own once-peaceful residential area; and as people concentrated more and more on piling up gold and less and less on living gracefully, the monster, industrialism, with its noise, filth, and smoke was slowly spreading its tentacles throughout the city.

This new problem he attacked in *The Turmoil* (New York, 1915), in which he sharply criticized American materialism and big business as the causes of the undesirable change. Once he had commenced analyzing the changing social and economic conditions, he kept at it for some ten years; three other novels were of a similar nature: *The Magnificent Ambersons* (Garden City, New York, 1918), *Alice Adams* (Garden City, New York, 1921), and *The Midlander* (Garden City, New York, 1924). These four novels together reveal the mature Tarkington as a social historian making his most sincere and probably his most significant contribution to American literature. They are all well written, utilizing an approach of commonplace realism, as initiated by Howells, and all are chronicles of Hoosier families and their relationship with business. Tarkington was attacking materialism five years before Sinclair Lewis began his criticism in *Main Street* (1920), followed by *Babbitt* (1922) and other novels.

In *The Turmoil* bigness and smoke become the symbols of commercialism and greed. James Sheridan, a self-made man, fights his way to the top as a millionaire, but can not adapt himself socially to his new life and ruins his family through his selfishness and shortsightedness, even forcing his sensitive poet son Bibbs to enter his business and remake himself into his father's likeness. The similarity to Howells' *The Rise of Silas Lapham* is apparent, and the novel was praised by Howells himself.[25]

[25] For an analysis of *The Turmoil*, see Holliday, *op. cit.*, 189-204.

In *The Magnificent Ambersons* Tarkington dramatizes the tragedy of a family on the road down hill. The grandfather, Major Amberson, had made the family fortune after the Civil War, and the next two generations spend it. The arrogant grandson, George Minafer, finally overcomes the effect of the possessiveness of his mother and his own idleness and bullheadedness just in time to save himself from utter ruin. Here the purifying effect of a woman's love, as seen in George's mother, becomes a recurrent theme.[20]

Alice Adams, probably his best work, was intended originally as the third of his trilogy published in 1927 as *Growth (The Turmoil, The Magnificent Ambersons,* and *The Midlander);* but he let *The Midlander* supplant *Alice Adams,* which is a study of mediocrity in an individual. *Alice Adams* utilizes his old theme of how greed corrupts. Here is a family neither on the upgrade nor on the downgrade but an average family struggling pathetically to rise in the economic and social world and failing miserably. In the spectacle of Mr. Adams, goaded by his wife to attempt to advance from the employee to the employer class in the drug business, in the despicable character of the son Walter, and particularly in the ineffectual attempts of the dreamy Alice to ascend into "society" through snaring the right young man as a husband, there is a mixture of humor and intolerably depressing pathos. The novel won the Pulitzer Prize, a repeated award, since it had been tendered also for *The Magnificent Ambersons.*

[20] Many places featured in *The Magnificent Ambersons* were recognized by Indianapolis residents. Amberson Addition was in reality Woodruff Place, a beautiful residential area on the east side, now hemmed in by industrial development; the old Amberson mansion, placed by the author in Amberson Addition, was modeled after the house used today as headquarters of the Knights of Columbus at Thirteenth and Delaware streets. Woodress, *Booth Tarkington,* 197-98.

Alice Adams received the plaudits of Sinclair Lewis and Ellen Glasgow and went through the usual routine of being issued in several editions, being translated, and made into moving pictures—with Katharine Hepburn playing one of the Alices.

Tarkington's fourth sociological novel, *The Midlander,* offers a glimmer of hope for the phase of ugly industrialism of his home city, in his realization that there were still beauty and spirituality to come from the new age. Yet it is, in another sense, tragic in bringing to an unhappy end Dan Oliphant, the young man who came home from college with a dream of the city's expanding northward from the boundary at Sixteenth Street and who promotes the new addition so enthusiastically and successfully that his absorption in it ruins his marriage, and he is thus destroyed by his own creation.[27] It is interesting that in 1923, when he wrote *The Midlander,* the author could stand the deteriorating character of the area around his old home no longer; and, with strong emotional tugs because of his desertion, he bought a home in an attractive new addition at 4270 North Meridian Street, where he lived the rest of his life and where he died.

In the meantime, Tarkington's strong interest in the theater had by no means been quenched, and in his second period of playwriting he had been turning out entertaining farces and comedies of manners, with varying degrees of success.

The Country Cousin, written with Julian Street (New York, 1916), is a farce-comedy about an Ohio girl who goes to New York to protect a friend from the wiles of Easterners.[28] It was in this play that Alfred Lunt got his

[27] See Woodress, *op. cit.,* for excellent discussions of *The Turmoil, The Magnificent Ambersons, Alice Adams,* and *The Midlander.*
[28] See *ibid.,* 207-11, for *The Country Cousin.*

start as an actor, and Tarkington was so taken with him that he wrote *Clarence* (New York, 1921) to provide Lunt with his first opportunity to star. And in *Clarence* a young actress, Helen Hayes, played one of her first adult roles. It is the story of how a shoddy, recently discharged veteran of World War I manipulates the family of a manufacturer and how the ex-soldier turns out to be a famous entomologist in disguise. The play's success on Broadway and on the road made theater history.[29]

The Gibson Upright, written in collaboration with Harry Leon Wilson (Garden City, New York, 1919), was a farce designed as anti-Communist propaganda, but proved amateurish and failed on the stage.[30] "Poldekin," an unpublished play of anti-Communist intentions, starred in by George Arliss, also failed, as did *The Wren* (New York, 1922), his first use of a setting in Maine in an important work, written for Helen Hayes and co-starring Leslie Howard.

One-act plays were not beyond the playwright's interest; and he dashed off such popular pieces as *Ghost Story* (Cincinnati, 1922), *The Trysting Place* (Cincinnati, 1923), *Bimbo, the Pirate* (New York, 1926), *Station YYYY* (New York, 1927), and *The Travelers* (New York, 1927), several of which were successfully produced by amateurs.

Of longer plays, *The Intimate Strangers* (New York, 1921), written for Maude Adams and produced by Florenz Ziegfeld, was a lively comedy scintillating in repartee; and "Rose Briar" was a good comedy of manners, featuring Billie Burke in the role of a cabaret singer, but it remained unpublished. *Tweedles,* a comedy written with Wilson (New York, 1924), achieved its humor in the opposing pride of two families, one of New England, the

[29] For a discussion of *Clarence,* see Woodress, *op. cit.,* 211-15.
[30] See *ibid.,* 215, for *The Gibson Upright.*

other of Pennsylvania. "Magnolia," dealing with the perversion of ideals in the Old South, written for Lionel Barrymore, failed for no apparent reason; and "Colonel Satan," a play about Aaron Burr, failed for lack of the revision which Tarkington, in ill health at the time, could not give it.

His last plays were *How's Your Health?* written with Wilson (New York, 1930), with a mediocre theme about hypochondria, and *Mister Antonio* (New York, 1935), the heart-warming presentation of a cheerful Italian organ grinder who shrugs off the evil in life. Otis Skinner starred in it successfully. In his plays, as in his novels, Tarkington was an optimist even when dealing with social problems and, most certainly, an excellent entertainer.[31]

From the time of the publication of *Alice Adams* in 1921 until his death Tarkington's work remained good, but it never again reached the level of the Pulitzer Prize winners. In the meantime, academic honors were thronging his way. After receiving honorary degrees from Princeton, DePauw, and Columbia universities, he declined all similar offers; and in 1940 his first alma mater, Purdue, was able to award him an honorary degree only by arranging a special presentation, accompanied by an academic procession, at his home.

Several collections of short stories appeared about this time. *The Fascinating Stranger and Other Stories* (Garden City, New York, 1923) is composed mostly of humorous tales involving the same two prosperous families, the Mearses and the Eliots, and their children. Renfrew Mears finally wins the hand of Muriel Eliot in spite of the complications created by younger children of the

[31] For discussions of these various plays, see *ibid., passim.*, and Russo and Sullivan, *A Bibliography of Tarkington, passim.*

families, somewhat in the tradition of *Seventeen*. *Women* (Garden City, New York, 1925) analyzes the problems of the feminine world of the suburbs during the daytime, when the husbands labor at the office and the wives are left to keep house, attend club meetings, gossip, and bicker. Later, having delineated the problems of the eleven-year-old in *Penrod* and of the adolescent in *Seventeen* and being at this time attracted to several great nephews and nieces, all of whom were about seven years of age, he wrote a series of stories about young children which were first printed in *The Saturday Evening Post* and then collected as *Little Orvie* (Garden City, New York, 1934), charming adult readers by the impulsiveness of the characters. In *Mr. White, The Red Barn, Hell and Bridewater* (Garden City, New York, 1935) one finds the four stories of the title, previously published in periodicals, all examining life and the hereafter from different points of view. *Rumbin Galleries* (Garden City, New York, 1937) contains six of the author's stories, previously printed in the *Post,* inspired by the New York art dealers, Abris and David Silberman, who had sold Tarkington many of the paintings which made up his excellent collection.

This interest in art was the genesis of a group of essays on art, entitled *Some Old Portraits* (Garden City, New York, 1939), which concentrated upon twenty-two paintings of his own collection and interpreted art for the nonexpert.

A curious item, written with Kenneth Roberts and Hugh Kahler, was a burlesque handbook for collectors of antiques, entitled *The Collector's Whatnot* (Boston, 1923).

Another collection of essays had been *Looking Forward and Others* (Garden City, New York, 1926), which discusses such problems as happiness, alcohol, and life after death, yet includes such delightful pieces as "Nipskillions" and "Discovering the Recipe for the Ideal Wife." *The World Does Move* (Garden City, New York, 1928), reflective and autobiographical essays, astutely analyzes the changes in American society from the Civil War until the time of writing, such as the expansion of the railroads, the emergence of political corruption, architectural developments, decline of the old-time religion, and the rise of a new society that attacked every belief and was smug in its abilities and grasp of facts. Yet Tarkington was always optimistic in his view of the United States and its future.[32]

As the times changed, so did Booth Tarkington; yet in another sense he remained much the same. His movie and radio scripts showed his interest in new means of communication. If he had lived a few years longer, undoubtedly he would have plunged enthusiastically into authoring scripts for television. Many of the scripts that he turned out were never published, but *The Help Each Other Club* (New York, 1934), a radio play about the troubles of the unemployed during the Depression, which he had been asked to write, did see print after being produced in 1933. It consisted of a sort of round-table discussion in which various youths talk over their futures. Another published radio play was *Lady Hamilton and Her Nelson* (New York, 1945), written in 1940 as propaganda.

In addition to his regular output he dashed off a large number of articles, stories, and essays which were never collected. Writing was always a serious affair to him, shut up in his study and wearing a comfortable bathrobe,

[32] Again, for more detailed reference to these collections of stories and essays, see Woodress, *op. cit.*, and Russo and Sullivan, *op. cit.*

and he often worked for sixteen to eighteen hours straight, protected by his wife from intrusion, and having his meals sent up to him. Yet he varied this strenuous routine by fellowship at the University Club in Indianapolis on some of the afternoons and by occasional vacations between projects. At one time he and Susanah spent some months in Europe.

Tarkington remained a conservative and a traditionalist, espousing the ideals of the Midwest of the preindustrial era and defending individuality. As an opponent of the New Deal of the thirties, he and his works were attacked by its defenders. Unmoved, however, he continued to write as he chose; and even when his eyesight grew worse and worse until he could hardly see, he worked on, aided by his secretary, Betty Trotter, to whom he learned to dictate. He opposed war, but during both the First and the Second World Wars his patriotism drove him to write propaganda for the American cause.

Even though he produced quantities of short stories and plays, his production of the novel was steady throughout nearly all his life. *Gentle Julia* (New York, 1922), the first one to follow *Alice Adams,* is a good tale something like *Seventeen;* for Jane Baxter, in the latter novel, a fascinating, uninhibited young girl, was so successful that she was later transferred to the role of the thirteen-year-old Florence Atwater in *Gentle Julia,* as a sort of feminine Penrod. Also, there is the same comedy involving children, parents, and young people in love, such as Florence's twenty-year-old beautiful Aunt Julia, who is surrounded by a bevy of suitors. Tarkington, always fond of dogs, adds to the tale the humorous antics of the black French poodle named Gamin, which so delighted Alexander Woollcott that he and Tarkington became fast friends.[33]

[33] For *Gentle Julia,* see Woodress, *op. cit.,* 192-94.

The Plutocrat (Garden City, New York, 1927) was the first novel written after his European trip in 1924-25 and was inspired by his traveling companion in North Africa, a Princeton friend who was so typically loud, uninhibited, and American in his reaction to everything they saw that Tarkington was greatly amused. This friend he exaggerated and transformed into the figure of the American millionaire manufacturer, Earl Tinker, a noisy braggart who makes himself a spectacle by lying to his wife, getting drunk, and pursuing women, but, on the other hand, is a good-natured, unassuming philanthropist whom the reader can not help liking. The most interesting aspect of the novel, however, is the author's conception of Tinker as representing America in the same relationship to the older but less progressive civilization of Europe as ancient Rome held to Greek civilization.[34]

Claire Ambler (Garden City, New York, 1928), the second product of his European trip, is a reworking of the theme of the innocent, flippant American girl, unschooled in European ways, flouting the foreign mores as she moves blithely and unchaperoned through society. This theme, of course, had been featured in Henry James's *Daisy Miller* (1878) and Howells' *A Fearful Responsibility* (1881); but in *Claire Ambler* the American girl, Lily Mayhew, of northern New York state, does not find tragedy or death at the end of her shocking peregrinations. Her flirtations in Italy and Sicily nearly bring death to an Italian prince, a pro-Fascist, who is ambushed by anti-Fascists because she has snubbed them. At length Claire awakens from her romantic posturings, returns home, and gets down to the real business of living.[35]

After these two novels Tarkington returned to the

[34] See *ibid.*, 265-69, for analysis of *The Plutocrat.*
[35] See *ibid.*, 269-71, for *Claire Ambler.*

familiar setting of Indianapolis for *Young Mrs. Greeley* (Garden City, New York, 1929), but this time he examined a new facet of urban living—life in the apartment house. This is a social and economic study of business and social rivalry, and in it occurs his themes of the selfish wife and social climbing.[36] He later treated the subject more thoroughly in *The Lorenzo Bunch* (Garden City, New York, 1936), an unhappy tale of a dangerously beautiful but selfish wife who brings misery to all with whom she deals, ruining the happiness of her husband, whom she then discards. Here is another of his Becky Sharps.

Mirthful Haven (Garden City, New York, 1930) is perhaps the author's most bitter book. It probably reflected his mental anguish when he thought he was losing his sight and also his defense of an aged Kennebunkport sea captain who had been unjustly dismissed from his position with the River Club. This novel of manners examines the antagonism between the natives and the summer residents of Kennebunkport, which he calls ironically Mirthful Haven, as seen particularly in the successful opposition of both sides to a marriage between the daughter of a native and the son of a summer family.[37] *Wanton Mally* (Garden City, New York, 1932) is the less usual type of work for Tarkington, for it is an historical novel woven about two seventeenth-century portraits which he owned and, with gallant gentlemen, masked women, and dueling thieves, smacks of the bold, romantic adventure of *Monsieur Beaucaire*. *Image of Josephine* (Garden City, New York, 1945) continues this interest in art, using the setting of an art gallery. *Mary's Neck* (Garden City, New York, 1932) again tells a story against the Kennebunkport background, here called Mary's Neck,

---

[36] See Woodress, *op. cit.*, 271-72 for *Young Mrs. Greeley*.
[37] For *Mirthful Haven*, see *ibid.*, 277-79.

and is a much more pleasant novel than *Mirthful Haven* in its dramatization of the comic amusements of a summer colony. Here the novelist takes the opportunity to satirize modern art. Following these books, Tarkington then took up again his old interest, the theater, in *Presenting Lily Mars* (Garden City, New York, 1933), which relates the tale of an ingenue who succeeds so well in her first try that she nearly wrecks the play by arousing the jealousy of the leading lady and who goes home in disgrace, but finds the producer pursuing her—not to retrieve her as an actress but to obtain a wife.[38]

In his last years the novelist returned to his all-consuming love, the Indiana scene. *The Heritage of Hatcher Ide* (Garden City, New York, 1941) is a continuation of the *Growth* trilogy, yet echoes the world of Tarkington's youth. Set in 1939, just before the outbreak of World War II, the novel tells how Hatcher Ide, returning from college, encounters the lingering effects of the chaotic Depression and witnesses the egoistic selfishness of Sarah Florian, veteran of two unsuccessful marriages (another of Tarkington's Becky Sharps), who does much devilment and remains unrepentant. When the older generation sinks under the economic buffeting of the times, the younger group takes over to regenerate the country. It is a realistic novel, yet one of hope and confidence in the ultimate triumph of wisdom and right. It is the best of the later novels.

The Fighting Littles (Garden City, New York, 1941) is so loosely put together that it is almost a book of short stories. In the character of the curmudgeon, Ripley Little, there is voiced much of the author's anti-New Deal con-

---

[38] Consult Woodress for fuller discussions of all these later novels of Tarkington. This book contains by far the best criticism—and, in some cases, about the only criticism available.

victions; the book serves as a rather mediocre outlet for
his opinions. *Kate Fennigate* (Garden City, New York,
1943), likewise, is not a pleasant book. In telling the story
of a woman who makes her husband a success in business,
Tarkington degraded the character of the husband so
much that the editors of the *Post,* who had requested
such a story, rejected it. It was not the pleasant magazine
type of fiction. Indianapolis residents, however, were interested to find that both this novel and *The Heritage of
Hatcher Ide* were set in Indianapolis.[39]

Tarkington's last novel, *The Show Piece,* published
posthumously (Garden City, New York, 1947), was only
two thirds completed at the time of his death; like many
other stories before it, it deals with egoism, a favorite
subject for the author. *Three Selected Short Novels* (Garden City, New York, 1947) contained "Walterson," "Un-
certain Molly Collicut," and "Rennie Peddigoe."

Booth Tarkington died on May 19, 1946, at his home in
Indianapolis at the age of seventy-six. He had lived a full,
interesting, and productive life—and one that was modest
and honest as well; he became a part of that infinity in
which he had come to believe that life flows. And with
the news of his passing Hoosierdom mourned; for Indiana
had lost one of her greatest interpreters and American
literature a distinguished figure.

As we look back over the titles of the author's many
books, we are struck by his great versatility and ability;
Tarkington used many kinds of materials and fashioned
them all to artistic and popular purpose. The public
thronged to buy a high percentage of his production, and
many of his books are still selling, with indications of continued demand. Although many pieces were written obvi-

[39] The old University Club and Tudor Hall, a private secondary school
for girls, are featured in *The Heritage of Hatcher Ide.*

ously for the purpose primarily of entertaining, still he tried always to say something, for he cherished the idea that an artist must have a belief of some kind to get across to the reader. As a humanitarian, he was interested in people and in character, and the later Tarkington particularly emphasized character and disparaged overattention to plot.

Proof of this emphasis on character lies in the many unforgettable personages that abound in Tarkington's stories, such as his host of Becky Sharps. Another strong element in his works is his universality. Readers easily recognize the people about whom Tarkington wrote, whether it was Penrod, Willie Baxter, the Sheridan family, or the Amberson family; these types were—and are—universal. In creating them the author fastened on the enduring in human nature, for every boy is (and every man was) a Penrod, and the family next door might be either on the way up, like the Sheridans of *The Turmoil,* or on the way down, like the Ambersons. Tarkington recorded the lives not only of Hoosiers and residents of Indianapolis for nearly the entire first half of the twentieth century but also the composite life of America. To read Tarkington is to read social history. In his social history and criticism, as in his *Growth* trilogy and *Alice Adams,* lies his greatest contribution to literature.

His literary attitude resists a pat generalization. Not only did he begin his work as a romanticist, but he continued this approach to life even into some of his later work; nevertheless, the great bulk of his production is more or less realistic in faithfully setting forth life with a variety of social and economic forces playing on it and supplying motives for action. Yet it must be recognized that both his romanticism and his realism tend seldom to be extreme. *Beaucaire* and *In the Arena* are the exception rather than the rule, and he never was really tempted by naturalism. His plays, although often built on a social problem, must be classified mostly as entertaining farces or as light comedies, and in none of them is there the serious study of a great problem that one finds in the plays of William Vaughn Moody. Still, Tarkington bears away the laurels as the most prolific Hoosier dramatist, even outdistancing that other Indiana writer of excellent farces and also of musical comedies, George Ade; and Tarkington is one of the most popular American playwrights of the first third of this century. Another element of his universality is his use of many settings, for he places his actions in the Midwest, Indianapolis, Terre Haute, Maine, the East, and at many points in Europe. It should be noted in passing that he utilized Hoosier settings more than any other Indiana author, except, perhaps, Riley. He followed the lead of Henry James in portraying (often in unflattering colors) the American traveler in Europe, as in *His Own People, The Man from Home, The Plutocrat,* and *Claire Ambler.* And perhaps a last element closely allied with his universality is his quiet optimism in seeing that underneath the complexities of all the many changes in society the best in humanity is still strong and that although this best element may be forced to adjust to new conditions, it will survive and can not be crushed.

To the young and to the young in heart the name of Booth Tarkington will always be associated primarily with his books of childhood and youth. And in spite of his sharing the leadership of Indiana literature with Meredith Nicholson and George Ade from about the time of the death of Riley in 1916 until the deaths of all three,[40] for many he will remain the best of all the numerous Indiana

[40] Meredith Nicholson died in 1947, George Ade in 1944.

authors, a complete Hoosier—the genial gentleman from Indiana.[41]

CAROLINE VIRGINIA KROUT

From this point forward in the history of the novel in the Golden Age of Indiana literature there is no figure of the stature of Tarkington, and the only names of particular importance are those of George Barr McCutcheon and Gene Stratton Porter. There are several lesser lights, however.

One of these is Caroline Virginia Krout (1852-1931), the author of only three novels and a book of juvenile stories, but a writer who realized a degree of fame in spite of her small production and her shy disposition.

In order to sketch her biography some attention must be given first to her eccentric father, Robert Kennedy Krout, "a sort of Hoosier Bronson Alcott."[42] He was brought as a boy from Covington, Kentucky, to the wild southwestern portion of Montgomery County, Indiana, locally known as the "Balhinch" district, where he learned Latin and Greek under the schoolmaster James Gilkey, in the town of Alamo. From this school Krout proceeded to Wabash College, in Crawfordsville, where he was graduated in 1848. He was considered a student of unusual promise, but for some unaccountable reason he never ful-

[41] Further study of Tarkington must begin with the very readable Woodress biography, which I heartily recommend. The best bibliography available is Russo and Sullivan. See also Albert D. Van Nostrand, The Novels and Plays of Booth Tarkington. A Critical Appraisal (MS. Ph. D. thesis, Harvard University, 1951). An anthology of Tarkington's writings, recently published, is John Beecroft (ed.), *The Gentleman from Indianapolis. A Treasury of Booth Tarkington* (Garden City, New York, 1957). The Indiana State Library has many Tarkington letters, but the main collection of Tarkington manuscripts is deposited at Princeton University.

[42] Banta, *Indiana Authors and Their Books*, 183.

filled it and spent the rest of his life dabbling in teaching, law, chemistry, selling, writing for newspapers, and, in general, rebelling quietly against the social order but getting nowhere—meanwhile letting his home in Crawfordsville deteriorate until it became an eyesore. His wife, Caroline Brown Krout, a Crawfordsville girl, bore him nine children. His perfectionist criticism of the writing of his literary daughters, Caroline and Mary, drove them toward success.

The older daughter, Mary Hannah Krout (1851-1927), became one of the leading feminists of the United States, a commanding public speaker, a pioneer in the field of women's journalism, and a traveling reporter for Chicago newspapers, writing about events occurring all over the world. She led an interesting life, bold and adventurous for the times before the adoption of woman suffrage and recognition of the professional abilities of women. She became well known partly because of her early verse, including the poem, "Little Brown Hands," which was reprinted all over the country. Unfortunately, however, she neither collected her poetry nor published the plays she wrote. After a trip to Australia she grew tired of traveling, retired to Crawfordsville, and continued her writing, helping her widowed friend, Mrs. Susan Elston Wallace, complete the autobiography left unfinished by her husband, General Lew Wallace.[43]

In contrast to her self-confident sister, Caroline Krout was always timid to the point of doing herself injustice. She was born on October 13, 1852, in Crawfordsville, and attended a local subscription school, then a public school.

[43] For the biography of Mary Hannah Krout, see Banta, *op. cit.*, 184-86, and Russo and Sullivan, *Bibliographical Studies of Seven Authors of Crawfordsville*, 13-68. The Indiana Division of the State Library has Mary Krout's manuscripts, scrapbooks, and other materials.

When she was sixteen, her mother died, leaving Caroline the care of the house and the four younger children. When relieved of this assignment three years later by a younger sister, Caroline taught for five years in the Crawfordsville schools until her health was broken and she found herself an invalid. During her illness she utilized her time by contributing short stories and feature articles to the Chicago newspapers. After a partial recovery, she became assistant court reporter in Crawfordsville and next served on the staff of the Newberry Library in Chicago. When ill health caused her to give up this position, she returned to Crawfordsville and wrote stories for periodicals, then turned to novel writing, adopting the suggestion of her friend Mrs. Lew Wallace that she employ the pseudonym, Caroline Brown (her mother's maiden name). Her shyness and the fact that she discovered belatedly that her nearly completed second novel, *On the We-a Trail,* was on the same subject as *Alice of Old Vincennes,* a novel being published by her fellow townsman, Maurice Thompson, almost moved her to quit writing completely. These two authors had been writing similar novels, completely unknown to each other; and when the fact was discovered, Thompson generously wrote to Caroline Krout, begging her not to let his book interfere with the completion and publication of her own. She was so sensitive to criticism and so aware of her own literary faults that after publishing four books she gave up writing and lived the last twenty years of her life as a recluse with her sisters in the family home in Crawfordsville, where she died, on October 9, 1931.[44]

Her first novel, *Knights in Fustian. A War Time Story of Indiana* (Boston, 1900), was inspired by her chance

[44] The biography of Caroline Krout was obtained from Banta, *op. cit.,* 182-84, and from Russo and Sullivan, *op. cit.,* 3-4.

contact with an old woman who shared with Miss Krout memories of her unfortunate experiences with the Copperheads of Indiana. The story is placed in mythical Middle County of southern Indiana, with Crofton as the county seat.[45] This is really the "Balhinch" district of Montgomery County, which she knew through her father. Frank Neal, son of a prosperous farmer, returns from the Union Army on furlough to recover from his experiences as a prisoner of war at Andersonville and finds the countryside in ferment with anti-Union sympathy aroused by the subversive Knights of the Golden Circle. After Frank and the heroine, Lucy Whittaker, suffer harrowing experiences at the hands of the Knights, Frank and a Federal detective foil the plot of the organization to seize control of the state, and the Knights are dispersed by troops sent by Governor Oliver P. Morton. Frank and Lucy then become engaged. The book is in many ways interesting but is better as history than as a novel and tends to be rather dull. The author is weak in characterization, often utilizing exposition clumsily interpolated into the story to develop her wooden characters, and the hero and heroine are incompletely drawn; also Miss Krout's ability in describing nature is not carried over to the description of persons. Governor Morton, however, makes a rather convincing minor appearance in the story, and the book is dedicated to him. The principal value of the novel lies in its picture of the secret society, not the uninteresting rustics who compose it.[46] Despite its faults, the book sold well. Governor Theodore Roosevelt of New York wrote to

[45] Another more modern novel by an Indiana author in which a mythical Indiana county is created is *Raintree County,* by Ross F. Lockridge, Jr., published in 1948.

[46] See the rather unfavorable review of *Knights in Fustian,* written perhaps by Maurice Thompson, in *The Independent,* 52 (January-June, 1900):1389-90.

Miss Krout, ". . . you have given me far and away the best and most vivid idea I ever had of the Indiana Copperheads and also an exceptionally good picture of life in the western farming communities."[47]

Although the author preferred her first book to her others, many readers have always liked better the second, *On the We-a Trail. A Story of the Great Wilderness* (New York, 1903), which had its genesis in her interest in early Indiana history and the Indian trail extending from the Wea Indian towns on the Wabash River about ten miles below Lafayette and running down to the Kentucky hunting ground, crossing Sugar Creek, four miles west of Crawfordsville, at Indian Ford. Perhaps having learned from her first novel about the use of history, Miss Krout relegated it more to the background here and told the tale of how a girl, Ferriby Benhem, the sole survivor of an Indian attack on her family's cabin (for she had been away at a spring, getting water) wanders dazed for some time through the wilderness while her lover searches for her. At length she is rescued and taken to Fort Sackville (Vincennes), where she is cared for by a French family. The taking of this fort from the British by George Rogers Clark and his band is woven into the fabric of the romance, and the book abounds in adventure and sympathetic description of the mysteries of the deep Indiana forests. On the other hand, there is an air of unreality in some of the action and descriptions, caused partly by a lack of detail and sufficient character analysis. Now and then characters are unrealistic in their actions, as when the hero, Robert Lancaster, having barely missed being hit by an Indian's tomahawk, stops to pick it up and examine it before defending himself or giving chase to the fleeing Indian.

[47] As quoted in Banta, *Indiana Authors and Their Books*, 184.

Bold Robin and His Forest Rangers (New York, 1905),
a juvenile, is a collection of six stories evidently written
earlier at the request of Mrs. Wallace and perhaps inspired by the interest in archery begun in Crawfordsville
by Maurice and Will Thompson. It consists mostly of
tales she had invented for her young nephews.

Her last novel, *Dionis of the White Veil* (Boston, 1911),
is a well-written romance suggested by the publication of
a pamphlet by the Indiana Historical Society[48] giving
the history of the attempt of a party of priests and nuns
to found the first Jesuit mission at the mouth of White
River in the wilderness that became Indiana, at about the
same time that the Sieur de Vincennes was establishing
the first trading post on the Wabash. Following the history
carefully, Miss Krout, added her usual idyllic yet accurate
descriptions of the forest and a love story. The gay Chevalier Fauchet falls in love with a novice, Dionis Montfort,
who is to take the veil in less than a week, and finally succeeds in wresting her from the Church just in time.

Caroline Krout, thus, is a writer with many faults; yet
one must admit, at least, that many parts of her narratives
move well, that her descriptions of nature—inspired perhaps by the "Balhinch" region—are skilfully written, and
that she suceeded in digging her materials from her native
soil. Her fame today remains chiefly local.

HENRY THEW STEPHENSON—CHARLES T. DALTON—
GEORGE W. LOUTTIT

So also are the next three writers mostly known locally.
They are Henry Thew Stephenson, Charles Test Dalton,
and George William Louttit.

[48] Jacob P. Dunn, *The Mission to the Ouabache (Indiana Historical
Society Publications,* Vol. 3, No. 4, 1904).

There are few facts to be found about Henry Thew Stephenson (1870-1957), for he lived the quiet life of a student, teacher, and scholar. Born in Cincinnati on April 22, 1870, he was awarded the B.S. degree from Ohio State University in 1894, the A.B. degree in 1898 from Harvard, and in 1911 the A.M. degree from Indiana University. In 1900 he married Agnes Reynolds, of Richmond, Indiana. He was a member of the English Department of Indiana University from 1895 to 1940. He died at Eau Gallie, Florida, December 29, 1957.[49]

Stephenson published many scholarly studies, mostly of Shakespeare and Elizabethan England, and, unprofessorlike, several romantic novels. *Patroon Van Volkenberg. A Tale of Old Manhattan in the Year Sixteen Hundred & Ninety-Nine* (Indianapolis, 1900) is a dashing, vibrant tale of Michael LeBourse, a French Huguenot, who as a young man is separated from his sister during the religious wars and spends most of the rest of the story in attempting to locate her, finally discovering her murdered in old New York. The book abounds in pirates, breathless fights and escapes, civil strife in New York, and strong, deadly feeling between Protestants and Catholics. Its main fault is the tendency of the author to summarize rather than to dramatize the action.

The Fickle Wheel. A Tale of Elizabethan London (Indianapolis, 1901) shows the same fault, but makes use of Stephenson's scholarly knowledge with happy results. It, too, is a stirring adventure story involving sword play and cloak-and-dagger business. He gives a good view of Elizabethan London, with the figures of Shakespeare and Ben Jonson and the reflection of Shakespeare's plays

[49] For the biography of Henry Stephenson, see Banta, *op. cit.*, 304; obituary in Indianapolis *News*, December 31, 1957, p. 15; *Indiana Alumni Magazine*, February, 1958, p. 14.

thrown in, as the author spins the thread of the love story of Cecily Coverdale, whose hard-bitten merchant father keeps her and her lover, Richard Allen, apart until the new sovereign, James I, brings the two together and knights Richard.

Christie Bell of Goldenrod Valley. A Tale of Southern Indiana and of Cincinnati in the Olden Time (Indianapolis, 1918) is the story of a beautiful schoolgirl, her farmer-father, and the father's unloved brother in Cincinnati, told against the background of the freshness both of beautiful rural surroundings and of such rural personalities as the sweet Christie Bell. As a parting shot at narration, Stephenson wrote a much different type of book in *The Mystery of the Murdered Bridegroom,* published in 1931, the title of which speaks for itself.

(Charles) Test Dalton (1875-1945) is remembered for one novel, *The Role of the Unconquered.* Born in Chicago in 1875, he was awarded the A.B. degree from Butler College in 1896 and then did a year's postgraduate work at Harvard University. He spent two years in London in the role of correspondent for American newspapers. In 1918-19 he served as drama director first at Camp Logan, Texas, and then at Camp Merritt, New Jersey. He lived in Indianapolis from 1920 to 1931 and then moved to New York, where he died on December 10, 1945.[50] *The Role of the Unconquered* (New York, 1901) is an amateurish, melodramatic, but spirited historical romance about Henry of Navarre's winning Maria de Medici as his bride in spite of the machinations of the villainous Duke of Savoy. Other novels, which are poorly written and lacking in description and action, are *For Brides Only. A Romance of the Mountains and the East*

[50] The biography of Test Dalton is from the Indiana Biography Series, 29:111.

Side (New York, 1930) and *The Richest Man on Earth* (New York, 1931). His plays, except for *The Mantle of Lincoln* (New York, 1922), are light and inconsequential farces, like *Adam's Apple* (New York, 1913), but encountered at least fair luck in being produced in Indianapolis and elsewhere.

The product of George William Louttit (1868-?) was likewise mediocre—or less. He was born on June 30, 1868, in Dayton, Ohio; his family moved soon to Fort Wayne, Indiana, where he was educated in the public schools. He studied law at the University of Michigan, in 1888 married Gertrude Britton, of Ravenna, Ohio, in 1890 began practicing law in Allen County, Indiana, where he was elected first judge of the municipal court in Fort Wayne, and in 1899 served in the Indiana legislature.[51] His first novel, *A Maid of the Wildwood. A Romance of the Middle West in Early Days* (Fort Wayne, Indiana, 1901), is a story of the times of the Indian chief Tecumseh and his death. The hero fires the shot that fatally wounds Tecumseh and then in compliance with the chief's last wish buries him in an unknown and unmarked grave.[52]

The Gentleman from Jay (New York, 1903) tells the absurd story of the hayseed, bewhiskered farmer, Thomas Tucker, from Pokeville, who gets himself elected to the state legislature in 1902 and makes a laughing stock of himself because of his unfamiliarity with the ways of the big-city capital—hotels, elevators, restaurants, theaters, and

[51] The biography of Louttit is from Barry, A Biographical and Bibliographical Dictionary of Indiana Authors, 455, and William E. Henry, *Legislative and State Manual of Indiana for 1899 and 1900* (Indianapolis, 1899), 1029.

[52] A recent biography of Tecumseh, written by the Indiana author Glenn Tucker is *Tecumseh. Vision of Glory* (Indianapolis, 1956). In this study Tucker points out that no one knows today who killed Tecumseh or where he was buried.

champagne. His ignorance, prejudice, and conceit are appalling, and his uncouth speeches in rustic dialect draw howls of derision from the assembly and spectators. His bills fail, and everything he does is wrong, with the result that he is hooted home. This outlandish novel is surprisingly bitter in spots but is often very funny; it undoubtedly reflects the author's experience in the legislature.

The Eddyite. A Christian Science Tale (Fort Wayne, Indiana, 1908) is a biting criticism of the beliefs and practices of that faith; and *King Fez* (Fort Wayne, Indiana, 1907) and *Bits and Hits in the Devil's Verse* (Boston, 1928) are collections of undistinguished poetry. Louttit did nothing outstanding.

George Barr McCutcheon

This is certainly not the case with George Barr McCutcheon (1866-1928), for he inaugurated a tradition in literature, a tradition which so appealed to readers that his nearly fifty books, almost all novels, sold over five million copies. Primarily a dreamer and romancer, though always professing a preference for realism, McCutcheon was cut from the same cloth as Charles Major, George Cary Eggleston, Lew Wallace, and Maurice Thompson. It was McCutcheon who wrote the famous Graustark series, high-flown romances about a tiny, mythical Balkan kingdom, weighed down by intrigue and suffocating, backward tradition, ruled over by a dazzlingly beautiful princess with a court full of other gorgeous creatures, fairly imploring red-blooded, ingenious Americans to come across the sea, assert American superiority by setting things to rights, and marry the abused, tempting females. Through his romancing and his feeding the American ego, McCutcheon rode the tidal wave of popularity that threatened for a time to engulf the more serious literature in the United States.

He came of no unusual antecedents, but of good stock. His father, John Barr McCutcheon, a Civil War veteran, was a farmer and cattle raiser whose ancestors had migrated from Scotland to Virginia, then had become pioneers first in Kentucky and next in Indiana, where they moved in 1826, ten years after the last became a state. John McCutcheon, a man of literary interests who was said to have written and produced a play, was selected to take charge of the first farm owned by Purdue University after it had opened its doors as the "agricultural and mechanical" college of the state. Later he served as sheriff of Tippecanoe County and then as county treasurer. The novelist's mother, Clara (Glick) McCutcheon, came of Dutch ancestors that settled in Pennsylvania. George had two well-known brothers: Ben Frederick McCutcheon (1875-1934), who became a columnist and later commercial editor of the Chicago *Tribune,* and John Tinney McCutcheon (1870-1949), the famous cartoonist, world traveler, and writer.[53]

George Barr McCutcheon was born on July 26, 1866, in Tippecanoe County, attended a country school and, when the family moved to Lafayette, the Lafayette schools. The creative impulse manifesting itself early, at the ripe age of eight, he wrote his first story, entitled "Panther Jim," which remained unfinished—perhaps happily so, since he later was to confess his addiction to dime novels. He learned to draw and taught the art to his brother John, the boys continuing their drawing and writing for many years, often in secret, by means of candlelight in the basement of their Lafayette home. In 1882-83 George was a student at Purdue University, where his companions were his brother John and George Ade, and he reported the college news for the Lafayette *Journal;* but the next summer he joined a traveling theatrical troupe, which

[53] For a discussion of John T. McCutcheon, see below, 417-19.

experienced financial disaster, forcing the young actor to trudge penniless some three hundred miles home—a walk which definitely dampened his enthusiasm for acting. He determined then to become a writer, taking a position as reporter on the Lafayette *Journal* for the princely salary of six dollars a week. He wrote a column and some poetry and in 1893 transferred his journalistic activties to the Lafayette *Daily Courier,* where he held the position of city cditor until 1901.

His dialect letters, "Waddleton Mail," achieved only newspaper publication. During this time he had been attempting, without much success, to write stories, and his first appeared in the *National Magazine* in 1896. His first novel, "Pootoo's Gods," was a romantic story of shipwreck in a savage land. The stimulus of the fame which the author acquired from Graustark and other books made it a success when it was published under the title of *Nedra* (New York, 1905).[54]

McCutcheon's second novel, *Graustark. The Story of a Love Behind a Throne* (Chicago, 1901), was written in the same manner and was sold, after several rejections, for only $500, but began his long series of tremendously successful Graustark romances, to say nothing of many romances on other subjects. After Graustark became a success, he resigned from his editorship, for he really disliked newspaper work; but he was induced to work half time until he moved in 1901 to Chicago, where his brothers Ben and John were living. He now settled down to a writ-

[54] "Pootoo's Gods" offers a problem, for I can not confirm its publication or find a date for its appearance by reference to Banta or any of the usual sources for bibliography, such as the Library of Congress or the *Cumulative Book Index.* Yet the article by Sarah G. Bowerman in the *Dictionary of American Biography, Authors Edition,* 12:12-13, definitely implies publication. It may have been printed privately and had only a small circulation.

ing career, publishing at least one book every year and in many years two books. In 1904 he married Mrs. Marie Van Antwerp Fay, and the couple lived in New York City. He maintained throughout his life a close friendship with George Ade and Booth Tarkington, and from 1924 to 1926 he was president of the Author's League. Living primarily in his writings, he pursued a life outwardly uneventful; he penned altogether forty-eight works, mostly romantic novels. A reporter who interviewed him in 1927 found him reserved to the point of being almost uncommunicative.[55] He died suddenly on October 23, 1928, at the Hotel Martinique in New York, at a luncheon of the Dutch Treat Club, and his ashes were buried in his home city, Lafayette, Indiana.[56]

McCutcheon's work can best be characterized by an analysis of his first successful work, *Graustark,* since most of what he wrote from that time henceforth was in the Graustark pattern—or, flavor—of romance. Perhaps a historical point of view will aid in placing this book in its proper perspective, for it was by no means the first of its kind; yet it began what became the most successful series of such novels.

The type can be traced back to the adventurous and sentimental *Prince Otto* (1885) of Robert Louis Stevenson, a story containing good psychological analysis of the mythical German state of Grunewald. In 1894 the prince was appropriated by Anthony Hope, his personality divided between Rudolph Rassendyl and Rupert of Hentzau, and his kingdom was reassigned as the princi-

[55] See Jean West Maury, "What George Barr McCutcheon Thinks About," in Boston *Evening Transcript,* December 10, 1927, article in clipping file in the Indiana Division of the State Library.

[56] Material on George B. McCutcheon was obtained from the article in the *Dictionary of American Biography,* the interview in the Boston *Evening Transcript,* and miscellaneous sources.

pality of Ruritania, the account being set forth in a swashbuckling thriller entitled *The Prisoner of Zenda.* In Hope's novel an English commoner, Rudolph Rassendyl, whose appearance is nearly identical with that of King Rupert of Ruritania, impersonates the king when Rupert's villainous brother, Black Michael, imprisons his kingly brother; and Rudolph thereby saves the monarch and his kingdom. This improbable but delightful romance about how a commoner brings nobility to their knees in thankfulness for his heroism appealed strongly to Americans, who at that time were thrilling vicariously to accounts of the weddings of rich Americans and titled Europeans, who were looking up the genealogy of their families, and who were decorating their houses with gingerbread turrets. As *The Prisoner of Zenda* went through twenty-six printings, Ruritania suddenly became more real to Americans than many existing European countries; and even today this novel can be found in most libraries. Anthony Hope thus began a type that flourished for several years, with the setting an imaginary small European kingdom, a feebly glittering aristocracy shot through with intrigue, but still having a small band of loyal followers of a king or a beautiful princess—the yarn being told to the accompaniment of the swirling of graceful cloaks and the flashing of weapons.

Imitations of *Zenda* were not slow to arise. Among others, Richard Harding Davis published *The Princess Aline* in 1895; two years later Harold McGrath included an American in his *Arms and the Woman;* in 1898 appeared *The Pride of Jennico,* by Agnes and Egerton Castle, which was set in an eighteenth-century Bohemian kingdom; the next year Davis followed his first Zenda novel with another, *The King's Jackal;* in 1900 came Harold McGrath's *The Puppet Crown.* All these novels were similar—indeed, in some ways almost carbon copies, one of the other.[57]

It was when this vogue had become well established that McCutcheon published *Graustark* in 1901. Although he claimed that he had not read *The Prisoner of Zenda* and was influenced only by the *Arabian Nights,* the resemblances to *Zenda* are unmistakable; and he must have been influenced at least by other Zenda stories and the feeling of romance which permeated the literary atmosphere. McCutcheon's novel, though a bit awkward in composition, was a success for two reasons: first, the more cultured readers, having begun to be surfeited with this subject, had relinquished such novels to the less sophisticated, for whom McCutcheon's style was well fitted; and second, he gave a new twist to the mythical kingdom plot by the happy idea of making an American the hero—a clean-cut, alert, and vigorous young man—the typical American that every American male fancied himself to be. So Grenfall Lorry, the American go-getter, falls in love at first sight with the Princess Yetive ("the most beautiful woman in the world"), who is traveling incognito in the United States, follows her to her tiny, picturesque Balkan kingdom, where amid a feudal world of black villains (dangerous in spite of being undersized), burning hates and loves and loyalties, he easily uses American ingenuity to save the kingdom and then marries the princess. In answer to the objection to the match raised by a handful of ignorant, though patriotic, courtiers, he observes that every American is the equal of every European nobleman, for is not every American boy the potential president of the greatest nation on earth?. And Princess Yetive can

[57] I am indebted to James D. Hart, *The Popular Book* . . . (New York 1950), *passim.,* for much of the preceding information, as well as some of that which follows.

not help falling in love with Lorry—for after all, what European woman could resist a courageous, red-blooded American male? The characters, however, with the possible exception of the princess, are all types with little individuality, even the hero himself being only the symbol of American manhood. The plot is essentially simple, consisting of throwing obstacle after obstacle in the path of happiness for the couple; but against the background of the ancient castle, dungeons, mountains, midnight rides, gorgeous uniforms, and dazzling virtue eventually love triumphs over all. Here, then, is ample food for the American ego—for could not every American do what Grenfall Lorry did? Here is irresistible escape literature!

During the first nine months after publication *Graustark* sold 150,000 copies; and soon the publishers, ashamed of the pittance of $500 paid McCutcheon for his manuscript and doubtless fearful he would seek another firm, began paying him royalties on the skyrocketing sales. Perhaps the greatest testimony to the effect of the book was the flood of letters that overwhelmed the author, asking him for information as to the quickest way to get to Graustark. People attempted to buy tickets to Graustark and claimed that they knew characters in the romance.[58] Soon the inevitable occurred, and a play based on the book was produced, which earned over $250,000 for its producers and after a long Broadway run spent years touring the nation.

McCutcheon realized that purely by accident his literary mining operations had struck gold, and he did not let the favorable opportunity slip by. He kept pouring out other Graustarkian romances until the year before his death and prepared an elaborate genealogical table of the rulers of Graustark. The others are *Beverly of Graustark* (New

---

[58] See "Buying a Ticket to Graustark," in *Literary Digest,* November 17, 1928.

York, 1904), *Truxton King* (New York, 1909), *The Prince of Graustark* (New York, 1914), *East of the Setting Sun* (New York, 1924), and *The Inn of the Hawk and Raven* (New York, 1927). The last named, a fast-moving tale of a robber band and its chieftain, Jonifer Dovos, who kidnaps Colonel Starcourt of the Graustarkian dragoons as a birthday present for his beautiful daughter Gerane, is the best written of all, and in order to follow the chronological development of the dynasty of Princess Yetive, should be read first. All of these Graustark books gave the reader the impression that the European male was dissipated, villainous, and of small stature—obviously not the equal of the invincible Americans; that Germany, Russia, and Austria were brewers of mischief, but England and France were peacemakers; and that America should have little to do with the corrupt European politics. What small part McCutcheon's books had in the development of the spirit of American isolationism—or conversely, how much the spirit of isolationism influenced McCutcheon—is a matter for historians to debate.

Once launched successfully into the field of romance by the grace of *Graustark,* McCutcheon wrote novel after novel in the romantic vein. It is true that only a minority of his huge production dealt with the distinctive Graustark theme, yet nearly all his other books were equally high-flown—as, for example, *The Man From Brodney's* (New York, 1908), in which an unconquerable hero and a beautiful princess figure in a complex plot in the exotic setting of a South Sea island. He published much that was unsubstantial and does not deserve mention here. Among his works one finds a large number of novelettes of equally flimsy character, and also two plays, privately published in only a handful of copies.

Still, some of his other books should receive at least a passing glance. *Brewster's Millions* (Chicago, 1903) is one of these. Published under the pseudonym of Richard Greaves in order to win a bet that this book would sell better than *The Sherrods,* issued the same year with his now-illustrious name, *Brewster's Millions* is a comic fantasy, a sort of comedy of manners. Montgomery Brewster, a mild sort of playboy, inherits a million dollars from his grandfather, then receives notice almost immediately that a forgotten uncle has left him seven millions provided that on his twenty-sixth birthday (one year away) he is absolutely penniless; the uncle had hated Brewster's grandfather and wanted none of the grandfather's money to be joined to his own in Brewster's pocket. So Brewster has the pleasant, but very difficult, task of spending the grandfather's million in a year. The terms of the will prevent him from bestowing much in charity and specify that he must provide evidence that he can manage his affairs wisely and shrewdly. The task of spending is misunderstood by everyone, and being considered a spendthrift, he loses respect in general until he successfully qualifies to inherit his uncle's fortune. This is, of course, a plot story, a brilliant plot story; but in reality it is a case of much ado about practically nothing. Nearly all the characters are merely types. There were social ramifications, however. The contemporary reader gladly identified himself with Brewster and his happy task and vicariously shared his reveling in the high life of competitive luxury—a life to which very few of the readers belonged but which they all endorsed and desired. The novel won the bet for the author in proving that it was not his name, but his creative fancy that made the book sell. *Brewster's Millions* sold more copies than any of his later books. Made into a play, it elevated Edward S. Abeles, in the role of Brewster, to stardom during the theatrical seasons of 1906 to 1908.

Others of McCutcheon's books are interesting, too. *Mr. Bingle* (New York, 1915) reflects his love of Dickens in his attempt to portray a Dickensian character. *The Day of the Dog* (New York, 1904) is a good—though slight—story which arose from a dream. A young, attractive widow and a lawyer who reveals the rascality of her brother-in-law are forced by the latter to flee a ferocious bulldog and are left prisoners, sitting on a beam in a coach house with the dog lunging at them from below. It took McCutcheon another dream to find a way to get the two down. The lawyer takes off his waistcoat, lowers it to the dog, which clamps his teeth upon it, and the lawyer then tosses the infuriated animal into an empty stall and brings the grateful widow down a ladder—and eventually to the altar. *Viola Gwyn* (New York, 1922) is a narrative of pioneer Indiana laid around 1832 in and around the mushrooming town of the novelist's native Lafayette, with its cabins abuilding among the forest trees and the courthouse yard full of stumps. It affords a good picture of the times with their rough, grotesque characters, but misses by miles being a *Hoosier School-Master* because this fascinating setting is used only to set off the love and adventure story of a stalwart hero and a proud, beautiful, and spoiled heroine, whose obstacle to love is disintegrated when the proper time arrives.

Nevertheless, McCutcheon attempted several times to turn his back on the romance which he loved and to write instead some sterner stuff in the field of realism. *The Hollow of Her Hand* (New York, 1912) is a story of crime but it is without success in analysis of the psychological motivation which the author attempted. In *The Sherrods* (New York, 1903) one finds the sympathetic study of a bigamist, a young artist of Clay Township, Indiana, who leaves his young wife to make his way, with his sketches, to Chicago, where he finds astonishing success and where he marries a beautiful heiress of the North Side, while still loving his first wife. This could be a psychological problem novel except for the fact that McCutcheon makes his three characters too unbelievable to be really tragic.

The only novel in which the author could be said actually to have attained to realism is his own favorite, *Mary Midthorne* (New York, 1911), which is completely unlike the rest of his work. This is the story of how the young and virtuous Eric and Mary Midthorne, brother and sister, are tyrannized over by their thin-lipped, self-righteous uncle and aunt, Mr. and Mrs. Horace Blagden, and are constantly told that they may grow to be sinful like their parents. The villainous Chetwynd Blagden, their cousin, steals from a bank and goads Eric until he finally knocks Chetwynd against a rotten bridge railing, which gives way and allows him to fall to his death. Eric at first conceals the death, then, conscience-stricken, confesses the "crime" when the Blagdens have emerged more human from the testing fires of sorrow; and eventually Eric and Mary come into happiness. In this grim story, written in an uneven style, but containing some good characterization, the reader feels that for the only instance in his entire writing career McCutcheon really comes to grips with life.

In spite of his attempts at realism, George Barr McCutcheon must go down in literary history as an inveterate romantic, who was quoted as saying, "Why read for realism when one can read for thrills?"[59] And though his popularity has diminished today, he will remain known, at least to many older readers, as the author of the passionate love and adventure narratives of the Graustark books and as an authority on the Balkans—which, incidentally, he never visited.[60]

[59] Kunitz and Haycraft, *Twentieth Century Authors,* 870.

[60] The papers of George B. McCutcheon are deposited in the Purdue University Library.

Gene Stratton Porter

Gene Stratton (Mrs. Charles Darwin) Porter (1863-1924) likewise is known as something of an authority; and her name for years has been practically synonymous with the out-of-doors and with wild life, which she reported on in detail, though actually she made practically no contributions to scientific knowledge. She was, instead, an excellent amateur naturalist. Her bid for literary fame rests mostly on her sugary-sweet, but immensely popular, novels of the simple rural life of man, animal, and bird. And by the time of the death of "the bird woman," as many called her, the sales of her books had reached the unbelievable total of ten million copies. Here, then, is a famous author indeed! But would that her books were as worth while as they were popular!

She was born Geneva Stratton on August 17, 1863, on a farm in Wabash County, Indiana, youngest of the twelve children of the Reverend Mark Stratton, a farmer and Methodist minister whose family claimed to be of ancient British origin, and Mary Stratton, of Dutch ancestry. Her father was a man of high character and strong purpose, who maintained an interest in literature and who shared with his wife a love of nature. As a child Geneva's family duty was to care for the chickens; and when her mother was compelled by failing health to relax the family routine, Geneva had freedom to wander in the woods, gathering Indian relics, butterflies, moths, and bird feathers, and observing wild life, encouraged in her gentle treatment of animals by her father's Biblical injunctions. The Reverend Mr. Stratton was later to appear as the character Abram in *The Song of the Cardinal;* the entire family eventually furnished much literary material in the form of characters and incidents.

In 1874 the Stratton family moved to Wabash, Indiana. Geneva continued in school until 1883, but did not receive a diploma because she withdrew to nurse a sick sister. Shortly afterward she herself became an invalid through slipping on the ice and fracturing her skull; but during her recovery Charles Darwin Porter, a druggist of Geneva, Indiana, succeeded in overcoming her timidity. The two were married on April 21, 1886, and took up residence at Decatur. In 1888, after their daughter Jeannette was born, the couple removed to a small cottage in Geneva, where Mrs. Porter, perhaps because of possible confusion with the name of the town, began calling herself Gene. At this time the town of Geneva was covered by heavy timber and surrounded by marshland; the area was called the Limberlost after an early native known, because of his suppleness, as Limber Jim, whose disappearance into the swamps had inspired the settlers to say, "Limber's lost."

Mr. Porter's interests prospered. He organized a bank which gained importance when oil was discovered in the vicinity, sixty producing wells being drilled upon the Porter farm. In 1895 he and his wife designed and built Limberlost Cabin, a red cedar log house of fourteen rooms.[61]

Mrs. Porter devoted much time to nature study in the marshes. She attempted to paint, then studied photography and succeeded so well in picturing wild life that she was soon sending photographs to the magazine *Recreation;* shortly afterward she became a member of the staff of *Outing.* She experienced a thrill when her first story, "Laddie, the Princess, and the Pie," appeared unexpect-

[61] The Limberlost cabin still stands today and has been made into a museum by the Indiana Department of Conservation. It is known as the Limberlost State Memorial.

edly in the *Metropolitan* in September, 1901, the editor having lost the address of his new author.

Thus encouraged by small success, she planned a writing career and soon sent a story of ten thousand words to Richard W. Gilder, editor of *Century*, who liked the narrative but advised her to expand the material into a novel. In a month of concentrated effort she did so, and the result was *The Song of the Cardinal* (Indianapolis, 1903). It is the sympathetic biography of a redbird, reflecting the author's love of nature, and was inspired by her chance finding, on a wintry day when she went to the woods to feed the birds, the body of a cardinal shot by a hunter, evidently in target practice. The book was illustrated by camera studies made by the author, and the work became so popular that it was translated into seven languages. Mrs. Porter suddenly found herself famous. Yet, the novel commenced the controversy concerning the scientific accuracy of her natural history, and from that time forth critics continually disputed her observations.

Mrs. Porter was not slow to capitalize on her first success. *Freckles* (Garden City, New York, 1904) had its genesis in her observing a beautiful black vulture feather falling from the sky. She and her husband traced the vulture to its nest in a hollow log close by, where from time to time they observed and photographed the nesting of the birds and the emergence of young from the eggs. But joined with this episode in the book are woodcraft, moralizing, romantic love, the figure of a Scottish logger, and sentimentality about the waif, Freckles, who guards the trees in the Limberlost and finally is discovered by his rich father. The novel was written much in the pattern of E. P. Roe's popular work, *Nature's Serial Story* (1885). In ten years, *Freckles* sold more than 670,000 copies, with sales eventually mounting to more than a million copies in the United States and 500,000 in Great Britain. By 1947 the total was nearly two million copies.[62] It has been said that the American trenches of World War I were littered with copies of *Freckles,* read by the dough-boys because of its idealized picture of home and sim-plicity and virtue—aspects of life conspicuous by their absence in wartime. To tell the truth, *Freckles* was not a real success immediately after publication but gained in reader interest after the issuance of its sequel, *A Girl of the Limberlost* (Garden City, New York, 1909), illustrated by a hundred pictures and telling the story of Freckles' friend Eleanora, who hunts moths in the swamps to sell in order to finance her education. *A Girl of the Limber-lost,* likewise, had sold nearly two million copies by 1947. Both these novels were read mostly in fifty-cent reprints.

Her next novels were mostly of a similar sentimental type, though not always containing the same mixture of nature and the out-of-doors. *At the Foot of the Rainbow* (Garden City, New York, 1907) features a triangle con-sisting of a dissipated Irishman, his forgiving wife, and a heroic Scot. *The Harvester* (Garden City, New York, 1911) was her first novel to deal with adults and the first one to sell many copies at the regular price of novels. It tells the story of the success of a young man in making a living in the woods. *Laddie* (Garden City, New York, 1913), a fic-tionized story of her own childhood experiences in the woods interwoven with her older brother's wooing, was followed by *Michael O'Halloran* (Garden City, New York, 1915), a conventional moralizing narrative of a plucky little newsboy. With the exception of *The Song of the Cardinal* all the novels thus far mentioned remained

[62] The figures for the sales of Mrs. Porter's works usually can be readily found in the discussions of her work. See particularly, however, Hart, *The Popular Book,* 212, and *passim.*

her most popular works, selling over eight million copies, mostly during her lifetime.

The Porters remained at their home in Geneva until 1913, by which time the Limberlost that Mrs. Porter had made famous had nearly disappeared, through the cutting of the timber and the draining of the swamps; accordingly, the family sought a new retreat from which wild life could be studied and written about. Such a place was discovered in Wildflower Woods at Sylvan Lake, near Rome City, Indiana, where there existed a nearly primeval wilderness. By 1914 a new cabin was constructed of Wisconsin cedar logs, a two-story building of fourteen rooms. Here Mrs. Porter lived and continued her writing until 1923, when she moved to California for the sake of her health.

Her later novels tended to deal more with the problems of ordinary life than her earlier ones. Yet *A Daughter of the Land* (Garden City, New York, 1918), a story of farm life, contrasted with *Her Father's Daughter* (Garden City, New York, 1921), which mirrored her fear of the Japanese living in California; and *The White Flag* (Garden City, New York, 1923), perhaps written because of the strong criticism of her sentimentalism by literary critics, surprised some readers because of its realism and was, therefore, less popular with her public. *The Keeper of the Bees* (Garden City, New York, 1925) and *The Magic Garden* (Garden City, New York, 1927) were both written at a home which she had built on Catalina Island. The latter book was concerned with the fate of the children of divorced parents. All these more serious novels, however, never enjoyed the following of her earlier sweet and simple tales.

Throughout most of her writing career she interspersed her novels with volumes that revealed, through enthusiasm in descriptions and excellence in drawings and photographs, a true insight into nature. These books are *What I Have Done with Birds* (Indianapolis, 1907), reissued as *Friends in Feathers* (Garden City, New York, 1917), *Birds of the Bible* (New York, 1909), *Music of the Wild* (New York, 1910), *Moths of the Limberlost* (Garden City, 1912), *Birds of the Limberlost* (Garden City, 1914), *Homing with the Birds* (Garden City, 1919), and *Tales You Won't Believe* (Garden City, 1925). *Morning Face* (Garden City, 1921) contains accounts of birds both in verse and prose. Her verse, never of high quality, but written in an attempt to please the literary critics, who refused to treat her work seriously, included *The Fire Bird* (Garden City, New York, 1922), a long narrative recounting a tragic Indian legend dealing with a woman's guilty conscience, and *Jesus of the Emerald* (Garden City, 1923), a description of Christ. *Wings* (Garden City, 1923) is a collection of nature stories, and *Let Us Highly Resolve* (Garden City, 1927) is a collection of mediocre essays containing much autobiography.

Taking advantage of the popularity of her books, Mrs. Porter organized her own motion picture company, Gene Stratton Porter, Inc., to film her novels. Assisted by her daughter and son-in-law, she screened the stories with fidelity to the text. She was building a second home on Catalina Island when her automobile was struck by a streetcar at an intersection in Los Angeles; and, fatally injured, she died on December 6, 1924, at the age of 61.[63] Several of her books were yet to be published.

She died as one of this country's most popular novelists, who had become a sort of American idea, "a public insti-

[63] The life of Gene Stratton Porter was obtained from miscellaneous sources, but particularly from the article in the *Dictionary of American Biography, Authors Edition, Supplement One,* 21:601-3, by Harry R. Warfel.

tution, like Yellowstone Park," as William Lyon Phelps put it.[64] Her publishers estimated that during her own lifetime she had more than fifty million readers in the United States, to say nothing of later generations and readers in foreign countries, where her books were translated into Spanish, Czecho-Slovakian, Danish-Norwegian, Swedish, Dutch, German, and even Arabic. Her publishers said also that during the last seventeen years of her life her books sold at the rate of 1,700 copies a day, including Sundays, and that if placed end to end, they would form a line of 1,110 miles, or the distance from Philadelphia to New Orleans.[65] Certainly she was the best known of the many popular Indiana authors and also one of the most widely read authors in the world. Her books are still read today, and chances of their remaining popular for some years to come seem good.

But just why were her writings, particularly the earlier books, so well received? The literary critics both of her own time and later have found only a saccharine sentimentality and a simplicity and naïveté in them. Living, they say, was never so ridiculously simple and so full of virtue of the Pollyanna variety; seldom does she face the realities of life. Mrs. Porter, nevertheless, continually lashed back at her critics, saying that fiction should be a great moralizing agent for humanity which should uplift the reader and make him a gentler, kindlier person with higher ideals. She angrily condemned realistic and naturalistic writing as impure and advocated censorship of books—an attitude which implied the suppression of books unlike her own—and she not only admitted her sentimental idealization of her characters but gloried in

---

[64] As cited in Hart, *op. cit.*, 211-12.

[65] See Samuel F. Ewart, *Gene Stratton-Porter. A Little Story of the Life and Work and Ideals of "The Bird Woman"* (Garden City, New York, 1915), 47, and *passim*.

that treatment of them, still claiming, however, that she had drawn them from actual life. Her argument thus runs close to contradiction.[66] Also, she stoutly defended the accuracy of her scientific observations, saying that in Norway or Sweden her writings would have won a Nobel Prize.

The truth is that her typical writings have always appealed essentially to the simple-minded—children, the old, and those who have been buffeted by the waves of life until they have nearly sunk or have been shipwrecked. Mrs. Porter received large quantities of letters of appreciation from the poverty-stricken, the sick, the inhabitants of reform schools and prisons, stating how much her books had helped them to face reality. These unfortunate people received a therapeutic effect from their imaginative return to nature and the idyllic simple life, releasing them from the world of men, where they had experienced disaster. And this type of reader, like the poor, we have with us always, hence the steady popularity of such writing. This public has always feasted upon Mrs. Porter's sparkling sweetness; and, besides, her sprinkling of selected scientific terms throughout her work gives the reader a sense of intellectual attainment.

Therefore, while recognizing the tremendous popularity of this writer and also what merit is contained in her work, we are forced to agree with the critics and put her down as a popular novelist only, a representative of the back-to-nature movement, stimulated by Theodore Roosevelt, John Muir, John Burroughs, Luther Burbank, and Ernest Thompson Seton, a naturalist in her study of the out-of-doors, a writer of the type of E. P. Roe and

[66] See H. E. Maule, "Gene Stratton Porter," in *The Country Life Press, Garden City, New York* (Published for the Friends of Doubleday, Page & Company, 1919), 145-47; also Ewart, *op. cit.*, 45-49.

Harold Bell Wright—but of practically no real literary value to the mature reader.[67]

The last thirteen of the Indiana novelists of the period of the Golden Age are of much less importance than many of those whom we have already treated in our discussion.

ELIZABETH MILLER HACK

The first of these minor figures is the historical novelist, Elizabeth Jane Miller (Mrs. Oren S.) Hack (1878-1961), whose stories of ancient and medieval times once thrilled thousand of readers, but are now little read. Mrs. Hack was born on August 17, 1878, near New Ross, Indiana. Her parents, Timothy and Samantha (West) Miller, taught schools in the wintertime but farmed during the summers. When in 1883 the family moved to Indianapolis to provide better educational opportunities for the children, Elizabeth went to the public schools, Manual Training High School, and Butler College, at which latter institution she commenced writing poetry. In 1908 she was married to an Indianapolis attorney, Oren S. Hack, who died in 1942. Mrs. Hack died August 18, 1961.[68]

Mrs. Hack produced four novels. *The Yoke. A Romance of the Days When the Lord Redeemed the Children of Israel from the Bondage of Egypt* (Indianapolis, 1904) is well explained by its subtitle. As a study of the

[67] Materials on the life and works of Gene Stratton Porter are usually of easy access. In addition to the sources cited above, the reader might consult pamphlets on her homes distributed by the Indiana Department of Conservation and also the biography by her daughter, Jeannette Porter Meehan, *The Lady of the Limberlost. The Life and Letters of Gene Stratton-Porter* (Garden City, New York, 1928). Mrs. Meehan also wrote a sequel to *Freckles* entitled *Freckles Comes Home* (Garden City, New York, 1929), which was rather well received.

[68] The material on Mrs. Hack is from Banta, *Indiana Authors and Their Books*, 127; Indianapolis *News*, August 19, 1961.

period of the Exodus and of the civilization of ancient Egypt it is evidently an accurate account, but the chief interest of the book lies in the love story of the heroine, a beautiful young Israelite, and the hero, an important Egyptian, and, also, to a lesser degree, in other love stories. The entire account forms a vivid religio-historical romance. *Saul of Tarsus* (Indianapolis, 1906) is an ambitious project, the story involving scenes in Jerusalem, Rome, Alexandria, and Damascus in the days following the Crucifixion and the characters, Saul of Tarsus, Stephen, and the emperors Tiberius and Caligula—all drawn authentically and imaginatively. *The City of Delight. A Love Drama of the Siege and Fall of Jerusalem* (Indianapolis, 1908) continues Mrs. Hack's interest in ancient times by sketching against this historical event a vigorous and charming romance involving the Judaean prince Philadelphus, great-grandson of Judas Maccabaeus, and the girl Laodice, who, having been united in a child marriage, in maturity are forced to fight against usurpers, Salome, and a jealous cousin. In her last novel, *Daybreak. A Story of the Age of Discovery* (New York, 1915), the author's stage shifts from antiquity to Spain in the days of Ferdinand and Isabella and the war against the Moors, with the usual love story, this time provided by the niece of the king, Antonia de Aragon, and her lover, Betran Ponce de Leon, who, under the displeasure of Ferdinand, escapes from Spain by joining the first expedition of Columbus and returns to effect a happy untangling of affairs. This last book was not so well received as the other three, being pronounced by a few critics somewhat artificial. Otherwise, Mrs. Hack's novels enjoyed, in general, good critical appraisal and popularity.

GRACE C. ALEXANDER

Grace Caroline Alexander (1872-1951) wrote only two novels, the first of which is more interesting to Indiana literature and, also, has more permanent appeal. She was born in Indianapolis in 1872, attended the public schools, and taught for several years; from 1891 to 1903 she was an editorial writer and music critic for the Indianapolis *News* and beginning in 1904 acted as a reader and associate editor for the Bobbs-Merrill Company. She died October 1, 1951.[69]

Her first book, *Judith. A Story of the Candle-Lit Fifties* (Indianapolis, 1906), is the love story of Judith La Monde, who returns from her studies in Paris to the narrowing horizon of the quaint, old-fashioned Indiana village of Camden, on the Ohio River (in reality Corydon, which Miss Alexander had visited), where she is to be married to an unsuitable mate; and she complicates an already unfortunate situation by falling in love with the new minister in town. Even though the book lacks humor and contains tedious digressions, still it reproduces the atmosphere of pioneer Indiana. *Prince Cinderella* (Indianapolis, 1921) is a completely different sort of story of contemporary life of the well-to-do of New England, involving a girl of twenty-two who is "sinfully rich," her mansion and its assortment of queer inhabitants, a mystery, and a happy ending.

HAROLD M. KRAMER

Harold Morton Kramer (1873-1930) wrote adventure stories, most of which are as ephemeral as *Prince Cinder-*

[69] Biography of Miss Alexander is from Banta, *Indiana Authors and Their Books,* 5; from obituary in Indianapolis *News,* October 3, 1951, p. 18; and from the records of the State Board of Health. The day and month of her birth have not been found.

ella. He was born on April 28, 1873, in Frankfort, Indiana, the youngest of the ten children of Philip Edward Kramer and his wife, Mary (Choate) Kramer. He attended the Frankfort schools, became a printer, and in 1897 he married a teacher, Nora Caroline Lee; then the Spanish-American War having broken out, in 1898 he enlisted in Company C, 158th Infantry, and received a first lieutenant's commission. When he returned to civilian life, he engaged in journalism, acting as night editor of the Frankfort *Daily Morning Times.* In 1910 he left journalism for lecturing, and during World War I he became a Y.M.C.A. secretary, serving at the front in France. Elected in 1925 the executive secretary of the International Lyceum Association with offices in Chicago, he carried on this work until his death in Chicago, March 20, 1930.[70]

In his first novel, *Hearts and the Cross* (Boston, 1906), one finds an amateurish, immature, yet dramatic story of how a young itinerant minister, befriended by an Indiana farm family, turns out to be a pardoned convict, who then clears his name and marries happily. *Gayle Langford. Being the Romance of a Tory Belle and a Patriot Captain* (Boston, 1907) is a swashbuckling tale with a love interest and features a sea fight and other deeds of violence. There is weaker action but still much adventure in the involved story of the melodramatic *The Castle of Dawn* (Boston, 1908), in which a young newspaperman and an attractive girl are imprisoned in the Ozark Mountains by Nicaraguan revolutionists. *The Chrysalis* (Boston, 1909) is another adventure book, the story of how a young lawyer grows out of his "chrysalis" by means of the influence of a Western girl and features financial and political intrigue and a setting in Spokane, Washington. Kramer's last novel, *The Rugged Way* (Boston, 1911), contains more

---

[70] Biography of Kramer is from Banta, *op. cit.,* 181.

substance in its dramatic presentation of a young man's fight against an unjust accusation and his deliberate choice of the role of true manhood. Harold Kramer, however, ranks only as a mediocre novelist. He wrote also *With Seeing Eyes. The Unusual Story of an Observant Thinker at the Front* (Boston, 1919).

JOHN T. McCUTCHEON

John Tinney McCutcheon (1870-1949), the brother of George Barr McCutcheon, who created the Graustark series of novels, is known more for his cartoons and newspaper reporting than for his novels and is hardly a literary figure. In fact, he drew some 10,000 pungent cartoons on politics and current events. In 1931 he won the Pulitzer Prize for a cartoon, "A Wise Economist Asks a Question," in which a man, labeled "Victim of Bank Failure," seated on a park bench, is asked by a squirrel, "But why didn't you save some money for the future when times were good?"—to which the man replies, "I did." Another famous cartoon was entitled "Injun Summer," which has been reproduced each year for many years in the Chicago *Tribune*.

He was born on May 6, 1870, on a farm near South Raub, Tippecanoe County, Indiana, and lived there till 1876, when the McCutcheon family moved to Lafayette, Indiana, where his father was made director of the first farm operated by Purdue University. John was graduated from Purdue in 1889, then joined forces with George Ade to work for the Chicago *Record* for two years; from 1901 to 1903 he was with the Chicago *Record-Herald* and from 1903 to 1946 with the Chicago *Tribune*. His political-cartoon work began in the campaign of 1896, when he drew a sketch of William Jennings Bryan making his "Cross of Gold" speech. In the course of his journalistic

career he was present at the Battle of Manila Bay, visited
the Philippines and Asia after the Spanish-American War,
went to Africa at the time of the Boer War, in 1909-10
accompanied for a time Theodore Roosevelt's big-game-
hunting safari, was in Mexico in 1914, and saw Europe
in 1916, when he covered the First World War. He
married Evelyn Shaw in 1917. For some time his family
maintained a summer home, Treasure Island, near Nassau
in the Bahamas. He retired from the *Tribune* in 1946
and died in Lake Forest near Chicago, on June 10, 1949.
Even though he spent most of his mature life in Chicago
or in globe-trotting, he still considered himself a Hoosier
and retained strong ties with his home state, which has
always looked upon him as a native son.[71]

In addition to journalistic works, books of travel, collections of cartoons, and miscellaneous books, John T. Mc-
Cutcheon published four novels, none of which, unfortunately, made a permanent impression. *Congressman
Pumphrey. The People's Friend* (Indianapolis, 1907) is
the clever story of the moral decline of a congressman
who is elected on promises to battle corruption in Washington but who falls victim to the very forces which he
has planned to combat. Having arrived in Washington,
he is showered with favors by Senator James B. Octopus
and Colonel Harrison K. Bunker, who let him win money
from them at poker, give him tips on stocks by which he
makes much money, see that the doors of the right society
are opened to his wife and daughter, and provide him and
his family with a trip to Europe with expenses paid—all
so that Pumphrey will vote the right way on their own
measures. Pumphrey, of course, succumbs to their cam-

---

[71] Biography of John T. McCutcheon is from newspaper clippings in
the Indiana Biography Series, 34:84-85, 86, 88, and 35:13. See also the
biography of George Barr McCutcheon, above, 394-404.

paign. This satire on the Washington life of a congress-man contains the author's well-drawn illustrations of the pompous Pumphrey.

Dawson '11, Fortune Hunter (New York, 1912), also accompanied by McCutcheon cartoons, is the slight story, told mostly in letters to his mother, of how a home-loving country boy, a recent college graduate, goes to Chicago to seek his fortune and the struggle which he makes to establish himself. Perhaps an autobiographical element can be detected here. *The Restless Age* (Indianapolis, 1921) is a somewhat similar book, depicting a country boy, who, after being wounded in France in World War I, returns for a year to his parents' farm; then, dissatisfied with farm life, he is lured by the prospects of the city, whence after many unsavory experiences in which he "learns about life the hard way" he goes back to the farm and marries his old sweetheart. McCutcheon's last novel, *An Heir at Large* (Indianapolis, 1923) reminds the reader of *Brewster's Millions,* by his brother, George Barr McCutcheon, in that it is the story of a young man of good character but meager income who suddenly falls heir to a fortune of fifteen millions left him by his uncle. But *An Heir at Large* concentrates on the hero's testing his wealthy sweetheart by retaining his pose as a poor boy and then working as a laborer in the steel mills, where he tries to manipulate affairs by means of his money. All in all, then, John T. McCutcheon is a clever but mediocre novelist. Yet, as a cartoonist who drew masterpieces of clean humor and satire he was one of the country's greatest.

FREDERICK LANDIS

Frederick Landis (1872-1934) made a name of sorts for himself through one of his two novels. One of seven

children of Abraham H. and Mary A. (Kumler) Landis,
he was born on August 18, 1872, at Seven Mile, Ohio,
and went to school in Logansport, Indiana. He was graduated from the University of Michigan Law School in
1895, and he practiced law in Logansport, then served
in Congress from 1903 to 1907. In 1909 he married Bessie
A. Baker. After he retired from Congress, he was a member of the editorial staff of the New York *American* for
three years. He joined the Progressive party in 1912, becoming its candidate for lieutenant governor of Indiana.
Later he was editor of the Logansport *Pharos-Tribune,*
made radio speeches as "The Hoosier Editor," and issued
a monthly magazine, *The Hoosier Editor,* from 1933 to
1934, made up of his own writings. Landis was re-elected
to Congress in 1934. He died from pneumonia on
November 16 of that year.[72]

The Glory of His Country (New York, 1910) tells, in
an undisciplined style, the heart-rending story of how an
old Indiana woodsman, a boyhood friend of Abraham
Lincoln, who was known as a Copperhead or Southern
sympathizer during the Civil War, finally discloses the
fact that in response to a request from Lincoln he
had posed as a Copperhead but was really a Union spy
who had gained valuable information for the North, but
had allowed himself, out of patriotism, to be reviled by
his neighbors. This novel was dramatized by August
Thomas as "The Copperhead," with John Barrymore
playing the leading role in the play. Another novel, *The
Angel of Lonesome Hill. A Story of a President* (New
York, 1910), features the tender sympathy of Theodore
Roosevelt, who reconsiders a pardon, previously refused,
of the unjustly accused and long-imprisoned son of an

[72] The sketch of Frederick Landis is taken from Banta, *Indiana Authors
and Their Books,* 186-87.

aged couple. The book constitutes a high tribute to Roosevelt.

ULYSSES SAMUEL LESH

Ulysses Samuel Lesh (1868-   ) was born on August 9, 1868, in Wells County, Indiana, the son of Joseph and Sarah Lesh. After graduation in 1891 from the law school of the University of Michigan, he practiced in Huntington, Indiana. In 1894 he and Minnie Fulton were married. He held the positions of Huntington city attorney from 1902 to 1904; county attorney, 1907 to 1909; assistant attorney general of Indiana, 1917 to 1921; and attorney general, 1921 to 1924. After 1924 he practiced law in Huntington.[73]

Lesh's two novels are quite unlike each other. *A Knight of the Golden Circle* (Boston, 1911) has something in common with *The Glory of His Country,* by Landis, in sketching the movements of Southern sympathizers in Indiana during the Civil War, with weird midnight initiations in abandoned houses and the adventures of the members. Governor Oliver P. Morton is treated as a hero. The story was suggested to Lesh by the fact that his own home had once been used as a center for a rebel organization.[74] Lesh's second narrative, *Three Profiteers* (Boston, 1934), provides a mere thread of plot on which a maximum of economic theory is strung. An oil baron imprisoned for bribery experiences a change of heart about his previously ruthless methods of business, so that he advocates control of excessive growth of individual

[73] The material on Lesh was obtained from *ibid.,* 191, and from Hubert H. Hawkins, director of the Indiana Historical Bureau. At this writing Mr. Lesh is still living and active.

[74] Compare *A Knight of the Golden Circle* not only with Frederick Landis' *The Glory of His Country* but also with Caroline Krout's *Knights in Fustian.*

fortunes and a wider distribution of the profits of business—yet, without threat of socialism or communism. The
book makes serious reading.

CAROLINE DALE SNEDEKER

One might expect Caroline Dale Parke (Mrs. Charles
Henry) Snedeker (1871-1956), the granddaughter of David
Dale Owen,[75] to write of Indiana history, particularly the
New Harmony experiment; and that is exactly what she
did—at least, in three of her books. She also turned out
other novels and several juveniles, using mostly as her
setting life in ancient Greece and Rome. Daughter of
Charles Augustus and Nina Dale (Owen) Parke, she was
born on March 23, 1871, at New Harmony. When Caroline was six months old, the family moved to near-by
Mount Vernon, Indiana, where she lived and attended
school until the age of thirteen, making frequent happy
visits with her father to New Harmony and eagerly learning all about the interesting history of that old town.
After she had had a year of school in Louisville, Kentucky,
her family removed to Cincinnati, where they all studied
at the College of Music. Caroline afterwards toured as a
concert pianist.

In 1903 she was married to the Reverend Charles Henry
Snedeker, rector of the old colonial church of St. George
on Long Island, where she lived in the hundred-year-old
rectory for seventeen years. Later Mrs. Snedeker lived
and wrote at various places: New Harmony; at the Mc-
Dowell Colony in Peterborough, New Hampshire; at Nantucket; at a farm on Long Island; and at Bay Saint Louis,
Mississippi. Always, however, she maintained a close asso-

[75] For David Dale and Robert Dale Owen, and the connection of the
Owen family with New Harmony, see above, 176-77n.

ciation with her beloved New Harmony.[76] She used the pen names of Caroline Dale and Caroline Dale Owen.

After six years of study about ancient Greece she began her writing in this field with books which were intended for older boys and girls, but can be read with enjoyment by adults. *The Coward of Thermopylae* (Garden City, New York, 1911, reissued in 1912 as *The Spartan*) is based on the passages in Herodotus that tell how two Spartan soldiers, part of the band of Leonidas, are stricken with an eye disease causing temporary blindness; one is led back to perish with his comrades, while the other returns to Sparta, is accused of cowardice, but later dies a lonely and noble death fighting for his country at the Battle of Plataea. The novel accurately reports the simplicity and beauty of Greek life and sets the style for similar books: *The Perilous Seat* (Garden City, New York, 1923) continues the story of the Greek struggle with Persia, but is rather dull; *Theras and His Town* (Garden City, New York, 1924) is a story of Athens and Sparata for younger children; *The Forgotten Daughter* (Garden City, New York, 1933) is a tale of the oppression and the slavery of ancient Rome; and *A Triumph for Flavius* (New York, 1955) is another story of ancient Rome, this time of the young son of a Roman general who disputes his father's right to whip a slave.

Other juveniles, but on a more modern theme, are *Downright Dencey* (Garden City, New York, 1927), a tale of old Nantucket, and *The Beckoning Road* (Garden City, New York, 1929), a story of a Quaker family which migrates from Nantucket to New Harmony, Indiana. *The Town of the Fearless* (Garden City, New York, 1931)

[76] The biography of Mrs. Snedeker comes from Banta, *op. cit.*, 298-99, and from the file of newspaper clippings in the Indiana Division of the Indiana State Library. The date of death is recorded in the *Wilson Library Bulletin*, 30:593 (March, 1956) .

is another narrative of New Harmony, telling more of local characters, such as Joseph Neef and Robert Owen; in fact, it is almost the author's family history. *The Black Arrowhead. Legends of Long Island* (Garden City, New York, 1929) speaks for itself. Later juveniles include *Uncharted Ways* (Garden City, New York, 1935) and *The White Isle* (Garden City, New York, 1940).

Seth Way. A Romance of the New Harmony Community (Boston, 1917) is a well-written adult novel based on the life and achievements of the famous but erratic Thomas Say (1787-1834), one of the foremost natural scientists in the early history of the United States, the latter part of whose life was bound up with the New Harmony movement. Students of the movement would do well to read this fictional account of it. *Luke's Quest* (Garden City, New York, 1947) is similar to some of Mrs. Snedeker's other novels in that it is another story of ancient times, but is much unlike her usual work in its sympathetic rendering of the story of Luke and of the beginnings of Christianity. It may be regretted that Mrs. Snedeker did not turn her talents more often to strictly adult literature, as in these last two books.[77]

BEDFORD-JONES

Henry James O'Brien Bedford-Jones (1887-1949) was one of the most prolific of all Indiana authors, having published more than a hundred books, mostly of the mystery or romantic adventure type; but none of these is worthy of long remembrance. Bedford-Jones is something of a shadowy figure. Born in Canada in Napanee,

---

[77] Anyone interested in studying Mrs. Snedeker's works may consult her semi-autobiographical introduction to *The Diaries of Donald Macdonald, 1824-1826,* which she edited for the Indiana Historical Society *Publications* (Vol. 14, No. 2, 1942).

Ontario, on April 29, 1887, he migrated to Evansville, Indiana, where he was married twice, first to Helen Williamson, then to a widow, Mrs. Mary Bernardin, and where he wrote many of his books. Later he removed to Ann Arbor, Michigan, and died on May 6, 1949, at his home in Beverly Hills, California. Some of his books appeared under the pseudonym of John Wycliffe. A few of his stories were juveniles.[78]

It is neither possible nor worth while to list and analyze the many works of this writer;[79] perhaps two or three titles will serve adequately to characterize his production. *The King's Passport* (New York, 1928) and *D'Artagnan. The Sequel to the Three Musketeers* (New York, 1928) are swashbuckling novels of renaissance France, complete with secret documents, dark streets, and flashing swords. *Drums of Dambala* (New York, 1932) is a tale of the revolt of Toussaint L'Ouverture in Haiti. Other titles, such as *Rodomont. A Romance of Mont St. Michel in the Days of Louis XIV* (New York, 1926), seem to follow the same pattern.

JAMES BALDWIN

In contrast to the huge number of novels of Bedford-Jones, James Baldwin (1841-1925) has only one novel to his credit, although his list of expository publications, textbooks, edited collections, and juveniles totals fifty-

[78] The biographical material concerning Bedford-Jones is from his obituary in the Indianapolis *Star*, May 7, 1949, p. 9.

[79] The absence of any available bibliography of the works of Bedford-Jones and the fact that only a few of his novels can be found in any one library that I have been able to consult tend to indicate the ephemeral quality of his writings and his lack of importance. Even the Library of Congress lists only 23 titles from 1912 to 1939 and gives a confusing cross reference to Lincoln Sayler, a writer of boys' stories, who evidently is not identical with Bedford-Jones. Perhaps one of the pseudonyms employed by Sayler was utilized also by Bedford-Jones.

four; and the aggregate sale of all the volumes with which he was associated reached the huge figure of more than 26,000,000 copies—which is more than Gene Stratton Porter and Harold Bell Wright claimed together. Baldwin was born on December 15, 1841, in Hamilton County, Indiana; his parents were Isaac and Sarah (Clayton) Baldwin. Though he attended the district schools, he mostly educated himself; and so well did he succeed that he taught school in Hamilton County three years and in 1869 was made superintendent of city graded schools in Indiana. He retained this position till 1887, when he became connected with Harper & Brothers publishing firm in New York, and from 1894 to 1924 he served as editor of school books for the American Book Company. His death came the next year, on August 30. His career was marked by publication in many fields.[80]

Baldwin's one novel—if novel it can be called—was published anonymously as *In My Youth. From the Posthumous Papers of Robert Dudley* (Indianapolis, 1914) and then was re-issued as *In the Days of My Youth. An Intimate Personal Record of Life and Manners in the Middle Ages of the Middle West* (Indianapolis, 1923). This book seems strongly autobiographical; and it gives a vivid reflection of the pioneer period in central Indiana, evidently in the area around Westfield.[81] It is the story, with practically no plot, of a very sensitive, shy boy as he was brought up in the drab environment of a frontier Quaker settlement, where the church was the center of life and the beauty and music which his artistic soul craved were strictly taboo. The author has no point to make or purpose in mind as he paints deftly and sympa-

[80] The life of James Baldwin is mostly from Banta, *Indiana Authors and Their Books,* 14, which also contains a partial list of his publications.

[81] See the letter of J. J. Baldwin, cousin of the author, to the Indianapolis *News,* September 10, 1925, in Indiana Biography Series, 2:39.

thetically the picture of this imaginative boy to whom
the harsh realities of life were unreal and to whom the
unrealities of life, like his imaginary playmate, were real—
all of this set against the background of the details of
pioneer living and written in a rambling style. The book
went through three editions and excited much favorable
comment, even before the author became known.[82] It is
to be regretted that James Baldwin did not turn his talents
more to such imaginative materials as this.

ELMER DAVIS

It is a pleasure to turn next to a consideration of Elmer
Holmes Davis (1890-1958), one of the most famous of
contemporary Hoosiers—a scholar, newspaperman, radio
newscaster and analyst, student of contemporary politics
and events, guardian of the liberties of a free press and
of a free people, prophet of the threatening doom of
civilization through nuclear warfare, essayist, short story
writer, and novelist.

The son of a bank president, Elam H. Davis, and his
wife, Louise (Severin) Davis, who before her marriage was
a high-school principal, Elmer Davis was born in Aurora,
Indiana, on January 13, 1890. When attending high
school he worked as a printer's devil for the Aurora
Bulletin, then did part-time teaching in the Franklin,
Indiana, High School while a senior at Franklin College,
from which he received the A.B. degree in 1910 and also
the A.M. degree in 1911, for work done while in residence. In 1910 he went to Oxford University as a Rhodes
scholar, where he studied the classics and took an interest
in foreign affairs and politics, traveling on the continent
during the summers. In Paris he met his future wife,

---

[82] See the review by Eleanor Kellogg, "Towhead," in the Chicago *Post,*
November 13, 1914. Clipping in Indiana Division, Indiana State Library.

Florence MacMillan, of Mount Vernon, New York. Returning from Europe in 1913, he found no promising openings in Aurora and went to New York, where, after some searching, he received a minor editorial position on the staff of *Adventure* magazine at ten dollars a week.

It was at this time that he wrote his first novel, *The Princess Cecilia* (New York, 1915), which was so unimportant that one looks in vain for a copy of it today or even for any reviews of it. Indeed, Davis was never proud of the book and later tried to ignore its existence.

After a year with *Adventure,* in 1914 he obtained a position at twenty dollars a week with the New York *Times,* where he remained ten years, the first five as a reporter and the second five as an editorial writer. Here he became a famous political reporter and created the well-known fictional character, the old Hoosier Democrat, Godfrey G. Gloom, from Amity, Indiana, who attended all the national conventions. In 1917 he and Miss Mac-Millan were married, and to pay for a house he began to write novels, often working late into the night; also about this time he began a limited amount of radio broadcasting.

Leaving the *Times,* he was a free-lance writer for some fifteen years, until with the outbreak of World War II in 1939 he began his distinguished career in radio with his series of nightly five-minute news summaries, to which millions of Americans listened. He quickly acquired repute as an expert news analyst, characterized by calmness, judgment in sifting facts from propaganda, and a firm devotion to the cause of truth and justice. In 1942, in consequence of Davis' complaint that there was an unfortunate confusion and overlapping in the various news agencies of the government and that there should be a single agency responsible for giving accurate news reports to the American people, President Franklin D. Roosevelt created the Office of War Information and surprised Davis by making him the director of it. He stepped from a salary of $1,000 a week in radio to a salary of $10,000 a year as a government employee. For his excellent service he received the Medal of Merit.

After the war he was recognized as the leading news analyst of the American Broadcasting Company. The most highly honored commentator in the history of radio, Davis received the Peabody Award (better known as the radio "Oscar") three times, the Overseas Press Club award four times, the National Headliners award twice, and once each the Sigma Delta Chi, Lauterbach, Dupont, the University of Missouri, and New York Newspaper Guild awards. In addition, he was given many other honors, such as several honorary degrees, a special prize from the Tamiment Institute for his book, *But We Were Born Free,* and a Stephen S. Wise award for his contribution to civil liberties. He was president of the Author's League of America and president of the Radio Correspondents' Association. Despite his diversified activities, however, throughout his entire life Elmer Davis always retained a close association and identification with his home state. He died on May 18, 1958.[83]

Following his first novel there appeared a group of rather light, humorous, and satirical novels characterized by improbable plots and a breezy style. *Times Have Changed* (New York, 1923) features a staid high-school

[83] The biography of Elmer Davis is from Banta, *op. cit.,* 82-83, and from miscellaneous sources such as clippings in the Indiana Division of the State Library. For evidence of Davis' continuance of ties with Indiana, see *Old Indiana and The New World* (Washington, D. C., 1951), such articles as "We Lived in Indiana Too," in *American Heritage,* Autumn, 1950, pp. 6-7, and also the many references to Indiana in his books.

principal who gets into trouble because of his innocent attentions to one of the alumnae of his school and because of certain misunderstandings; and this general situation is repeated in *I'll Show You the Town* (New York, 1924), in which a respectable Latin professor is put in a doubtful light by his innocuous association with three ladies. In *Friends of Mr. Sweeney* (New York, 1925) a frustrated journalist who has to write editorials contrary to his own opinions takes an out-of-town friend to see the city and in a series of hilarious adventures finally obtains the upper hand over his hidebound employer and regains his own individuality and self-respect. *The Keys of the City* (New York, 1925) is a miniature of *The Man That Corrupted Hadleyburg* in the story of how a tramp brings about the downfall of Hollisburg, Indiana; but the book was damned by faint praise in reviews. Davis recaptured his stride, though, in *Strange Woman* (New York, 1927), which repeated his old plot situation of respectable people who are discomfited by being placed in doubtful circumstances, in presenting a college president who is saved from a pitfall laid by a clever and seductive woman opera singer by the offer of his wife to step out of the way of her husband's new romance. *White Pants Willie* (Indianapolis, 1932) is a light story of a young man from a small Illinois town who makes good in pleasure-mad Florida during the land boom there; and in *Bare Living* (with Guy Holt, Indianapolis, 1933) the hero hides from public view in a nudist colony until his difficulties are solved for him.

A much different sort of novel, however, is *Giant Killer* (New York, 1928), a fictional account, based on careful research, of the Biblical David. In Davis' version, David becomes a coward and an irresponsible king verging on villainy, whose throne is upheld by the virtuous and patriotic Joab. Although the book is highly imaginative, to some reviewers it seemed overlong and uninspired.

Davis wrote other types of literature. *Morals for Moderns* (Indianapolis, 1930) is a collection of serious, but not exactly successful, stories dealing with sexual conduct; and a second collection of stories, *Love Among the Ruins* (Indianapolis, 1935), gives a fair picture of the Depression. A book of essays collected from magazines, *Show Window* (New York, 1927), shows a serious turn of mind in attacking popular idols in his treatment of modern literary movements and modern luxury. He includes personal sketches, such as "Have Faith in Indiana," in which he records both his pride and sorrow in revisiting his native state. The book abounds in wit and satire. His serious, careful analysis of society is continued in a second collection of essays, *Not to Mention the War* (Indianapolis, 1940), which arose from his desire to think of something besides the war and which deals with such varied subjects as Karl Marx, Hilaire Belloc, and cats. The piece entitled "On Being Kept by a Cat" is very humorous.

It is through his last two books, however, that Davis achieved the greatest prominence as a writer. *But We Were Born Free* (Indianapolis, 1954), a best seller, shows him to be a champion of liberty and freedom in attacking the forces in contemporary American society which, he thinks, tend to destroy individual thought and action, such as the Congressional investigating processes, as seen in the activities of Senators McCarthy, McCarran, and Jenner. *Two Minutes Till Midnight* (Indianapolis, 1955) depicts a grim future for the country and the world because of the Russian attainment of the means of advanced nuclear warfare and is a stern warning to America to have a consistent foreign policy, to abandon the hope of co-existence, and to prepare to defend herself. As might be expected, this book caused much comment.

Elmer Davis, we may say, then, is significant not so much because of his literary activities as on account of his public life and his radio broadcasting. As a novelist he has contributed practically nothing of permanent value.

WILLIAM WINTER

This same judgment should be rendered in the case of William West Winter (1881-1940), except that, unlike Davis, Winter was not eminent. The son of Ferdinand Winter, a distinguished Indianapolis lawyer, William Winter was born in Indianapolis, attended the public schools, the Massachusetts Institute of Technology, and the Yale Forestry School. After holding a position for several years with the United States Forestry Service, he married Mary Major, of Brooklyn, New York, and returned to live in Indianapolis. During World War I he served in France as captain in the aviation section of the Signal Corps. Winter practiced law for some years in Indianapolis before moving to Brooklyn, New York. He died in Rutland, Massachusetts, in 1940, evidently on May 18.[84]

Two of his books may be considered as representative. *The Winner* (Indianapolis, 1915) is the success story of a young mechanical engineer, who, after study in France, develops a radically new design for an automobile engine, but who meets only misunderstanding and scorn in his attempt to get the Crescent automobile manufacturers to produce it; nevertheless, a car powered by his engine beats the Crescent Company car in an important auto-

[84] Biographical material on Winter was obtained from the obituary in the Indianapolis *Star*, May 19, 1940, Part 1, p. 3.

mobile race, and the engineer wins recognition—also, it should be added, the daughter of the president of the Crescent Company. The scene is laid in Centralia, a thin disguise for Indianapolis and its famous speedway. The book is amateurish, but the plot holds the reader. *The Boss of Eagle's Nest* (New York, 1925) is a Western with the difference from the type that the scene is laid on the Mexican side of the border, the hero is a Mexican rancher, and the villain is an unscrupulous rich American rancher who seizes the property of others. Other books by Winter are *Louisiana Lou. A Western Story* (New York, 1922), *Quemado. A Western Story* (New York, 1923), *Millions in Motors. A Big Business Story* (New York, 1924), *The Lone-Hand Tracker* (Garden City, New York, 1926), and *When Death Rode the Range* (Garden City, New York, 1926).

DAVID W. ANDERSON

The three books of David Wulf Anderson (1878-1938) represent Hoosier local color, and the first two achieved a fame of sorts by being made into motion pictures. Biographical facts about Anderson are scarce. He was born in Missouri, spent his youth in the so-called Flatwoods region southwest of Lafayette, Indiana, and taught school for a time, then traveled for a teachers' magazine and became a lecturer on patriotic and literary subjects, journeying over the country. At the time of publication of *Thunderhawk* in 1926 he was living at Stockwell.[85] He died on April 2, 1938, in Piqua, Ohio, and was buried at Montmorenci, Indiana.[86]

[85] See "A New Indiana Novel," in the Indianapolis *Star,* November 28, 1926, Part 3, p. 30.

[86] Biographical information on David W. Anderson is mostly from various clippings in the Indiana Division of the State Library and obituary notice in the Lafayette *Courier and Journal,* April 4, 1938.

Anderson utilized the region of his youth as the setting for all his novels. *The Blue Moon. A Tale of the Flatwoods* (Indianapolis, 1919) relates the narrative of a youth, a fresh-water pearl hunter on the Wabash River in the 1840's, who finds a wonderful pearl which was then named the Blue Moon. The conventional revelation of the mysterious ancestry of the woodland hero and heroine forms the denouement, but the book abounds in physical action and in the atmosphere of the Wabash region. *The Red Lock. A Tale of the Flatwoods* (Indianapolis, 1922) continues this setting and is the story of a bound boy in 1849, who, though bound to a money lender to satisfy his dead father's debts, through sensational adventures carries on a romance with the daughter of his oppressor. *Thunderhawk. A Tale of the Wabash Flatwoods* (Garden City, New York, 1926) is the last of his books about the same locality and period, featuring another pearl hunter, mystery, and sensational action. Altogether, it may be said that David Wulf Anderson made interesting and vivid use of his Hoosier setting, but his romantic novels are only ordinary.

<h3 style="text-align:center">KATE MILNER RABB</h3>

The last Indiana novelist of this period is Kate Milner (Mrs. Albert) Rabb (1866-1937). Although she wrote a newspaper column for many years, she published only one novel—and that of a strange sort. She was descended from pioneers who had come from Kentucky to Indiana before the Civil War and was the daughter of Dr. Isaac Livingston and Henrietta (Parsons) Milner of Rockport, Indiana, where she was born on August 9, 1866. After attending the Rockport schools, she studied at Indiana University, from which she received the A.M. degree; then she taught in Jeffersonville and Rockport. In 1891 she was married to Albert Rabb, to whom she had become engaged in college. The couple lived in Indianapolis, where Mr. Rabb established himself as a successful lawyer. After he died in 1918, Mrs. Rabb concentrated on the writing which she had seriously undertaken after her marriage. During her literary career she contributed stories to many magazines and composed a weekly column, "The Hoosier Listening Post," for the Indianapolis *Star*, which dealt often with stories, sketches, and sidelights of Indiana history and which had a large following of readers. In addition, she translated a German juvenile, wrote a study of various epics, edited a collection of humor in ten volumes, and published two books on the history of Indianapolis: *"No Mean City"* (Indianapolis, 1922) and *An Account of Indianapolis and Marion County* (with William Herschell, Dayton, Ohio, 1924). Mrs. Rabb died, July 3, 1937, in Indianapolis.[87]

Her novel, *A Tour Through Indiana in 1840. The Diary of John Parsons of Petersburg, Virginia* (New York, 1920), though disguised in the form of a diary of a person who was, perhaps, a relative of Mrs. Rabb, and which has been edited by her, is actually a clever work of historical fiction. Fortified by a picture of John Parsons, "taken from a daguerreotype," as the frontispiece, and all the apparatus of scholarly editing, including footnotes from historical works, Mrs. Rabb succeeded in passing off this fraud, with few ever discovering her trick. The material had first been published in the Sunday editions of the Indianapolis *Star* and had attracted much interest.

[87] Information concerning Mrs. Rabb is from Banta, *op. cit.*, 262, and the Indiana Biography Series, *passim*. In May, 1961, Indiana University dedicated in her honor the new Kate Milner Rabb residence hall for women students.

It is to be regretted that the author resorted to this deceit, for the book can stand well on the basis of a historical novel. Though there may have been a John Parsons, historians have found no evidence of the existence of his diary; Mrs. Rabb simply used research and her knowledge of Indiana history to create the diary and the letters, sending her hero traveling about the state, visiting the leading towns, such as Indianapolis, Madison, Logansport, Greenfield, Lafayette, Terre Haute, Greencastle, and Vincennes, bearing letters of introduction to the leading citizens in each community. In fact, these letters must have been numerous enough to fill a small trunk, since Parsons met and recorded his impressions of almost all the people of importance in Indiana in 1840. He was very observant and was interested in everything, attending parties, political meetings, camp meetings, observing colleges and comparing them with those in Virginia, becoming acquainted with merchants, politicians, preachers, judges, pretty young girls, and fine ladies. Also, there is introduced a love element in that the handsome Parsons becomes engaged to a beautiful maiden; but this happiness is nipped in the bud by the death of the hero on his trip home to Virginia.

With Mrs. Rabb we end our study of the novel in the Golden Age of Indiana literature. Perhaps a summation and analysis of this type may now be in order.

In the first place, we should note that the most important novelists of the period are Edward Eggleston, George Eggleston, Lew Wallace, Mary Catherwood, Maurice Thompson, Meredith Nicholson, Charles Major, Booth Tarkington, George McCutcheon, and Gene Stratton Porter. At least one author, George Eggleston, has long been undervalued and should be accorded a higher critical esteem than heretofore bestowed on him; and Tarkington, though he received considerable attention during his lifetime, has since suffered neglect and merits more complete appreciation today. Of this list of ten writers, those still read today are Edward Eggleston, Wallace, Thompson, Nicholson, Major, Tarkington, and Porter, whereas the others—George Eggleston, Catherwood, and George Mc-Cutcheon, and all the minor novelists discussed in this chapter—either are little read at the present time or have been largely forgotten. In most cases of neglect by the general public and by literary critics we are forced to agree that it has been just, although many of the writers remain interesting from the historical point of view, if not otherwise significant.

The great majority of the thirty-four novelists of the period are confirmed romanticists, with only a handful of definite realists and a small group exhibiting tendencies toward both points of view. The romantics are Lew Wallace, Maurice Thompson, Mary Lamb, Charles Embree, Charles Major, Millard Cox, Caroline Krout, Henry Stephenson, Test Dalton, Elizabeth Hack, Grace Alexander, Harold Kramer, Frederick Landis, Caroline Snedeker, Henry Bedford-Jones, James Baldwin, Elmer Davis, William Winter, David Anderson, and Kate Milner Rabb. The realists include the significant figure of Edward Eggleston, whose work was so important in the beginning of realism in American literature. He was followed by certain minor figures: Maurice Egan, who was much more interested in Catholicism than in realism, Otto Stechhan, Frank Myers, George Louttit, and Ulysses S. Lesh.

The group who wrote both in a romantic and a realistic vein, usually favoring in different degrees one point of view or the other, were George Eggleston, who was primarily a romanticist; Mary Catherwood, whose early contribution was significant in American literature in exhibiting a type of realism which anticipated the work of Edgar Watson Howe and Sherwood Anderson, but whose later output was entirely romantic; the minor writer, Dwight Armstrong; then Meredith Nicholson, who usually could not bear to bring a realistic story to its logical conclusion and spoiled it with a happy ending, and who also penned much romance; Booth Tarkington, whose romantic, popular novels have too much obscured his serious social studies; George McCutcheon, who wrote mostly the thrilling Graustarkian romances and published only one completely realistic novel; Gene Stratton Porter, who attempted late, but unsuccessfully, to introduce realism into her sentimental writing; and John T. McCutcheon, a writer of light books, only one of which contains much realism. We must conclude, therefore, that the novel of the Golden Age was primarily romantic. The typical novel of this period is one written for entertainment.

And what are the various types found among this tremendous production? In spite of some unavoidable overlapping they can be placed under the headings of the historical novel, the romantic novel (which excludes the historical), the realistic novel, satire, religious stories, and juveniles. In addition, perhaps we may list the writers of novels about Indiana. Let us investigate each group briefly.

The historical novel, with seventy titles, is one of the favorite types of Hoosier writers of the era. Commencing with Edward Eggleston's realistic *The Hoosier School-Master* (1871), which began the Golden Age, it continues till long past the close of the period in 1921; in fact, the type is still popular today. Its greatest period was from 1900 to 1910. Its subjects were various, Indiana being a favorite. Most of the books—for example, those of both

Egglestons, Wallace, Catherwood, Major, Tarkington, Krout, and George McCutcheon—were very readable; few however, were serious in nature, the greatest exception to this observation being the books of Lew Wallace. The more serious subjects tend to come with the minor writers, as with the Biblical novels of Mrs. Hack. The most significant historical novels were *The Hoosier School-Master* (1871) and *The Circuit Rider* (1874) of Edward Eggleston, Wallace's *Ben-Hur* (1880), Major's *When Knighthood Was in Flower* (1898), and Tarkington's *Monsieur Beaucaire* (1900). Most of the historical novels were primarily romantic in nature.

The next type of novel, including altogether sixty-four titles, which we shall call loosely the romantic novel, excludes the historical but includes adventure fiction, nature narratives, and other kinds of nonrealistic writings. Of this group only two are at all significant, George McCutcheon's *Graustark* (1901) and Nicholson's *The House of a Thousand Candles* (1905). Clearly the romantic novel tended to be slight and entertaining, but contained little worthy of being remembered.

Not so with the realistic novel, for much of the best of all Indiana literature comes under this heading, which comprises forty-two books. The best ones are Eggleston's *The Hoosier School-Master* (1871), Tarkington's *The Gentleman from Indiana* (1899), George Eggleston's *Blind Alleys* (1906), George McCutcheon's *Mary Midthorne* (1911), and Tarkington's long list, made up of *Penrod* (1914), *Penrod and Sam* (1916), *Seventeen* (1916), *The Turmoil* (1915), *The Magnificent Ambersons* (1918), *Alice Adams* (1921), and *The Midlander* (1924). Clearly, then, Booth Tarkington dominates the realistic novel. And the period in which one finds the greatest concentration of this type is from about 1908 to 1921.

There are only two authors who concern themselves primarily with religion—Maurice Egan, who writes always about the Catholic Church and the Catholic faith, and Mrs. Hack, who has contributed three Biblical novels, employing material from both the Old and New Testaments. Of course, Elmer Davis, with his *Giant Killer* (1928), is really beyond the period.

Only three writers delved into satire: Tarkington with *Cherry* (1903), a burlesque of the historical romance; Louttit, with *The Gentleman from Jay* (1903), an absurd story of the Indiana legislature; and John McCutcheon with *Congressman Pumphrey. The People's Friend* (1907), a satire on the corrupting influence of the Washington life of a Congressman.

Finally, we should record the fact that many of the novelists dipped into the field of juvenile literature: Edward Eggleston, George Eggleston, Catherwood, Thompson, Major, Tarkington, Krout, and Snedeker.

The spread of the novels within the date limits of the Golden Age appears to be more even than one might assume at first. However, the historical novel is concentrated in the period from 1900 to 1910, the romantic novel from about 1900 to 1910 or 1915, and the realistic novel from about 1908 to 1921. Yet, one must not overlook the fact that many of the significant Indiana novels of the Golden Age were produced before 1900.

And why was romantic and sentimental fiction preferred at the turn of the century and the first ten years or so of the twentieth century? The answer is not easily come by, but one should recognize the fact that this idealism, this desire for love and adventure and for escape from the vexing problems of the opening of the century, were evidence partly of the spirit of isolationism that pervaded the American people at the time, from which they were to be awakened roughly by World War I. Americans tended then to be cheerful and self-assured, not concerning themselves greatly with problems outside their own country and often thinking that they had their own problems somewhat in hand. Perhaps the disillusionment occasioned by the war spurred the development of realism. Even President Theodore Roosevelt provided an example for the American people by his confidence, lightheartedness, and his gusto and physical vigor, to say nothing of his indirect advertising of the West. But whether or not these are the correct reasons, the Indiana novel of the period tended to be primarily romantic.

Before concluding, we should take note of a few other interesting facts. Two novelists, the Eggleston brothers, were also historians of some stature; and Edward's contribution to dialect literature was unique. Three writers held honored positions as diplomats—Maurice Egan, Lew Wallace, and Meredith Nicholson—and the authors who contributed the best studies of government, politics, and society in general are Nicholson and Tarkington. Mrs. Porter is the only nature novelist, and she had an interesting theory that fiction is a moralizing agent in society. Lew Wallace, however, fitted, unwittingly, rather well into her theory, even though much in his novels was constructed only for the enjoyment of the reader; yet, he popularized the novel and the drama as a moral influence. *Ben-Hur* was widely imitated; also, Mrs. Catherwood's French romances and Thompson's *Alice of Old Vincennes* served as models for the majority of the later historical novels. In addition, in contrast to the novelists of the earlier period of Indiana literature, the novelists of the later period often were professional writers, such as the Egglestons, Catherwood, Thompson, Nicholson, Major, Tarkington, George McCutchcon, Porter, and that writer of swashbuckling romances, Bedford-Jones. Some of these people, especially the Egglestons and Tarkington, circulated freely in the Eastern literary circles.

The greatest novelists of the Golden Age were two realists—the pioneer in American realism, Edward Eggleston, and the versatile, optimistic Booth Tarkington, who as a social historian evidenced sympathy and universality. Because of his early position in the chronological development of realism the former takes precedence in the larger field of American literature; and the latter assumes the lead in the novel of the Golden Age of Indiana literature. Nevertheless, the typical Indiana novel tended to be romantic and, as already indicated, written for entertainment only.

7

HUMOR, SHORT STORY, ESSAY, AND DRAMA

HUMOR

THE READER who has perused much of the writings of Hoosiers need not be told that humor is a favorite ingredient in their literary cookery; and even though he may chance upon many volumes of imaginative work without much humor, he can not progress far in the study of Indiana literature without encountering it again and again. The whimsical but natural fun, the drollery, the dry witticism, the story told with a straight face, often at the expense of the narrator himself, the deflating of someone's ego, the wholesome irony of exposing human frailties, based on the knowledge of human nature, a knowledge such as the pioneer stump speakers possessed—all these are characteristics of Indiana humor. Much of Indiana literature is shot through with it. However, it is difficult to classify many authors as strictly humorists, for, while a large number have elements of humor in their works, they belong primarily in other categories.

We have seen that there are aspects of humor in the works of many authors already studied, particularly of the poets Phoebe Cary, John Finley, James Whitcomb Riley, Silas B. McManus, and William Herschell, and in the fiction of Baynard Rush Hall, Edward Eggleston, Maurice

Thompson, Booth Tarkington, and Elmer Davis.[1] Also, one might add the name of the essayist, to be considered shortly, Juliet V. Strauss. Nevertheless, there are three writers whom we can designate essentially humorists— George Ade, Strickland Gillilan, and Kin Hubbard. They form a small but significant—and enjoyable—category of Indiana literature of the Golden Age.

GEORGE ADE

George Ade (1866-1944), the "warm-hearted satirist,"[2] is one of the most famous of Indiana authors; and his name is linked with those of the other Hoosier greats in literature. A humorist, social historian, moralist, adventurer in language, entertainer, short-story writer, and author of successful plays and smashing musical comedy hits, the Aesop of Indiana, this small-town boy rose rapidly through the medium of journalism to become one of the most popular of Hoosiers and of American literary figures in his day. He demonstrated the fact that the golden touch of King Midas could be applied to one's manuscripts; and his famous country estate, called Hazelden, and his bountiful hospitality to friends and neighbors gave ample evidence of his material success. Yet he should be known mostly as a clever writer who keenly and sympathetically observed, and boldly reported on, human nature. He was the literary descendant of that maker of

---

[1] Of course, humor is evident also in such nonliterary presentations as the cartoons of John T. McCutcheon. Then, one tends to laugh at the antics of such versifiers as Alfred J. Cotton and James B. Elmore, but one could hardly call the writings of these men typical Indiana humor.

[2] See Fred C. Kelly, *George Ade. Warmhearted Satirist* (Copyright 1947 by the Bobbs-Merrill Company, Inc., Indianapolis). This is the best biography of Ade and it includes an account of his works. I have made liberal use of it in my discussion of Ade. Quotations from the volume are used by permission of the publisher.

maxims Benjamin Franklin and the vernacular or dialect philosophers—Hosea Biglow, Jack Downing, Josh Billings, Artemus Ward, Mark Twain, and Mr. Dooley. Thus, George Ade was steeped in a certain literary tradition, and, like each of his predecessors, he had to seek and establish his own idiom. In this quest he was most notably successful.[3]

George Ade was born in Kentland, Indiana, on February 9, 1866; however, unlike many other Indiana writers, such as Nicholson and Tarkington, his family was not native Hoosier. His father, John Ade, had been brought by his parents as a boy from England to Cheviot, Ohio, a town near Cincinnati, where later John met and married Adaline Adair, an unsmiling young woman of great common sense. The couple soon moved, in 1853, to a *Hoosier School-Master* type of society in the swampy wilderness country of northwestern Indiana, where John Ade first managed a store in the tiny backwoods cluster of cabins called Morocco and then became a blacksmith. In 1860, when the last of Indiana's counties (Newton) was organized, John Ade found himself elected recorder and moved his family to the new county seat, a muddy prairie town called Kent (afterwards Kentland), where they occupied the second house built in the town. George's father served also as cashier of a bank. Here George was born and grew up in a happy environment in the town of less than six hundred; as the next to the youngest of six children, he became known as something of a work dodger and an impractical dreamer. Kentland proved a good laboratory in which to learn much about human nature. Here he developed a love of theatricals and selected Mark Twain as the object of his hero worship.

---

[3] See Carl Van Doren's essay on George Ade, "Old Wisdom in a New Tongue," in *Many Minds* (New York, 1924), 18-33.

After much doubt whether George would ever be able to make a living at anything, his father sent him to Purdue University, which was then little more than ten years old and had about two hundred students. He enrolled in 1883 and took the scientific course so that he might avoid some of the usual requirements in mathematics, a subject he always disliked; he gained the reputation of being a hard-working student, but one who did nothing sensational. However, he did eventually get a few serious essays published in the student monthly, *The Purdue,* and he made many friends among the students.

Soon after his arrival, his room in the dormitory, like Tarkington's room at Princeton, became a place of relaxation for many students, who were amused at Ade's witticisms. He became president of the Irving Literary Society and joined the Sigma Chi fraternity; but never let it be said that his interests—literary, scholarly, or fraternal—could ever keep him from attendance at the Grand Opera House in Lafayette when a good show came to town! In such attractions he reveled! Yet perhaps the most notable events that occurred during his Purdue career were a love affair with a coed, Lillian Howard, which was to turn out unsuccessfully—evidently the only true love of his entire life, for he never married—and his forming of a friendship with a fellow student, John T. McCutcheon, an attachment of literary significance which lasted most of the rest of his life.

Ade's commencement oration for his class of 1887 was "The Future of Letters in the West"; and in it he predicted that "the hub of the literary universe was about to shift from Cambridge, Massachusetts, to an indefinite region which included Crawfordsville, Indianapolis and Tippecanoe County, Indiana."[4]

[4] As reported in Kelly, *George Ade,* 64.

Having nothing special in mind in the way of a vocation after graduation, but hounded, like Tarkington, by his family and friends to "do something," Ade drifted, after a time, into a sporadic attempt to study law in Lafayette, then joyfully leaped at the chance to work on Lafayette newspapers, mostly the *Call*. Next, after a brief fling at advertising patent medicines, he accepted the invitation of John McCutcheon, who had gone to Chicago and had a job as artist on the *Morning News,* to join him and try his luck in the big city.

So it was in 1890 that George Ade, jobless, descended upon Chicago, shared McCutcheon's double bed in a rooming house, and soon was a reporter on the *Morning News* (later the Chicago *News-Record,* then the Chicago *Record*) at a salary of twelve dollars a week. It was now that the real George Ade began to develop, for he was an eager student of human nature and human affairs; and the raw, growing city of a million, teeming with many nationalities and interests, a center of finance, political intrigue, and vice, moved him strongly. He carefully studied the city and got to know as many as possible of the people in it, from all walks of life, his keen observation and knowledge of human nature showing him much that other reporters overlooked.

Assigned first to write a daily piece on the weather, this cub reporter carefully read back files of the paper to orient himself in the new job. His big chance came one evening when news arrived of an explosion on a freighter in the Chicago River, and the managing editor, finding no other reporter about, was forced to dispatch Ade to cover the event. His story, the lead story on the first page the next morning, was so accurate and so dramatic that it attracted wide attention. Another of his early journalistic triumphs was the achievement of an interview with the atheist, Col. Robert G. Ingersoll, a feat no one else could then accomplish; henceforth his newspaper sent him to interview other notables. His acquaintance with famous personages dates from this time. Before long, as the star reporter on his paper, he was helping fledgling reporters, one of them an insecure youngster named Theodore Dreiser, whose job was saved by Ade's sympathetic advice.[5]

It was about this time that Ade and McCutcheon made a visit to Purdue and there met a promising new student, Newton B. Tarkington, not yet called Booth, who had become a member of their fraternity, but who disappointed them because he wanted to become an artist. George remarked, "He's such a good observer, he might do well as a writer."[6]

Ade's newspaper stories soon took on a slant toward human interest. Not only did the news-making events attract him; stories of attempts to start balky horses, yarns about streetcar conductors and shop girls, or accounts of the smells of the city took his fancy. His ear caught the twang of conversation, which he began to reproduce in his writings. Since so much of this kind of material was cut by the proofreaders or editors, Ade was finally given a department of his own, "Stories of the Streets and of the Town," which, beginning in 1893, was earmarked to get by the make-up men. Here, thanks to his distinctive style, the new George Ade emerged; and he and his friend McCutcheon formed a team, Ade writing the copy for the "Stories" and McCutcheon supplying the sketches illustrating them, often drawn on the spot.

All sorts of inconsequential but interesting subjects

---

[5] Kelly, *George Ade*, 89-90. Kelly reports many other interesting details of Ade's newspaper life.

[6] *Ibid.*, 84. For a discussion of Tarkington, see above, 350-85.

appeared in this flourishing daily column, served up with the flavoring of Ade's ready wit: actual, revealing conversations overheard on the street; descriptions of small shops, detective stories, real or imagined; a search for an acceptable boardinghouse; the Chinese of Clark Street; the excitement of a fire; the frightening experience of a visitor to the violent ward of an insane asylum. Ade wanted to become known as "a realist with a compact style and a clean Anglo-Saxon vocabulary and the courage to observe human virtues and frailties as they showed on the lens."[7] He desired to report people as they were, neither to caricature nor exaggerate. In these wishes he was eminently successful; and his unsigned column, together with Eugene Field's column, "Sharps and Flats," rose to the rank of literature, helping to establish the Chicago *Record* as a newspaper of quality.

With Ade's column building up a large following among readers of the *Record,* it was only natural for the newspaper to seize the opportunity to publish selections from it, which appeared in a paperback series sold at twenty-five cents each. *Stories of the Streets and of the Town* (Chicago, 1894), accordingly, made George Ade an author. Eight numbers were issued altogether from 1894 to 1900.[8]

Ade kept improving his stories both in variety and in worth. Since his settings and characters reflected many aspects of contemporary life, his columns became an interesting sort of social history. All his later writing was tested here in miniature; for he experimented with the short story, the fable, dialogue, verse, and drama. More ideas came to him in a few weeks than bless many writers

[7] As reported by Kelly, *op. cit.,* 110.
[8] Second Series, 1894; Third Series, 1895; Fourth Series, 1895; Fifth Series, 1897; Sixth Series, 1898; Seventh Series, 1899; Eighth Series, 1900.

in an entire lifetime; and he often got them from such sources as the Newspaper Club, rival newsmen, barbershops, from readers,[9] from boys met on the street, from conversations overheard—from everywhere and nowhere.

Before long he conceived the device of using continuing characters. Thus was born Artie Blanchard, a colorful youth speaking an amazing slang, based on a real-life artist protégé of Ade's, Charlie Williams. Ade had got Williams a job on the *Record*, where he began his life work. He was later to become famous, illustrating, among many other things, the earlier editions of Tarkington's *Monsieur Beaucaire*. After Ade's "Artie" series had run for a while in the *Record*, it was succeeded by the Doc' Horne series, based on a queer old gentleman liar whose character was quickly sketched in a typical Ade sentence: "If they had built the Mississippi levees as I told them to, long before the war, they wouldn't be washed away every year."[10] About the end of 1896 appeared Pink Marsh, a shiftless but lovable colored bootblack of questionable but interesting ethics, who told stories to the Morning Customer, such as how he took a girl away from a better educated rival by promising her a bicycle which he did not intend to buy, then getting out of bringing her candy by pretending to be " 'conomizin' " for the bicycle. In these sketches Ade was the first writer to present successfully the northern Negro.[11]

Ade's characters were perpetuated in collections: *Artie* (Chicago, 1896), *Pink Marsh* (Chicago, 1897), and *Doc' Horne* (Chicago, 1899). One evidence of the popular appeal of these writings was the naming of a cigar for Artie!

---

[9] One reader who sent him useful suggestions was Franklin P. Adams, then a student at the Armour Scientific Academy.

[10] Kelly, *George Ade*, 125.

[11] *Ibid.*

But the critics also were impressed; and Mark Twain and William Dean Howells both became ardent Ade fans, Twain thanking Howells in a letter for introducing him to Pink Marsh.[12] This letter eventually was published in Ade's *One Afternoon with Mark Twain* (Chicago, 1939). Ade remained a favorite author of Howells. Hamlin Garland so liked Ade's work that in 1895 he urged him to write a novel.[13]

But other jewels were yet to be fashioned from the gold of the *Stories*. A football tale that had come out in the *Sunday Record-Herald*, November 24, 1901, was reprinted in a small edition as *Grouch at the Game* (Madison, Wisconsin, 1901); and a selection of other *Stories* appeared in *In Babel* (New York, 1903). H. L. Mencken pronounced two or three of the stories in the latter book among the best American short stories.[14] *Bang! Bang!* (New York, 1928) was a collection of burlesque detective stories of the type of the nickel library, based on George's boyhood reading in the haymow. The final compilation, edited by Franklin J. Meine and printed by the Caxton Club of Chicago, came only three years before Ade's death, *Stories of the Streets and of the Town* (Chicago, 1941).[15]

In the meantime, however, Ade was engaged in other enterprises. Having seen more of the country through an invitation to the Midwinter Fair of San Francisco in 1894, McCutcheon and Ade developed a zest for travel and determined to visit Europe. This they did the next year and sent back articles and accompanying sketches to the *Record* twice a week entitled "What a Man Sees Who

[12] *Ibid.,* 125-26.
[13] *Ibid.,* 122.
[14] *Ibid.,* 171.
[15] Copies of this edition are reported to have been sold for as much as $150. Copies of the original editions of the stories have long been collectors' items, usually selling at high prices.

Goes Away from Home." These were mostly straight, colorful reporting of interesting details about European life, and a collection of the articles under the same title was issued in 1896 in Chicago. From this time Ade thoroughly enjoyed travel. He wrote also two juveniles, *Circus Day* (Chicago, 1896) and *Stories from History* (Chicago, 1896), the latter published under the pseudonym of John Hazelden. Four more juveniles were to come from his pen before he was finished with this type: *Handsome Cyril* ... (Phoenix, Arizona, 1903, Strenuous Lad's Library, No. 1), *Clarence Allen* ... (Phoenix, Arizona, 1903, Strenuous Lad's Library, No. 2), *Rollo Johnson* ... (Phoenix, Arizona, 1904, Strenuous Lad's Library, No. 3), and *Fred Stone Jingles for Good Little Girls and Good Little Boys* (n.p., n.d. [1921]).

Yet, in spite of the success of nearly all these early books, the most typical work of George Ade was yet to come. It lay in his fables. In his continual efforts to keep a variety in his column, "Stories of the Streets and of the Town," he conceived one day the idea of writing a fable, which appeared on September 17, 1897, in the *Record* and was later rewritten as "The Fable of Sister Mae Who Did As Well As Could Be Expected." In this story hard-working Luella, who was short on looks but long on virtue, slaved in a factory for three dollars a week, while her lazy, empty-headed, but shapely sister Mae became cashier of a lunchroom, had practically to fight off her masculine admirers, and landed a wealthy husband and crashed society. But did Mae then forget Luella? Certainly not. She gave Luella a job in her house as assistant cook at five dollars a week. The moral was phrased as: "Industry and Perseverance bring a sure Reward."[16] Nevertheless, even

---

[16] George Ade, *Fables in Slang* (Chicago, 1900), 135-42.

though this first fable was a success, Ade had no intention of writing other fables.

However, goaded by friends to produce more, ten months after the appearance of the first fable he published two more in the *Record* under the title, "Fables in Slang"; and the genre was established. Ade found that by the use of slang, compression of thought, unusual figures of speech, and a strange capitalizing of important words he could produce a startling and amusing effect. So popular did the fables become that even though he claimed to be no expert in the use of slang and complained that he was really wasting time in keeping his attention from larger work—for publishers had been urging him to write a novel, and Stone & Co. had even gone so far as to make up a dummy with a title, "The College Widow," stamped on it and had sent out a salesman to sell the book on a subscription basis—still he acquiesced to the demand and wrote fables madly. Finally the publishers despaired of Ade's ever writing the great American novel and influenced him to produce enough of the fables to make a book. The fables began to be published by other newspapers and soon were syndicated as a weekly feature in many papers in the East and Midwest.

So when *Fables in Slang* (Chicago, 1900) was issued, the stage was set and the audience assembled. By the end of 1900, sixty-nine thousand copies of the book had been sold, and the young author awoke to find himself famous. This success followed immediately on that of the first novel of Ade's friend, Booth Tarkington, entitled *The Gentleman from Indiana.* Everyone read and quoted the fables— the rich, the poor, the educated and uneducated, young and old; all found an element of universality in them which carried strong individual appeal. William Allen White, editor of the Emporia (Kansas) *Gazette,* wrote

Ade: "I would rather have written *Fables in Slang* than
be President."[17] And instead of being attacked by the
critics for his liberties in the use of the language, he was
complimented by Brander Matthews of Columbia University; and his friend, William Dean Howells, wrote that
"His portrayal of life is almost absolute in its perfection—
you experience something of the bliss of looking at your
own photograph. . . ."[18]

The book and the many later collections of other fables
bear careful analysis. They contain a large variety of
tales. The reader finds in them first an amusing distrust
of people who leave the tested and beaten path of life and
thereby make unnecessary errors in judgment or who take
up ridiculous poses. For example, the parents of Clarence
and Joseph are so demanding with one and so lax with
the other that both boys are failures. The Coming Champion is considered greased lightning until he boxes with
a real fighter, who knocks him out. Lutie, putting on airs
in her village, fancies herself a great singer until she is
given the acid test of the box office and a good critic. The
Benevolent Lady, who has little to do, decides to look,
through her lorgnette, on the poor, but they resent her
helping hand, and she turns angrily to other occupations.
Handsome Jethro, who considers himself above physical
labor, saves in ten years only nineteen dollars of his
salary in a ten-cent store, while his brother Lyford buys
and develops a valuable farm. The moral of the fables
seems to be that one should use common sense, mind one's
own affairs, and make no pretense to be other than what
one is.

However, this moral can not be applied nearly so
easily and universally as the old maxims, such as those of

[17] Kelly, *George Ade,* 144.
[18] *Ibid.*

Franklin. We know these old saws by heart; yet experience leads us to doubt the ultimate truth of some of them. Thus, one of Ade's characters, a caddy who sees wealthy golfers forever playing, wonders why his hard-working father "could seldom get one Dollar to rub against another." And then there is the shabby brother who does all the hard work in the law office, while his gay, flashy brother flits about and gets all the credit. The implication is that perhaps, after all, honesty is not always the best policy, and hard work and virtuous living do not continually pay off.

An excellent example of this rather indefinable hinting is found in one of the most famous of the fables, which will merit setting forth in its entirety.

The Fable of The Two Mandolin Players
And the Willing Performer

A Very Attractive Debutante knew two Young Men who called on her every Thursday Evening, and brought their Mandolins along.

They were Conventional Young Men, of the Kind that you see wearing Spring Overcoats in the Clothing Advertisements. One was named Fred, and the other was Eustace.

The Mothers of the Neighborhood often remarked, "What Perfect Manners Fred and Eustace have!" Merely as an aside it may be added that Fred and Eustace were more Popular with the Mothers than they were with the Younger Set, although no one could say a Word against either of them. Only it was rumored in Keen Society that they didn't Belong. The Fact that they went Calling in a Crowd, and took their Mandolins along, may give the Acute Reader some Idea of the Life that Fred and Eustace held out to the Young Women of their Acquaintance.

The Debutante's name was Myrtle. Her Parents were very Watchful, and did not encourage her to receive Callers, except such as were known to be Exemplary Young Men. Fred and Eustace were a few of those who escaped the Black List.

Myrtle always appeared to be glad to see them, and they regarded her as a Darned Swell Girl.

Fred's Cousin came from St. Paul on a Visit; and one Day, in the Street, he saw Myrtle, and noticed that Fred tipped his Hat, and gave her a Stage Smile.

"Oh, Queen of Sheba!" exclaimed the Cousin from St. Paul, whose name was Gus, as he stood stock still, and watched Myrtle's Reversible Plaid disappear around a Corner. "She's a Bird. Do you know her well?"

"I know her Quite Well," replied Fred coldly. "She is a Charming Girl."

"She is all of that. You're a great Describer. And now what Night are you going to take me around to Call on her?"

Fred very naturally Hemmed and Hawed. It must be remembered that Myrtle was a member of an Excellent Family, and had been schooled in the Proprieties, and it was not to be supposed that she would crave the Society of slangy old Gus, who had an abounding Nerve, and furthermore was as Fresh as the Mountain Air.

He was the Kind of Fellow who would see a Girl twice, and then, upon meeting her the Third Time, he would go up and straighten her Cravat for her, and call her by her First Name.

Put him into a Strange Company—en route to a Picnic— and by the time the Baskets were unpacked he would have a Blonde all to himself, and she would have traded her Fan for his College Pin.

If a Fair-Looker on the Street happened to glance at him Hard he would run up and seize her by the Hand, and convince her that they had Met. And he always Got Away with it, too.

In a Department Store, while waiting for the Cash Boy to come back with the Change, he would find out the Girl's Name, her Favorite Flower, and where a Letter would reach her.

Upon entering a Parlor Car at St. Paul he would select a Chair next to the Most Promising One in Sight, and ask her if she cared to have the Shade lowered. Before the Train cleared the Yards he would have the Porter bringing a Foot-Stool for the Lady.

At Hastings he would be asking her if she wanted Something to Read.

At Red Wing he would be telling her that she resembled Maxine Elliott, and showing her his Watch, left to him by his Grandfather, a Prominent Virginian.

At La Crosse he would be reading the Menu Card to her, and telling her how different it is when you have Some One to join you in a Bite.

At Milwaukee he would go out and buy a Bouquet for her, and when they rode into Chicago they would be looking out of the Same Window, and he would be arranging for their Baggage with the Transfer Man. After that they would be Old Friends.

Now, Fred and Eustace had been at School with Gus, and they had seen his Work, and they were not disposed to Introduce him into One of the most Exclusive Homes in the City.

They had known Myrtle for many Years; but they did not dare to Address her by her First Name, and they were Positive that if Gus attempted any of his usual Tactics with her she would be Offended; and, naturally enough, they would be Blamed for bringing him to the House.

But Gus insisted. He said he had seen Myrtle, and she Suited him from the Ground up, and he proposed to have Friendly Doings with her. At last they told him they would take him if he promised to Behave. Fred warned him that Myrtle would frown down any Attempt to be Familiar on Short Acquaintance, and Eustace said that as long as he had known Myrtle he had never Presumed to be Free and Forward with her. He had simply played the Mandolin. That was as Far Along as he had ever got.

Gus told them not to Worry about him. All he asked was a Start. He said he was a Willing Performer, but as yet he never had been Disqualified for Crowding. Fred and Eustace took this to mean that he would not Overplay his Attentions, so they escorted him to the House.

As soon as he had been Presented, Gus showed her where to sit on the Sofa, then he placed himself about Six Inches away and began to Buzz, looking her straight in the Eye. He said that when he first saw her he Mistook her for Miss

Prentice, who was said to be the Most Beautiful Girl in St. Paul, only, when he came closer, he saw that it couldn't be Miss Prentice, because Miss Prentice didn't have such Lovely Hair. Then he asked her the Month of her Birth and told her Fortune, thereby coming nearer to Holding her Hand within Eight Minutes than Eustace had come in a Lifetime.

"Play something, Boys," he Ordered, just as if he had paid them Money to come along and make Music for him.

They unlimbered their Mandolins and began to play a Sousa March. He asked Myrtle if she had seen the New Moon. She replied that she had not, so they went Outside.

When Fred and Eustace finished the first Piece, Gus appeared at the open Window, and asked them to play "The Georgia Camp-Meeting," which had always been one of his Favorites.

So they played that, and when they had Concluded there came a Voice from the Outer Darkness, and it was the Voice of Myrtle. She said: "I'll tell you what to Play; play the Intermezzo."

Fred and Eustace exchanged Glances. They began to Perceive that they had been backed into a Siding. With a few Potted Palms in front of them, and two Cards from the Union, they would have been just the same as a Hired Orchestra.

But they played the Intermezzo and felt Peevish. Then they went to the Window and looked out. Gus and Myrtle were sitting in the Hammock, which had quite a Pitch toward the Center. Gus had braced himself by Holding to the back of the Hammock. He did not have his Arm around Myrtle, but he had it Extended in a Line parallel with her Back. What he had done wouldn't Justify a Girl in saying, "Sir!" but it started a Real Scandal with Fred and Eustace. They saw that the only Way to Get Even with her was to go Home without saying "Good Night." So they slipped out the Side Door, shivering with Indignation.

After that, for several Weeks, Gus kept Myrtle so Busy that she had no Time to think of considering other Candidates. He sent Books to her Mother, and allowed the Old Gentleman to take Chips away from him at Poker.

They were Married in the Autumn, and Father-in-Law took

Gus into the Firm, saying that he had needed a good Pusher for a Long Time.

At the Wedding the two Mandolin Players were permitted to act as Ushers.

MORAL: *To get a fair Trial of Speed, use a Pace-Maker.*[19]

In the above fable the reader finds himself in the curious position of attempting to sympathize with the two luckless suitors, but actually he admires the go-getter and laughs at the absurd position of the unfortunates. It is the realization of the truth of such stories, of the fact that the extrovert, the "pusher," does get ahead at the expense of the less ostentatious and the more conscientious and humble person, that strikes home. There may be something topsy-turvy in the moral order. This is life, and the reader knows it. Perhaps it is really true that "Early to Bed and Early to Rise and you will meet very few of our best people." Yet, whether he endorses this attitude toward living, he is pleasantly surprised at the way things turn out in the tales and at the revelation of human nature.

Through all his fables, Ade is consistently Hoosier, or, at least, Midwestern, in the derivation of his wit and point of view. His native Hoosier philosophy and common sense, like Riley's, are revealed everywhere. As Carl Van Doren points out:

As a satirist of genius Mr. Ade goes, of course, beyond the folk in his perception of the ironies which attend prosperity, and yet he derives the body of his wit from a very general Hoosier wisdom. His fulcrum and his point of view are Hoosier. His people no less than he, whatever illusions they may cling to, have a steady suspicion of saints and poets and reformers, of snobbishness and eccentricity and af-

[19] *Fables in Slang*, 181-94, as reprinted in *The America of George Ade (1866-1944)* . . ., edited by Jean Shepherd (Copyright 1961 by G. P. Putnam's Sons), 93-97. Reprinted by permission of the publisher.

fectation. Like him they are tickled by tales of townsmen who come off second best in bargains with rustics or with villagers; of rude Westerners who do not suffer by comparison with Easterners of a higher polish; of simple Americans who, having tried the shining routes of Europe, come joyfully back to the familiar habits of their inland home. They like to laugh at windy statesmen, but are willing to smile at politicians who hoodwink the populace cleverly. They encourage aspiration, but they snicker at the mean arts by which mean persons seek to make themselves conspicuous in the world without real excellence. They look askance at rhetoric, at rebellion, at ecstasy. For the most part they confine their talk to the essential topics of work and play and love, but they will take none of these too seriously: they hold that work must have its interludes, that play must not degenerate into hard labor, and that love must be regarded, or at least discussed, as one of the aspects of comedy. Inveterately middle class themselves, they feel for proletariats a contempt which is modified by democratic sentiment, and for aristocracies a contempt which is modified by a sneaking curiosity. Inveterately nativist themselves, they despise all foreigners and newcomers and do not pretend to understand them. At the same time they are sure enough of their position in a settled order to delight in jokes at their expense, or at the expense of their neighbors, provided the jokes are in their own language and are made by some one whose standing is established.[20]

George Ade is well qualified to write such fables inasmuch as he presents himself as subject to many of these same errors, and he is one of the very people whom he ridicules. His laughter is directed toward himself as well as his characters. He does not pose as occupying a position above them; rather he seems to think that perhaps the characters would themselves enjoy the joke. Since he is a product of the folk, coming from a small-town back-

[20] Quoted from Van Doren, *Many Minds*, 23-25, by permission of the estate of Carl Van Doren.

ground, he knows intimately the beliefs of the people, the types of human folly that he censures, and how far he can go without dissenting from popular ideas or well-grounded doctrines. And yet, strangely, though based on small-town standards—for in his day the city was formed largely of rural and small-town people, with their typical behavior—this is still a chiseled, urban wit.

His method is to characterize quickly and deftly with a few words, using the vernacular and some of its slang and bold and original figures of speech, then to add a few illuminating details. He is a moralist in that he constantly demolishes pretense, greed, selfishness, foolish reformers, climbers, Bohemians. One should not look into his fables for deep philosophy; instead one finds here a social record of how many Americans live—and how ridiculous they make themselves. His liberties with the language both astonish and delight. As he remarked, the dictionaries never have caught up with him. Of course, some of his diction is dated and as such can not endure, but most of it is so universal as to need little or no footnoting today and may require little in the future. Yet one must recognize that it is distinctively American and that foreigners will always have trouble with it. As Ade said, "Andrew Lang once started to read my works and then sank with a bubbling cry and did not come up for three days."[21]

Not long after the appearance of the first volume the fables were published in more and more newspapers, and Ade issued many collections of them. Now more than able to support himself by his pen, in 1900 he left the *Record* to devote himself exclusively to authorship. The other collections of the fables and books drawn from his fables are *More Fables* (Chicago, 1900), *Forty Modern Fables* (New York, 1901), *The Girl Proposition* (New York,

[21] *Ibid.*, 32. I have obtained several of my ideas here from Van Doren.

1902), *People You Know* (New York, 1903), *Breaking into
Society* (New York, 1904), *True Bills* (New York, 1904),
I Knew Him When— (Chicago, 1910), *The Revised Legend of One Who Came Back* (New York, 1912), *Knock-
ing the Neighbors* (Garden City, New York, 1912), *Ade's
Fables* (New York, 1914), *The Fable of the Hostess and
the Hikers and the Party Under the Trees* (issued by the
American Red Cross, 1918), *Hand-Made Fables* (New
York, 1920), and *Thirty Fables in Slang* (New York, 1933).
The Ade fables finally became so popular that they
reached the inevitable stage of being made into motion
pictures about the time of World War I and being transformed into a comic strip, drawn by Art Helfant, in 1927.
So they reached by various means a widespread audience.
Many literary figures, including Carl Sandburg, treasured
them.

When George Ade found himself a famous writer, he
discovered that he was also a wealthy one; and he soon had
an unneeded $500 to $1000 a week. Instead of depositing
his money in a Chicago bank, he sent it all to his amazed
father, who was still cashier of the small Kentland bank,
so that he might show the checks to the well-wishers who
had originally advised that it would not be worth while
to send George to college. One can imagine the effect
produced! Another evidence of George's growing fame
was the appearance in Chicago of George Barr Mc-
Cutcheon, for some years now city editor of the *Courier*
in Lafayette, to ask Ade's advice about how to break into
print with the six novels which he had in manuscript but
in which no publisher had shown much interest. Mc-
Cutcheon had finally received an offer of the paltry sum
of $500 for *Graustark,* and he wondered if he should
accept. Ade advised him to do so in order to get his name
in print, but not to commit himself for other books. Mc-

Cutcheon took his advice and, as a result, became shortly, like Ade, a famous and wealthy author.

Having money on his hands, Ade, acting on the advice of his brother William, decided to invest it mostly in farm land around Kentland; and he eventually owned nearly 2,400 acres in his native Newton County. On one farm near the town of Brook he built an Elizabethan-style house with rooms for guests and employees which became the famous Hazelden estate. Living here for varying periods of time, Ade often entertained his friends and neighbors and, secure from the interruptions of city life, did some of his writing. He combined a homey quality of living (he insisted that his neighbors were never to knock on the door but rather to walk in) with great hospitality, acting as host to an annual large community party, political conventions, and conventions of his college fraternity. His golf course became a club. It is no wonder that for reasons personal as well as literary George Ade was loved by Newton County, and by Indiana. When not at Hazelden, Ade either lived in Chicago, traveled, or, later in life, wintered in Florida, where his next-door neighbor was his author friend, Hervey Allen.

Yet, this account of his writing is far from complete, for nothing has yet been said about his work as a playwright. When he was still on the *Record* he acquiesced in the requests of friends and wrote several slight bits for the stage: a skit, "The Back-Stair Investigation"; a one-act play for the comedienne May Irwin, entitled "Mrs. Peckham's Carouse"; and a farce comedy, "The Night of the Fourth." The last two were very successful, but Ade never would permit his name to be used with them, and evidently none of the three was ever published. The main result of this writing was to sharpen his interest in the theater.

It was not, however, until he took a trip to the Far East
in 1900 that his interest was quickened to the extent of
writing a full-length stage production. In Manila he stayed
with John McCutcheon and found the scene interesting,
for the Philippines had just been freed from Spanish
domination. One series of Ade's columns had been "Stories of Benevolent Assimilation," in which he had satir-
ized American foreign policies in the Far East. From correspondents such as McCutcheon, who were reporting the
Aguinaldo insurrection, he heard the interesting and amusing stories of the American negotiations with a Moro
chieftain, Hadji Jamalol Ki-Ram, the Sultan of Jolo, which
was the main island of the Sulu archipelago. Since Sulu
practiced slavery and polygamy, the American government
was attempting to "assimilate" Ki-Ram tactfully without
insulting him and yet slowly educating and changing both
the monarch and his people. It was a delicate situation—
and, as Ade sized it up, one just made for a comic opera
satirizing the American attempt to civilize his "brown
brother."

Upon returning home, he set to work on his first light
opera, with Gilbert and Sullivan as his guiding star. Working with a young composer, Alfred G. Wathall, *The
Sultan of Sulu* (New York, 1902) was soon readied and
attracted the attention of Col. Henry W. Savage, the head
of a Boston stock company, who offered to try it out. It
ran for eleven weeks in Chicago in 1902, took to the road
for a time, Colonel Savage requiring his authors to make
constant revision, then reached Boston and New York, in
which latter stand it lasted 192 performances, making
theatrical history. The text of the play, published in New
York in 1903 and sold in the lobby of the Wallack
Theater, has become a collector's item. The libretto deals
with the amusing attempt of the American government

to civilize Ki-Ram and his kingdom. Ki-Ram becomes governor, is given a silk hat as his sign of office, has to divorce all his wives except one, the unfortunate wives then demand alimony on the American pattern—and so the story proceeds! One of the songs which Ade wrote for this piece, entitled "R-E-M-O-R-S-E," is sung by Ki-Ram after he has imbibed too many American cocktails and contains the line that has since passed into common American usage, "The cold, gray dawn of the morning after."

Ade followed this successful stage production with another, a musical comedy, *Peggy From Paris* (Chicago, 1903), which, although successful, was not such a hit as the *Sultan*. It concerned a girl from a small Illinois town who, after studying singing in Paris for several years, returns to masquerade in Chicago as a French opera singer; but her "hayseed" father, hearing she has come back, appears and tries to get her to accompany him home—thereby making exposure of her fraud possible.

A somewhat different sort of play was *The County Chairman*, published finally in New York in 1924. In spite of the fact that in it Ade departed from his usual style and wrote without slang, and despite the absence of singing and dancing numbers, it was a great success. This is a story of life and politics in a Midwestern country town of the early eighties, and the hero finds himself in the agonizing situation of running for election as state's attorney in opposition to the father of the girl he wishes to marry. Many small-town types are utilized as characters, such as the old settler, the confident drummer, the soapbox orator. The play ran for a long time in Chicago in 1903, enjoyed an unbroken run of 272 nights in New York, where critics dubbed it the best of the rural dramas, then toured for three or four years, had a revival in 1937 with Charles Coburn as the Chairman, and was made into a Hollywood movie with Will Rogers playing the lead.[22]

The County Chairman was followed by a comic opera, *The Sho-Gun* (New York, 1904), another satire laid in the Far East, satirizing commercial expansion in the person of an American businessman who tries to revolutionize the commercial life of an island near Korea, where live such people as the Sho-Gun of Ka-Choo, the Princess Hunni-Bun, the dowager Hi-Faloot, and Omee-Omi. This show opened in Chicago and ran a few weeks, then followed *The County Chairman* at Wallack's in New York, where it lasted 125 nights. It was received better on the West Coast, however, and Ade always considered it his best musical production.

The first work that he wrote in his newly built Hazelden, in 1904, was *The College Widow* (belatedly published, New York, 1924). Instead of writing the story as a novel, as he had planned six years before, he now turned it into a play, a play about college life and college football, a subject new to the American public and, what is more, a play not about a large university, but about Wabash College, at Crawfordsville, Indiana—although the college is never identified by name. Ade dashed off the four acts in less than three weeks and went to New York to read the play to his producer, Colonel Savage, who was doubtful whether the public would be interested in a play about college life.

It was tried out, however, at the Columbia Theater in Washington, D.C., in September, 1904, with everyone, George Ade most of all, very skeptical about the reception. The Sigma Chi chapter of George Washington University desired to attend the first night as a group and to hold a reception afterward; but Ade was so jittery that

[22] Kelly, *George Ade,* Chapter 17.

he refused the honor, saying that "he might be hiding under a bed or perhaps his body would be floating down the Potomac."[23] But to everyone's surprise the play went over—and it went with a bang, indeed! The audience laughed, applauded, and during the scene of the football game in the third act was in an uproar. George was forced to make a curtain speech at the end of the third act and found himself looking into a box, where Admiral George Dewey was sitting, the hero of the Battle of Manila Bay, who called out, "George, it's wonderful!"

George replied, "Admiral, God bless you for them kind words!"[24]

In brief, the play was one of the most popular American productions. After a successful run in Washington, it went to New York, where the audience on the opening night applauded continually and even cheered, and Ade had to make another speech. The critics all acclaimed the production; and adulations came from such fellow dramatists as the Hoosier poet and playwright, William Vaughn Moody, and the British novelist and playwright, James M. Barrie. *The Widow* ran almost a year in New York and has been given steadily from that day till the present, by professional and amateur groups; at one time three companies were on the road in different sections of the country. It has grossed at least two million dollars. It "made" at least one actor, Thomas Meighan, who afterward became famous in motion pictures. Of course, George Ade emerged from his new triumph more loved than ever—and, incidentally, was called the most successful playwright in America. One could not avoid his plays on Broadway. As evidence of his popularity in Indiana is the fact that a town in Newton County was now named after him.

[23] *Ibid.*, 188.
[24] *Ibid.*, 189.

The plot of *The College Widow* is typical of Ade's clean and humorous stories. It concerns the rivalry between two small colleges, Atwater, a Presbyterian institution, and Bingham, a Baptist school. Hiram Bolton, president of a railroad, has endowed Bingham with chapels and quadrangles in gratitude for his having been expelled during his freshman year and thus given the opportunity to enter a worth-while business. He and his son Billy, an excellent halfback, stop at Atwater on the way to Bingham, where Billy is to enroll, to see Mr. Bolton's old friend, Dr. Witherspoon, the president of Atwater. Mr. Bolton leaves Billy and goes off to London on a business trip. The Atwater students, in desperate need of a halfback for their football team, persuade the beautiful Jane Witherspoon, called the "college widow" because she loses a suitor with each graduation, to entice Billy into enrolling at Atwater and playing on the team. He succumbs to her charms and is instrumental in winning the crucial football game with the arch football rival, Bingham.[25] At the height of the furious and exciting game Mr. Bolton returns and denounces his son, saying, "You're a hell of a Baptist!"—a statement quoted for many years after the appearance of the play. Billy, having fallen in love with Jane, is chagrined when he discovers why she led him on, but the play ends happily.

One of its unforgettable aspects is the inclusion of about ten good character parts, such as "Silent" Murphy, the burly foundry worker, who has been drafted into taking an art course so that he may play center on the team, and the "hayseed" "Bub" Hicks, who is at first homesick but changes later into a sport, wearing extreme college styles, and "knows a lot of things the faculty can't find out."

[25] If Atwater represents Wabash College, as Ade said, then Bingham must stand for DePauw University, the arch rival of Wabash in football for about seventy years.

When the play went to London in 1908, the manager of the theater foresaw the need to translate American slang into the Londoner's idiom and distributed a glossary with the program, defining such things as "prexy," "the campus," and "pin-head."[26] The play was soon transmuted into the mediums of a musical show and a motion picture.[27]

The many other Ade plays need not be covered in such detail, for they exhibit a great similarity to those already discussed. Next in the order of their production, but not necessarily their publication, was the successful *Just Out of College* (New York, 1924). It featured as principal character Edward Worthington Swinger, a character previously used in "Stories of the Streets and of the Town," who is paid $20,000 by a "pickle king" to stay away from his daughter for three months and to demonstrate if he has any business sense; but Swinger uses the money to buy a rival pickle company which the "pickle king" has been planning to buy and in the end placates the father and wins the girl.

Another play, "The Bad Samaritan," was a failure, as were "Artie" and "U.S. Minister Bedloe." *Father and the Boys* (New York, 1924), however, about how an old man turns the tables on young folk, was very successful. A popular musical play written for the Purdue Harlequin

[26] For a fuller discussion of *The College Widow,* see Kelly, *George Ade,* Chapters 19 and 20.

[27] The musical play made from *The College Widow,* produced 1918-19, was "Leave It to Jane," which was revived as an off-Broadway show in 1959-61. There were various movie versions. A talking movie issued in 1930 was "The Widow from Chicago," and one issued in 1936 was entitled "Freshman Love." The play was revived for the Purdue Varsity Show of 1941. It was translated into French as *L'Opéra La Veuve Académie* (n. p., n. d. [Chicago, 1924]). See Dorothy R. Russo, *A Bibliography of George Ade, 1866-1944* (Indianapolis, 1947), 95, 121. This is the definitive bibliography of the works of Ade.

Club, *The Fair Co-Ed* (New York, 1908), starred Elsie Janis, who was featured also in another musical, *The Slim Princess* (Indianapolis, [1907]), a travesty on *The Prisoner of Zenda* and based on a magazine story, one of many written by Ade. The musical, *The Old Town* (New York, 1909), played 171 performances in New York in 1910 and marked the close of Ade's career of some ten years as a playwright.

He had even done a group of one-act plays, of much the same type as his longer, nonmusical pieces: *Marse Covington* (Washington, D.C., 1918), *The Mayor and the Manicure* (New York, 1923), *Nettie* (New York, 1923), and *Speaking to Father* (New York, 1923). All these were comedies except *Marse Covington,* which told the story of how a proud Southerner of the old school was shielded from embarrassment while gambling by a former Negro servant.

In all his dramatic work Ade surely had not been what one would call a great dramatist. William Vaughn Moody's *The Great Divide* contained more substance than Ade's complete dramatic production. Yet the Hoosier dramatist still occupied a place as a corrective influence on the foibles of society and was significant in the development of American drama. Thomas H. Dickinson says in his *Playwrights of the New American Theater:*[28]

> Our interest in George Ade as a corrective influence in American writing is enhanced by the fact that he definitely turned his hand to the stage. . . . [His plays] were milestones in the history of our native drama. His importance lies not so much in the musical plays (though of these "The Sultan of Sulu" had a satiric quality that gave point to its lighter graces) as in his comedies. In "The College Widow," "The County Chairman," "Father and the Boys," we have, among a number of Hick types from the yokel drama of the

[28] (New York, 1925), 150-51.

time, an assortment of characters that were new to the American stage. College students, the president of the Freshwater college, the political figures of a small middle-western community, the "college widow" who buries one every commencement, the athletic hero, the new capitalist, the state's attorney, the store porch orator, the members of the fife and drum corps, the subscription book agent—these characters have today receded far into the past, but they have not receded from memory. They were handpicked from the streets on which Ade walked as a young man. The actions in which they engaged, the caucuses, political campaigns, football contests, gossiping matches at the railroad depot and in the store, were the material of the life he and his neighbors had lived. Let it be granted that these characters and materials were treated with a sportive levity, that the fable of the play was never of the slightest significance. It remains that the author had brought observation to the theater. George Ade was a humorist. Like the best of humorists his humor consisted in having a good eye. As this was a rare endowment in the theater of his time, he occupies in my opinion a higher position in the history of our stage than the themes of his plays would seem to indicate. Urged by a self-judgment as sure as his observation was keen, Ade laid down his pen at the height of his success. His had been a pungent, corrective wit. He set many on the right way.

A few miscellaneous publications of Ade's, not yet listed, should attract only passing attention and will close our consideration of his works. His verse, both some that appears in his musical shows and some that was rejected, is represented in *Verses and Jingles* (Indianapolis, [1911]) and is appropriately entitled, for of poetry in the higher sense there is none. The book is full of typical satire. Travel letters are found in *In Pastures New* (New York, 1906) and present a common-sense view. *The Rolling Peanut* (Detroit, Michigan, [1904]), an endorsement of a one-cylinder Oldsmobile roadster, has become a collector's item; *Chapter Houses, with Particular Reference to*

Purdue University (Lafayette, Indiana, [1910?]) was written for his fraternity, as was *A Picture Book for Purdue Sigs* (Lafayette, Indiana, [1912]); *Hoosier Hand Book and True Guide for the Returning Exile* (Chicago, 1911) was edited for the Indiana Society of Chicago. An edition of selections from Indiana literature was compiled by Ade: *An Invitation to You and Your Folks from Jim and Some More of the Home Folks* (Indianapolis, [1916]). *Not a Fable* (New York, [1919]) was issued for Jewish war relief during World War I. *Single Blessedness and Other Observations* (Garden City, New York, 1922) is a collection of essays, now considered a very rare item; and other essays are found in *John Hertz. An Appreciation* (Miami, Florida, 1930), *The Old-Time Saloon Not Wet—Not Dry Just History* (New York, 1931), *Revived Remarks on Mark Twain* (compiled by George Hiram Brownell, Chicago, 1936), and *Notes & Reminiscences* (with John T. McCutcheon, Chicago, 1940). In addition to all these items Ade also wrote much for magazines and turned out movie scripts.

The latter part of Ade's life was filled not only with literary activities but also with civic duties, philanthropy, great friendships, and honors. He was the most famous graduate of Purdue University and served as a member of the Board of Trustees. He and David Ross, another member of the Board, purchased land, contributed heavily, and secured the erection of the great Ross-Ade Stadium at Purdue. Ade served as national president of the Sigma Chi fraternity. His service as director of publicity for the Indiana Council of Defense during the First World War reminds the reader of a similar role that Elmer Davis held as director of the Office of War Information during World War II. He was a warm friend of Theodore Roosevelt, Booth Tarkington, James Whitcomb Riley (for whom Ade named a tree at Hazelden), and of hundreds of other well-known people of his day, to say nothing of thousands of people of much less importance. Everyone was important to Ade. He received honorary degrees from Purdue and Indiana universities. And after a full life of hard work, accomplishment, laughter, and sincere love for his fellow man, George Ade died at Brook, Indiana, on May 16, 1944, at the age of seventy-eight. Indiana —and the nation—had lost a talented writer, a great wit, and a wonderful friend. His Hazelden House and estate were given to Newton County for a George Ade Memorial Hospital; his farms he divided among relatives; and his library and manuscripts he left to Purdue.

George Ade must go down in Indiana literature as one of the greatest writers of the state. Though he did not probe deeply into the human heart or pen formal philosophy, and though much of his work has proved ephemeral, still he was a moralist, a social historian, an entertainer of vitality, a liberalizing influence on the use of language, a shrewd satirical observer and commentator on life, a thoroughgoing American. As a national humorist he was the successor to Mark Twain. The state and nation can never forget George Ade.[29]

STRICKLAND GILLILAN

Sandwiched in between the two giant humorists, George Ade and Kin Hubbard, is Strickland Gillilan (1869-1954), a humorist and lecturer of interest but not nearly of their stature, for he is known today mostly for one poem. He was born on October 9, 1869, in Jackson County, Ohio,

---

[29] The Indiana State Library has a good collection of letters of George Ade. A careful selection of representative writings of Ade is given in Fred C. Kelly (ed.), *The Permanent Ade. The Living Writings of George Ade* (Indianapolis, 1947).

attended country schools and Ohio University. He followed first the career of a journalist, being associated with the *Jackson Herald* in 1887 and the Athens *Herald,* 1888-92; served as city editor of the Richmond (Indiana) *Daily Telegram,* 1892-95, and conducted a daily column of humor; was city editor of the Richmond *Daily Palladium,* 1895-1901; editor of the Marion (Indiana) *Daily Tribune,* 1901; a member of the staff of the Los Angeles *Herald,* 1901-02; then moved to the Baltimore *American,* where he wrote a humor column from 1902 to 1905. After 1905 he became a free-lance writer and humorous lecturer, traveling about the country. He was twice married. He died on April 25, 1954, in Warrenton, Virginia.[30]

Gillilan had achieved only local fame for his humor by 1897, when, in a dearth of news for his Richmond newspaper, he wrote his famous poem, "Finnigin to Flannigan," based on a story told to him by one of Richmond's many "railroad Irish." This bit of verse in Irish dialect recounted the tale of Finnigin, the boss of a section, who so tired his superintendent Flannigan with detailed reports of frequent derailments in his section that he was ordered to be brief. When another derailment of minor importance came and the train had been righted and again dispatched on its way, Finnigin worked all night in his shanty "bilin' down his repoort."

> An' he writed like this: "Musther Flannigan:
> Off agin, on agin,
> Gone agin.—Finnigin."

Immediately the poem became popular in Richmond, and Gillilan sent it to the old *Life* magazine, whose editors

[30] Information about Gillilan is taken mostly from *Who's Who in America,* Vol. 20 (1938-39), Barry, A Biographical and Bibliographical Dictionary of Indiana Authors, 352, and Leon W. Russell, "Man Who Made World Grin at Finnigin Dies," in Indianapolis *Star,* April 26, 1954, p. 1.

snapped it up and asked for more. From that time the humorist's verses sold easily to magazines and were printed in the Indianapolis *Journal* and newspapers over the country.

His collections of humorous and dialect verse are five in number: *Finnigin to Flannigan* (Richmond, Indiana, 1898), *Including Finnigin* (Philadelphia, 1908), *Including You and Me* (Chicago, 1916), *Laugh It Off* (Chicago, 1924), and *Gillilan, Finnigin & Co.*, compiled by Homer Rodeheaver (Winona Lake, Indiana, 1941). All this verse is composed of homely themes with such titles as "A Baby the Size of Mine," "An Old Man's Retrospect," "The General Store," and "When Work Is Through." There are geniality, optimism, moral counsel, high spirits, and sentiment aplenty. Of course, these are ingredients found in the poetry of Riley, but appear here without the strength and appeal of that master of sentimental verse. Also, they are couched in a form that often approaches unmitigated doggerel.

Gillilan issued other types of material: two books of humorous essays growing out of his lectures—*Sunshine and Awkwardness* (Chicago, 1918) and *A Sample Case of Humor* (Chicago, 1919); two juveniles, *Danny and Fanny* (New York, 1928) and *Danny and Fanny and Spot, the Fox-Terrier Hero* (Chicago, 1939); a book of Republican campaign songs and a work on public speaking. In his humor he is far below Mr. Dooley (Finley Peter Dunne) and George Ade; and, all in all, his reputation will remain chiefly local.

KIN HUBBARD

No so, however, with Frank McKinney (Kin) Hubbard (1868-1930), for he has been known throughout the nation and has been reprinted so long after his death that his fame seems secure. Originally an artist who merged into a humorist, a crackerbox philosopher whose work lies within the main stream of American humor and whose prototype in the preceding century was Josh Billings, Kin Hubbard became one of the most popular of American humorists, yet maintained all the while his distinctive Hoosier characteristics.

The early portion of his life was varied in experience. From his maternal grandfather, Captain John B. Miller, who for years toured the Middle West by wagon with a dramatic stock company, the humorist evidently inherited a love of all things theatrical; and from his father, Thomas Hubbard, the publisher of the Bellefontaine *Examiner,* an important newspaper which had been in the family for a number of years, he must have inherited an interest in the world of journalism. Both interests were to play dominant roles in his life. Kin, as the boy soon came to be known, was born in Bellefontaine, Ohio, on September 1, 1868, was reared by his father and his mother, Sarah Jane (Miller) Hubbard, attended the Bellefontaine public schools, and learned printing in his father's print shop. He varied the school routine by employment. After his father was appointed postmaster with the election of Cleveland, he spent five years in desultory work in the post office, during which period, among other adventures, he toured the South as a silhouette artist, loafed around a theater and a newspaper office in Detroit, and excelled in amateur theatricals back in Bellefontaine.

A letter he had sent to a friend in Indianapolis, which contained some thumbnail sketches, was shown to John H. Holliday, founder of the Indianapolis *News,* who hired Kin in 1891 as the first newspaper artist of Indianapolis. He remained with the *News* three years as a completely self-taught artist, using the chalk-plate process, illustrating, from memory, local happenings, and receiving a salary of twelve dollars a week.

Being ousted by a new managing editor who desired a more versatile artist, Kin returned to Bellefontaine, organized minstrel shows, barnstormed in Atlanta, worked on the Cincinnati *Tribune,* went back home for more minstrel shows, was employed by the Mansfield (Ohio) *News,* barnstormed again with a vaudeville troupe, then worked for a year on the Indianapolis *Sun.* In 1901 he brought this vagrant life to a close when he was rehired by the Indianapolis *News,* where he remained the rest of his life.

At first his work on the *News* was to draw caricatures, many of a political nature. In 1904 while touring Indiana on a campaign train he made sketches of several rural characters; and when, on November 16, one of these was printed in the *News* along with a quip of only two sentences, it attracted the attention of the editor, who asked Hubbard to begin a series, the first of which appeared on December 31 of that same year. Kin christened his character Abe Martin. A daily crude drawing of this ludicrous rustic person, complete with baggy pants, ragged coat, shapeless hat and shoes, button eyes and chin whiskers, placed against a rural background, such as a rail or barbed-wire fence or country store, which carried beneath it a sentence or often two unrelated sentences in the nature of observations on contemporary life and manners, became a great favorite. Almost overnight Hubbard became a sort of Old Man Indiana. Soon the feature was syndicated and eventually appeared regularly in three hundred newspapers across the country. His collections of these drawings, with their accompanying sentences, were issued regularly from their first publication in 1907 as *Abe Martin of Brown County, Indiana* until the appearance of *Abe Martin's Town Pump* in 1929.

He also wrote another syndicated feature, a weekly dialect essay, begun on October 7, 1911, and published in the Saturday edition of the *News,* entitled "Short Furrows"; but although this was popular, it did not arouse the interest attached to Abe Martin. For some time during this period the three men—Hubbard, the poet William Herschell, and the cartoonist "Spin" Williams—formed what was known as the "Idle Ward" on the Indianapolis *News,* which was the pride of the paper. The three worked under a sign provided by Don Herold: "Visitors not allowed to loaf here—we do our own loafing."

In 1905 Hubbard married Josephine Jackson of Indianapolis; with her and their two children he was very happy, preferring his home life to a career of lecturing and making lucrative personal appearances, which he could have followed. He took a trip around the world in 1924. He died, a thorough Hoosier, on December 26, 1930.[31]

Kin Hubbard's compilations of cartoons with their accompanying quips and also collections of his essays were usually issued at the end of the year for Christmas sale, often in almanac form and accompanied by monthly calendars and illustrations by the author. In the typical book of cartoons the two sentences under each cartoon, printed together in the *News,* were divorced by space between them. The Abe Martin Publishing Company, which supposedly issued some of the books, was only a name under which the author published and distributed his own books.

The complete listing of his publications is as follows:

[31] Biographical information about Kin Hubbard comes mostly from the article by Stephen Noland in the *Dictionary of American Biography, Authors Edition,* 9:324, and from Banta, *Indiana Authors and Their Books,* 160-64.

Collection of Indiana Lawmakers and Lobbyists (Indianapolis, 1903); *Caricatures of Law Makers, Clerks and Doorkeepers of the Sixty-Fourth General Assembly of Indiana* (Indianapolis, 1905); *Abe Martin of Brown County, Indiana* (Indianapolis, 1906); *Abe Martin's Almanack* (Indianapolis, 1907; other editions in 1908, 1911, and 1921); *Abe Martin Scrapbook* (n.p., [1908]); *Abe Martin's Brown County Almanack* (Indianapolis, 1909); *Brown County Folks* (Indianapolis, 1910); *Short Furrows* (Indianapolis, 1912); *Back Country Folks* (Indianapolis, 1913); *Abe Martin's Primer. The Collected Writings of Abe Martin and His Brown County, Indiana, Neighbors* (Indianapolis, 1914); *Abe Martin's Sayings and Sketches* (Indianapolis, 1915); *New Sayings, by Abe Martin and Velma's Vow, a Gripping Love Tale by Miss Fawn Lippincut* (Indianapolis, 1916); *Abe Martin's Back Country Sayings* (Indianapolis, 1917); *Abe Martin on the War and Other Things* (Indianapolis, 1918); *Abe Martin's Home Cured Philosophy. The Writings of Abe Martin and His Brown County, Indiana, Neighbors* (Indianapolis, 1919); *Abe Martin, the Joker on Facts* (Indianapolis, 1920); *These Days* (Indianapolis, 1922); *Comments of Abe Martin and His Neighbors* (Indianapolis, 1923); *Fifty Two Weeks of Abe Martin* (Indianapolis, 1924); *Abe Martin on Things in General* (Indianapolis, 1925); *Abe Martin, Hoss Sense and Nonsense* (Indianapolis, 1926); *Abe Martin's Wise Cracks and Skunk Ridge Papers* (Indianapolis, 1927); *Abe Martin's Barbed Wire* (Indianapolis 1928); *Abe Martin's Town Pump* (Indianapolis, 1929); Kin Hubbard (ed.), *A Book of Indiana. The Story of What Has Been Described As the Most Typically American State in the American Democracy Told in Terms of Biography* (Indianapolis, 1929); *Abe Martin's Broadcast, Kin Hubbard Announcing* (Indianapolis, 1930); and *Abe Martin's Wisecracks, by 'Kin' Hubbard, Selected by E. V. Lucas* (London, 1930).[32]

Even though the titles—or the subtitles (some of which are set forth above)—of Hubbard's work indicate his type of material, a rather close analysis is in order. He was a keen observer of his age, and through a natural feeling for contrast he expressed his criticism of life humorously through dialect and drawing and indirect allusion. His formula was simple: under his crude drawing of the rustic Abe Martin engaged in some homely task or simply lounging about, he placed a sentence or two of aphorism, in the nature of social criticism or of close observation of life. Frequently Hubbard remodeled old sayings. "Someone is always taking the joy out of life" becomes "Ther's somebuddy at ever' dinner party what eats all th' celery"; and "All that glitters is not gold" is transmuted into "Th' first thing t' turn green in th' spring is Christmas jewelry."

As a continuing vehicle for his humor, Hubbard created Hoosier rustic characters who appeared frequently in Abe Martin's sayings. They were usually composites, but were easily recognized as true to human nature, both in country and town. Lafe Bud, for example, was a dandy; Miss Fawn Lippincut, a village belle; Miss Tawny Apple was rather daring in her dress and in matters of conduct; Tell Binkley, a failure, pretended to be at home in the world of finance; Mr. and Mrs. Tilford Moots constantly experienced marital difficulties. Utilizing these characters as a means whereby we may laughably recognize our own weaknesses in someone else, Kin polished sentences with telling phraseology which slowly unfolded in their impact in accurately reporting human situations. Thus, when in 1928 several widows were cleared of the charge of

[32] Several of the earlier books of Hubbard have been collectors' items for some time.

murdering their husbands, we find this saying: " 'I'll be glad when I'm found guilty, an' git a new trial, an' go free, an' have this mess over with,' said Mrs. Tilford Moots' niece, whose late husband wuz insured for eighteen thousand dollars." Also, " 'If she comes in t'night I'll try t' catch her in th' mornin' an' tell her,' said Mrs. Tipton Budd when somebuddy left a message for her daughter." This startling and tragic contrast between the older and the younger generations is developed likewise in "Uncle Mort Hickman, nearly ninety-eight, after cuttin' and splittin' four cords o' wood yisterday afternoon, wuz found frozen stiff in th' lane leadin' t' th' house by his four sons, who had been attendin' a billiard tournament."

Such compressed stories, saving the climax for the very last, are Hubbard's chief contribution to American humor. In other ways he trod mostly in the paths worn by the feet of Josh Billings long before.[33]

Yet there were other aspects of his humor. Hubbard took careful note of fads that swept the country, and it would be in character for Abe Martin to remark solemnly that a man down the road fell off a hay wagon and died before anybody could X-ray his teeth. Also, Kin had a sense of the past, as seen in his remark that once people mowed their lawns by means of a borrowed cow. Then, he often successfully parodied the local items found in small-town newspapers, such as "Mrs. Tilford Moots will take her little boy t' see Niagary Falls next week, as he'll soon be too old t' ride fer nothin' "; "Lafe Bud wuz showin' a dollar around today that he saved out o' last week's salary"; "Miss Irma Moots got almost halfway home last night before she was knocked down an' robbed"; and " 'We may buy a little coal t'use in case of sickness, but

[33] See Walter Blair, *Horse Sense in American Humor* (Chicago, 1942), 261-63.

th' engine keeps our sedan het up jest fine,' says Mrs. Art Beasley."[34]

In addition, Hubbard was expert in coining short sayings that caught the public fancy, such as "Of all th' home remedies a good wife is th' best," "Ther's some folks standin' behind the President that ought t' git around where he kin watch 'em," and "What the country needs is a good five-cent cigar." This last remark became even more famous years later when it was repeated by Vice-President Thomas Marshall, an ardent Abe Martin fan. Lastly, it should be noted that Hubbard was clever in his usual device of putting together two unrelated sentences, such as "There was a ole fashioned one-ring weddin' at th' Tiford Moots home t'day. Some folks git credit fer havin' hoss sense that hain't ever had enough money t' make fools o' themselves."

Hubbard protected his reader from his barbs by always directing them at his characters, thus allowing us to laugh at other people instead of having to admit how close home the barb came. And placing his scene in rather remote Brown County, Indiana, an area renowned then and to a certain extent today for its backwoods atmosphere and rusticity, gave the reader an opportunity to look down upon these grotesque figures. Hubbard's longer essays were another vehicle of his humor and often took the form of interviews with his characters, such as "Criminals an' Home Trainin'," by Constable Newt Plum, and "Th' Generous Distribution of Trouble," by Rev. Wiley Tanger.

Hubbard's type of humor is, of course, Middle Western and of the village or of the country. The emphasis is on the Midwestern character and the informality of life.

[34] Quoted in Jennette Tandy, *Crackerbox Philosophers in American Humor and Satire* (New York, 1925), 168.

Thus, he was immediately accepted by his fellow Hoosier and Midwestern authors, such as George Ade. When he proclaimed Will Rogers the country's best humorist, Rogers returned the compliment. Rogers gave his photograph to Hubbard inscribed: "To my friend Kin Hubbard. If I was as humorous as Kin, I would be one of the two funniest men in America."[35] Irvin S. Cobb said, "Thank the Lord for Abe Martin."[36] Franklin P. Adams remarked, ". . . perhaps, years after he is dead, the lofty critics will speak, as they now do of Artemus Ward, of the great and American satire of Kin Hubbard (Abe Martin)."[37] And when early in his career Hubbard drew a caricature of James Whitcomb Riley, he feared that he had offended the poet; but to his surprise and relief, Riley was so pleased with it that he asked for the original, and he penned a tribute to Abe Martin, which Hubbard included in his first Abe Martin book. The first two stanzas are as follows:

> ABE MARTIN!—Dad-burn his old picture!
> P'tends he's a Brown county fixture—
> A kind of comical mixture
>   Of hoss-sense and no sense at all!
> His mouth, like his pipe, 's allus goin'
> And his thoughts, like his whiskers, is flowin'—
> And what he don't know ain't worth knowin'—
>   From Genesis clean to baseball!
>
> The artist, Kin Hubbard, 's so keerless
> He draws Abe 'most eyeless and earless;
> But he's never yit pictured him cheerless
>   Er with fun 'at he tries to conceal—

[35] See Blanche Stillson and Dorothy R. Russo, *Abe Martin—Kin Hubbard. A study of a character and his creator intended primarily as a check list of Abe Martin books* . . . (Indianapolis, 1939), 10.

[36] Quoted in Tandy, *Crackerbox Philosophers*, 170.

[37] *Ibid.*

Whether onto the fence er clean over
A-rootin' up ragweed er clover,
Skeert stiff at some "Rambler" er "Rover"
Er new-fangled automobeel.[38]

But Hubbard's popularity was by no means confined to America. The essayist E. V. Lucas introduced him (but not very successfully) to English readers through a selection of sketches and sayings entitled *Abe Martin's Wisecracks;* and when Hubbard died, sincere tributes appeared in London newspapers.

His death was lamented by cartoonists and editorial writers across the country as the nation's tragedy. Millions felt a sense of personal loss, for they had grown to love Abe Martin and his creator. The well-known cartoon of John T. McCutcheon expressed the national grief in showing all Hubbard's characters bowing, grief-stricken, before Kin's home; and the desire to attend his funeral was so universal that the services were broadcast over a radio network. The flags of both the Indianapolis city hall and the Indiana state capitol were flown at half mast.

The state moved swiftly to carry out plans that were being formulated even before Hubbard's death to perpetuate the memory of this famous native son. Brown County, which Kin had first visited only some eight or ten years after he began the Abe Martin series because he feared—needlessly—that the residents might resent this publicity, was selected as the site for a great state park of 17,000 acres preserving not only the wonders of Brown County scenery but also the name of Kin Hubbard and the characters that made the county famous. In the heart of the Brown County State Park stands the Abe Martin

[38] *Abe Martin of Brown County, Indiana,* by Kin Hubbard (compiled from the Indianapolis *News,* 1906). This and other selections from Kin Hubbard's books are quoted with the permission of Mrs. Hubbard.

Lodge surrounded by twenty guest cabins named for some of Kin's best-known characters, such as Lafe Bud, Ez Pash, Tell Binkley, Fawn Lippincut, Constable Newt Plum, and Squire Marsh Mallow. The park was dedicated in 1932 on what was named Kin Hubbard Ridge.

But, after all, the best memorial to Kin Hubbard remains in the hearts of his readers. At this writing, Abe Martin is still being republished, from old newspaper files, daily in many papers, including the Indianapolis *News,* thirty-one years after the death of his creator.[39]

That is a rigorous test of humor.

THE SHORT STORY

The reader does not need to have pointed out to him the fact that the short story is one of the favorite forms of literature of Indiana authors; yet, in accordance with the limitations previously laid down, we have not found it possible to include in this account stories published in other than the minimum quantity of one collection. In spite of this limitation, however, there are a number of works which clamor for recognition. All but one of the writers of the short story have already been covered elsewhere, for they are essentially producers of poetry, the novel, or humor, and have been treated in these respective sections; and before dealing with the writer who published short stories only—Anna Nicholas—it would be wise to retrace our steps to remind ourselves of the other publications in this field.

The Indiana short story in the Golden Age began with the publication by Maurice Thompson in 1875 of *Hoosier Mosaics,* which are graceful dialect stories and sketches.[40] James Whitcomb Riley made a few contribu-

[39] For further study of Kin Hubbard see the sources cited above.
[40] See above, 315.

tions of stories, but these are negligible. Maurice Francis
Egan wrote three books of stories: *The Life Around Us*
(1885), *A Garden of Roses* (1887), and *How They Worked
Their Way* (1892), all heavily dominated by preoccupation with the Catholic Church.[41] Except for his plays, most
of the writings of George Ade, as before noted, sprang from
his production of the short story, his several collections of
"Stories of the Streets and of the Town" beginning with
the publication of the first volume of that title in 1894
and his many collections of fables commencing with
Fables in Slang in 1900.[42] A writer of unimportant stories
is Charles Fleming Embree, whose *For the Love of Tonita*
(1897) is made up of slight, Western materials.[43] One of
the best volumes of short stories is *Southern Soldier Stories* (1898), by George Cary Eggleston, a volume of realistic accounts of the Civil War of such quality, as before
indicated, that it deserves being revived.[44] This volume is
to be contrasted with the spirited group of pieces on student life at Harvard by Max Ehrmann, *A Farrago* (1898);
and Ehrmann also published several pamphlets containing
stories, such as *The Gay Life* (1925) and *Scarlet Sketches*
(1925), which were sermons against sexual immorality.[45]

The early local color and realism of Mary Hartwell
Catherwood is evident in *The Queen of the Swamp and
Other Plain Americans* (1889).[46] A different kind of
short story, one for juveniles and adults alike, is found in
Charles Major's *The Bears of Blue River* (1901) and
Uncle Tom Andy Bill (1908).[47] Booth Tarkington, in

[41] See above, 320-24.
[42] See above, 444-73.
[43] See above, 338-39.
[44] See above, 279-80.
[45] See above 227-32.
[46] See above, 304.
[47] See above, 346.

addition to turning out prize-winning novels, also penned short stories: *In the Arena. Stories of Political Life* (1905), realistic accounts of the inner workings of a state legislature; *The Fascinating Stranger and Other Stories* (1923), a work somewhat in the tradition of *Seventeen; Women* (1925), presenting the daytime, feminine world of the suburbs; *Little Orvie* (1934), tales of children about the age of seven; *Mr. White, The Red Barn, Hell and Bridewater* (1935), examining life and the hereafter; and *Rumbin Galleries* (1937), reflecting his interest in art.[48] Of course, it might be added that the Penrod books are little more than short stories loosely connected. Another famous novelist, Meredith Nicholson, in *Best Laid Schemes* (1922), writes stories, many of which are on the dim borderline with the familiar essay[49]; and Gene Stratton Porter presents nature stories in *Wings* (1923).[50] Finally, Elmer Davis examines the problem of sexual conduct in *Morals for Moderns* (1930), which, contrary to the impression given by the title, is a collection of stories; and in *Love Among the Ruins* (1935)[51] he paints a picture of the Depression.

Thus the Indiana short story was strong during the Golden Age; the best practitioner was George Ade, with Tarkington deserving second place. But it is a peculiar fact that all these writers were stronger in types other than the short story. Only one person, Anna Nicholas, is known chiefly for the short stories that she wrote.

To the name of Anna Nicholas (1849-1929) is attached mostly local fame, for her two books of short stories evidently did not attract much attention nationally; yet she

[48] See above, 362, 375-76.
[49] See above, 334.
[50] See above, 410.
[51] See above, 431.

was widely respected in Indianapolis for her journalistic ability and literary judgment. In inspiring Hoosier authors she did much for Indiana literature.

Miss Nicholas was born in Meadville, Pennsylvania, in 1849, the daughter of Dr. John and (Rachel) Gardiner Nicholas. After attending public and private schools, she taught a country school, then came to Indianapolis, where, for the remainder of her life, she followed the career of a successful journalist. She was employed first in the business department, then as a reporter and as a member of the editorial staff of the Indianapolis *Journal* from 1881 till 1904, when that newspaper became the Indianapolis *Star;* and she continued with the *Star* as literary editor, editorial writer, book reviewer, and feature writer until her death in Indianapolis on January 29, 1929. With her fifty-three years she probably established a record for continuous service as a newspaper woman. Devotion to her work was her life. In her office at the *Star,* hung with autographed pictures and letters from such authors as Eugene Field, Lew Wallace, James Whitcomb Riley, and Maurice Thompson, she carried on her professional activities and quietly advised young reporters and authors who frequently sought her sympathy and understanding. She helped Riley make his debut as a poet; and as a reader for the Bowen-Merrill Company (now The Bobbs-Merrill Company) she was the first to recognize the literary ability of Charles Major and to advance his cause.[52]

The two books of short stories by Miss Nicholas, *An Idyl of the Wabash, and Other Stories* (Indianapolis, 1898) and *The Making of Thomas Barton* (Indianapolis, 1913), are interesting and pleasant expositions of Midwestern

---

[52] Biographical material on Anna Nicholas comes from the Indiana Biography Series, 3:175-76, 181, 300-2, and from *Who's Who in America,* Vol. 15 (1928-29).

and Hoosier character, but though rather well written are not unusual. The former collection concentrates on Indiana village life with emphasis on the various manifestations of religious belief, the revival spirit, evangelization, and the social importance of churches. The atmosphere of humble town and country life, and the tragedy often underlying it, are portrayed realistically, yet sympathetically. The latter collection of stories also reveals optimism and humor. One of her best is the title story of the first book, "An Idyl of the Wabash," in which the differences between New England and Indiana life are exemplified in the romance and marriage of Callista Rogers, a schoolteacher from Vermont, and the Reverend Mr. Littledale, the Campbellite minister of Honeyport, Indiana.

Besides these collections of short stories Miss Nicholas published two works on the history of Crown Hill Cemetery in Indianapolis. We may say, then, in summary, that here is an author whose journalistic writing and whose personality overshadowed her imaginative endeavors.

THE FAMILIAR ESSAY

That it is often difficult to distinguish between the familiar essay and the formal or more serious essay is a fact of which students of literature are well aware, for the boundary is ill defined. The familiar essay, of course, is usually more personal, somewhat whimsical, and of a lighter touch than the formal essay; yet, the familiar essay may still embody a serious purpose. It is not our intention here to go into the details of the distinction between these two types. Let it suffice to say that although the familiar essay category is not large in the Golden Age of Indiana literature, it is worthy of recording.

We have already seen that several novelists and one humorist each wrote at least one collection of essays. Meredith Nicholson made a significant contribution in three books: *The Valley of Democracy* (1918), *The Man in the Street* (1921), and *Old Familiar Faces* (1929). Perhaps we might include also *The Provincial American* (1912), because of Nicholson's personal touch here evident.[53] In these books one finds mostly familiar essays differing considerably in style, some being of a rambling nature and some containing narratives, enlivened by racy humor, sentimentality, and an expert sense of timing. Through this material there shines forth Nicholson's belief in tolerance, democracy, and the desirability of good self-government. George Ade wrote *Single Blessedness and Other Observations* (1922) and *Notes & Reminiscences* (with John T. McCutcheon, 1940), the titles of which indicate something of the contents.[54] Booth Tarkington penned three books of essays: *Looking Forward and Others* (1926), in which he discusses alcohol, happiness, and immortality, and which contains the delightful "Discovering the Recipe for the Ideal Wife"; *The World Does Move* (1928), reflective and autobiographical pieces analyzing the changes in American society since the Civil War; and *Some Old Portraits* (1939), art essays based on his own art collection.[55] Gene Stratton Porter wrote a group of mediocre, autobiographical essays, *Let Us Highly Resolve* (1927).[56] Finally, Elmer Davis in *Show Window* (1927) attacks popular idols and modern luxury and includes personal sketches, such as "Have Faith in Indiana"; and in *Not to Mention the War* (1940) he deals with mis-

[53] See above, 333.
[54] See above, 472.
[55] See above, 376-77.
[56] See above, 410.

cellaneous subjects, as, for example, the humorous "On Being Kept By a Cat."[57]

Nicholson and Tarkington, then, are the leading writers of the familiar essay in the Golden Age. But there are three authors, not of the quality of Nicholson and Tarkington, writing primarily in this genre, who have yet to be considered.

Juliet Strauss

The first of these is Juliet Virginia Humphries (Mrs. Isaac) Strauss (1863-1918), who built first a local then a national reputation for herself as "The Country Contributor." The daughter of William and Susan Humphries, she was born on January 7, 1863, in Rockville, Indiana, and spent her life there. She attended the local schools, married Isaac Strauss, the publisher and editor of the Rockville *Tribune,* taught school, made contributions to her husband's paper, which eventually were placed in a column called "Squibs and Sayings," and contributed also to the Indianapolis *Journal.* A series of personal essays which she signed as "The Country Contributor" began in the Saturday issues of the Indianapolis *News* in 1908 and became immediately popular. These, along with essays published in the *Woman's Home Companion* and *Ladies Home Journal* under the title of "The Ideas of a Plain Country Woman," received national attention, and she continued to write the rest of her life. She also enjoyed a strong reputation as a lecturer. She died on May 22, 1918.[58]

Mrs. Strauss's one book takes its title and materials from the essays published in the *Ladies Home Journal. The*

[57] See above 431.

[58] The biography of Juliet V. Strauss is from Banta, *Indiana Authors and Their Books,* 308. See also clippings in the Indiana Division of the State Library.

Ideas of a Plain Country Woman (Philadelphia, 1906) contains only seventeen essays, evidently her pick of those published in the magazine. It is not difficult to see why they took such a hold upon the public fancy in their day. Her usual subject is the correct position, attitude, and conduct of women; and, contrary to what one would imagine, here is no suffragist or agitator for women's rights. Quite the contrary. Her constant message to women is of the quiet dignity and worth of the simple home, the merit of household drudgery, the mockery of the fashionable, elegant life with its attendant glitter of materialism and undercurrent of unhappiness and immorality, the respectability and happiness of sincere family life with husband and children, even though spent one cut above poverty, the worth of the spirit, of individuality, of a true marriage of love and companionship—of the use of courage and common sense and old-fashioned contentment with one's lot in life. Speaking of the face of the really good woman in "The Woman Who Wears the Halo" she says:

I think it will always be an old-fashioned face, a little worn with time and toil, a little touched with sorrow, a little lacking in that hard, manly knowledge one sees in the faces of woman-suffrage speakers. Woman's lot will change with changing times, but the conditions for wearing the halo will remain the same. Women may attain a certain freedom of action, but there will be no more freedom of mind. Mind is always free. We have been told that the book, the picture, the piece of music must, if it is to be called true art, be of a great simplicity, that the wayfaring man can understand. So this face that wears the halo must be written in lines that every human being can read. It must not show too many of the refinements of life, or much pride of culture or learning. It must be a rugged face, warmly touched with tenderness, lightly brushed with ladyhood to endear it to the truly refined, but with no affectations nor superfluous elegancies to frighten the timid or repel the humble.[59]

[59] *Ideas of a Plain Country Woman*, 26-27.

In this manner, through a simple, personal, and sincere style, Mrs. Strauss endeared herself to thousands of readers.

A tangible proof of the influence of this writer may be seen at Turkey Run State Park, near Rockville, where in one of the small canyons close to the hotel a large memorial fountain dedicated to Mrs. Strauss was placed in 1921 by the Woman's Press Club of Indiana.[60]

JOHN TARKINGTON

We turn next to a father who had the misfortune to be overshadowed by his son. The son is Booth Tarkington. The father, Judge John Stevenson Tarkington (1832-1923), wrote only two thin books, which he published under the pseudonym of John Steventon, perhaps to avoid an unfortunate comparison with his gifted son.

John Tarkington was born on June 24, 1832, in Centerville, Indiana, his mother being Maria (Slauson) Tarkington and his father, the Reverend Joseph Tarkington, a Methodist circuit rider; and he spent his childhood there. After graduation from Indiana Asbury (now DePauw) University in 1852, he came to Indianapolis and served as secretary to Governor Joseph A. Wright; then he studied law and served as a Republican in the legislature in 1863. He had received the Master of Arts degree from Indiana Asbury in 1855. Organizing the 132d Indiana Volunteers in 1864, he served as captain and provost marshal through the remainder of the Civil War. Returning to civilian life, he was elected in 1870 judge of the Fifth Judicial District, practiced law in Terre Haute and in Indianapolis, and for the last twenty-five years of his life lived in retirement in Indianapolis. His first wife was

[60] "Strauss Memorial Artist, Myra Reynolds Richards," in the Indianapolis *Star,* July 17, 1921, pt. 4, p. 33.

Elizabeth Booth, whom he married in 1857; his second wife was Linda H. Schulz. He died on January 30, 1923.[61]

One of Judge Tarkington's two books grew out of a European tour which he took with Booth; though it is pleasantly written, it is not of much moment. It derives interest partly from the writer's association with his famous son. *The Hermit of Capri* (New York, 1910) is cast in the form of letters to an unnamed correspondent; but embedded in descriptions of the sights and history of the island of Capri is much of the author's philosophizing about such subjects as the nature of truth, religious belief, occultism, transmigration of souls, and sin. *The Auto-Orphan* (Boston, 1913) is a reflective autobiography in which he tells interesting stories of his childhood and youth spent mostly in rural surroundings and ending with the belated recognition of a lost childhood friend who, as a Confederate prisoner of war, was wounded in attempting to escape.

LOUIS HOWLAND

The last writer, Louis Howland (1857-1934), was a newspaperman who wrote religious essays. He was born on June 13, 1857, in Indianapolis, received training in a private school there, and was graduated from Yale University in 1879. For some time he held a position with *Forum* magazine; then in 1892 he returned to Indianapolis and until his death was a member of the staff of the Indianapolis *News,* serving as editor from 1911 to 1934. He was one of the founders of the Indianapolis Literary Club. Mr. Howland died on March 26, 1934, in Indianapolis.[62]

[61] The material on John Tarkington is from the Indiana Biography Series, 1:73-75, and 4:234. Also, see above, 350-51.

[62] Banta, *Indiana Authors and Their Books,* 160.

In addition to some expository materials, he published two books of essays: *Day Unto Day* (Indianapolis, 1911) and *Case and Comment. Meditations of a Layman on the Christian Year* (Indianapolis, 1927). The materials forming these books are of the same type, for the essays were originally printed weekly in the Indianapolis *News* under the title "Case and Comment," the second book being a collection from a single year. These essays come close to the status of the formal essay, since they are often expository of fundamental Christian doctrine, as in "The Advent Message," "A Christmas Talk," "The Future Life," "Epiphany," and "Holy Week and Good Friday." These subjects are presented as seen by a layman, and there is a somewhat personal air in many of the pieces, as in "The Lust for Fame," in which the author discusses the hollowness of much human aspiration, and in "Growing Old," which presents a careful optimism. One must agree, at least, that here is a devoutly Christian newspaper editor.

DRAMA

Of the four more specialized types of literature of the Golden Age of Hoosier letters—humor, the short story, the familiar essay, and the drama—the last named was participated in more freely by more authors than any other. Many Hoosiers wrote plays, but only three can be designated as playwrights primarily, Joseph Arthur, William O. Bates, and Jackson Boyd. George Ade and Booth Tarkington wrote many successful dramatic productions but because of the larger quantity of their other publications they cannot be classified as dramatists. Therefore, before treating the three playwrights not before discussed, it would be well to survey briefly the history of the drama in the Golden Age, recalling those plays having previously been dealt with elsewhere.

Lew Wallace began the work of this period with his single closet drama in blank verse, *Commodus* (1876), having Roman history as its subject. It is a long jump, then, to the distinguished poet and dramatist, William Vaughn Moody, who published the first of his trilogy of verse dramas, on the subject of sin, *The Masque of Judgment,* in 1900, following it with *The Fire-Bringer* (1904), and leaving the third of the trilogy, "The Death of Eve," unfinished at his death. Moody's well-known prose plays, appearing next, were *The Great Divide* (1909) and *The Faith Healer* (1909), both continuing his treatment of the subject of sin.[63]

In 1902 George Ade commenced production of his thirteen published plays and musical shows (to say nothing of several which were staged but never printed) with the musical comedy, *The Sultan of Sulu* (1902), which was followed by the musical plays: *Peggy from Paris* (1903), *The Sho-Gun* (1904), *The Slim Princess* (1907), and *The Fair Co-Ed* (1908). Some of these musical plays were in the nature of satires. Ade's nonmusical shows, which were all comedies or farces, were *The County Chairman* (1924), *The College Widow* (1924), *Just Out of College* (1924), *Father and the Boys* (1924), and also four one-act plays: *Marse Covington* (1918), *The Mayor and the Manicure* (1923), *Nettie* (1923), and *Speaking to Father* (1923). Ade's plays, therefore, were light, usually very light, with only a modicum of serious thought.[64]

Booth Tarkington did not write any musical shows; otherwise his plays were much the same general kind

[63] See above, 240-48.
[64] See above, 464-70.

as Ade's.[65] Beginning with *The Guardian* (written with Harry Leon Wilson, 1904), which presented the inimitable Hoosier, Daniel Voorhees Pike, who continually disparaged Europe and bragged ridiculously about Indiana, the playwright continued with other farces: *The Country Cousin* (written with Julian Street, 1916), *Clarence* (1921), *The Intimate Strangers* (1921), *The Wren* (1922), *Tweedles* (written with Wilson, 1924), *How's Your Health* (with Wilson, 1930), *Mister Antonio* (1935), and also five one-act plays—*Ghost Story* (1922), *The Trysting Place* (1923), *Bimbo, the Pirate* (1926), *Station YYYY* (1927), and *The Travelers* (1927). Only three of Tarkington's plays contained much in the way of solid matter: *The Gibson Upright* (with Wilson, 1919), which was anticommunist propaganda, and the two propaganda radio plays, *The Help Each Other Club* (1934) and *Lady Hamilton and Her Nelson* (1945). One does not go, therefore, to Tarkington or to Ade for essentially thought-provoking drama; indeed, Tarkington never really considered himself a dramatist. Yet, almost all their plays were successful on the stage, some establishing record runs.

The next dramatist was Max Ehrmann, four of whose plays are much more serious and idealistic, yet they made small lasting impression.[66] These were *The Light of the Sun* (1910), *The Wife of Marobius* (1911), *Jesus: A Passion Play* (1915), and *David and Bathsheba* (1917), his best work. Ehrmann also wrote *Farces: The Bank Robbery; The Plumber* (1927) and the comedy, *Eternal Male and Female* (1949). William Dudley Foulke wrote *Maya. A Drama* (1911),[67] a closet play in verse, based on his

[65] See above, 364-65, 373-75, 377.

[66] See above, 230.

[67] See above, 236.

novel of the same title; Meredith Nicholson wrote only one play, a three-act comedy, with Kenyon Nicholson, *Honor Bright* (1923).[68] The last writer of plays was Test Dalton, who penned *The Mantle of Lincoln* (1922) and farces, like *Adam's Apple* (1926).[69]

The above listing, lengthy as it may be, still does not include the many dramatizations of novels of the Golden Age by persons other than the novelists, such as that of Major's *When Knighthood Was in Flower*, by Paul Kester. Nor does it include unpublished dramatizations of novels by the novelists, like that of *The Gentleman from Indiana,* by Tarkington. And it is evident that these Indiana dramatists wrote mostly to entertain. The only playwrights who had much to say were William Vaughn Moody and Max Ehrmann. Ade and Tarkington provided the greatest quantity—and also quality—of pure entertainment, the musical shows of Ade giving an added popular touch. The greatest Indiana dramatist obviously is Moody, who came near to writing a masterpiece of literature in his trilogy on the subject of sin and who contributed the greatest single play written by a Hoosier during the Golden Age, *The Great Divide.* The best plays portraying the Indiana scene and Hoosier character are Ade's *The County Chairman* and *The College Widow,* even though both are exaggerated. Consideration of the following three dramatists does not force us to modify these generalizations.

JOSEPH ARTHUR

Joseph Arthur was one of the most popular and successful American playwrights of the 1880's and 1890's, but now both the author and his plays are largely for-

[68] See above, 334.
[69] See above, 393.

gotten. He had a decided leaning toward melodrama, believing that was what the majority of theater-goers wanted. Arthur's real name was Arthur Hill Smith; he was born in Centerville, Indiana, in 1848 (or 1849), the youngest of the three sons of the Reverend John C. and Margaret (Hill) Smith. His father was a Methodist circuit rider, who served many Indiana churches before illness forced his retirement from the active ministry in the 1850's, at which time the family moved to Indianapolis. The father was the author of *Reminiscences of Early Methodism in Indiana* (Indianapolis, 1879).

Young Arthur grew up in Indianapolis, and it remained his official residence the remainder of his life. A youthful ambition to become an actor was born after witnessing performances at the old Metropolitan Theater in Indianapolis. According to his own statement, he served two years in an Army regiment during the Civil War, then transferred to the Navy, but his name does not appear in the official records, and his age would have precluded such service. We next find him with a circus, but when that folded up, leaving him stranded, his father persuaded him to enter college, but he remained for only one term. His interest in the stage had continued, and in 1875 his first play, "Colorado," was produced in Indianapolis; it was not a success. Three years later "The Great Encounter" was produced in New York and proved more successful than his first play.

The next few years were spent touring the British Isles and the Far East with a minstrel show and an opera company, after which he returned to New York. In the meantime, he had married the former actress, Charlotte Cobbe, who aided him in his writing. His next play, "The Still Alarm" (1887) proved to be a hit; it was soon followed by his greatest success, *Blue Jeans,* the only one of his plays still available in published form. It was copyrighted by the author in 1888, and the copyright was renewed by his wife in 1915. An acting edition was published by Samuel French in 1940. This thriller has held many an audience in New York and elsewhere on the edge of their seats.

The story, laid in Rising Sun, Indiana, traces the tempestuous love of June, the girl from the poor house, and the rich city boy, Perry Bascom. Perry, tricked into a bogus marriage to Sue Eudaly, flees from her and marries June. But Ben Boone, who is in love with Sue and is her accomplice, becomes jealous of Perry, knocks him unconscious and throws his body onto a saw band, then starts the machinery, which moves the hero slowly toward the buzzing saw. He is saved in the nick of time by June, who breaks down the door. Perry, now threatened by Sue with arrest, is gone for three years, then returns, and there is a happy ending. The characters are folksy Hoosier types.

Blue Jeans is characteristic of Arthur's plays in that he introduces a piece of machinery that sweeps the play and the audience into an exciting climax. In "The Still Alarm" there was a speeding fire engine; in "Corncracker" (1893) there was an elevator. In all his melodramas complex mechanical and scenic effects were part of the plan. His characters were chosen from people that had come within the scope of his own observation. Other plays were "The Cherry Pickers" (1896); "On the Wabash" (1898); "The Salt of the Earth" (1898); and "Lost River" (1900). The last named had an Indiana setting and utilized real Hoosier characters. Arthur's career as a successful playwright was cut short by his death in New York City on February 19, 1906.[70]

[70] Material on Joseph Arthur was obtained from an unpublished biography of the playwright written by William G. Sullivan, in the Indiana Divi-

WILLIAM OSCAR BATES

William Oscar Bates (1852-1924) was a minor drama-tist who lingered about the periphery of literary attain-ment and could not quite step into the glowing light of the inner circle. He was born on September 19, 1852, in Harrisburg, Fayette County, Indiana, was educated in the public schools there, attended Northwestern Christian (now Butler) College, and received the Ph.B. degree in 1875 from Cornell University. He did journalistic work from 1877 to 1899, being associated with the Indian-apolis *Journal,* the Cincinnati *News-Journal,* the St. Paul *Pioneer Press,* the New York *World,* and the New York *Commercial Advertiser;* then he returned to Indianapolis in 1900 to write plays. His death occurred on October 29, 1924.[71] He was one of the leading figures in the Little Theatre Society of Indiana, which was organized in 1915 to produce both proved and untried plays, to encourage Hoosier playwrights, and to inspire interest in the theater in Indiana. His preface to the volume of *Indiana Prize Plays, As Presented by The Little Theatre Society of Indi-ana During the Season of 1922-23* (Indianapolis, 1924) indicates his strong part in this movement. The Little Theatre Society produced a number of the plays of Hoosier dramatists, such as Tarkington and George Ade, but these were usually one-act plays. It is unfortunate for Indiana literature that the movement resulted mostly in the writing of one-act plays, the greater part of them not too substantial in character, and that the interest engendered so strongly for a time was soon diminished.

Bates published several one-act plays in *Drama,* wrote and produced some plays that were never printed, and secured publication of only two.

sion of the State Library, and from articles in the Indianapolis *News,* December 22, 1900, p. 9, and February 20, 1906, p. 1.

[71] Banta, *Indiana Authors and Their Books,* 19.

Jacob Leisler. A Play of Old New York (New York, 1913) is Bates's longest play—four acts and an epilogue—and gives in good dramatic form, following history closely, an account of how in 1689 Jacob Leisler, a German merchant, was proclaimed governor of New York by the people, in a rebellion against the regime of the Stuart kings of England, the last of whom, the hated James II, had just been deposed by William of Orange. But even with William securely on the throne, the changing currents of politics turn against Leisler, and his enemies eventually hang him. The play, though far from brilliant in execution, contains good characterization, suspense, action, and careful plotting. Probably it suffered in its reception from the public's lack of knowledge of the historic Leisler and also from their lack of interest in history. *Polly of Pogue's Run* (New York, 1917) is a slender one-act patriotic composition, the action taking place in the office of Indiana's Governor Morton on May 20, 1863, when a Copperhead uprising has just been quelled. The character of Morton is presented in its most attractive aspects as he goes effectively about his business of running the state and aiding the Union cause, dealing forgivingly with the Southern sympathizers, showing a misguided judge the error of his ways, and braving the pistol of a would-be girl assassin. "Where Do We Go From Here?" printed in the volume of *Indiana Prize Plays* mentioned above, is a clever farce—a satire on reformers, probably liquor reformers—in presenting an organization which has been instrumental in getting tea and tea-drinking outlawed. The play is overdone, however. Thus, Bates's plays are evidence of the dramatist groping, but not quite finding.

JACKSON BOYD

The last dramatist, Jackson Boyd (1862-1920), wrote only one play, a poetic drama, and that a strange sort of thing. Boyd, the son of William F. Boyd of Kentucky and Catherine (Eller) Boyd of North Carolina, was born in Greencastle, Indiana, on March 28, 1862. His father, a Union soldier in the Civil War, died of starvation at Andersonville prison; and the boy, growing up in poverty, took up a trade, but he educated himself by wide reading and then held several teaching positions in Indiana and in other states. At about the age of thirty-five he decided to become a lawyer, and after studying, he practiced in Greencastle the rest of his life. He served four years in the Indiana legislature. He established a reputation as a man of honesty, principle, and generosity, and as a self-made scholar. After hard labor on a philosophical book, *The Human Situation in Nature* (Chicago, 1921), he died in Greencastle on March 16, 1920.[72]

To say that *The Unveiling. A Poetic Drama in Five Acts* (New York, 1915) is a weird production is an understatement. This long allegorical and unactable play, in mediocre blank verse, covering twenty-three years of action, is a fantastic attempt to explain the philosophical and theological questions as old as man, such as what is truth, what is reality, what is life, and why do we live.

[72] Material on Jackson Boyd was obtained from Indiana State Bar Association, *Proceedings,* 1920, pp. 149-51; and the *Legislative and State Manual of Indiana,* 1905, p. 138.

Literature Since The Golden Age

8
POETRY

THE BEST-KNOWN FIGURES in Indiana literature had begun writing by 1921; and lists of Hoosier authors who commenced publishing after that date include no one of such prominence as James Whitcomb Riley, William Vaughn Moody, Edward Eggleston, Lew Wallace, Booth Tarkington, or George Ade. Still, the production of interesting books continued steadily. Those who attracted the most attention in the period from 1922 until the outbreak of the Second World War in 1939 were the poets Sister Mary Madeleva, E. Merrill Root, Margaret E. Bruner, and Marguerite Young, and the novelists McCready Huston, Charles E. Scoggins, and Robin E. Spencer, to say nothing of Jeannette Covert Nolan and Bertita Harding, who are both well known primarily for types of writing other than the novel.

We shall follow the procedure established in dealing with other periods in presenting here a chapter on poetry, then a chapter on the novel. There was no worth-while production of the short story, the familiar essay, or the drama by writers who began publishing after 1921.

ETHEL ARNOLD TILDEN

We commence with a woman who claims only a single modest book of verse. Ethel Arnold (Mrs. Francis C.) Tilden (1876-1950) was born in Greencastle, Indiana, on February 29, 1876, was educated in the public schools, in

Asbury Academy, and received the Ph.B. degree from DePauw University in 1897. After she had taught school for a time, she married, on September 13, 1900, a classmate, Francis C. Tilden, who later became professor of comparative literature at DePauw; the couple spent nearly all their married life in Greencastle. Three children were born to them. Mrs. Tilden wrote poetry, stories, and articles for various magazines and also lectured. In 1932 she was made the first poet laureate of the Indiana Federation of Clubs. Except for her one collection she was known mostly for the poetry of the oratorio, "The Evangel of the New World," which was performed in 1935 in commemoration of the 150th anniversary of the founding of Methodism. Her death occurred on October 31, 1950, at the home of her daughter in Wilmette, Illinois.[1]

In *Quest and Acceptance and Other Poems* (Westport, Connecticut, 1925) the reader finds a sensitive and delicate soul, searching for beauty and perfection in life. There are influences of Wordsworth discernible in the poet's quest for beauty in the out-of-doors, in the countrysides of both England and Indiana, and of Amy Lowell, in her attraction to imagism. She finds beauty in old houses, gardens, and market stalls, in moods—in the life of the imagination. Much of her work is descriptive, as in "Indiana Beech Woods," but she can be satirical, as in "Sophistry," and often she plumbs a surprising depth, becoming poignant and almost bitter, as in "Enough." "Isolation" expresses the solitude of the human spirit. Mrs. Tilden's poems are all short, and she uses well various verse forms and rhyme patterns. One wishes that she had produced more than this one collection.

[1] The biography of Mrs. Tilden comes from miscellaneous sources but mostly from Jerome Hixson, "She Will Go Sure," in *DePauw Alumnus*, December, 1950, p. 2.

Sister Mary Madeleva

The next poet was much more prolific. For in the work of Sister Mary Madeleva (1887-   ) one finds a very articulate writer who has published twelve volumes of poetry, to say nothing of other works.

Sister Mary Madeleva, whose secular name was Mary Evaline Wolff, came of German stock, all her grandparents having been born in Germany and having emigrated to Wisconsin, where they became pioneers. Sister Madeleva was born on May 24, 1887, in Cumberland, Wisconsin, the daughter of a harness maker, August Wolff, and his wife, Lucy (Arntz) Wolff. She was educated in the local schools, then attended the University of Wisconsin for a year and received her B.A. degree in 1909 from St. Mary's College, Notre Dame, Indiana. Other degrees received were the M.A. in 1918 from the University of Notre Dame, the Ph.D. in 1925 from the University of California at Berkeley, the Doctor of Literature degree from Manhattan College in New York City in 1938, and the LL.D. from Indiana University in 1958. In addition, she attended Oxford University in England in 1933-34. She has taught in various academies and colleges, has held administrative posts in education, and has lectured in the United States, Canada, and at Oxford University. Her travels have included Europe and the Holy Land. She is a member of the Sisters of the Congregation of the Holy Cross and from 1934 to 1961 was president of St. Mary's College, Notre Dame.[2] Here then is a poet who is very well educated and who should be prepared to write good verse.

The unprejudiced observer may well agree that she has

[2] Biography of Sister Mary Madeleva was found in various sources, particularly *The American Catholic Who's Who* (Grosse Pointe, Michigan), 1958-59, p. 303. For further information, see Sister Madeleva's interesting autobiography, *My First Seventy Years* (New York, 1959).

fulfilled this promise. In her first volume, *Knights Errant and Other Poems* (New York, 1923), the touch is not quite so sure as in her later collections, but the book marked a strong new voice in Hoosier poetry. There is some nature verse here, but the subject matter is mostly religious, one of the best pieces being "A Young Girl Writes to Her Father." The father, one discovers, is God, and the girl is longing for heaven. There are several good sonnets. *Penelope and Other Poems* (New York, 1927) received some reviews which noted that Sister Madeleva had talent for composing lyric poetry and a clear, simple, and beautiful utterance, but that she was still a novice in writing. It may be added that the book contains much love poetry, both secular and religious, and that there is a sure touch in the construction of her Italian sonnets. *A Question of Lovers and Other Poems* (Paterson, New Jersey, 1935) continues her simple but beautiful style and presents again love, but with much emphasis on the spiritual, as in echoes of Bible stories. There are accents of her travels in England and elsewhere in Europe. Along with her free verse are more of her well-wrought sonnets. As the title implies, *The Happy Christmas Wind and Other Poems* (Paterson, New Jersey, 1936) is a Christmas issue; it contains some poetry published previously. All the material here is religious. A similar small volume is *Christmas Eve and Other Poems* (Paterson, New Jersey, 1938), likewise religious in tone. *Gates and Other Poems* (New York, 1938) reflects her travels in the Holy Land and elsewhere, her continuing concern with religion, and her sensitive musings.

Selected Poems (New York, 1939) is her first publication of length and reprints much material which had appeared in previous volumes. In its more than a hundred pages one finds a collection of graceful lyrics and sonnets, again many of them religious, full of energy and warmth. *Four Girls and Other Poems* (Paterson, New Jersey, 1941) was written to commemorate the founding at Le Mans, France, on August 4, 1841, of a new religious congregation—the Marianites, Sisters of the Holy Cross. *A Song of Bedlam Inn and Other Poems* (Paterson, New Jersey, 1946) is a small book of lyrics, containing the interesting "To a Very Old Harness-Maker (My Father)."

Collected Poems (New York, 1947) reprints many earlier poems and some new ones in which she demonstrates a perfection of form along with an excellent technique. It includes the dedication, "To My Favorite Author," reprinted from *Knights Errant and Other Poems,* as follows:

> Dear God,
> Herewith a book do I inscribe and send
> To Thee Who art both its Beginning and its End;
> A volume odd,
> Bound in some brief, allotted years,
> And writ in blood and tears;
> Fragments of which Thou art the perfect whole
> Book of my Soul
>
> Break Thou the sealing clod
> And read me, God![3]

American Twelfth Night and Other Poems (New York, 1955), dedicated to Saint Mary's College, Notre Dame, is made up entirely of religious poetry, much of which had previously appeared in her books. *The Four Last Things. Collected Poems* (New York, 1959) repeats with minor changes the dedication, "To My Favorite Author." It contains a preface in which the author says that this is

[3] From *Four Last Things,* copyright by Sister Mary Madeleva, C. S. C., 1923, 1927, 1935, 1936, 1938, 1941, 1946, 1951, 1954, 1955, 1956, 1958, 1959. Used with the permission of The Macmillan Company.

the record of her writing of verse while she has been a nun over a period of forty-five years and remarks that "I have never had leisure for writing, save such times as one takes to recover from flu, winter colds, fatigue, if these can be counted leisure."[4] This volume stands as the most complete edition of her works and groups poems under the headings of some previous volumes.

Sister Mary Madeleva's poems, all short and simple in construction and thought, reveal a person of a very sensitive spirit and great depth who is closely observant of life and who is always searching for a closer communion with God. Her poetry is usually cast in conventional form, although some free verse is in evidence; she is at her best in her sonnets, which are often flawless. She seldom says much that is particularly new, but she is one of the best of the American nun poets and is one of the leading Indiana writers of the twentieth century.[5]

In addition to her verse, Sister Madeleva has also published other materials: *Chaucer's Nuns and Others Essays* (New York, 1925); *Pearl. A Study of Spiritual Dryness* (New York, 1925), which is a careful consideration of the medieval poem, *The Pearl; Addressed to Youth* (Paterson, New Jersey, 1944), convocation addresses for the students of St. Mary's College; *A Lost Language and Other Essays on Chaucer* (New York, 1951); and her interesting autobiography, *My First Seventy Years* (New York, 1959).

[4] P. viii.

[5] When asked by students what books are best to read as helps in writing, Sister Madeleva's answer was, "The Bible, the Oxford Dictionary, seed catalogues," meaning the words of God, of man, and of nature. *My First Seventy Years*, 148.

E. Merrill Root

Another rather prolific poet is Edward Merrill Root (1895-   ), although he did not produce as many volumes as did Sister Madeleva. Son of Edward Tallmadge and Georgiana (Merrill) Root, he was born on January 1, 1895, in Baltimore, Maryland, received the B.A. degree from Amherst College in 1917, attended the University of Missouri 1917-18, rendered service in the Friends' Reconstruction Unit in France, and attended Andover Theological Seminary 1919-20. He became assistant professor of English at Earlham College, in Richmond, Indiana, in 1920, was advanced to professor in 1930, and retired from active teaching in June, 1960, receiving at the time from the Earlham Board of Trustees a citation for "faithful and meritorious service." In addition to studying and teaching his career has included positions as one of the editors of *The Measure* and *The Poetry Folio*. He has studied with Robert Frost and Alexander Meiklejohn, has lectured at various universities, and has taken part in radio and television programs.[6]

The greater part of Root's first book, *Lost Eden and Other Poems* (New York, 1927), was written after he began to teach at Earlham College. It is a collection of pieces, mostly short, which give evidence of a sensitive spirit, seeking for beauty and spiritual values. His verse is rhymed in various patterns, and he does well with the sonnet. Some poems evidence more maturity in form and diction than others. Here are a strong appreciation of nature; fancy, as in "The Unicorn"; furious protest, as

[6] The life of E. Merrill Root was obtained from *The Biographical Dictionary of Contemporary Poets—The Who's Who of American Poets* (New York, 1938), p. 408; William Murray Hepburn (ed.), *Who's Who in Indiana* (Hopkinsville, Kentucky, 1957), p. 188; and *The Earlhamite*, July, 1960, p. 3.

in the description of the torture-death by whites of a
Negro in "Southern Holiday"; anti-war feeling, as in
"The Mountains of Skeletons"; and sympathy for the
underdog, as in "Suicide: Out of a Job." *Bow of Burning
Gold* (Chicago, 1929) marks an improvement in quality.
One sees a strong cosmological interest; the facetious,
as in "Noah"; rebellion against the present, wherein he
desires a new America with a second Columbus who will
arise and rediscover America; the historic, as in "Tren-
ton"; and sympathy with the underdog, the victim of
the machine world. Root's touch here is surer, the poems
tend to be longer, and his diction is often so well chosen
and the lines so carefully balanced that the reader is much
moved.

Before the Swallow Dares (Chicago, 1947) received
more attention and better reviews than his other two
volumes; and the praise is deserved, for this is the best of
the three. The subjects cover nature, philosophy, humor,
love, history—as in "God's Fool (Columbus, Dying)" and
"MacArthur on Luzon"—stories told with a thrilling zest,
as "Ballad of the Wolf Den," which recounts how Israel
Putnam crawled into a wolf's den and shot the killer, and
"The Iron Door" (the fight of the "Monitor" and "Merri-
mac"), tender poems written to those he loves, like "Your
Candles Shine" (on his daughter's tenth birthday), and
sonnets of pure beauty. The life of the mind, the senses,
and the heart blossoms in fresh bouquets, astonishing in
their variety and richness. The verse is mostly smooth,
descriptive, and tender. Indiana poetry of the period produced nothing better than this collection. One of the best
examples is the following sonnet:

Reveille

Death does not only waken us I think
To strange horizons past the world we know,
Where new dimensions spread, new powers grow . . .
First, first, we waken on that awful brink
To retrospection of the days that sink
Behind us in the world from which we go:
Fragrance of bread, a river's lapsing flow,
Sunrise of April in the redbud's pink . . .
Limned in that mighty moment we perceive
The wonder and the poignance and the awe,
The grief and glory, of the life we leave,
Which,—seeing too close and clear,—we never saw.
Breathless, at last we breathe; eyeless, we find
Dying the eyes which living kept us blind.[7]

Root also produced other types of books. *The Way of All Spirit* (Chicago, 1940) gives something of his philosophy of life and religious views. *Frank Harris* (New York, 1947), an appreciative biography; *Collectivism on the Campus. The Battle for the Mind in American Colleges* (New York, 1955); and *Brainwashing in the High Schools. An Examination of Eleven American History Textbooks* (New York, 1958) complete the list of his writings.

MARY E. BOSTWICK

A much different sort of poet is the newspaperwoman, Mary E. Bostwick (1886-1959), for she wrote only humor—of the slapstick sort. Indeed, her verse is mere doggerel, but reading it is usually a hilarious experience.

Miss Bostwick was born on February 11, 1886, in Denver, Colorado, and attended school there but abandoned formal education in the second year of high school because of difficulty with mathematics and went to an

---

[7] P. 71. Reprinted by permission of Hendricks House, Inc., New York, which now holds the copyright on *Before the Swallow Dares*.

Episcopalian school in Kentucky. She began newspaper work on the Denver *Post*, migrated to the Kansas City *Post* in 1913, and left it that same year for the Indianapolis *Sun*. She changed to the Indianapolis *Star* in 1914, where she spent the remainder of her professional career, though she took a leave of absence during World War I to work with Base Hospital 32 in Contrexeville, France. For some thirty years she covered the news in Indiana for the *Star*, doing feature articles, and at times she even helped make the news. She was that kind of person perhaps best described as a rugged individualist, for she disliked cosmetics and the evidences of femininity, loved auto racing, and was an aviation enthusiast. She was respected in her field for clear prose and flashing wit; her column, "As the Day Begins," had a wide following. She died on July   '959.[8]

She is remembered now, however, mostly for her "Last Page Lyrics," which were published for years, as the title indicates, on the last page of the *Star*. A collection of them was issued under this title (Indianapolis, [1929]). The book is ephemeral, but the reader will get many a laugh from its stories and commentary on life. She uses as subjects peculiar and ludicrous happenings which she gleaned from the newspapers and then magnified. For example, she writes of a soup competition among six New York hotel chefs, ground-hog day, burglaries, and the fine levied on a Milwaukee woman for kissing a policeman. As her poetry made readers chuckle over their morning coffee, so also can the reader today obtain much enjoyment from her verse, which in one sense, is dated, and in another is timeless in appeal.

[8] The biography of Mary Bostwick comes from the unsigned sketch in *Last Page Lyrics* and miscellaneous sources.

Edith Lombard Squires

In contrast to Miss Bostwick, Edith Lombard (Mrs. Walter) Squires (1884-1939) published two books of serious poetry, which received favorable comment. Daughter of Josiah and Alice (Rathbun) Lombard, Mrs. Squires was born in New York City and was educated at the New York Collegiate Institute. She moved from Zanesville, Ohio, to Richmond, Indiana, in 1924. There she married Walter Squires, who was building inspector of the Richmond schools, and five children were born to them. She was a member of the Friends Church and was the poet laureate of the Indiana Federation of Clubs. She died at her home in Richmond on June 2, 1939.[9]

Her first book of verse, *Sails That Sing* (New York, 1928), gave excellent promise of a rich poetic utterance. The poems show strong feeling, good dramatic power, and clear imagery, particularly in the Shakespearean sonnet. A sensitive awareness of life is evident. *Luminous Dust* (Dallas, Texas, 1939) continues her lovely sonnets, now in a sequence, and includes other types of verse, such as the narrative. The collection is well named, for she sings of the common dust which is luminous in its beauty— sometimes the dust of the garden, star dust, or the dust of the heart, glistening in sadness or in dreams. Here is beauty in many forms—of fields, old houses, of nature, of simple emotions, embracing a brave philosophy that accepts life in all its manifestations.

Straight Through the Western Gate. A Play Dealing with Three Episodes in the Life of George Rogers Clark (Richmond, Indiana, [1928]) follows the historical narrative and is written in appreciation of the services of Clark

---

[9] There is little information available on the life of Mrs. Squires. What I have found was obtained from the Indiana Biography Series and from *The Biographical Dictionary of Contemporary Poets*, 454.

in winning the Northwest for the United States. Other
plays of Mrs. Squires are as follows: *Ten Little Plays for
Little Tots* (Boston, 1930), *The Christmas Shadow*
(Franklin, Ohio, 1931), *Eleven Plays for Little Children*
(New York, 1931), *Turning the Corner* (Lebanon, Ohio,
1931), *Six Little Plays of Early Quaker Life* (Franklin,
Ohio, 1932), and *The Topaz of Ethiopia* (Boston, 1939).

HENRY BRENNER

The Reverend Henry Brenner, O.S.B. (1881-   ),
published more verse than did Mrs. Squires. It is difficult
to list many biographical facts about Father Brenner, for
he has lived the life of a recluse. He was born in Louisville, Kentucky, on April 21, 1881, and from 1896 to 1907
was a student at St. Meinrad's Abbey, St. Meinrad, Indiana, where he was ordained a priest in the Roman Catholic Church in 1907. He then remained at St. Meinrad's,
where he served in several capacities, such as novice master, teacher of expression, director of dramatics, and director of the Abbey symphony orchestra.[10]

Most of Father Brenner's publications are booklets
printed by the Abbey press; the titles indicate the subject
matter. *Liberty Aflame, 1773-1781. An Epic Narrative
Setting Forth the Heroes and Battles of the American
Revolution* (St. Meinrad, 1931) is in rather good blank
verse. *Christ and Caesar. A Drama of Political and Spiritual Combat in the Days of Ancient Rome* (St. Meinrad,
1932) is a curious play in blank verse with the lines interspersed with description and exposition, the whole somewhat mystifying the reader. *Faithful Adelaide. A Tale
of Two Hearts* (St. Meinrad, 1932) retells in blank verse

---

[10] Information concerning the Reverend Henry Brenner was obtained
from catalogues of St. Meinrad's Abbey, from the registrar of the Abbey,
and from one of his former students, Father Francis Kull.

the old tale of Griselda found in Boccaccio. *The House We Live In* (St. Meinrad, 1932) is a social comedy of animals, in blank verse, interspersed with description, satirizing government, politics, the judiciary, and private citizens. It is not very effective.

In spite of its title, *Modern Canterbury Tales* (St. Meinrad, 1932) is not an attempt to imitate Chaucer; instead the author presents, in rather mediocre blank verse and by means of allegory, an analysis of world social conditions. Old Father World is depicted as sick because he has not lived according to nature, and friends are called on to tell stories in order to give him moral remedies. The book is introductory to its prose sequel, *Back to Christ or The Christian's Rule-Book* (St. Meinrad, 1932). *The Poetry Contest. A Dramatic Contest in Three Acts with a Prologue and Epilogue* (St. Meinrad, 1932) is a dramatic phantasy in blank verse telling the story of how on a camping trip a merchant, a banker, and an heir scoff at poetry read by their guide, a learned man, who then gets them to agree to sponsor a poetry contest for thirty poets to be judged by ten critics. The poems are divided into "modern," "psychologic," and "noble"; the whole is a satire on modern poetry. *Titanic's Knell. A Satire on Speed* (St. Meinrad, 1932) is on the sinking of the "Titanic." In general, then, Brenner's poetry is interesting, but it is not distinguished. His best work is probably *Liberty Aflame*. His books appear not to have enjoyed wide circulation.

In addition to verse, Father Brenner also published the following works: *Messages of Music. Mood Stories of the Great Masterpieces* (Boston, 1923); *The Ruler with the Ruled; or The Love of King Manuel, an Allegory on Daily Communion* (St. Meinrad, 1927); *A Guide for Modern Life* (St. Meinrad, 1935); *The Art of Living Joy-*

fully (St. Meinrad, 1942); *The Courageous Shall Conquer* (St. Meinrad, 1943); *Seek and You Shall Find* (St. Meinrad, 1944); *Brother to Brother* (St. Meinrad, 1947); *Our Loving Father* (St. Meinrad, 1947); and *As Others See Us* (St. Meinrad, 1948).

MARGARET E. BRUNER

The next poet, a housewife of New Castle, Indiana, Margaret E. Baggerly (Mrs. Vate) Bruner (1886-   ) has published nine books of very good verse. Born at West Fork, in Crawford County, on September 25, 1886, the daughter of Vardamon David and Henrietta Shannon (Saunders) Baggerly, she was educated in the public schools and at a business college in Louisville, Kentucky. She came to New Castle in 1913 and was married to Vate Bruner, a local businessman, on October 7, 1916. She has lived in New Castle ever since, being employed at times as a secretary and stenographer and writing a weekly column for the New Castle *News Republican*. Her husband died in 1947.

She was the first poet laureate of the Indiana Federation of Poetry Clubs and poet laureate of the Indiana Poetry Society for twelve years. Various other honors have come to her. Her verse has appeared in more than 160 publications in America and England and in a large number of anthologies, and she has been awarded more than forty cash prizes, such as a first prize for the best lyric of the year in the *American Poetry Magazine* in 1947. Her poetry has been broadcast over various radio stations and has also been set to music.[11]

[11] Biographical details concerning Mrs. Bruner are from *The Biographical Dictionary of Contemporary Poets*, 64; Geoffrey Handley-Taylor (ed.), *The International Who's Who in Poetry* (2 vols., London, 1958), 1: 16; from miscellaneous sources, and from correspondence with Mrs. Bruner.

Mrs. Bruner's first volume, *The Hill Road* (Dallas, Texas, 1932), is a collection of verse that appeared first in many periodicals. Its publication heralded a strong new Indiana poet with a sure touch in diction, a delightful imagery, a mastery of various verse forms, particularly the sonnet, and many arresting thoughts beautifully developed. The poet's maturity has deepened in *Mysteries of Earth* (Dallas, Texas, 1934), and here the reader finds a sincerity, a sympathy for all mankind, a beauty in the commonplace, and a quick portrayal of character. Her verse obtains its themes from ordinary life and from the life of an observant, sensitive housewife, as in "The Spring," "I Listened to a Young Girl Singing," and "Death of a Spinster." She is adept in the short lyric, as in "Misnomer":

> I once thought poetry would be
> A sturdy cloak to cover me;
> Instead, I found it ice and fire,
> Deep frozen pools and flame's desire.[12]

In Thoughtful Mood (Dallas, Texas, 1937) contains more of the same types of verse, beautifully executed, and much nature poetry mingled with human interest. *Midstream* (Dallas, Texas, 1940) is well titled, for she follows a middle course in life and poetry, and she often uses understatement, such as is found in Edwin Arlington Robinson or Robert Frost. Human values and sincere feeling for simplicity and humble life again appear, along with reflection of the poet's girlhood amid rural surroundings. *Be Slow to Falter* (Dallas, Texas, 1941) reveals an introspective and somewhat philosophical spirit searching for significance in all of life—in gates, in gardens, in her home, in threshholds. It contains some accents of World

[12] P. 35. Quoted with the permission of the author.

War II. *The Constant Heart* (Dallas, Texas, 1952), dedicated to the memory of her husband, is a collection of tender verse, some of it reminiscent of life with her husband and containing more of her beautiful sonnets.

Above Earth's Sorrow (Boston, 1955) takes its title from one of her sonnets and gives her calm optimism derived from her experiences. The sonnet begins:

> In spring, when Easter time returns once more—
> The season that means victory—life anew,
> We feel that we must let our vision soar
> Above earth's sorrow, toward a fairer view;[13]

One of her best sonnets is "Old Man Alone":

> He keeps the house arranged the same as when
> His wife performed the usual, daily tasks;
> Her work-box, mending, stationery, pen,
> Are as she left them, and if some one asks
> To move them out when tidying the room,
> He says, "She liked them near her during times
> Of rest from other work—instead of gloom
> They re-create her presence and her rhymes."
>
> His days are half reality, half dream;
> He goes through yellowed manuscripts—old books
> They both loved; ponders over many a theme
> Of past and present, as a seer who looks
> With philosophic gaze on life . . . alone,
> And yet with one whose spirit meets his own.[14]

Her eighth book, *The Deeper Need* (Boston, 1957), dedicated to her mother and "the scenes of my childhood," takes its title from a poem explaining that a worker to whom she once gave food showed her that it was she,

[13] P. 23. This and the following sonnet are reprinted with the permission of the publisher, Bruce Humphries, Inc.
[14] P. 17.

not he, who had "the deeper need." Serenity and memories, including those of her rural home and friends, pervade the book. There are also some good poems on Indiana, such as "Indiana" and "Indiana's Autumn," and the usual sonnets.

The Road Lies Onward (Boston, 1960) won the award at the Indiana Authors' Day held at Indiana University in April, 1961, for the most distinguished book of poetry published in 1960 by an Indiana author. It continues the same kinds of verse before published, though perhaps here and there the diction is not quite so delicately woven. Many familiar subjects reappear—although not the same poems—and the calmness of her view of life and of her sympathy with all humanity is evident. The sonnet form sparkles again, and three of the most powerful and beautiful sonnets are those evidently reminiscent of her dead husband.

Margaret E. Bruner, then, is one of the best of the poets of this period. Her versatility is great; she can use many forms, such as the quatrain, sonnet, ballad, rondeau, villanelle, and triolet; she excels particularly in the sonnet, which she polishes to a luster near perfection. Her diction is well chosen, with no clichés, and her meter is smooth. The subjects treated are the usual ones of poetry —the home, nature, people, marriage, religion, life and death, love. Her short poems are as seemingly careless and as beautifully pointed as some of Emily Dickinson's. Truth shines forth through excellent imagery and imagination; there is a calmness that satisfies the reader through its quiet philosophy. In short, here is a true poet, one who has not received the recognition due her. She should be known better.

J. GRAYDON JEFFRIES

In contrast to her, J. Graydon Jeffries (1901-1936) is a rather pitiful figure. Born in Sedalia, Ohio, on August 29, 1901, he received as a boy of ten an injury at school when he was pushed from a bench by an older boy. Two years later, when his parents died, he came to Clay County, Indiana, where he lived with a brother. His injury resulted in making him an invalid. For a while he sold popcorn and magazines, studied painting, and then collapsed, finding himself shortly a patient in the Clay County hospital at Brazil, Indiana, where he wrote poetry by means of a specially constructed typewriter. He founded the poetry contribution section in the Brazil *Gazette,* entitled "Let Us Sing." For two years after he became blind he dictated his poems. After ten painful years in the hospital, he died on August 4, 1936.[15]

His published poetry may be treated as a unit, for all six slight books apparently contain much the same type of verse. They are *Flame Points* (Callahan, Florida, 1928), *New Moon* (c. 1931), *Carved in Frost* (c. 1932), *Star-Gazer* (North Montpelier, Vermont, 1934), *Miniature Cortège* (North Montpelier, 1935), *Chips from the Workshop of J. Graydon Jeffries* (North Montpelier, 1936), and *Last Poems* (North Montpelier, 1937). The volume entitled *Chips from the Workshop of J. Graydon Jeffries* is really a collection of prose sayings and original maxims that are strikingly original and poetic.

Jeffries' poetry is in free verse and is highly romantic, an escape from life in the form of a pursuit of beauty.

---

[15] Facts concerning J. Graydon Jeffries were obtained from miscellaneous sources but especially from Benjamin F. Musser, *Star-Gazer. Biographical Essay on the Early Days and Handicap of the Poet J. Graydon Jeffries Together with Seventeen of "Jimmie's" Exquisite Poems* (North Montpelier, Vermont, 1934).

The clouds, the sun, the moon, twilight, love, hope, appreciation of God's creation, idealism—all are embodied in his poems. His writing is often Keatsian, a sort of worship of beauty in every shape, but it is essentially a spurning of the material facts of life and a soaring away in fanciful flights. One is often moved by his emotion, as in his "Song For Deliverance," in which he manfully foresees his death. The main criticism one can raise is that often his verse is so ethereal that it is essentially about nothing. Still, one might expect this kind of verse to come from an invalid—or else a bitter realism and a cursing of fate. Be it said to the credit of Jeffries that he chose the former and made his wretched life and his poetry a blessing to others!

MARY W. PLOUGHE

Mary Wimborough Ploughe (1872-1945) has only one book to her credit, but it is at least of fair quality. She was born in Clinton County, the daughter of William H. and Celia (King) Wimborough and married Dr. Martin Ploughe in 1892. She died on January 31, 1945, at her home in Kempton, Indiana.[16] Her collection of conventional verse, *At Anchorage* (Philadelphia, 1937), exhibits at times rather rough meter and faulty diction. The title poem sets the tone for the book in revealing her long-desired acquisition of peace of mind, and "Revelation" registers her happiness achieved through acceptance of life as it is. Love, death, love of nature, duty, patriotism, religion, and day-dreaming form the subjects of her verse; she condemns war, gives sympathy to children, and at-

[16] Information about Mary Wimborough Ploughe comes from the obituary in the Indianapolis *News,* January 31, 1945, Pt. 2, p. 7, and from Tipton County records in the Genealogy Division of the Indiana State Library.

tempts to understand the strange workings of the hand of God.

A second publication of Mrs. Ploughe's is a religious essay, *Listening In On God* (Boston, 1938).

Marguerite Young

Our next author, Marguerite Young (1908-   ), with her two books of poetry and one novel, made a considerable impression on both the state and the country. The daughter of Chester and Fay Daphne (Knight) Young, she was born in Indianapolis on August 26, 1908, and attended Manual Training High School. She went to Indiana University for a year and in 1930 was graduated from Butler University, where she reveled in the study of verse offered by Professor Alice Bidwell Wesenberg. Miss Young was an enthusiastic member of the Butler Poetry Club, sponsored by Mrs. Wesenberg. After her graduation she was employed for several years as a real estate broker; but disliking the business world, she studied literature at the University of Chicago for two years, earning a Master's degree in 1936. While in Chicago she became a friend of Harriet Monroe, the well-known editor of *Poetry*. Returning to Indianapolis, she taught English for three years at Shortridge High School, then studied on a fellowship at the State University of Iowa. Her three books caused something of a sensation in Indianapolis, where she was hailed as a new literary star in the Hoosier skies, became the center of parties, was entertained by the mayor, and gave public readings from her poetry. She was described by interviewers as an attractive young woman who was demure and shy and very slow to talk about her own work. She next took up residence in New York City, where she engaged in various kinds of writing; soon she went to Europe, taught creative

writing at the State University of Iowa, and returned to
the East, where she has taught at Fairleigh Dickinson
College.[17]

Prismatic Ground (New York, 1937) was dedicated to
Mrs. Wesenberg. Professor William Lyon Phelps of Yale
called it an important publication. Reviewers[18] pointed
out the fresh talent, the objectivity, the original approach,
the subtle sensitiveness of the diction, and the author's
keen ear for the sound of words. They noted her ability
to make the unimportant seem momentous by surrounding it with subtly implied connotations and of leading the
reader through fragile images of delicate beauty.[19] The
imagistic quality of her verse is seen in "Wild Deer":

> Within a ring of moonlight
> The lettuce beds were clear
> Like cold and silver water
> To the wild and gentle deer.
>
> They came from down the mountain
> To where her garden lay
> From village streets and laughter
> A long, long mile away.
>
> And in the brittle morning
> She sighed and shook her head;
> She thought to burn a white fire
> To fill the deer with dread.
>
> But in the limpid evening
> She quite forgot her loss;
> She listened for their coming
> Like leaves that fall on moss.

[17] Biographical details about Marguerite Young were obtained from
the authors' file in the Indiana Division of the State Library, from Mrs.
Alice Wesenberg, and from miscellaneous sources.

[18] See, for example, J. N. N. (Jessica Nelson North?) in *Poetry*, November, 1937, and William Rose Benét in *The Saturday Review of Literature*,
July 17, 1937.

[19] See, for example, the poem, "Death in Lilliput," page 32.

> She knew, in all her dreaming,
> How one, with steps of fear,
> Would softly, softly follow
> The wild and gentle deer,
>
> Wherefore, who reached to touch her,
> Touched empty space instead;
> And no more come in moonlight
> Wild deer, now she is dead.[20]

The book is full of images, changes of pace, and carefully calculated surprises.

Moderate Fable (New York, 1944) was accorded more of a mixed reception than was her first book. It marks something of a development in the work of the poet in two directions—both toward a refinement and polishing of her idiom and also toward an obscurity that makes reading her verse something of an arduous task. Critics made diverse comments—that the verse was affected, nebulous, strained, and lacked spontaneity, and yet that it was crystalline and more subtle, complex, more varied and individual and mature. It concerns itself with heavy philosophical themes—being, time, perfection, reality, and probability. Its style is detailed and ornate; Miss Young herself called it rococo. An example of the strength, the depth, and yet in this writer's opinion the obscurity of the poetry can be seen in "A High Subjectivity":

> The idea of the universe is inconclusive
>
> As albino nuns with partridge eyes and silk eye lashes,
> As choirs of widows veiled in snowlight,
>
> A negative magnitude having also its existence,
>
> Such flocks of seraphim blue heron winged
> Who surpass by one item at least the real

---

[20] From *Prismatic Ground*, 13-14. Copyright 1937 by The Macmillan Company, and used with their permission.

As does the deer-footed mouse with the deer's gold eye
In the nest abandoned by orioles

Or red geranium toothed flower
Outside the wind which circles earth

Or painted Pharaohs on a star exploded
Like a concept.

Impossible, in crucial analysis,
That man, at his extreme, has not excessively willed

Non-being of being, and being of non-being

And Saturn, ringed by moons like daughter buds—
That truth should not reside in failing truths.[21]

Her third book, *Angel in the Forest. A Fairy Tale of Two Utopias* (New York, 1945), was completed partly with the help of the Kathryn McHale Fellowship, State of Indiana, given by the American Association of University Women. It struck a responsive note, particularly in Indiana, where interest in the social experiments at New Harmony, on the Wabash, has always been strong; reviewers also hailed it as a contribution to American history. It is difficult to classify, as it is neither pure history nor pure fiction; it is a psychological study of the utopian experiments conducted by Father Rapp and Robert Owen in the early nineteenth century. The history is recreated and interpreted in a strong style that is dramatic, metaphorical, metaphysical, and yet warm and beautiful. In fact, the style, though repetitive and obscure, makes the book, as the characters and the times are portrayed in swift, broad, and yet subtle, strokes. The result is something which appeals more to the intellectual

[21] Page 2. Quoted with the permission of the author.

and careful reader, rather than to the general public.
In introducing the book, Miss Young says:

> It is difficult to visualize this secluded area as once the scene
> of two Utopias, like the Cartesian split between body and
> soul—The Rappite, a Scriptural communism, founded by
> Father George Rapp, a German peasant, who believed his
> people to be future angels—the Owenite, founded by Robert
> Owen, an English cotton lord, who believed all men to be
> machines. The end result of Father Rapp's community, a
> celibate order, was heaven—and the end result of Robert
> Owen's, while also incalculable, was the British labor move-
> ment.[22]

She tells the story of the Rappites, taking them from
Pennsylvania to New Harmony and returning, then setting forth the career of Robert Owen in England and
Scotland before he came to America, his vision of Utopia
on the Wabash, the dream of its fulfillment, and the quick
failure of his experiment. The interconnection of the
past of New Harmony with modern life is subtly indicated throughout.

It is to be regretted that Miss Young has not published
more. She is a scholar and a creative artist and master
of a distinctive, difficult style that is both her strength and
glory and, perhaps, her greatest obstacle.

HELEN McGAUGHEY

The last poet to be considered in this period is (Florence) Helen McGaughey (1904-   ). Daughter of
Charles E. and Sallie Edith (Brumfield) McGaughey, she
was born in Roachdale, Indiana, on March 1, 1904, and
attended the Roachdale grade school and Greencastle
High School. After a year at Western College for Women,
she was graduated from DePauw University in 1926, re-

---

[22] Quoted with the permission of the author.

ceived the A.M. degree from Middlebury College in 1932, and did further graduate work at DePauw, Indiana University, Indiana State Teachers College, and Colorado University. She taught in high schools at Kentland, Cloverdale, Plymouth, and Greencastle; and for some years has taught at Indiana State College, where she is now professor of English. She has been a member of various professional and honorary organizations, has held scholarships to the Indiana University Writers' Conference, and has won national prizes for her stories and also for her verse. In 1959 she received an alumni citation from DePauw University. Her articles and essays have been widely published, and her verse has appeared in more than fifty anthologies.[23]

Her first volume, *Wind Across the Night* (Atlanta, Georgia, 1938), is a group of graceful, melodious lyrics composed mostly on the beautiful and miraculous aspects of nature. She writes sincerely and with feeling. *Music in the Wind* (Atlanta, Georgia, 1941) continues the same general type of verse. For her there is music in the wind and in the mystery of moon and stars and sunshine. The fragrance of spring hillsides and the splash of autumn color permeate the book. Excellent sonnets abound in this collection and also in her first. *Spring As a Blue Kite* (Atlanta, Georgia, 1946) has much of the same delicate nature poetry, but it also marks a broadening of her interest to include much more of human values, as in reflections of World War II and in her interest in individuals and their characters and problems—for example, in "Grinder" and "Lodestar."

Her fourth volume, *Reaching for the Spring* (New York, 1958), happily continues the emphasis on meaning in life. There are the usual sensitive lyrics appreciative

[23] Information concerning Helen McGaughey has been obtained mostly through personal correspondence with her.

of nature and the woods and changing seasons; but also there is affirmation in the complex and difficult world of today and in warm poems of love composed with a new touch, often in her best sonnet form. One of her loveliest poems is the sonnet, "Request."

> O Lord, who made this golden day to share,
> This meadow lark to sing, this field to bloom,
> These trees to scent the gold-diluted air—
> O give my filling heart abundant room
> That I may love each blessed gift from Thee:
> The gold-streaked butterfly on purple phlox;
> The hummingbird; the thrush; the chickadee;
> Tall daisies; white alyssum low on rocks.
> And let me not forget the solemn dirge
> Of sea aroused, or scent of woods in rain;
> The way wan daylight and pale darkness merge;
> The sound of sighing wind in soft refrain.
> And let my state be never so forlorn
> That I would miss the rose because of thorn.[24]

This fourth volume of Miss McGaughey is probably her best, for it adds more thought, an ingredient which the nature verse of her first two collections could perhaps have used.

A few words of summation of the poetry of this period in Indiana literature are now in order. The quality of the production, though not great in the Shakespearean or Miltonic sense, is still high; and it is suprising to find so many poets with the sensitive, imaginative spirit, the awareness of beauty and of the hidden meanings of life, the striving toward perfection that we here encounter. These writers, usually working alone, have well continued the tradition of Indiana poetry of the Golden Age

---

[24] Page 15. Quoted with the permission of the author.

and have given testimony to the fact that the muse makes her dwelling place on the banks of the Wabash as well as in Gotham or London town. The themes of the verse of this period seem to be mostly the usual areas of poets everywhere, and the form in which there is greater success than any other is the sonnet, in which several writers have excelled.

It is difficult to assign leadership among so many talented authors; however, it seems evident that the verse of Marguerite Young, though difficult for some to appreciate because of her singular style, has caused the most favorable comment. And perhaps following closely behind her is Margaret E. Bruner with her many books of excellent lyrics. In fact, we may say that several of these poets have never received their just recognition, and Hoosier letters have been much more advanced through them than has been generally recognized.

Many writers of verse who began publishing after 1939 can not be studied here. The strong tradition of Hoosier poetry continues. And all followers of the poetic muse in the state may enjoy the fellowship of many other Hoosier worshipers at the shrine!

9

THE NOVEL

LIKE POETRY, the novels published by Indiana authors between 1922 and 1939 show considerably less talent than those of the Golden Age. However, the production of novels continued at a strong rate, with many new writers appearing, and the novels of this period include many interesting and worth-while books.

JOHN F. BARNHILL—McCREADY HUSTON

The first novelist is Dr. John Finch Barnhill (1865-1943). One of eight children of Robert and Angeline (Shirts) Barnhill, John Barnhill was born on January 2, 1865, at Flora, Illinois, and was taken by his parents at the age of two to Nora, Indiana. He was educated in Westfield, where he was graduated from Union High School, and attended Central Normal College, at Danville. For six years during this period he taught school. He then studied medicine with a physician in Cleveland and with Dr. Joseph Eastman of Indianapolis and was graduated with honors in 1888 from the Central College of Physicians and Surgeons in Indianapolis. Beginning medical practice that same year in Indianapolis, he continued his medical studies at various times in this country and in London, Paris, Berlin, and Vienna. In 1889 he married Celeste Terrell, of Lynchburg, Ohio. For forty years he was in active practice as a physician and surgeon in Indianapolis, specializing in diseases of the ear, nose, and throat. During the latter part of his life he divided his time between teaching at the Indiana University Medical School and at the University of Southern California and resting and writing at Miami Beach, Florida. He held offices in many professional organizations. In 1929 he was awarded the LL.D. degree from Indiana University. After retiring in 1935, Dr. Barnhill died at Miami Beach on March 10, 1943.[1]

Except for several publications in the field of medicine, Dr. Barnhill is known for only two books. The first, *Not Speaking of Operations* (Boston, 1925), is a light, whimsical story of hospital patients in the convalescent period that follows an operation—during which, of course, their tendency is to do the opposite of the title. Putting together many experiences that he had over a period of years in various institutions, the author had to add little in the way of fiction to present some fascinating characters, such as the happy boy, Nick, who can not walk, and little Peggy, of the angel voice—both in the children's charity ward. This brightness is contrasted with the grouchiness of many of the adults. But the Negress from the South, Aunt Mandy, with her quaint comments, gives the reader many a laugh.

A much more serious book is *Hatching the American Eagle. A Narrative of the American Revolution* (New York, 1937). Narrated in the first person, the book deals with a portion of the Revolution not usually covered in history and story—the civilian front—and shows that many Americans were Tories during the war, as evidenced particularly by their activities during the winter of 1777-78,

[1] The biography of Dr. Barnhill was obtained from the Indiana Biography Series, 25:34-35, and from the clipping file, both in the Indiana Division of the Indiana State Library, and also from Jacob P. Dunn, *Greater Indianapolis. The History, the Industries, the Institutions, and the People of a City of Homes* (2 vols. Chicago, 1910), 2:1095-97.

when the British occupied Philadelphia. The persecution directed by the American patriots against Tories and Quakers is pictured with sympathy for both sides, as are the attacks made by Congress and by jealous officers on General Washington. Many of the most important figures in the early history of the American nation are introduced in a familiar and casual manner—such persons as Paul Revere, Patrick Henry, Betsy Ross, the Marquis de la Fayette, Samuel Adams, and the aged, gout-inflicted Benjamin Franklin, whose presentation might, perhaps, have been improved by the author if he had shown more of Franklin's humanity and wit. Probably characterized best of all is "Mad Anthony" Wayne. This is not the greatest book ever written on the Revolution, but it is one of the most interesting.

A much more prolific author is McCready Huston (1891-   ), who has published eleven books. He was born on March 11, 1891, in Brownsville, Pennsylvania, the son of Joseph Andrew and Elizabeth (Fishburn) Huston. After attending the University of Michigan for a brief period, he began his career in the field of journalism by working on the Uniontown (Pa.) *Morning Herald,* 1912-13, and the Pittsburgh *Gazette-Times,* 1913-19. In 1913 he married Daryl Greene, and three children were born to this couple. Deciding in 1919 that if he was to follow a career in writing he must leave big cities and take a less demanding position, he was attracted by the literary reputation of Indiana and became associate editor of the South Bend *Tribune;* then he was editor of the South Bend *News-Times,* 1929-32. Other positions followed: with the Philadelphia *Public Ledger,* 1933-34; the Scranton *Republican,* 1934. He was professor of journalism at the University of Pittsburgh, 1934-35; associate editor of the Indianapolis *Times,* 1935-36; a member of the editorial staff of the United Feature Syndicate, New York, beginning in 1936, and held positions with the Pittsburgh *Sun-Telegraph* and the Philadelphia *Inquirer*. Since 1940 he has been director of public relations of the Academy of Natural Sciences of Philadelphia, and editor of their magazine, *Frontiers*.[2]

Huston's first novel, *Hulings' Quest* (New York, 1925) tells the story of an idealistic architect and his contact with a self-made millionaire coal baron, whose empire suddenly collapses. *The Big Show* (New York, 1927) is not so much a tale of a circus, as the title implies, as it is the vigorous account of the search for freedom of the stepson of a circus man. The boy is sent to college, becomes a lawyer, and is enslaved by the law firm which he joins and by his marriage to the daughter of the head of the firm, but regains his self-respect with his first case. World War I enters as side dressing. As the reader would guess, *Dear Senator* (Indianapolis, 1928) is a novel of politics, but it is mixed with a love story, with the love interest losing eventually to the ambition of the hero. Although some reviewers complained of a lack of vitality and sufficient interplay of characters, the Indiana novelist, Elmer Davis, accorded the book high praise, saying that it was correct reporting of politics.

The King of Spain's Daughter (Indianapolis, 1930) is a narrative of the compromise which it is often necessary for the steady, intelligent wife to make between ideals and reality in waiting for her unfaithful husband to come back to her. In spite of some improbability, the nicety and clarity of the writing suggest Galsworthy. In *Solid Citizen* (New York, 1933) Huston attempts to create a

[2] Material on McCready Huston has been found in various editions of *Who's Who in America* and in the clipping file in the Indiana Division of the State Library.

modern Babbitt. In some respects there is a strong similarity between his Mr. Todd and the hero of the Sinclair Lewis novel, but Huston falls short of Lewis in having Todd be rescued from the amusing pitfalls brought on by women's flattery through efforts of his secretary and his wife. *The Right People* (Philadelphia, 1949) is a strong endorsement of virtue in narrating how a priest brings two wealthy, erring couples back to the ways of righteousness after the tragic deaths of their children.

Huston's last three novels show interest in psychological motivation, and all three deal in some way with rebelling against the society of Philadelphia. *The Prodigal Brother* (Philadelphia, 1952) contrasts the psychological make-up of two brothers and the lives they represent. Lawrence Kinlock, a steady, tradition-minded Philadelphia businessman, is a self-satisfied pillar of society, while his divorced brother Roger is an unsteady, prodigal whom women like. The story is of how Roger eventually finds himself. In *The Saving Grace* (Philadelphia, 1954) another stuffy, dignified Philadelphian, Hume Probyne, a university teacher and the bachelor son of a rich old family, goes complainingly to New York City to attempt to dissuade his sister's son from rejecting a "nice" Philadelphia socialite for Rose Martin, a refreshingly different, self-made business girl who has pulled herself up by her own bootstraps from a Pennsylvania coal-mining background. The story has the unexpected ending in the marriage of Rose and Hume. The rebel against Philadelphia society in *The Gates of Brass* (Philadelphia, 1956) is Reese Entrikin, a junior banker from the same general Philadelphia background as in the other two books. Rebelling against his mother's snobbishness, he breaks his pattern of life by obtaining a more interesting position, and he marries a girl who approves of some of his new ideas.

In the bulk of Huston's writing one sees the careful and smooth technique of the experienced novelist and reporter. Perhaps at times, however, the technique may impress the reader as being a bit too smooth and predictable; but here, at least, is a gifted writer in whose novels there is not only good style but also something of virtue, presented in a satisfying manner.

Two nonfiction books of Huston's are *Salesman from the Sidelines. Being the Business Career of Knute K. Rockne* (New York, 1932) and the humorous *The Family Meal Ticket. The Letters of a Modern Father* (New York, 1933).

LOUIS LUDLOW

The next novelist, Louis Leon Ludlow (1875-1950), is better known than Huston, but it is because of his journalistic and political career rather than for his novels.

One of eight children of Henry Louis and Isabella (Smiley) Ludlow—his mother was the daughter of Ross Smiley, who was a state senator, lieutenant governor, and a member of the convention which drew up the Indiana Constitution of 1851—Louis Ludlow was born on June 24, 1873, in a log cabin in Fayette County near Connersville. He later recalled the large chinks between the cabin logs through which lizards ran. He was graduated from the Connersville High School in 1892. Shortly thereafter, having a dream of becoming a newspaperman, he presented himself in the city room of the Indianapolis *Sun*, wearing a Prince Albert coat and pancake hat. The staff laughed at him, but soon he was hired as a reporter at a salary of ten dollars a week, and he was launched upon a journalistic career. That fall he entered Indiana University, but illness soon forced him to withdraw, and he returned to the *Sun*, where he stayed until 1895. He

served in other journalistic positions: on the Indianapolis
Sentinel, 1895-99; as a political reporter for the Indianapolis *Press,* 1899-1901; as the well-known Washington
correspondent of the Indianapolis *Sentinel,* 1901, of the
Indianapolis *Star* and of the Star League of Indiana,
1903-13, of the Columbus (Ohio) *Dispatch* and of the
Ohio *State Journal,* Columbus, and other newspapers,
1913-29. On September 17, 1896, he married Katherine
Huber, a society reporter on the *Sentinel;* the couple became the parents of four children. He was devoted to his
family and to the Methodist Church.

Then after twenty-eight years as a member of the Congressional press gallery, during which time he had viewed
with disgust the antics of many irresponsible congressmen, he decided to run for Congress himself. Kin Hubbard, the politically inexperienced creator of Abe Martin,
became his campaign manager. In spite of the seemingly
hopeless odds against a person running as a Democrat in
the predominantly Republican Indiana seventh (now the
eleventh) district, Ludlow's personal popularity secured
his election in November, 1928, by a margin of over
6,000 votes, while Herbert Hoover carried the district as
a Republican presidential candidate by 36,000 votes.
Everyone, including Ludlow, was surprised.

Ludlow proceeded to become the kind of congressman
he thought his constituents should have—capable, conscientious, friendly and helpful to everyone, outspoken
and fearless, with the reputation of being the hardest-
working congressman in Washington. He always answered
every communication and letter directed to him; he was
always present at committee meetings and at sessions of
the House and always voted, unless he was sick. He made
a distinguished record as a liberal devoted to economy in
government, prohibition, the rights of labor, and pacifism,

though he supported World War II as the means of achieving lasting peace. He made so many friends and did his work so well that he usually did not campaign for re-election, yet filled his post for ten consecutive two-year terms. He retired in 1948 with the record of being the first newspaper correspondent to change from press gallery to the floor of Congress, as the congressman with the longest continuous service in the history of Indiana, and as one of the most loved, respected, and distinguished congressmen in the history of the state. His motto was "Do all the good you can, in all the ways you can, to all the people you can, just as long as you can, and you will have always around you the arms that never fail." After retirement, Ludlow resumed his former role of a Washington correspondent until his death in Washington on November 28, 1950. He had received the honorary Doctor of Laws degree from both Butler and Indiana universities.[3]

In addition to Ludlow's many journalistic pieces and speeches he wrote *From Cornfield to Press Gallery. Adventures and Reminiscences of a Veteran Washington Correspondent* (Washington, D.C., 1924); *America Go Bust. An Expose of the Federal Bureaucracy and Its Wasteful and Evil Tendencies* (Boston, 1933); and *Hell or Heaven* (Boston, 1937), an argument for his proposed peace amendment to the Constitution.

His two novels, as one might expect, deal with virtue, but from different approaches. *In the Heart of Hoosier-*

[3] Biographical materials on Louis Ludlow abound in biographical dictionaries and in publications on the political history of the state. I have used particularly *Who's Who in the Central States. Volume One* (Chicago, 1947), 728; *The National Cyclopedia of American Biography,* Current, Vol. C (New York, 1930), 322; Kin Hubbard (ed.), *A Book of Indiana* (n. p., 1929), 141, 350; *Who Was Who in America,* Vol. 3 (1951-60); and the Indiana Biography Series, Vol. 35.

land. A Story of the Pioneers, Based on Many Actual Experiences (Washington, D.C., 1925) is dedicated to the memory of his parents, who "... guided my footsteps, as best they could, in the way of Truth and Honor." Indeed, the book is written to picture, with humor and pathos, the spirit, sturdy simplicity, and purity of the still crude rural society of southeastern Indiana in the seventies and eighties where the author grew up. This was the period between the time of the pioneers and the age of materialism and industrialism. Here one sees all the types of people of the day—admirable, humorous, and pathetic—with their differing proportions of good and bad. The characters that he draws fall somewhere between those of Edward Eggleston and Booth Tarkington. The early community, with its schools, social customs, husking bees, debates, love, marriage, and death, comes to interesting life.

In contrast to this presentation of a generally excellent way of life, *Senator Solomon Spiffledink* (Washington, D.C., 1927) shows through good-natured humor the greed, shallow pomposity, and general use of bunkum of an absurd senator such as Ludlow had so disliked as he observed Congress as a correspondent. This is a burlesque and political satire aimed at no political party. The rambling narrative tells how Spiffledink, son of an eminent lawyer of his Hoosier home town, is goaded into running for senator by the selfish girl who makes him her captive husband, is guided by clever managers, and, in spite of blunders, through the use of various shenanigans is elected and becomes a suave and politically wise senator. Although Ludlow was accused of modeling his hero on Senator James E. Watson of Indiana, he denied the charge, saying that Spiffledink is a composite. The book was very popular in Washington.

CHARLES ELBERT SCOGGINS

A much more prolific novelist was the much-traveled Charles Elbert Scoggins (1888-1955), who gleaned most of the material for eleven exciting adventure books from his wanderings in Mexico, Central America, and elsewhere. His stories often appeared first in serial form in *The Saturday Evening Post.*

Scoggins was a Hoosier by adoption, and then for only a portion of his life. Son of Jefferson Davis Scoggins and Catharine Josephine Minerva (Grant) Scoggins, he was born on March 17, 1888, at Mazatlan, Sinaloa, Mexico. His father was an American Methodist missionary who moved frequently from place to place. After his father's death his mother brought her three small children to Texas, where Charles did odd jobs to earn money for the family. He was graduated from high school in Denton, Texas, then worked his way through two years of study of engineering at the University of Texas, 1905-07, partly by painting posters for football games.

Leaving the University, he found himself attracted back to Mexico, where he embarked upon his adventures as an engineer connected with the construction of dams and railroads. He worked on the relocation of the Southern Pacific Railroad in 1907, the construction of the Mexican Central Railroad in 1908, and the railroad and dam of the Mexican Light and Power Company in 1909. Next, he was a machinery salesman, still in Mexico, 1909-12, and a saw salesman in Mexico and Central America, also in Florida, Georgia, and Cuba, 1912-20. In the meantime he had married Lois Lovett Durham of Muncie, Indiana, on December 26, 1913, and a daughter was born to the couple. Though they traveled in Spain in 1928, from about 1915 until 1930 the Scoggins family lived in Muncie, where he began his writing career, completing many of his short stories and novels; then they moved to Boulder, Colorado, where he continued to write. He died there on December 6, 1955.[4]

Scoggins' short first novel, *The Proud Old Name* (Indianapolis, 1925), set the pace for the rest. It is a story of two American miners in Mexico. The younger man, Jimmy Brown, of an undistinguished ancestry, becomes enamored of the daughter of a neighboring Spanish grandee and of their proud old family name and desires to marry the girl and take the name for himself until dissuaded by an insurrection and the timely appearance of an appealing American girl, whom he marries instead. The well-written narrative is a fascinating one, told in the first person. *The Red Gods Call* (Indianapolis, 1926) continues the type. The tale begins and ends in Milo, Indiana, which is really Muncie, but the bulk of it takes place in Mexico and Central America. A successful young businessman of Milo, Howard Pressley, is transformed by the call of adventure into "Buck" Pressley, soldier of fortune and companion of the colorful and notorious Ben Murchison, who, in turn, is the center of interest in an account of intrigue, duels, assassination, searches for unknown mahogany forests, the finding of a lake of asphalt, wild rides, and escapes. Again, the story is told in the first person, with an eye to colorful description and irony. Lew, the picturesque old American miner living in Mexico who narrated the first novel, also tells the story of *White Fox* (Indianapolis, 1928). This relates how the handsome young, dignified Indian of that name, the last of the royal line of Aztecs, who has been taught to think that some day he will deliver his people and restore to them

[4] Facts in the life of Charles E. Scoggins come from *Who Was Who in America*, Vol. 3, and the clipping file in the Indiana Division, Indiana State Library.

their past glory, is given a part in a motion picture film-
ing the last days of Montezuma on location and is then
invited to go to New York to make a personal appearance
at the show's premiere. While there he comes to see that
his hopes for his own race are futile. In *John Quixote*
(Indianapolis, 1929) we have more romance—this time in
Spain, where an American medical student, John Harvey,
follows a pair of beautiful eyes from a bull fight to a
castle. The aristocratic girl is fleeing from an unwanted
match to her wise grandfather, who becomes the most interesting character in a story of rather worn romantic
materials, but told in Scoggins' usual intriguing manner.

The Walking Stick (Indianapolis, 1930) is another tale
involving Muncie, here called Mumford, Indiana. It deals
with the revolt of Fred Harper, who inherited his father's
grocery and membership in the Rotary Club, but who
desires to be different and to become a musician and carry
a walking stick. When he returns from New York as a
rather successful musician—but having learned a little
humility—he re-establishes himself in the respect of his
neighbors. There is social criticism here, both of the rebel
and of small-town conformity, but the book fails to be
another *Main Street*. With *The House of Darkness* (Indianapolis, 1931) Scoggins returns to his former subject
matter, spirited adventure in Central America. Four men
and a girl search by airplane for the House of Darkness,
a fabled temple of riches of the ancient Mayas lost in the
Yucatan jungle. The plane is wrecked, and the group fight
the fierce, trackless jungle, but are rescued at last by
descendants of the Mayas and discover the temple and its
treasures. Three of the five survive to tell their thrilling,
deadly experiences. *Flame* (New York, 1932) is another
book of violent, hair-raising action involving picturesque
characters. A group of Americans vacationing on a yacht

visit a Caribbean island and find themselves in the middle of gun-runners and a revolution. In *Tycoon* (New York, 1932, 1934) one discovers a story similar to *The Proud Old Name;* this time a young, red-headed American engineer helping to construct a railroad in Central America falls in love with the daughter of the leading citizen of the near-by town; his disregard of local customs leads to adventures. *The House of Dawn* (New York, 1935) is something like *The House of Darkness* in that it narrates a search for gold hidden in the Andes Mountains of Peru, presented with the usual excitement and memorable characters. *Pampa Joe* (New York, 1936) does not quite keep up the quality of most of the other books; still, it offers an interesting tale in recounting how a Texan goes to Argentina to recover a mortgage on a ranch located in the pampas, where he meets a powerful old man and falls in love with his granddaughter. The author had used the main element of this plot before. His last book, *Lost Road* (New York, 1941), tells, with accompanying frills of Mayan lore, airplanes, gold mines, Indians, and love, a breathless yarn of four people who are stranded in an impenetrable jungle in Brazil.

Charles Elbert Scoggins, therefore, was a writer who inherited the mantle of highly romantic fiction from George Barr McCutcheon. He could pen very exciting, intensely gripping adventure stories, nearly all with a locale south of the border in lands strange, exotic, wildly beautiful, but of deadly danger for gringo travelers. He is excellent in characterization, usually having at least one physically powerful, able American leader of commanding personality in each book surrounded by a group of lesser characters, one or two of them often sullen and evil, and including an inexperienced pretty American girl, who adds zest and love interest to the tale. There is a quest, which is often a search for something like treasure or ancient lost cities hidden in impenetrable jungles and guarded by the arrows and throwing sticks of savages. The style is sophisticated, without the usual mass of details and artifice added to an adventure story to prolong it. All the details and incidents contribute to the denouement and final effect. It may be said that there is little substance to his work, that it amounts to hammock reading alone, and that it does contain a certain amount of hokum. However, one must admit that all these novels are so fascinating that the striking of the bedtime hour or the jangling of the telephone comes as a very unwelcome interruption before the reader sees his courageous but harried adventurers safely through to the end of their quest.

MARGARET WEYMOUTH JACKSON

Our next writer, Margaret Weymouth (Mrs. Charles C.) Jackson (1895-   ), wrote warm, imaginative narratives of domestic life, often utilizing Indiana locales for her entire action. Although she has six novels to her credit, the great bulk of her writing has been in the form of short stories of which she has published hundreds in magazines, such as *The Saturday Evening Post*.

Fifth child in a family of seven children of George L. D. and Martha Stuart (Connell) Weymouth, Mrs. Jackson was born on February 11, 1895, in Eureka Springs, Arkansas. The family must have had a streak of printer's ink running in their veins, for both the parents were interested in writing, and six of the children ultimately took up positions in publishing or advertising. After graduating from Lake View High School in Chicago in 1914, Mrs. Jackson attended Hillsdale (Michigan) College for two years, then came to Spencer, Indiana, where her father edited and published *Farm Life* magazine, which at that

time had a circulation of over four hundred thousand.
Following a period as a secretary in Pennsylvania and
Boston, she served as woman's editor of *Farm Life* in 1918
and as associate editor of *Better Farming,* published in
Chicago, 1918-19. On January 10, 1920, she was married
to Charles Carter Jackson, of New York City and Spencer,
Indiana. Three children were born to them. The family
lived in Manitoba, Canada, 1920-24, and returned to
Spencer, where, except for a sojourn in Irvington in Indi-
anapolis, 1930-33, they have lived ever since. For a time
her husband and her father published jointly *The Poultry
Journal* at Spencer.

In addition to her journalistic work, Mrs. Jackson began
her personal writing early, receiving her first compensa-
tion, ten dollars, for an article, "Babies in the Zoo,"
from the Chicago *Tribune* at the age of nineteen. Shortly
thereafter she was given twenty dollars by the old Chicago
Blade and Ledger for a mystery story. But she did not
attempt to concentrate on writing until after her marriage, when she was living in Spencer. She placed her
first story with a national magazine of large circulation,
Good Housekeeping, in 1925 and one with *McCall's* the
next year. She has put her efforts mostly into stories
rather than novels, with her husband as her collaborator
and critic. She has combined writing with being a wife
and mother, and in recent years she and her husband have
operated a gift shop at Spencer.[5]

Mrs. Jackson's first novel, *Elizabeth's Tower* (Indianapolis, 1926), is a simple, heart-warming story of a
neglected orphan girl living with an aunt and uncle on

[5] The biography of Margaret Weymouth Jackson comes from *Who's
Who in America,* Vol. 26 (1950-51); *Who's Who in the Midwest* (Chicago,
1949), and from the clipping file in the Indiana Division, Indiana State
Library.

a bleak North Dakota farm. She develops an inner stability and strength of character which enables her to withstand adversity and, as she grows up, to give friendship and counsel to others. Though Elizabeth is almost too good to be real, still the story is optimistic and presents a realistic picture of North Dakota, where the author had lived for a time. *Beggars Can Choose* (Indianapolis, 1928) is a novel about marriage, contrasting two sisters of a wealthy, socially prominent Chicago family. One girl marries in her class, but is less happy than the other, who marries against her family's will a poor young newspaper artist; and in spite of vicissitudes the couple maintain a true affection. In some ways the novel is not very impressive, but the author keeps interest in her characters and in the central problem.

In *Jenny Fowler* (Indianapolis, 1930) there are glimpses of Indiana in the nineties—Spencer (called Hilltown), Bedford (Stone City), Bloomington (University City), and Culver, French Lick, and Brown County, which latter places appear with their correct names. The characters, also, are Hoosiers, speaking in Hoosier idiom and living amid Hoosier traditions and atmosphere. This is the story of how Jenny as a young girl marries the sweetheart of her best friend, Marian Caruthers, then after his death, marries her own former sweetheart, while Marian teaches school all her life. Yet, at the end of their lives, the two women are both lonely, and Jenny is still feeling guilty for having treated Marian as she did many years before. The characters are well drawn, and the story is one of much interest. *First Fiddle* (Indianapolis, 1931, 1932) is very much a Hoosier book featuring many familiar sights in Indianapolis. The action moves in and around such landmarks as the Soldiers and Sailors Monument on the Circle, Washington Street, the Claypool Hotel, Irvington,

Market Street, North Meridian Street with its mushrooming automobile business, and Butler University. It is a well-written narrative of the problems that a young veteran of World War I, John Moore, a graduate of Thornton College, which is "forty miles from Indianapolis," has in getting on in the world, when the best jobs have been taken by those who stayed at home. His war bride, Cecily, whom he married while on leave—their honeymoon was spent in the Claypool Hotel—having begun in the business world while he was in uniform, is much further ahead than he. He finds himself playing second, not first, fiddle in the family. Perhaps the story deals too much with a money-mad class of people, but it holds the reader—be he Hoosier or not—to the end. Bobbs-Merrill brought out an Indiana Edition of the book, limited to a thousand copies.

With *Sarah Thornton* (Indianapolis, 1933) Mrs. Jackson moves her locale to Chicago and writes a novel of the family life of middle-class Americans covering the first quarter of the century. At seventeen Sarah falls in love with a neighbor boy, Kurt, but the two are kept apart by their youth, by Kurt's possessive mother, by his own weakness, and by the war. Their marriage is thus delayed twenty-five years, during which period Sarah is the mainstay of her family. It is a story of sentiment and of the importance of love in human relationships; but some reviewers complained that the author was too heavily burdened with message. Her last book, *Kindy's Crossing* (Indianapolis, 1934), covers the years 1895-1933 in an industrial town which could perhaps be Spencer and deals particularly with three generations. There are the farsighted and industrious Bert Inness, who, with his pretty wife Estelle, started from small beginnings and emerged a rich automobile manufacturer; their daughter, Blanche, who is spoiled by the wealth; and Blanche's daughter, Nancy, who, facing the ruin of the business during the Depression, is strong enough to roll up her sleeves and buckle down to work. Nancy marries a farm boy, a neighbor of the simple old mother of Bert, who all this time has been living on her farm and quietly observing the other three generations. The book is hardly a brilliant social study; yet it is well constructed and contains some excellent writing, as well as some material dealing with illicit love which annoyed at least one Hoosier reviewer.

In conclusion we might remark that Mrs. Jackson seems not to have any one burning message for humanity, but she is a social historian, particularly of Hoosier society and locales; she has an easy uninvolved style which is good in rapid narration, and she can create believable characters. The whole results in very readable books.

John Calvin Mellett

Another of the Hoosier journalists turned novelist and short story writer is John Calvin Mellett (1888-   ). Though he has only three adult novels to his credit, he has published many short stories in magazines and three juvenile novels.

One of the seven sons of Jesse and Margaret (Ring) Mellett, John Mellett was born on August 4, 1888, in Elwood, Indiana, into a heritage of journalism; for his father was founder and publisher of the Elwood *Free Press,* and all his six brothers went into newspaper work. Mellett, therefore, took naturally to the family profession. After graduating from high school in Anderson, he worked on the Anderson *Daily Bulletin* and spent two years as a cub reporter on the Indianapolis *News,* then was graduated from Indiana University in 1912, where he served as editor of *The Daily Student* and took part in athletics. He married Harriet Brooks on November 17, 1913, and they became the parents of three children. After attendance at the Pulitzer School of Journalism, he returned to the *News* for two years. Next, he became assistant professor of English at the University of Maine, where he founded the Department of Journalism. Following this academic venture he was sports editor of the New York *Mail,* worked on other New York papers, and was business manager for the International News Service. During World War I he took a position on the publicity staff of Secretary of War Newton D. Baker; also he did investigative work for the Treasury Department and promoted the sale of War Savings Stamps. Returning to Indiana, he established an advertising business and from 1920 to 1927 was executive secretary of the Indiana Public Utility Association, resigning in order to write stories, which were published in popular magazines, and novels. In 1932 he was made publicity and advertising manager of an Insull group of Indiana utilities. He was management representative for the Public Service Company of Indiana when he was made director of the Indiana Economic Council in 1953. He retired in 1957.

Mellett started his writing career when he submitted a story of horse racing to *Collier's* under the pen name of Jonathan Brooks, because his brother was managing editor of the magazine and the author wanted no favoritism shown. To his surprise the story brought $500, and for some time he turned out hundreds of other stories. His first two novels were also published under the same pseudonym.[6]

[6] Information about John C. Mellett has been obtained from *Who's Who in America,* Vol. 23 (1944-45), the Indiana Biography Series, 22: 99-100; the clipping file in the Indiana Division, Indiana State Library, and the Indiana Department of Commerce and Public Relations.

Mellett's first novel, *High Ground* (Indianapolis, 1928), reflects his newspaper background. It is the story of James Andrew Marvin, the redheaded, high-principled, fighting editor of *The Monitor* of the town of Summit, Indiana, which is experiencing the growing pains of becoming a city. In a sense the book is a fictional biography or character sketch, told from the point of view of each of Marvin's five children—Matthew, Mark, Luke, John, and Ruth. Each of these children loves and admires the father, yet can not completely understand his moral greatness, and each helps him in one way or another run the newspaper. One by one they slip away, however, for reasons good or otherwise, leaving him a gallant old man defeated in one sense in his constant battle against vice, but triumphant spiritually. Here is the spirit of Greek tragedy. The book may be considered a tribute to the greatness of the courageous old-time Indiana editors; it is an uplifting experience to read the story of a man who, in any controversy, could always be relied upon to take "the high ground." *Chains of Lightning* (Indianapolis, 1929) reflects Mellett's work with public utilities. It continues the same literary device of building a character sketch and telling a story from different points of view. But here the central figure is Jason M. Wheeler, a millionaire electric power magnate, who, instead of being a dishonest, greedy person, as the reader might conceive such persons to be, turns out to be a pillar of honesty and virtue—a sort of James A. Marvin. The story is told by several persons: Wheeler's wife, the girl his son is in love with, an antagonistic senator, Wheeler's enemy, and a local politician (who had also figured in *High Ground*). Wheeler is shown to be hard working, human, and kindly; and the arguments for government ownership of public utilities come out second best as against those for honest, private ownership.

The characters are more types than individuals. The book is near propaganda, but it makes good reading.

In Mellett's last novel, *Ink* (Indianapolis, 1930), he returns to his love, journalism, in presenting the story of Arthur Morton, a civic-minded, red-haired young newspaperman, who unexpectedly falls heir to a dying newspaper in the complacent city of Columbia and quickly sets the city on its ears by his courageous exposure of vice, such as in the connection of the corrupt police force with liquor interests. The book is close to melodrama but holds the reader. Perhaps it reflects the experience of Mellett's brother Don, the publisher of the Canton *News,* who was murdered when he attacked vice in his city.

In these books, Mellett's presentation of high-mindedness and civic responsibility approaches propaganda. His other publications were the juveniles: *Jimmy Makes the Varsity* (Indianapolis, 1928), *Pigskin Soldier* (Garden City, New York, 1931), and *Varsity Jim* (Indianapolis, 1939).

LeRoy Oliver MacLeod

We turn next to a writer who became, through fiction, a historian of the Wabash Valley, particularly of the rural community around Browns Valley, about ten miles southwest of Crawfordsville. Although his main occupational interest has been advertising and public relations, he has published a book of verse and three novels.

LeRoy Oliver MacLeod (1893-   ) was born in Anderson, Indiana, on October 20, 1893, the son of David Penn and Martha Agnes (Jones) McLeod (the son changed his spelling of the family name). He grew up on a farm near Browns Valley then attended DePauw University, where he majored in English composition and served as editor of *The DePauw*, the student newspaper. After receiving his A.B. degree in 1915, he soon married a DePauw classmate, Irene Ruth Miller, by whom he had two children. The couple was subsequently divorced. Spending some time in farming at Browns Valley, MacLeod evidently observed this rural community well, for it is featured in his four books, which have about them much of the aroma of good Hoosier soil. He was a newspaper reporter in Colorado and California, 1919-21 and from 1921 to 1929 was a partner in the Waters and MacLeod Advertising Agency in Los Angeles. In 1928 he and his second wife, Geraldine Seelemire, were married. After 1929 he was engaged in advertising in New York. In 1958 he retired as the advertising manager of the New York State Electric and Gas Corporation.[7]

MacLeod's first published work was a volume of poetry. *Driven* (New York, 1929) is a reflection of farm experience by a sensitive observer who understands and appreciates rural life and sees much of the tragic in it. There is found here a strength deriving from nature itself. Probably the best piece is "Drouth," a group of narrative sketches, which mirror the physical and spiritual results of a period without rain as seen in the crops and in the isolation of a family. The sonnets and shorter poems are not so successful. There is much about the collection which reminds one of Robert Frost, even though a grim philosophy similar to that of A. E. Housman is often evident.

[7] The biography of LeRoy MacLeod has been obtained from *Who's Who in Commerce and Industry* (Eleventh International Edition, Chicago, 1959) ; *Who's Who Among North American Authors,* Vol. 6 (1933-35) (Los Angeles, 1935) ; Martha J. Ridpath (ed.) , *Alumnal Record, DePauw University* (Greencastle, Ind., 1920) ; the Alumni Office of DePauw University; and from the clipping file in the Indiana Division, Indiana State Library.

His three novels are all placed in the setting of the Wabash Valley, evidently near the town of Browns Valley. *Three Steeples. A Tragedy of Earth* (New York, 1931) is a story of power and quality. A Hoosier farm boy "gets religion," becomes a Methodist preacher, converts the sluggards of his village, but finds them largely unchanged by their experience. When his church catches fire, he loses his life in the conflagration by rushing into the building thinking to save the village idiot, who, it turns out, was gibbering in a near-by barn all the while. The entire community is here revealed in realistic, vivid detail, along with poetic touches. The young preacher comes to realize that people want mostly to be left alone. Another Indiana novelist, McCready Huston, in reviewing the book, pronounced it "as important as *Main Street*";[8] William H. F. Lamont, of the English Department of Rutgers University, included the book in his list of fifty great modern novels. Few other reviewers, however, seemed to be so greatly impressed.

The Years of Peace (New York, 1932) became a selection of the Book League of America. The title is ironical, for even though the action is following the Civil War, still those years were hardly peaceful for the farm couple, Tyler and Evaline Peck, who live in secret warfare under the marriage bond and misunderstand each other's true nature as they go about the monotonous farm tasks. The talent of the author is evident in the manner by which he makes warmly dramatic and fascinating the lives of these two average people, as well as those of the entire farming community. His character delineation and his style are excellent.

MacLeod's last novel, *The Crowded Hill* (New York, 1934), is the sequel to *The Years of Peace* and is the second

[8] See Huston's review in the South Bend *News-Times*, March 15, 1931.

of a proposed tetralogy, the last two volumes of which have never appeared. *The Crowded Hill* covers the years 1876 to 1878 and takes its title from the crowding of the huge farmhouse inherited by Tyler Peck from his Uncle Lafe, when he and Evaline and the six children move into the house, which is still occupied by Aunt Mary and Cousin Lucy. Though Tyler is elated by the acquisition of this new farm in the Wabash Valley near Terre Haute (called "Terry Hut" in the Hoosier vernacular) and tries to become like his uncle, the women find living under one roof a trying experience. Tyler can sometimes laugh off his shortcomings, but a former sin, in which his uncle had discovered him, haunts him continually. There is about the novel an earthiness, a smell of the fields, a careful description and depiction of Hoosier farm life that makes these seemingly uninteresting characters important and transforms the microcosm of their small community into a macrocosm.

In this and MacLeod's other two novels one finds an unhurried style—at times perhaps too leisurely—which breathes pulsating life into the picture of the Wabash Valley and its people with all the glory, inadequacy, humor, and bitterness found in life. All MacLeod's novels are absorbing.

ROBIN EDGERTON SPENCER

Absorbing also are the four novels of the meteorologist, Robin Edgerton Spencer (1896-1956), who stole time from his charts and weather machines to write, not of Hoosierdom, but of ghosts, mental derangement, and the plight of incompetent persons.

Spencer, whose father, William Sterling Spencer, was a train dispatcher, and whose mother was Nellie Constance (Tierney) Spencer, was born on December 23, 1896, at

Ogden, Utah, and lived for six years in Utah, California, Nevada, Idaho, Montana, and Wyoming. Then his mother, finding it necessary to support the family, took him and his brother and sister to Salt Lake City, where she secured employment. The family found itself in poverty, however, and at age ten Spencer left school and started working in a department store. After three years he became an office boy for the Oregon Short Line Railroad, finding the work light enough that he could read during office hours—Dickens, Dumas, and Poe—and he began to write stories. The years from fifteen to twenty were spent as a tariff clerk, file clerk, and rate clerk, while on the side he read Hugo and Emerson, and studied the violin. During World War I he was rejected for regular enlistment because of his eyes, but served in the Army Medical Corps.

Upon being discharged, in 1919 he entered the service of the United States Weather Bureau on the North Pacific Coast, studied hard, was promoted and sent to Bismarck, North Dakota, whence he was transferred in 1921 to Moorhead, Minnesota. In 1921 he married Cornelia Louise Leick, by whom he had a daughter. After he was transferred to Washington, D. C., in 1923, he chanced upon a short story of Henry James and was so enthralled that he bought James's complete works—paying for the set at six dollars a month. During the winter months of the next few years Spencer attended night classes at George Washington University, but spent the hot summer evenings writing his first book, *The Lady Who Came to Stay*. In 1930 he became assistant meteorologist of the United States Weather Bureau in Indianapolis, where he was located till 1938 and where he wrote the rest of his novels. In the latter year he returned to Washington, where he remained for some time. His first wife died in 1947, and he married Evelyn Tracy Scott in 1948. *Who's Who in America* for 1950-51 gave his home as Laramie, Wyoming. He died in 1956.[9]

Spencer established a name for himself with his first novel, *The Lady Who Came to Stay* (New York, 1931), for it was snapped up by the first publisher to whom it was submitted, was selected as a "book of the month" by the Book League of America, and was published also in England. None of his other books aroused so much interest or brought forth so much discussion.

The book is based on the idea that love and hate can transcend death. It tells a gripping story of the supernatural, evidently inspired by Spencer's admiration for Henry James's story, "The Turn of the Screw."

The locale is a large, gloomy old house where dwell four old, forbidding unmarried sisters. Into their midst comes an unwelcome guest, Katherine (the lady who came to stay), who is their only brother's widow, stricken with a mortal ailment, and forced to seek shelter with her sisters-in-law. Katherine protects her child, Mary, from the four, particularly the vicious and violent eldest, Phoebe. Phoebe conceives a terrible hate for Katherine; and after Katherine dies, Phoebe, turning her vengeance upon Mary, loses her life in an encounter with Katherine's ghost. All the other sisters now love Mary, but the apparition of Phoebe continually attempts to bring disaster to Mary; yet the presence of Katherine hovers about and protects her daughter. The neurotic Aunt Milly, curious about love, romances vicariously with the growing Mary, who marries; then Milly passes also and joins forces with

[9] Facts in the life of Robin E. Spencer have been found in *Wilson Library Bulletin*, 6:nos. 3, 4:262, 320 (November, December, 1931); *Who's Who in America*, Vols. 21, 22, 26; and the clipping file in the Indiana Division, Indiana State Library.

the spirit of Katherine in the house. The last two aunts, the twins, Emma and Lucia, observe and help Mary's little son, who is forced to stay for a lonely period in the dismal old house and who peoples it with spirit playmates. The presence of Katherine likewise protects him against Phoebe. The conflict between the spirits of Katherine and Phoebe comes to a conclusion only with the death of the last sister, Lucia, in the conflagration of the house. In a sense this is a sort of morality play, with personified virtues and vices contending for representatives of mankind.

The author has written in a style so fitting to the material that he makes the impossible appear probable, and he secures temporarily what Coleridge calls the "willing suspension of disbelief" on the part of the reader. Yet, his work here is derivative of Henry James in its suspended, involved sentences and its ambiguity. The popularity of this book resulted in its transformation by Kenneth White into *The Lady Who Came to Stay. A Play in Seven Scenes* (New York, 1941).

Spencer's next novel, *The Incompetents* (New York, 1933) was not so successful. It is totally different from his first book in subject matter and approach, but his style continues to be complicated and his sentences long and involved. The title arises from the lack of competence seen in a family in which the wife realizes that her smug, selfish prig of a husband has turned out to be incompetent because of the manner in which she has handled their married life and also that she has never trained her daughter to be competent. After the daughter marries, the mother seizes the opportunity to divorce her husband and to search in Europe for some of the aspects of life that she has missed. But upon her return she finds her former husband living with their daughter and son-in-law and disrupting the marriage through his daughter's attachment to him. When appeals to the husband, the daughter, the daughter's husband, and even to the son-in-law's mistress, whom he has been driven to seek, all fail, the wife solves the problem by remarrying her husband. The solution is a little too pat and artificial for most readers.

Felicita (Indianapolis, 1937) was Spencer's favorite book. He called it a "grownup fairy story." It is a carefully constructed romantic tale of how an author and literary critic, exhausted by driving himself for a long time, suddenly breaks all ties and goes to visit a friend, who lives in a large old rural house just beginning to decay. The old friend is called away, leaving the author in the care of a servant; and the author is so fascinated by the house, which seems to have a vaguely malign influence, that he determines to write a novel about it. From small bits of facts discovered in the house, he creates in his imagination a beautiful heroine, Felicita, who ultimately becomes so real to him that when he dies he achieves an ecstatic union with his beloved. Again, in this novel, as in his first, Spencer makes this beautiful, strange story credible. Perhaps he wished to point out the values that the modern world neglects.

In the last book, *The Death of Mark* (Indianapolis, 1938), one finds more of Spencer's interest in psychology. It is a study of the effects of an accident on three people. The domineering Mark, becoming a cripple in a mine accident, receives doubled affection from his wife, Rita. He insists that she show friendship to his younger brother, but when she does so, he becomes deranged, then in the end regains his sanity. Again, this is a well-written, intense novel, with unnecessary externals omitted. It was included by Dr. William Lyon Phelps of Yale University on a list of noteworthy books.

Phelps characterized Spencer as very original, imaginative, spiritual, and as one who ventures into uncharted lands.[10] Yet, just as Phelps was predicting that Spencer was "one of the future really great writers of America,"[11] Spencer ceased publication. Why? One can only guess.

JEANNETTE COVERT NOLAN

The next novelist, however, seems never to have experienced any difficulty in continuing to publish. Jeannette Covert (Mrs. Val) Nolan (1897-   ) has to her credit, at this writing, thirty-six books, not counting reissues. One of the most prolific of contemporary Hoosier authors, she has written both for adults and for children of various ages, primarily for the latter. Her works are penned mostly for entertainment—in which purpose they have indeed succeeded, to judge by their popularity—though there is a strong instructional element in the juveniles.

Mrs. Nolan came of strong Hoosier antecedents. Jacob Covert, her paternal grandfather, the first white male child born in Wells County, Indiana, owned and edited a newspaper in Washington, Indiana, in the Civil War era and was also editor of an Evansville paper. When she was born at Evansville, Indiana, on March 31, 1897, her father, Charles Grant Covert, was city editor of the Evansville *Tribune* (later called the *Journal-News*), though he later turned to law and politics and became mayor of Evansville. Her mother was Grace Louise (Tucker) Covert.

The printer's ink in her veins moved her so early to write that at the ripe age of nine she received a silver

---

[10] See William Lyon Phelps, "May I Suggest," in *The Rotarian* (Chicago), August, 1938, p. 46.

[11] See "Spencer Called Future Great," in Indianapolis *Times*, November 26, 1938, p. 1.

badge from *St. Nicholas* magazine in recognition of the publication of her first poem. When she was in high school at Evansville, she served as editor of the school paper and was also editor of the yearbook during her senior year. Since at the time of her graduation her family was not experiencing financial prosperity, she could not go to college like her sisters, but instead obtained a position in 1915 on the Evansville *Courier,* where, at the age of seventeen, she became for a short period "Betty Brown," conducting the lovelorn column. But the editor soon relieved his much-worried columnist, who was lying awake nights trying to think up answers to the problems of women of forty who were having trouble holding onto their husbands, and assigned her to straight reporting, feature articles, and a weekly short story. A year later she transferred to the *Journal-News* and soon was doing, among other assignments, a weekly short story with an Evansville setting.

In 1917, after three years of newspaper work, she was married at the age of twenty to a childhood friend, Val Nolan, a young attorney of Evansville; and for some time her interests were domestic rather than literary. Two boys and a girl were born to this couple. Mr. Nolan became city attorney of Evansville.

Acting on doctor's orders, Mrs. Nolan took her children to stay for several winters in Florida. During these months her interest in fiction returned; she made up stories to amuse the children, then after they had been put to bed, wrote them down. The children were her first critics. Her sister, an Evansville librarian, now suggested that she write clean, thrilling juvenile stories to market. When Mrs. Nolan sold her first story to *St. Nicholas,* she found herself back in the writing business. In 1933, the same year that her first book was published, the Nolan family moved to Indianapolis, where Mr. Nolan served as U.S. district attorney until his death in 1940. Having published only a few books by that time, she decided to concentrate on her writing as a means of livelihood and of education for her children. The family moved to Bloomington, Indiana, in 1941, returning in 1945 to Indianapolis, where Mrs. Nolan has lived ever since. In addition to writing, she has occasionally taught classes in juvenile writing at Indiana University extension in Indianapolis and has conducted workshops on children's literature at the annual Indiana University Writers' Conference and at the University of Colorado Writers' Conference. From 1943 to 1945 she contributed a column, "Lines With a Hoosier Accent," to the Indianapolis *Star,* alternating on the same page with Hoosier novelist Meredith Nicholson.

Many honors have come to this well-known author. Her work has been included in anthologies and school readers and has been dramatized and transformed into radio presentations. Ten of her books have found publication and popularity in England. Her juvenile, *The Story of Joan of Arc,* was published also in India and Portugal. *The Story of Clara Barton of the Red Cross* was translated into German and Japanese and was used by the Federal government in its re-education program in Germany, Austria, and Japan following World War II. This book and six other juveniles—*The Young Douglas, Hobnailed Boots, Treason at the Point, Florence Nightingale, Andrew Jackson,* and *George Rogers Clark, Soldier and Hero*—were Junior Literary Guild selections. Her *George Rogers Clark* received the Indiana University award in 1955 for the best juvenile written that year by an Indiana author. In 1959, she received the highest recognition of Theta Sigma Phi for the outstanding woman journalist or author: the Frances Wright award for excellence in writing. In 1961 she again received the

Indiana University award, this time for *Spy for the Confederacy: Rose O'Neal Greenhow.*[12]

Mrs. Nolan's works may be considered as belonging to various classes. The juveniles can be divided into fiction, biography, and a combination of these two, which may be called fictional biography, while the adult publications can be divided into expository books and the novel.

The juvenile fiction consists of *Barry Barton's Mystery* (New York, 1932); *Hobnailed Boots* (Philadelphia, 1939), which deals with George Rogers Clark's expedition to the Illinois; *Treason at the Point* (New York, 1944), concerned with Benedict Arnold; *Patriot in the Saddle* (New York, 1945) on Andrew Jackson; and *The Victory Drum* (New York, 1953), about George Rogers Clark's expedition to Vincennes.

Mrs. Nolan's juvenile biographies include *The Story of Clara Barton of the Red Cross* (New York, 1941), *James Whitcomb Riley, Hoosier Poet* (New York, 1941), *The Little Giant. The Story of Stephen A. Douglas and Abraham Lincoln* (New York, 1942), *O. Henry. The Story of William Sydney Porter* (New York, 1943), *Florence Nightingale* (New York, 1946), and *Spy for the Confederacy: Rose O'Neal Greenhow* (New York, 1960).

Her list of juvenile fictional biography is the longest of all. It consists of *The Young Douglas* (New York, 1934), the story of the rescue of Mary, Queen of Scots, from imprisonment in the Castle of Lochleven by Alan Douglas; *Red Hugh of Ireland* (New York, 1938), the tale of Hugh Roe O'Donnell, one of the heroes of Ireland; *The Gay Poet. The Story of Eugene Field* (New York, 1940); *An-*

---

[12] The biography of Jeannette Covert Nolan has come from *Who's Who in America*, Vol. 31 (1960-61), from the clipping file in the Indiana Division of the Indiana State Library, and from Mrs. Nolan herself, who supplied information upon request.

drew Jackson (New York, 1949); *John Brown* (New York, 1950); *LaSalle and the Grand Enterprise* (New York, 1951); *The Story of Ulysses S. Grant* (New York, 1952); *Abraham Lincoln* (New York, 1953); *The Story of Joan of Arc* (New York, 1953); *George Rogers Clark. Soldier and Hero* (New York, 1954); *The Story of Martha Washington* (New York, 1954); *Benedict Arnold. Traitor to His Country* (New York, 1956); and *Dolley Madison* (New York, 1958).

Mrs. Nolan's juveniles are clean, well constructed, smoothly written, and highly interesting—both to young readers and adults alike. Many are very exciting.

Her first adult expository book was *Hoosier City. The Story of Indianapolis* (New York, 1943), advertised as "not a guide book, not a history, but the engrossing quick-paced *story* of a great city."[13] It is a well-written account that in spite of a few omissions makes history fascinating, particularly in the earlier portions. The second is *Poet of the People. An Evaluation of James Whitcomb Riley* (Bloomington, Indiana, 1951), written with Horace Gregory and James T. Farrell.

Our main interest here in Mrs. Nolan's work, however, lies in her adult novels, which are ten in number. She began with rather heavy material. *Second Best* (New York, 1933) is a dramatic story of the frustration of a small soul in a small town who finds it her lot to accept second best instead of her first choice in regard to a career and a husband. Janice Carl's domineering father is horror stricken at his daughter's desire to go on the New York stage and disapproves of her choice of a young man; instead of rebelling, she stays home and marries her second choice, later becoming something like her father—unsympathetic, self-centered, and bitter. Life in the small

[13] See dust jacket of the book.

Indiana town is well pictured. *New Days, New Ways* (New York, 1936; English edition, 1937) is a study of the problems of adoption, particularly whether a woman who intelligently rears the child of another merits the child's affection and confidence. Marjorie Blakely grows up in a Midwestern college town never doubting that the wise Lynn Blakely is her mother until the arrival of her real mother, Lynn's cousin Berta, who is much different from Lynn.

In *Where Secrecy Begins* (London, 1938) a new interest is shown, in the form of a mystery. As a reaction to the devices of contemporary murder mysteries, such as having many characters killed off in a general blood bath, the author makes use of but one murder. This is a Hoosier story laid in the artists' colony of Dugger County (Brown County), Indiana, and in Capital City, which is evidently Indianapolis. A new ingredient in murder mysteries here is the featuring of Miss Lace White, a woman writer past fifty, who is made an honorary lieutenant in the state police and who solves a murder, which is laid at her very door. *Profile in Gilt* (New York, 1941) continues this interest in mystery stories. Likewise it has a single murder. The detective in the story is again the alert, indefatigable Lace White, who solves the murder of a former maid of the family of the heroine, whose marriage to the son of a professor of Redding University has been opposed by the professor. Another mystery, *Final Appearance* (New York, 1943), evidently based on the historic Indiana town of New Harmony, features Lace White, who solves a mystery stirred up by the strange Jonathan Ingle, upon returning to the town of Felicity. There is something of an air of unreality both in the strange setting and in the tale itself, but the book is exciting in some parts. *"I Can't Die Here"* (New York, 1945) is another Lace White murder mystery with perhaps too many characters and loose ends, yet with the usual interest. The last two Lace White mysteries are *Sudden Squall* (New York, 1955), with a setting of a lake resort in Kentucky, and *A Fearful Way to Die* (New York, 1956), in which the clever detective solves the problem of why a Midwestern industrial leader was literally frightened to death. All these Lace White mystery stories make good escape reading, but like most mystery stories, leave one little to remember—except the pleasure.

More serious are two other books. *Gather Ye Rosebuds* (New York, 1946) is a warm, pleasant period piece about life in a blue-blooded family in 1910, which was inspired by Mrs. Nolan's home town, Evansville. The story is rather quaint in action and in its carefully described setting and re-creation of the period, but the plot is perhaps too neat in its several happy endings. Many characters, particularly the old Confederate soldier, "Major" Cameron, are well drawn against the kindly society of the Midwest. The book was later made into the motion picture, "Isn't It Romantic?" *This Same Flower* (New York, 1948) likewise is a historical novel, continuing the story of the Cameron family of *Gather Ye Rosebuds* in the person of Sidney Cameron, who boldly (for her day), answering an advertisement in a city newspaper for a private secretary, finds herself in the midst of the exciting suffragette movement and the struggle for women's rights. Again one discovers a sympathetic re-creation, not only of a period of the recent past, but also of interesting characters. Suffragette parades, band wagons, and local inertia and opposition all are breathed into life, along with a love interest.

In general, we can say that though Jeannette Covert Nolan's four serious adult novels are not great, they make

interesting and profitable reading. The sum total of her
contribution to Hoosier literature has been large. And it
may be remarked in passing that the interest in writing
seen for three generations in Mrs. Nolan's family seems
to have been transmitted to the fourth; for her son, Alan
T. Nolan, an Indianapolis attorney, is the author of *The
Iron Brigade* (New York, 1961), the history of volunteer
infantry regiments from Indiana, Wisconsin, and Michigan in the Civil War. This book has been well received.

HERBERT OSBORNE YARDLEY

Like an earlier writer, Robin Edgerton Spencer, our
next author, Herbert Osborne Yardley (1889-1958), was
also engaged in government service, but of a more exciting
nature. He was the father of American cryptography and
the nation's foremost expert on codes. His writing of
novels was only a side line to his brilliant work in military
intelligence and in the breaking of the codes of foreign
nations. In this vocation it may be safe to say that he was
a genius.

The son of Robert Kirkbride and Emma (Osborne)
Yardley, the author was born on April 13, 1889, at Worthington, Indiana, and was educated at the local high school.
He became a telegrapher in Indiana; then having passed a
Civil Service examination, in 1912 he was employed by
the United States Department of State as a telegrapher and
code clerk. In 1914 he married Hazel Milam, by whom
he had a son.

His professional progress was now meteoric. He helped
develop a new diplomatic cipher code in 1914. Through
study at night he increased his knowledge so that he became America's foremost expert on ciphers and codes.
When the United States entered World War I in 1917,
he was given a commission as lieutenant in the Signal

Corps and was assigned by the War Department to establish the Cryptographic Bureau, known as Military Intelligence No. 8, under the department of Military Intelligence. He served as head of this Bureau and was promoted to captain in 1918 and to major in 1919. Under his guidance the Bureau deciphered the most difficult codes that the enemy could devise. In August, 1918, he was a military observer on the staff of General Pershing and was in charge of Military Intelligence C-17 at the peace conference in 1918. As a reward for his services, he received the Distinguished Service Medal in 1922. He was honorably discharged and soon found his Bureau, with himself still in charge, reconstituted as the Cryptographic Department (which he later called "The Black Chamber") of the Department of State; it was housed secretly in an old house in New York. During the Washington Arms Conference in 1921-22 Yardley and his staff were able to decipher the most intricate codes of foreign countries, even keeping the American delegates advised about the messages that the Japanese delegation was sending home. His Bureau, nevertheless, was abolished by Secretary of State Stimson in 1929 under the theory that diplomatic correspondence should be inviolate—an idea which seemed absurd to Yardley.

His sixteen years of government service at an end, the author thereupon returned to Worthington, Indiana, and soon began writing his books, some of which became well known and one of which turned out to be famous—as well as infamous. He also spent some short periods in Hollywood as a writer and technical advisor. Called again to the international scene, from 1938 to 1940 he was secret advisor to Generalissimo Chiang Kai-shek, helping the Chinese government with his knowledge of codes (this experience was to give him the background for one of his novels). Then in 1940 he returned to Washington for a special assignment with the United States Signal Corps, and in 1941 he served as secret advisor to the Canadian goverment. In 1942 he re-entered government service in Washington, taking a position with the enforcement division of the Office of Price Administration, from which position he retired in 1952. His first marriage having ended in divorce in 1944, he and Edna Ramsaier were married that year. He died in Washington on August 7, 1958.[14]

Yardley's first book, *The American Black Chamber* (Indianapolis, 1931), not only attracted great attention in the United States; it was also a bombshell bursting upon the diplomatic scene, with embassies of every country purportedly rushing to secure copies in America or in London, where an edition was published the same year. The reason for the popularity was obvious. It is a thrilling autobiographical account of his sixteen years of service with the State and War departments. It tells, among other things, of the beginning of his work as a telegraph operator in the Code Room of the Department of State in 1913, his learning how to manipulate codes and ciphers, his solving the supposedly unbreakable American diplomatic code and the codes of friendly nations, his receiving a commission in the army at the outbreak of World War I with the assignment of establishing a cryptographic bureau, which he called "The Black Chamber," the fascinating activities of that bureau with its breaking of the German code, its discoveries of the use of secret inks for messages, the apprehension of various German spies, the peace conference, the breaking of the Japanese secret code

[14] Information about Herbert O. Yardley has been obtained from the clipping file in the Indiana Division and the Indiana Biography Series, 23:29; 50:104, and from information provided by Mrs. Edna Yardley and Mr. Yardley's son Jack, of Indianapolis.

used at the Washington Armament Conference, and the final dissolution of the Chamber in 1929. Great figures of the United States and of other powers walk through the pages as the fate of nations hangs in the balance. The book has much suspense and reads like a novel. So sensational was this true detective story that the Japanese government found itself embarrassed and filed a formal protest with the American government; Yardley's book was then ordered to be suppressed.

Word that Yardley had prepared a second manuscript, evidently of much the same type, aroused the State Department. Fearing that another book would upset diplomatic relations even more, the Department got Congress to pass a law specifically against Yardley, though it was couched in general terms, stating that no former government employee could disclose or publish information obtained during government service regarding any official diplomatic code. Thus, Yardley found himself in the dual role of having been both of great service to his country and yet emerging as something of a trial to it.

When publishing in the field of cryptography he now had to content himself with puzzle books designed for entertainment only; so his only other works on this subject were *Ciphergrams* (London, 1932) and *Yardleygrams* (Indianapolis, 1932). A later book was *The Education of a Poker Player, Including Where and How One Learns to Win* (New York, 1957). However, it must be added that he managed to get his first book republished in London in 1940 as *Secret Service in America. The American Black Chamber.*

As one might expect, Yardley's three novels are romantic tales of espionage based upon his experiences. *The Blonde Countess* (New York, 1934) is a breath-taking story of World War I, telling of the search for a beautiful

German spy and her final apprehension. The book is based upon the actual workings of The Black Chamber and is full of the use of codes, secret inks, chases, and cloak-and-dagger tactics. It is difficult to put this book down. *Red Sun of Nippon* (New York, 1934) is likewise an exciting book, recounting how an intelligence officer of the State Department and Major Greenleaf, former head of the disbanded Black Chamber, who figured also in the preceding book, uncover a network of espionage and intrigue which leads all over Washington and discover that Japan, preparing for her Manchurian expedition, is attempting to prevent an understanding between the United States and Russia. Stolen messages, broken codes, social glitter, black rascality, and a love affair involving a beautiful Chinese-American girl are all featured. The tale is sometimes fantastic. *Crows Are Black Everywhere* (New York, 1945), written jointly by Yardley and Carl Grabo, professor of English at the University of Chicago, reflects Yardley's experience in China. The title is a famous Chinese saying. Here is a narrative of international intrigue in 1940 in Chungking. An American reporter, Peggy Cameron, comes to the city to write unbiased stories of the Sino-Japanese War but is soon swept up in a web of intrigue that includes loyal Chinese, Japanese spies, Americans working as advisors to the Chinese, secret codes, Japanese bombings of Chungking, and a plot to kill the Generalissimo. Again there is excitement and suspense, but the material might perhaps have been put together in a more orderly manner.

We must conclude that Yardley knew whereof he wrote, for his breathless tales of espionage and codes came directly from his personal experiences—which is an element lacking in many writers of exciting, but artificially constructed, tales.

Clarence E. Benadum

It is a far cry from the cloak-and-dagger tales of Yardley to the kind of work published by Clarence Edward Benadum (1889-   ), the Muncie trial lawyer, who obtained his inspiration for his best-known novel when he read a bronze plaque on the wall of an Indianapolis hotel and then produced an exciting story of the Civil War.

Benadum was born on June 7, 1889, on a farm eight miles northwest of Muncie, Indiana. His father, Spencer A. Benadum, whose family had come from Lancaster, Pennsylvania, to Lancaster, Ohio, then to Indiana, had seen Civil War service in the 121st Regiment of the Ninth Indiana Cavalry and told his son many stories of the War. This was the genesis of the novelist's interest in the Civil War era. He attended Valparaiso University, at twenty-one was a homesteader and gold miner in the Black Hills region of South Dakota, and crossed the Arctic Circle, searching for gold. In his travels he met and talked with Jack London about writing. Returning to Muncie, he studied law and was admitted to the bar in 1910. In 1917 he married Mary Brandt, a teacher who also had attended Valparaiso University, and enlisted in the army, serving in the Quartermaster Corps and in the field artillery during World War I. After the war he became a trial lawyer in Muncie, where he has practiced for many years, making a name for himself with his courtroom pleas. For one term he was prosecuting attorney of Delaware County; in 1940 he was the Republican candidate for the gubernatorial nomination in Indiana.[15]

Benadum published only two novels. *Blackshirt* (Philadelphia, 1935) is heavily weighted with politics. A young

[15] Biographical data on Benadum has been obtained from the clipping file in the Indiana Division, Indiana State Library, and from *Indiana Today* (Indiana Editors Association, 1942), 361, 428.

man becomes involved in politics because of a labor strike, which he opposes. Being called "blackshirt," he is encouraged to become the leader of an independent party, which makes magic of the term and sweeps him into election to Congress. But the most important aspect of the book is the insight it gives into political intrigues and trickery in Indiana. Republicans, Democrats, Socialists, and Communists are all bitterly criticized. The New Deal also comes in for its share of condemnation. One will note that the dialogue here is usually stilted and unreal.

Bates House (New York, 1951) is a much better novel. It arose from the author's interest in the stories that his father and other Civil War veterans had told him about the battles of Stone's River, Shiloh, Nashville, and Franklin. The particular impulse to write the book came on a cold February evening when, after having finished a jury trial in Indianapolis, he reread the historic plaque on the south side of the Claypool Hotel (on the site of the Bates House) commemorating the speech made by Abraham Lincoln from the hotel balcony in February, 1861,[16] as he traveled from Springfield to Washington, D. C., to be inaugurated President.

The novel is a mixture of historic fact and fiction and re-creates dramatically the fever of war emotions both of the North and the South, together with the inclusion of battle scenes and a love element. The story begins with the speech of Lincoln at Bates House. In the assembled crowd are Margaret Manning, a girl who has come from her home in Alabama to claim an inheritance left her by an uncle in Indianapolis, and David Stone, a young Indianapolis attorney, who had helped her obtain the inheri-

[16] The balcony of the Bates House was later built into the home of Mr. and Mrs. Urban Charles Brenner at 1306 Park Avenue, Indianapolis.

tance. David admires Lincoln, but Margaret hates him
and soon leaves for her home. Her train is wrecked, however, and she is fortunately rescued by a slave, whom, in
gratitude, she later buys from his master and sets free.
After she attends the inauguration of Jefferson Davis, she
is accused, because she had met Lincoln in Indianapolis
and had freed a slave, of being pro-Union; and she has to
flee. Likewise, David, because he had championed Margaret's rights to her inheritance in Indianapolis, is accused of being a Southern sympathizer. Finally at the
close of the bloody war, in which David serves in the
Federal Army and shoots Margaret's Southern suitor in
battle, David and Margaret are reunited, Margaret is
cleared of charges of being a Southern spy, and they are
married. But many years later David dies thinking re-
gretfully of the Confederate he had shot. The book is
full of salty dialogue, adventure, the hate each side felt
toward the other (as that of the Indianapolis residents
toward the Southern sympathizers known as the Knights
of the Golden Circle), love, faith, ambition, and suspense.
Even though there is much fruitless questioning of the
ethics of wars and why they arise and though good and
evil are often inextricably intertwined and there seems
to be no moral in the narrative, still it is a moving, realistic story. It holds the reader to the end.[17]

[17] An interesting commentary on *Bates House* is the fact that shortly
after the book was published Charles F. Rutledge, a textbook publisher
of Elwood, Indiana, asked the Delaware Circuit Court to ban further sales
of the novel on the ground that it portrays General Grant as being
intoxicated at the Battle of Shiloh, that Booth, the killer of Lincoln, is
represented as visiting Indianapolis following the assassination, and that
the book "completely falsifies American history" and "promotes the
Dixiecrat political party." See "Ban Asked on 'False' Novel of Civil
War," in Indianapolis *News*, November 29, 1951, p. 29.

Bertita Harding

An entirely different sort of writer is the glamorous Bertita Harding (1907-   ), who, because she has spent most of her romantic life in flitting between the United States, Mexico, Brazil, and various parts of Europe, has been a Hoosier more incidentally and legally than actually. She is a marginal inclusion in this literary history. Still, she evidently wrote several of her books at her home in Indianapolis. Most of her work has been biographical in nature, tracing the royal glitter of former European royalty, such as various members of the Hapsburg family, in Europe and elsewhere. Only three of her books are novels.

Daughter of a mining engineer, Don Emilio and Countess Sarolta (Karolyi) Leonarz, Bertita Carla Camille Leonarz (she added "de Harding" after her marriage) was born in Nuremberg in Bavaria, Germany, on November 1, 1907, of Rhenish-Hungarian parentage. In her father's family had been many talented painters, while in her mother's family there were musicians. The parents wanted their daughter to become a concert pianist, and her education was planned with that in mind. Mexico early cast a strong influence over her life. Her forebears had come years before to that country in the retinue of the ill-starred Austrian royalty, Maximilian and Carlota, Emperor and Empress of Mexico. Her parents, having been commissioned by Emperor Franz Josef of Austria to find and return the Hapsburg crown jewels, which had been scattered over Mexico after the reign of Maximilian, brought her to Mexico at the age of two. She grew up close to the romantic old castle-fortress, Chapultepec, and learned to speak German, Hungarian, and Spanish, hearing many sad stories from former ladies-in-waiting to the Emperor and Empress. She later added French, Italian, and Portuguese to her languages. Her formal education was obtained at the Convent of Sacré-Coeur in France, the Drexel-Lankenau School in Philadelphia, and the National University and Conservatory of Music in Mexico City in 1922.

As a visiting student at the University of Wisconsin in 1923 she met Jack Ellison de Harding, of Manchester, England, who was working on a Master's degree in English literature. The couple were married on October 7, 1926, in Indianapolis. Mrs. Harding became a naturalized American citizen the next year. Since that time she has called Indianapolis and Monterrey, Mexico, home and has engaged in a career of traveling, writing books and motion picture scripts, and lecturing. Also, she is a singer of Hungarian and Spanish folk songs.

Her husband, an Indianapolis advertising executive, who published *I Like Brazil* (Indianapolis, 1941), died in 1954. On October 2, 1957, Mrs. Harding was married in Vienna to Count Josef Radetsky, of an old noble Hungarian family and descendant of the famous Austrian field marshal of the same name. The marriage, however, soon ended in divorce in Vienna and a prison term for the Count, who, it is reported, attempted to swindle his new wife out of $50,000.[18]

Mrs. Harding's nonfictional books are as follows: *Phantom Crown. The Story of Maximilian & Carlota of Mexico* (Indianapolis, 1934), parts of which were utilized for the motion picture, "Juarez," and which the Indiana novelist, Meredith Nicholson, stayed up all night to read; *Golden Fleece. The Story of Franz Josef & Elisabeth of Austria* (Indianapolis, 1937); *Imperial Twilight. The*

[18] See Irving Leibowitz' column in the Indianapolis *Times*, September 29, 1958, p. 13. For the biography of Mrs. Harding I have used *Who's Who in America*, Vols. 20-30, and the clipping file in the Indiana Division, Indiana State Library.

Story of Carl and Zita of Hungary (Indianapolis, 1939); *Hungarian Rhapsody. The Portrait of an Actress* (Indianapolis, 1940), the tragic story of Camille Fehér de Vernet, godmother of Mrs. Harding, and once a great European actress; *Lost Waltz. A Story of Exile* (Indianapolis, 1944), memoirs of the family of Archduke Leopold Salvator of Austria, concentrating on Archduke Franz Josef; *Age Cannot Wither. The Story of Duse and d'Annunzio* (Philadelphia, 1947)—the romance of the famous Italian actress, Eleonora Duse, and Gabriele d'Annunzio, the poet-politician; *Southern Empire. Brazil* (New York, 1948), an analysis and appreciation of that country; *The Land Columbus Loved. The Dominican Republic* (New York, 1949); *Mosaic in the Fountain* (Philadelphia, 1949), an interesting autobiography of the author, following closely her fascinating life; *Magic Fire. Scenes Around Richard Wagner* (Indianapolis, 1953), which was made into a motion picture presented in Europe and in the United States; and *Concerto, the Glowing Story of Clara Schumann* (Indianapolis, 1961). In all these publications Mrs. Harding presents history accurately and in a popular, interesting fashion.

The same general technique is used in her novels, except that where fact runs out fictionalized dialogue and description are added. *Royal Purple. The Story of Alexander and Draga of Serbia* (Indianapolis, 1935) was inspired by her father's close connection with the hero. Mrs. Harding wrote the story of Alexander I of Serbia and his love for the beautiful peasant girl, Draga, and their assassination in 1903, out of pity for the pair. The book is rich in dramatic, colorful action and also has dialogue which is Balkan in style, yet is tailored somewhat to the American reader. In spite of the use of modern slang and some sensationalism, the book carries the reader along. *Farewell 'Toinette. A Footnote to History* (Indianapolis, 1938) is a light and gay historical romance revolving around a little-known incident in history. When the fourteen-year-old Marie Antoinette, having been married by proxy for reasons of state to the loutish French dauphin, who was to become Louis XVI, is taken by her brother, Emperor Joseph II, across Swabia on the way to Versailles, they decline the invitation of the Duke of Württemberg to rest at his castle of Sibyllengard, saying they would stop at an inn; but the Duke, desiring sport, shrewdly proclaims the castle an inn and disguises his family as servants of the hostelry. Here Marie Antoinette meets and falls in love with Prince Eugene of Württemberg. There is pathos in the picture of the homesick young girl and the suggestion of the deluge that was to engulf her, her husband, and France in the French Revolution. The result is a combination of fiction and history that is not easily classified.

Amazon Throne. The Story of the Braganzas of Brazil (Indianapolis, 1941) is hardly a novel, for it records the history of Brazil from 1808 through 1889 in the persons of the three Braganza kings: Dom João, Dom Pedro I, and Dom Pedro II. The interest is kept in the persons of these three monarchs rather than in their country; they are depicted as handsome, intelligent, and dedicated to their realm, though their private lives are not above questioning.

In short, Bertita Harding can barely be called a novelist, for her novels are on the borderline between history and fiction—and incline more to the former. Nevertheless, her many fascinating books involving history, with her careful research well camouflaged, read like the most contrived fiction and make the reader a spectator—practically a participant—in the events portrayed. She is a remarkable writer.

Evangeline Ensley

A much different sort of author is (Wilma) Evangeline Ensley (pen name Evangeline Walton, 1907-   ), who whisks the reader away, not to the dazzling courts of Europe, Mexico, or Brazil, but rather to Druidic Wales, Anglo-Saxon England, and a modern witch house.

Miss Ensley came of a family of professors, writers, and Quaker scholars. Her paternal grandfather served in the Civil War as a Union officer, and her mother's ancestors deserted Virginia and the Carolinas for the North because of slavery. The novelist's maternal great-grandmother was a Quaker. Her parents were Marion Edmund Ensley, an Indianapolis businessman, and Wilma Coyner Ensley. She was born on November 24, 1907, in Indianapolis. Since frail health prevented regular attendance at school or at college, she was educated by private tutors and through her own reading in folklore, mythology, and philosophy. Interest in writing came early, for at age five she made up narratives and at eighteen wrote short stories. She wrote her first two books at her home in Indianapolis and her third after she had moved to Tucson, Arizona, for her health, where she lived with her mother.[19]

Becoming much interested in Celtic materials, she turned soon to the Welsh Mabinogi, the collection of ancient Welsh tales, and chose the fourth book as the basis for her first novel, *The Virgin and the Swine* (Chicago, 1936). Her research she did mostly at The Indianapolis Public Library. She had once abandoned the uncompleted manuscript in discouragement, but her mother found it and urged her to continue her labors.

[19] Facts in the life of Evangeline Ensley were obtained from the clipping file in the Indiana Division of the State Library; from *Who's Who of American Women. Volume I (1958-1959)* (Chicago), 58-59; and from the Division of Vital Records, Indiana Board of Health.

This is a well-constructed story of the life of the Druidic Prince Gwydion of Gwynedd in his role as both a philosopher and a lover. The swine are featured as the first to be introduced into the island of Britain. The book is a combination of drollery, poetry, history, and myth and presents a picture of the era when magic was taken as fact and when the use of swine and the rights of fatherhood were new ideas. Readers not interested in this historic age may find the book a bit tedious. Nevertheless, the novel was warmly welcomed by people interested in Welsh materials.

Witch House (Sauk City, Wisconsin, 1945) is well titled. It tells the story of a large old forbidding house erected in the seventeenth century on a bleak island close to the New England coast by an accused sorcerer, Joseph de Quincy, who had fled France and who then founded a queer family that seemed destined to the accursed fate of harboring witchcraft, evil, and misfortune throughout all its generations. The dark house seems to have an indefinable malignity that makes all its inhabitants come to grief. But the tale concentrates on how Dr. Gaylord Carew, a nerve specialist trained in Eastern hypnotism and occult powers of the mind, is called to the Witch House by a descendant of the original de Quincy, the widowed young Elizabeth Stone, in order to save her daughter, Betty-Ann, from evil spirit influences there. He encounters hatred from two distant cousins of Elizabeth, Quincy Lee and Joseph Quincy. Horrible events occur. A chess board is repeatedly overturned by an unknown force, objects are moved from their places on shelves, tables and pictures and stones are hurled at people by invisible hands, an ominous black hare occasionally materializes to frighten the child, an evil old aunt arises from the dead to stalk about the house, mysterious forces influence thinking. But Dr. Carew's keen intelligence and calm spiritual strength baffle all the forces of evil, protect the child, and unmask Joseph Quincy as the author of most of the trouble. When at the last the house burns—with Joseph trapped in it—the doctor finds himself the victor in the contest, and with Elizabeth and Betty-Ann as his prizes. Though the book begins slowly, it soon gathers such tempestuous force that one finds himself believing the eerie tale. The reader is advised either to follow these pages in broad daylight or if he chooses to take this flight into the blackness of sorcery by night to fasten his seat belt first!

The Cross and the Sword (New York, 1956) is a story of Anglo-Saxon times in England and Norway, rich in historic detail and atmosphere of that savage warring era. It is the first-person account of the Norseman Sweyn, known as Black Thrym, son of Firebeard, Jarl of Wolves' Dale, and also the beautiful Swan-White, a captive taken on one of Firebeard's many raids, whom he later denounced as a witch. Sweyn was reared by his father's one-time friend, Thorbrand, became a friend of Ketil the Lapp, and groped his way toward a new religion, Christianity, that was spreading slowly into England and the North, attended by much misunderstanding and bloodshed. This is a stirring, imaginative tale, abounding in tenderness, courage, and brutality between Danes and English, heathens and Christians, with the author not so much taking liberties with history as filling in vacancies in extant records.

RUTH LININGER DOBSON

Ruth Lininger (Mrs. Gilbert) Dobson (1911-   ) has written only two novels, both of them about rural or small-town life. Born in Latrobe, Pennsylvania, on October 28, 1911, she spent her first seven years in Chicago. Her family so liked the town of Middlebury, Indiana, near South Bend, on a summer visit that they lived there the next five years. After two years of high school in Pennsylvania and two more years in Middlebury, she attended Purdue in 1928-29, taking an active part in student activities—debating, dramatics, and work on the school paper. But finding no particular interest in home economics, she spent her last three years following a literary course at the University of Michigan, where she was graduated in 1933. The next year she was married to Gilbert Dobson, an engineer.[20]

Mrs. Dobson began writing early in her life, turning out poems and stories. When in school in Middlebury she became interested in the Amish who lived in the area. Several of her schoolmates were Amish, there were Amish maids in her home, and her family bought vegetables and antiques from Amish farmers. It was natural, therefore, for these people to attract her attention as possible subjects for fiction. Her first Amish story was penned at age sixteen, when she was a freshman at Purdue. It received honorable mention in a contest which a famous Indiana writer, a Purdue alumnus, George Ade, helped judge.

Then came her first novel, *Straw in the Wind* (New York, 1937), a narrative of Amish life that received the major award in the Avery Hopwood and Jule Hopwood contest in fiction in 1936, for which she received $1500. It is an account of a small community of Indiana Amish farmers who are hard working and prosperous, but their picturesqueness is offset by their domineering bishop, Moses Bontrager, who relentlessly runs the lives of his

[20] Information about Ruth Lininger Dobson has come from "Former Co-ed Author of 'Straw in the Wind,'" in *The Purdue Alumnus,* February, 1937, p. 18; from "Today is Enough," in *ibid.,* December, 1938, p. 4; and from miscellaneous sources.

family. After his daughter watches a dance, she is exhorted to confess her supposedly sinful life; but when she continually refuses, saying she is conscious of no sin, Moses reads her out of the church, and she flees from the family and eventually marries an "outsider." Moses' wife dies, almost unwept by the husband. When his favorite son steals money that his father had cached in order to buy some valuable adjoining land, Moses' regret is the loss of the money, not the sinfulness of the son, and the blow kills him. He had sacrificed everything to his stern way of life and his greed.

Many scenes about Middlebury are found in this colorful book; but its plot is weak, and its picture of Amish life is probably one-sided. Though much of the presentation of customs and dress is undoubtedly authentic, still the Amish objected to what they called the incorrect dialect and errors in customs and religious practices and condemned the bigotry of Moses as untypical of their sect.[21] Nevertheless, the book went through several printings.

Mrs. Dobson's second novel, *Today Is Enough* (New York, 1939) is an appealing story of a city girl who finds herself the wife of a minister in his first charge, which is a small Indiana village. The book depicts her adjustment to her marriage and to small-town living. The town ways are shown to be simple and virtuous and neighborly, and there is much detailed description of the country and country people. One finds a dearth of plot and also an incomplete handling of social problems.

To summarize, we might observe that of the fourteen novelists covered here only five—McCready Huston,

[21] See Elizabeth Horsch Bender, "Three Amish Novels," in *The Mennonite Quarterly Review*, 19 (1945):273-84.

Charles E. Scoggins, Margaret W. Jackson, Jeannette C. Nolan, and Bertita Harding—could be called professional authors. All the others published so much less, comparatively, that literature seems to have been to them something of an avocation.

Preoccupation with high-mindedness or virtue can be found particularly with Huston, Louis Ludlow, and John C. Mellett. Concern with the supernatural is seen in two novels of Robin E. Spencer and one of Evangeline Ensley, while two writers penned mysteries: Herbert O. Yardley with three books and Jeannette C. Nolan with six. There are many exciting, intense novels in this period, but perhaps the laurels for excitement go to Scoggins and Yardley. And several persons wrote historical novels: John F. Barnhill, Louis Ludlow, Margaret W. Jackson, LeRoy MacLeod, Clarence E. Benadum, Bertita Harding, and Evangeline Ensley. The Indiana novel in this period, as well as in others, tends to be predominantly romantic, though several writers—Huston, Jackson, Mellett, Spencer, Nolan, and Dobson—have some elements of realism in their work.

One of the most significant aspects of the novel of this period is the wide use of Indiana as a locale. For example, the following novels have a Hoosier setting: Ludlow's *In the Heart of Hoosierland,* which is laid in southeastern Indiana; Scoggins' *The Red Gods Call* and *The Walking Stick,* both dealing with Muncie; Jackson's *Jenny Fowler,* the action of which covers Bloomington, Bedford, Spencer, and other places, and *First Fiddle,* which moves in Indianapolis; Mellett's *High Ground,* set in the imaginary town of Summit; MacLeod's three novels about the Wabash Valley; Nolan's *Second Best,* which takes place in an Indiana town, *Where Secrecy Begins* (Brown County and Indianapolis), *Final Appearance* (New Harmony), and two novels inspired in some way by Evansville—*Gather Ye Rosebuds* and *This Same Flower;* Benadum's *Blackshirt,* about Indiana politics, and *Bates House,* picturing Indianapolis in the Civil War era; and Ruth L. Dobson's *Straw in the Wind,* which portrays the Amish of northern Indiana, and *Today Is Enough,* telling of an Indiana town.

Finally, we might ask, who are the best novelists of this period? It is very difficult to make such a pronouncement, for no one stands forth head and shoulders above the rest. Perhaps, however, we might venture to say that worthy of especial note are Huston, Scoggins, Jackson, Mellett, Spencer, and Nolan. The bulk of the production of this period is somewhat in the order of escape reading. Although a few, like Jackson, who is something of a social historian, of Hoosier society in particular, have serious purposes in writing and messages to communicate, the typical Indiana novelist simply wanted to tell a good story.

Of the success attained in this endeavor, let the popularity of these novels serve as evidence!

Index

INDEX

(591)